Research: New & Practical Approaches
2nd Edition

Tony Bastick
Faculty of Education and Humanities
University of the West Indies, Mona
Kingston, Jamaica

Barbara A. Matalon
Institute of Education
University of the West Indies, Mona
Kingston, Jamaica

Chalkboard Press, Materials Production Unit
University of the West Indies, Mona Campus
Kingston, Jamaica, W. I.

Research: New & Practical Approaches
2nd Edition, 2007

Authors: T. Bastick and B. Matalon
Cover design: Louis Matalon

Email inquires at mpu_uwi@yahoo.com

Includes bibliographic references, index and footnotes.

ISBN: 978-976-632-039-3

Printed in the USA

Table of Contents

Forward ix

Part 1: On Your Mark 1

Chapter 1: An Introduction to Research 2

Types of Research 2
    The Real Reason for Doing Research 5
Some Common Types of Research 5
Quantitative or Qualitative Research 5
    Step 1: Preliminary Thinking 6
    Step 2: Narrowing Down Your Topic 7
Building Your Research I 10
    Step 3: Reading More About your Research Topic 11
Where to Find Information 13
Building Your Research II 15
    Step 4: Beginning to Form Your Hypothesis 15
    Forming Your Hypothesis 16
H_0 or H_1? 17
    The Null Hypothesis (H_0) 17
    The Alternate Hypothesis (H_1) 19
Test Yourself 1 19
Building Your Research III 19
Test Yourself 2 20

Chapter 2: Learning About Variables 21

Knowing What Your Variables Are 21
    Qualitative and Quantitative Variables 21
A Word or Two About Measurements 22
Test Yourself 3 23
    Continuous, Discrete and Dichotomous Measurements 24
Independent Variables (IV) and Dependent Variables (DV) 25
Perception or Prevalence Variables 26
Building Your Research IV 27
Test Yourself 4 28
Confounding Variables 28
Making Operational Definitions 29
Test Yourself 5 31
How Terms Are Used 31
Finally 32
Building Your Research IV 32

Part 2: Get Ready 33

Chapter 3: As You Begin 35
Parametric or Non-Parametric Research Designs? 35
    What on Earth is a Parameter? – Sampling Procedures 35
    What is a Normal Population? 36
    How Many People (or Things) in a Sample? 37
Randomization Techniques 38
Non-Parametric Research 40
Conclusion: Parametric or Non-Parametric Research 41
Time for a Decision! 42
    Using the Decision Chart 43
    Related or Non-Related? 45
    A Decision Chart for Testing Your Hypothesis 46

Chapter 4: Parametric Research Designs 47
"True" Experimental Research Designs 47
An Introduction to "Word Maps" of Your Research 48
Word Map 1 49
A Pretest/Treatment/Post-test Research Design 49
    Participants, Treatment Conditions and Time Constraints 50
Factorial Research Designs 52
    About Interaction Effects 52
Word Map 2 56
    Making a Table of Your Research Design 57
More Types of Research Designs 59
As If This Wasn't Enough 62
Word Map 3 63
Solomon Four-Group Design 64
Word Map 4 64
A Checklist When Planning an Experimental/Quasi-Experimental
    Research Design 66
Test Yourself 6 67

Chapter 5: Non-Experimental Research 68
Correlational Research Designs 68
    Planning Correlational Research 69
Word Map 5 71
Causal/Comparative Research Designs 72
Simple Linear Regression Designs 73
    Incorporating Correlational Research Designs into the "Big Picture" 74
    Commonly Made Mistakes in Correlational Designs 74

Chapter 6: Non-Parametric Research Designs 75
    Spearman's rho 75
    Word Map 6 75
        The Chi-Square Design 76
    Other Methods of Testing Hypotheses Using Non-Parametric Statistics 77
        Research Design Using the Wilcoxon Matched-Pairs Signed Rank Test . 77
        Research Design Using the Friedman Test 78
        Research Design Using the Mann-Whitney U Test 78
        Research Design Using the Kruskal-Wallis Test 79

Part 3: Get Set! 81

Chapter 7: Why Use Questionnaires? 82
    The Many Uses of Questionnaires 83
    Questionnaire Items 85
        Item Types 85
        Perception Responses Versus Prevelance Responses 86
    High or Low Discrimination Response Format? 88
    Reverse Scoring Items 89
    Lie Scales, Consistency Questions and T/F Combination Questions 90
        Coding for Missing Values 92
    Rating Scales 92
        The Likert-type Scale 92

Chapter 8: GAMTEAP – The Psychology of Questionnaire Responding 96
    To Group or Not to Group? That is the Question! 96
        A Word About Space Saving 97
        Language Style and Meaning 97
    Formatting Your Questionnaire 98
        The Introduction 98
        Ensuring that ALL Questions are Answered 100
    The "Look" of a Questionnaire 101
        Questionnaire Design: Example 1 101
        Questionnaire Design: Example 2 105
    The Need to Train Your Respondents 109
        Questionnaire Design: Example 3 110

Chapter 9: The "Nitty Gritty" of Pre-Planning Your Questionnaire Items 112
    Question Content 113
    Pretesting Your Items and Pilot Testing Your Questionnaire 114

Part 4: Almost There! 117

Chapter 10: Reliability, Validity, Ethics and Cover Letter 118
The Classical Test Theory and Measurement Error 119
Validity 121
Ethics in Carrying Out Research 122
    The Use of Deception 124
The Cover Letter 125
    Extras to Give Your Research Project Some Validity 126

Chapter 11: Writing the Proposal 128
A Suggested Format for the Research Proposal 128

Part 5: Go!!! 137

Chapter 12: Data Entering 138
    Step 1: Entering Your Raw Data 138
Using the Formula Wizard in Excel 141
    Step 2: Checking Your Data 142
    Step 3: Entering Your Data into SPSS from an Excel File 143
Checking Your Categorical Data Using Frequency Counts 147
    Finding Frequencies for Categorical Data Using Cross Tabs 148
Getting the SPSS Output into Your Written Report or Thesis 150

Chapter 13: Data Entering 152
Measures of Central Tendency 152
Measures of Variability 153
Why Do You Need Descriptives Statistics? 154
    Descriptives Using Continuous Variables 154
Do Your Scores Come From a Normal Distribution? 156
Choosing a Level of Significance 157

Chapter 14: Parametric Tests (1): Bivariate Correlations 159
Exercise 14.1 160
Drawing Scatterplots with SPSS 160
Estimating the Correlation from a Scatterplot 164
Test Yourself 7 166
Drawing Pie Charts, Bar Graphs and Histograms 167
Drawing Pie Charts 168
Drawing Bar Graphs 170
Drawing Histograms 173
    Drawing a Histogram Using the Graph Option 173
    Drawing a Histogram Using the Frequencies Option 174

Drawing a Histogram Using the Explore Option 176
Outliers 179
Calculating Correlations – Pearson *r* 180
Using the SPSS Programme to Determine the Value of Pearson *r* 180
Calculating the Reliability Coefficient (r^2) 183
Introduction to Partial Correlations 183
Test Yourself 8 185
Calculating Partial Correlation using SPSS 186
Interpreting SPSS Output from the Partial Correlation Programme 189

Chapter 15: Increasing the Reliability and Efficiency of Your Questionnaire

**Chapter 15: Increasing the Reliability and
Efficiency of Your Questionnaire** 192
Cronbach's Alpha 192
Using the SPSS Programme to Determine the Value of C-Alpha 193
Data Reduction – Exploratory Factor Analysis 198
Varimax Factor Analysis 199
Using Varimax Factor Rotation to Develop a Questionnaire 199
Interpreting the Factors: What is Each Factor Measuring? 206

Chapter 16: Parametric Tests (II): The t-test

Chapter 16: Parametric Tests (II): The *t*-test 209
An Explanation of What the *t*-test Does 209
Using SPSS for the *t*-test Statistic 210
Levine's Test of Equality of Variance 215
Test Yourself 9 216

Chapter 17: Parametric Tests (III): ANOVA

Chapter 17: Parametric Tests (III): ANOVA 218
What is the ANOVA? 218
The One-Way ANOVA 219
The Effect Size (η^2) 226
Interpreting Multiple Comparisons 227
Why Make Multiple Comparisons? 231
Things to Think About – Type 1 and Type 2 Errors 231
The Two-Way ANOVA and Three-Way Analysis of Variance (GLM in SPSS Talk) .. 233
Word Map 7 235
Levene's Test of Equality of Error Variance (from Step 6) 237
Reading an ANOVA Table 238
The Effect Size (η^2) 239
Looking at the Interaction Effects 240
What is an Interaction Effect???? 240
Interpreting the Results of the Three-Way ANOVA 242
More About Main Effects and Interactions 242
Recognising and Interpreting Main Effects Only 243
Recognising and Interpreting Interaction Effects 248

Chapter 18: Non-Parametric Tests 255

Chi-Square Test for Independence 255
  Example 1: Using the Chi-Square Test – a 2 X 2 Research Design 256
  Example 2: Using the Chi-Square Test – a 2 X 3 Research Design 258
Spearman's *rho* 259
Mann-Whitney U Test 261
Wilcoxon Signed Rank Test 263
Kruskal-Wallis Test 265
The Friedman Test 266

Part 6: The Finish Line

Part 6: The Finish Line 269

Chapter 19: A "Basic" Recipe for Your Research Thesis 271

In Order of Appearance 271
The "Preliminaries" 271
Abstract 273
The Main Body of the Text 274
Chapter 1: Introduction (Nature of the Study) 275
Chapter 2: A Review of Related Literature 278
Chapter 3: Methods 280
Chapter 4: Results 283
  Figures and Tables 284
Chapter 5: Summary, Discussion and Recommendations 285
References 289
Appendices 290

Chapter 20: When to Write What 291

Suggestions for Effective Research Writing 292
  Making an Outline 292
  Pseudo-Academic Language 294
  Using the Appropriate Tense 294
  Citations, Quotations and Paraphrases 295
  References 297
  Tables and Figures 298

Test Yourself Answers 301
Appendices
  Appendix A: Detail of Descriptives.13 data file 308
  Appendix B: Detail of Data for Correlate.13 and Non-Linear.13 ... 309
  Appendix C: Detail of Data for Covariate13 310
  Appendix D: Recommended Style Manuals for Theses and
    Research Papers for Faculties at UWI 311
References 313
Glossary 316
Subject Index 327

Forward

Research: New and Practical Approaches has been written primarily as a guide for students who "have to complete a research project or thesis" in order to graduate but we also believe that those who are already carrying out research will find this text a useful companion. The text is an amalgam of information that is usually found in a variety of different texts – an introduction to research, statistical analyses, and research writing. It is not intended to be the ultimate text on research writing, *or* for statistical analyses, *or* to provide all the answers to all of the problems that many researchers face when carrying out investigations. We believe, however, that this text will remove some of the mystery that surrounds the research process and thesis writing.

We think that you, as the researcher and thesis writer, do not have to reinvent the wheel. There *are* standard procedures for basic research and you should not have to do a lot of extra research to find out how to carry out these procedures and then do even more research to be able to write them up for your final paper. In a way, this text can be considered a "cook book" approach to the research process! We provide the essential ingredients and give you some basic recipes – show you what is available and offer advice as to what is required when you have made your choice. Although we can offer advice and warnings, it is up to you to select the most appropriate procedures for the different parts of your research.

Be aware that there is NO one approach acceptable for every type of research.

Research procedures have four main parts – how to collect your data, how to analyse it, how to interpret the results of your analysis, and how to write about it. In order to collect data, you must first determine what type of research you want to do and exactly what you want to investigate (your topic). Once you have decided on your topic, you have to determine the most suitable research design for it. This text offers guidelines on how to choose a project or research topic that fits your circumstances and then how to choose the most suitable research design for it.

Next, you must know what types of statistical analyses are most appropriate for the different designs, and, importantly, how to analyse and interpret your data. We show you how to enter the raw data into Excel, put it into the SPSS programme and how to interpret the output. Finally, you have to write everything that you have done in an acceptable format. It has been written, "The process of research is not complete until the findings have been written up[1]" and once you have decided on your research design and exactly what you are going to do, we give you an outline of the formal conventions for writing the final paper and what goes in which section.

The text has been divided into six main parts. Each part is presented in order of knowledge steps and each part builds on the preceding one – from **Part 1: Getting Ready** through to **Part 6: The Finish Line.**

---

1. Denscombe, 2003, p. 284.

Part 1: On Your Mark starts you thinking about how to pick a topic for research that fits your interests, experience and special circumstances, how to narrow the topic down so that it is do-able, and how to research the subject matter. It also contains some helpful hints for collecting and organising material for the literature review.

Part 2: Get Ready is about choosing the right research design. If you do not know which type of research design best fits your project, it will be difficult to know where to go! This part also serves as a basic guideline to help students decide what statistics would be most appropriate for their research before they even start to collect the data. Thinking about how you are going to analyse your data, before you start to collect it, ensures that you don't waste your time, energy, and money collecting a lot of useless information.

Part 3: Get Set is all about questionnaire (survey) designs. We placed this in its own special section because we realised that a large majority of students rely on questionnaires to form the backbone of their research. (In the student version of this text, it was originally included in Part 2.) We quickly realised, however, that this was an important aspect of research carried out by our students. Making up questionnaires and administering them to large groups of people is not as easy as it looks so we have added this section about item types, item formation, and GAMTEAP – Getting As Much Targeted Effort As Possible (from your respondents).

Part 4: Almost There. After all the time spent thinking about your topic, narrowing it down, defining your variables, and all the other things you have to think of in order to carry out effective research, it is now time to take a short rest! This section was included because we realised that our researchers needed to take a breather and think about certain aspects of research that are often neglected. Even though the topics of reliability, validity, ethical considerations and the important cover letter are discussed throughout the text, we felt that they were important enough to merit individual attention.

We also realised that students had limited knowledge about how to write a proposal and so we enlarged this and put it in this section. This is in keeping with our initial "cook book" concept and provides a basic format so that students can ensure that their proposals are accepted – provided, of course, that they have followed all the initial steps!

Part 5: Go!!! We have found that after students have narrowed down their topics, defined the variables and collected all the necessary data, they often do not know what to do with it. This section shows you how to enter your data into Excel and then how to import it into the SPSS programme. Probably more importantly, we show you how to interpret the SPSS outputs.

The different steps for each statistical technique are illustrated and data are provided on the CD and also in Appendices A, B and C so that you can do each step while it is being explained. Do not worry, we have used the minimum amount of data! The best way for you to become comfortable with the different SPSS programmes is to enter the data given and follow each step. This way you will be able to compare your results with ours and know that you have done it correctly when your output corresponds with ours. This is one of the best teaching methods we know – hands on experiences.

Remember, however, that this is not a statistics text book and only the most elemental statistics are described here. For more advanced research, you should take an advanced research course or be able to refer to one of the many texts about statistical analysis.

Part 6: The Finish Line. At last! This part is all about writing the final thesis. This is an important section because we have found that many students do not have an idea of what part of their research goes into which section. This can be considered another example of the "cook book" concept that we have used throughout the text.

Conventions decree that a thesis paper consists of five sections and the basic "ingredients" of what should be in each section is described in detail. Follow the recipe and the thesis will, at the very least, be in an acceptable format!

Remember that your thesis is not necessarily a chronological report of what you did, but it is a report, usually written in the standard five-chapter format that best enables the reader to believe in your research project. This section concludes with warnings about the overuse of technical jargon and plagiarism.

Research Exercises

Throughout the first two parts, we have included some different exercises that will help you to organise your thoughts about your research. The *Building Your Research* exercises will help form the basis for writing your research proposal. *Making Word Maps* takes you the next step and helps you to focus on exactly what has to be done during your research. We have also added a few questions, *Test Yourself*, for you to answer (answers are provided!) For the exercises in Part 5, we have placed data on a CD and in Appendices A, B and C so that you can enter it into an Excel file on your own computer. Once this has been entered, you can follow the directions given in each chapter of this section and see if you get the same results. This is a good method of a "hands-on" approach which will help you become acquainted with the SPSS programmes.

All of these exercises require extra time and effort, but we have found that when or students do them, they find that each step of the research process becomes clearer to them.

Special Thanks to ...

Our students in our research classes who have been so patient in waiting for the "next chapter" to be printed off and who have shown us where the text needed to be revised. Based on their questions about the different aspects of research, we were able to revise and clarify many of the issues that they found difficult to understand. We thank you for the feedback that you have given us over the past three years. You have provided us with invaluable knowledge of your needs and we hope that we have met them.

Particular thanks to Karen Matalon who put this book into its final format (and printed off extra chapters for the students on request.) She spent many long hours making sure that the cross references matched, finding appropriate graphics and that the final version was as reader-friendly as we hoped it would be.

The Second Edition ...

We printed the initial version of this text in haste in order to meet the needs of our research students. But, as they gleefully pointed out, the first version contained many typos! We have spent the past year talking to our students and have (hopefully) corrected the errata.

Based on the comments we received, we have added some more "Test Yourself" exercises and increased the data to be copied by students so they can do more of the hands-on SPSS exercises. Additionally, we have placed most of the data on a CD in order to make the hands on exercises easier!

Finally, in Section 6, in keeping with our cookbook theme, we have added 'recipes' showing the basic ingredients required for each chapter. This 'recipe' has two purposes: (1) to serve as a checklist and (2) to act as a guide for the order of writing. As we have noted throughout the text, this recipe can be altered and amended according to the requirements of your faculty supervisor or journal editor, but the basic format for each chapter is based on universally accepted principals of thesis writing.

Thanks again to all our students who have provided comments about the text and to Karen Matalon who painstakingly formatted this text into its present form.

Over the years of working with and guiding students, we have found that most come up with some wonderful ideas for research that are pertinent, important and can be used to increase knowledge – prerequisites for good research. Unfortunately, we have also found that many have no idea how to ensure that what they want to do can be observed, measured, analysed and reported. Thus, they often become discouraged, never complete their theses and just drop out of university – having done years of hard work with no degree to show for it.

These are the students we call the ABDs (means **A**ll **B**ut **D**egree!)

The first part of this text, **On Your Mark**, starts the reader thinking about how to pick a topic for research that fits his or her interests, experience and special circumstances, how to narrow the topic down so that it is do-able, and how to discover information about the chosen topic. It contains some useful and important tips for collecting material for the necessary background information (to be included in both the proposal and the literature review chapter of the thesis), explains what hypotheses and variables are and how to operationally define constructs. In short, **On Your Mark** shows how to get started in the field of research without making too many costly mistakes.

To the Student Researcher...

As a fledgling researcher, one of the easiest paths to success is to replicate the success of others, but in your own way. When you begin your search for background information, look carefully for other studies that appear similar in content and/or method to the research that you want to do. You should be able to recognise the type of research that was carried out, why it was carried out, what was involved and how the results were analysed and reported. Then you can adapt, change, amend and carry out your own research.

Finally, we cannot stress enough the role of a dedicated and knowledgeable academic advisor. For the novice researcher, a committed mentor is the most important factor in your research project!

1
An Introduction to Research

Before you even begin to think of a research topic, it is a good idea to look at some of the reasons why people do research. The type of research that we focus on in this text is scientific in that the processes are reported in sufficient detail for a reader to evaluate an imaginary replication of the work. The four common purposes of scientific research of scientific research are to *explain*, *describe*, *improve* or *predict*. Experimental researchers test theories to explain and describe the statements more fully, investigate outcomes and look at the effectiveness of specific treatment conditions. For practical interest, researchers evaluate programmes to provide information to policy makers as a basis for decisions to be made or for any improvements that may have to be carried out. Other research produces measurements that may predict the likelihood of future events as either a basis for current decisions (as in the case of using test results to predict success at college or the benefit of adding fluoride to drinking water) or as the basis for selecting or rejecting a different course of action. But always, to be accepted as 'good' research, researchers must use **presentation, collection, processing** and the **provision of evidence** that their audience finds convincing.

Types of Research

Examine the different types of research that are carried out. As you read about each one, think of the purpose or reason why this type of research is being carried out. As you read, also think of the research you may want to do and why you want to do it.

Argumentative/Critical

- The purpose of this type of research extends beyond mere investigation. The primary aim of an argumentative or critical paper is to interpret an issue and argue for or against a particular opinion *based on previous research*.
- You must have a central thesis but all sides of an argument should be presented. The arguments must be firmly based upon findings in primary and perhaps, secondary source materials (but, preferably primary source material). It requires careful assimilation and presentation of evidence.
- In an argumentative or critical paper, you must develop a position (your thesis statement) so you can arrive at a judgement *based on research findings*. Use specific quotations (with references) to show that the position you have chosen has been presented accurately.
- You must ensure that your own judgements and opinions are supported by reference material. In other words, you just cannot state that something is wrong or right, you must show proof!

Descriptive

- Descriptive research is intended to produce information of interest to policy makers. This type of research should accurately and precisely depict natural or experimental effects. Data can be derived from surveys, opinion polls, questionnaires, interviews, scales, case studies, treatment groups and experimental conditions.
- Descriptive research papers can consist of (i) a report of the characteristics of a sample at one point in time or of the characteristics of a sample taken over an extended period of time (i.e., a longitudinal study) or (ii) a detailed examination of one or more case studies, some particular feature or aspect of a group within the case study, (iii) responses from questionnaires, interviews or surveys that have been given to a sample of a specific population, or (iv) findings from some experimental or treatment conditions.
- In a qualitative study, the data may be obtained from transcripts, field observations and archives and does not necessarily have to consist of new research.
- In a quantitative study, the researcher selects measures that will give the most valid and accurate description of the phenomena being studied, analyses the obtained data and reports the findings based on the analyses.
- In a descriptive paper, you report *only* what has been observed and your observations must be precisely and accurately described in detail. It requires careful assimilation and presentation of evidence.

Analytical

- This type of paper analyses issues in order to draw general conclusions or arrive at some meaning, cause or consequence based on facts and basic evidence. For example, an analytical paper can examine the effectiveness of interventions such as a drug therapy, an educational programme, and so on.
- You have to analyse component parts of an issue to arrive at these meanings, causes and/or consequences.
- Data can be based on surveys, interviews, treatments, conditions, etc.
- Conclusions are drawn from facts and basic evidence. Note that when causal factors are discovered, then further research is required to make sure these factors really did account for the observed changes.
- For quantitative research, you analyse responses from questionnaires, interviews, etc., according to specific demographic/organismic data (similar to a descriptive paper).

Explanatory

- In explanatory research, you gather and summarize facts. This type of research is concerned with functions, processes and factual results.
- Reasons for an explanatory paper include applied research, market research, and technical reports.
- An explanatory paper can include graphs, charts, tables, listings in addition to other statistical data.
- Explanatory research generally subsumes that descriptive, predictive and improvement research has already been carried out. In other words, if researchers are able to explain a phenomenon, it usually means that they can describe it, predict it, and are aware of the most suitable methods for improvement.

The "Real" Reason for Doing Research!

It is unfortunate (but true) that the real reason why most students carry out research is *because they have to*, so here the operative word is *interest*. If you are not interested in finding out answers to the questions you are asking, your research paper will reflect this. Ideally, you should be passionate and really care about making a difference in the world with your completed research. This passion will lead you to battle against all the difficulties that will be thrown against you in the months to come.

Some Common Types of Research

Causal-Comparative Research[1]

- Causal-comparative research is a common approach to exploring relationships between variables, in determining whether relationships exist between variables and in the investigation of cause-and-effect relationships.
- The objective of this type of research is to describe how an event (or what happens during a condition) is related to other events (treatments, conditions, groupings). Results are explained in terms of strength and magnitude of the relationship(s).
- To show that there is a strong relationship between variables, researchers doing this type of research should use a well-planned strategy and be systematic in relating scores on one variable to scores on another variable measured at another point in time.
- Causal-comparative research is useful because it allows the study of possible cause-and-effect relationships under conditions where experimental manipulation is difficult or impossible (for example, investigating the relationship between putting fluoride in water and tooth decay). It is also useful to explore relationships between variables prior to, or as a substitute for, carrying out an experiment.
- Results of causal-comparative research must be interpreted with care because, generally speaking, there can be more than one causal effect. It is, however, a very useful research design for exploratory investigations.

Correlational Research

- Similar to causal-comparative research, this type of descriptive research investigates the possibility of a relationship between two variables but does not require the use of any form of intervention or treatment conditions – the research is carried out under naturally occurring situations.
- Data may be collected in the form of responses to questionnaires, interviews, or other information-gathering instruments.
- The two sets of responses are analysed according to how these two sets of variables are related (linked) to each other.
- Results are explained in terms of the degree of the direction and magnitude of the relationship(s).

---

1. Causal-comparative research is used mainly for testing for *relationships* that exist (or do not exist) between two variables. Very few studies (other than those used in the medical and other scientific fields) can prove conclusively that one variable can *cause* or *effect a change* in the other.

- The major uses of correlational research are to (i) allow inferences to be made about the relationship between two or more variables; (ii) offer a descriptive explanation to describe the actual behaviour, and (iii) predict likely outcomes of behaviour or help explain the effect of one variable on another variable.

Experimental (and Quasi-Experimental) Research

- In experimental and quasi-experimental research, the researcher carefully and systematically observes the effects of a treatment or condition to determine whether this treatment or condition has any statistically significant effect on another variable.
- The researcher examines contrasting results from samples that are different on one critical variable but are otherwise similar (for example, all males but of different age groups). Measures from the results form the data to be analysed.
- Experimental research can also involve comparing participants with different characteristics. For example, research can compare the type of prenatal health care for mothers who are from very low SES with those mothers who are from a high SES, examine the effects of teaching programmes, drug treatments, and so on. The number and types of variables are almost unlimited for this type of research.

Quantitative or Qualitative Research?

We have found that some of our students are not sure of the differences between qualitative and quantitative research. When we ask students why they want to write a qualitative research paper, they reply that they are frightened (or have no foundation) of the statistical analyses required in quantitative research. The majority feel that a qualitative research paper requires only a literature review, some interviews and then a collation of the information. They do not seem to realise that qualitative research is one of discovery and interpretation and that an in-depth study of their topic is necessary. The researcher must be prepared to go "...into sufficient detail to unravel the complexities of a given situation".[2] Above all, the qualitative researcher must be good at writing and like to write!

The major difference between qualitative and quantitative research is that qualitative research "...involves the natural setting as the direct source of data...qualitative data are collected in the form of pictures and words rather than numbers"[3].

Quantitative research entails collecting numerical data on observable behaviours of samples and then subjecting these data to numerical analysis.[4]

---

2. Denscombe, 2003, p. 31.

3. Fraenkel, & Wallen, p. 502

4. Gall, Gall, & Borg, p. 23

In quantitative research, a statistic is just a number – one number that stands in place of a lot of other numbers. This number summarises the many measurements that have been collected on the sample of the population you want to study. For example, suppose you wanted to find the average height of 200 children, you would need only one number (the average or the mean) to stand in place of 200 other numbers (the heights of all 200 children). This is why statistics (quantitative methods) are such powerful descriptions. They can describe many numbers with just one number. In fact, along with one or two other numbers, statistics can even describe the accuracy of this description of the average height. On the other hand, it would take many pages of language description (qualitative methods) to describe the heights of all 200 children and even more pages of writing to describe the accuracy of this written description.

Using the example of researching the average height of 200 children, a large amount of writing is unnecessary for quantitative research because the concept of height and its measure is understood in a standard way – an average number means the same thing to almost everyone. If, however, you wanted to describe aspects of the children's height that did not correspond to the common standard and you were unable to operationally define that particular aspect, you would then have to use qualitative descriptions. For most research projects, writing about each of the 200 children would require too many words (well over the limit set by your faculty or publisher!) Thus, you would be forced to look at a much smaller amount of children or use just a few of them for case studies. In both of these scenarios, you would have to summarise your descriptions as part of your analysis.

Both research methods have their uses. The advantage of using qualitative research lies in choosing a very important, but small, aspect to describe in your research paper. The strength of qualitative research is in its high validity within a specific context. The main advantage of using quantitative research with a sample of the population under study (particularly if they are randomly selected) is that you can make wider generalisations that would be of interest to a larger group of people. It is unlikely that you can make generalisations from a few case studies – no matter how in depth they are.

Now...

Once you have thought about the various reasons why research is carried out and you have decided to do quantitative research, you should be ready to start thinking seriously about your topic. Remember to keep the different reasons for research in mind when you follow the first steps essential for an effective research paper.

STEP 1 ▶ Preliminary Thinking – Choosing a Research Topic

Choosing a topic for your research is the most important step in research writing – the step that can make your life unnecessarily difficult and waste your time, energy and money, or the step that can set you on the road to success. The topic of research and your reasons for doing it can be based on almost anything that interests you: scientific study, practical concerns, an evaluation of a programme, the provision of information for an existing programme, effectiveness of a treatment plan, differences in perceptions, how many defective items are produced per month in a large factory, does Pill X work better than Pill Y, and so on......the list can be endless!

> When looking for a research topic,
> the operative word is interest!
>
> *Don't Forget*

To think of a valid research topic, the first thing you need to do is ask a wide variety of questions. When discussing concepts during class lectures and when you are going about your everyday life, ask yourself a lot of *why*, *what*, or *how* questions. You can ask, "Why has this happened?" "What has gone on here?" "How did this happen?" "What really makes me angry about what I see happening?" "What needs to be changed somehow or other?" "Why is this happening?" Most research is based on the "what", "why" and "how" questions. When you look with fresh eyes and from your own viewpoint, you will find there are many things that interest or puzzle you and you need to find the answers! Once you have identified an area where you think your efforts will be most effective – you have identified your research topic.

> The purpose of asking these questions is to frame,
> shape and focus on:
> what you are going to do and .....
> how you are going to do it in such a way that
> will gain you your qualification or journal article.

The best research is original and significant. But, you think, "How can I be expected to do original research?" Well, remember that although you may be in a classroom full of students who appear to be like you, you are different from the others. You have had a different childhood and other unique experiences that can enable you to see things differently from everyone else. Now is the time for you to look at the world from your own perspective and to use that special knowledge to think of a topic that is different from the others or a way of measuring a concept that has not been done before.

Keep in the back of your mind the word *suitability*. In addition to answering the questions you are asking, the topic you choose and the way you do it must match the administrative requirements of your institution or the interest of a specific journal. In a college or university setting, ask, "Is my topic an area of research and interest that matches that of a supervisor who is willing to help me?" "Are there so many aspects to my topic that I may not be able to explain it fully and to write it up in the number of words that are required?" If the answer is no to the first and yes to the second, then you will need to rethink what you want to do or narrow your focus to just the main, most important aspects.

STEP 2 ▸ Narrowing Down Your Topic

Once you have decided what interests you, you have to start "narrowing down" your topic. Although you have started with some big ideas, you must now set definite limits on what you want to research. Actually, setting limits on what you want to research ensures productive and effective reading times. This narrowing down of your topic is an important step in defining your research because as your research develops, you may find many other interesting ideas that are relevant to your topic but you must resist chasing them at this time. Keep notes on these other interesting ideas and do not waste them because they might come in very useful as "suggestions for further research" (see **Part 6: The Finish Line!**).

When you begin to narrow down your topic, you first try to make a reasonably explicit statement of exactly what you want to do or what question(s) you are trying to answer. To put this in plain language, you ask yourself, "Why I am doing this research?" This narrower aspect of the problem will become the official statement or reason for your research and eventually will turn into your thesis or problem statement. This reasonably explicit statement is actually more than just a statement – it will have a very special significance and a special meaning for you. It will represent what you care about and will be symbolic of what drives you to do the research. It will become the anchor that keeps you centred on the main problem.

Remember we stated that research should be original as well as, ideally, being useful to the community? There is a third proviso. Once you have decided what interests you and found that the topic is original and useful, you have to ensure that your research is do-able. 'Do-able' means that you have the resources to carry out your research within the limitations set by your ability, your institution, your time, your energy and your pocket book.

Two very sobering limitations on any research paper are the limitations on time and the word count set by the university or the number of pages accepted by a journal. Any time you become overwhelmed by the seeming enormity of your task, just remember that you only have to write a few words (in most faculties, between 15,000 and 20,000 words for a master's thesis and, at the maximum, 80,000 words for a PhD thesis) and you are expected to finish it in a relatively short time.

> Check your faculty for guidelines that will help you. These guidelines list the characteristics that distinguish the levels of research projects, sample size, number of variables, types of analysis, etc., for an undergraduate project, a taught Master's project, a Master's thesis and a PhD thesis. By looking at these requirements, you can judge how much work you need to do and this will set limits on the width and depth of your topic. Journals also set rigid requirements and if you propose to send your work to a journal, check on "Instructions to Authors" as requirements may differ according to the journal.

Remember that your research project is limited in time and size by the requirements of your qualification or of the journal you will submit it to. Also, remember that you cannot change the world – nor should you be expected to! You can make your mark in a different way, by finding a special area that others have not focused on directly. This is where your own experiences come in to help you to identify that area.

Two Examples of Narrowing Down a Topic

Example 1: A researcher heard complaints that students at a university did not complete their requirements and dropped out of university before graduation. Because of her background and personal experiences, she was highly motivated to investigate this and make it her research topic. The big picture, therefore, was "drop-out students at a university." This topic had to be narrowed down to fit the level of her award. As she was doing a research project and not a thesis, the initial significance and level of originality were not overburdening, so a simple descriptive, analytical or explanatory research would suffice as long as it described the current situation. The major thrust of her final research centred around five questions:

1. How many students drop out of the university before they graduate?
2. What reasons do students give for dropping out of university?
3. In which departments there are more drop-outs than others?
4. Are there more male than female drop-outs?
5. Do the reasons differ by department and/or gender?

For this researcher, "drop-out from college" was operationally defined as "students who attended college for at least three years and then did not re-enroll." This researcher could have narrowed the topic even more and "drop-outs" could have been defined as students who had completed their academic courses but did not complete their theses (a requirement for graduation in many faculties). Note that the general topic of "student drop-outs" was narrowed down until it became something that could be observed, measured and analysed. This is an example of *operationally defining* the topic that you are examining (see Step 6).

The questions asked by the researcher formed the basis for a strong, interesting and worthwhile research paper. Above all, the research questions could be answered! The significance of this research is that it reported base-data for a current situation of concern. Who is concerned, why they are concerned and what their concerns are, would be researched as the rational for the design of this survey and act as a guide to interpreting and reporting the results.

Example 2: Another researcher was interested in finding out about aggression in schools. But first, the construct, aggression, had to be operationally defined. Aggression is a construct – a construct is a name we give to abstract concepts that are symbolic of how things in the world are perceived or thought of, for example, emotion, depression, motivation, patriotism. You should use published studies to find precise definitions of your terms as they are used by experts in the area to be studied. However, as a start, and just to give you a clearer understanding of some of the constructs you want to define, you can see how the terms are generally used by non-experts by looking them up in a dictionary. For example, in our small dictionary, aggression was defined as "an unprovoked attack or warlike act." Then, you must think of all the things that are involved in unprovoked attacks or warlike acts: pushing, shoving, fighting, using a weapon, swearing, shouting, throwing stones, and so on. Now, you have something that can be observed and measured! When you start looking at published research involving aggression, you can then ensure that your definitions are valid and acceptable.

To narrow down the topic, the researcher decided that he wanted to examine aggression in both government and private elementary schools but not in high schools. This meant that the research questions involving aggression in schools could consist of something like the following:

1. What types of aggressive behaviours are exhibited by children attending elementary schools?
2. What reasons do the students give for acting aggressively?
3. Are more aggressive behaviours exhibited by students in private or in government schools?
4. Do boys or girls display more aggressive behaviours?
5. Do the reasons for aggressive behaviours differ by school type and/or gender?

You will notice that these questions have the same form as in the last example, but the context is different. What is similar is that data will be collected and analysed to answer the questions. What is different is that in order to answer Question 3 in the second example, you will need a reliable way to decide which behaviours are considered aggressive and which ones are considered more aggressive, not just your say-so, but an agreed order of aggressiveness.

When you are trying to narrow down your topic, you must also think about how you are going to collect the data for your research. In other words, what will you be measuring? and what participants will you be requiring? In the first example, the researcher might find it difficult to track down enough college drop-outs to complete her data. In the second example, the researcher might decide it might be too costly to travel to schools in the country and so would decide to keep his participant selection to elementary schools in an urban area. This is another example of what we mean when we say your research must be do-able!

One effective way of narrowing down your research topic is to talk about it to other people. Try to explain to them (in plain language) exactly what you are going to do or what you are trying to find out. Ask your friends to ask you questions about your explanation. Often, just having to explain it to someone else (or answer questions about what you are trying to do) puts your topic into perspective and gives you a clearer idea of what you should be doing. Telling others about what you are doing can also help to build your commitment to doing the work. If you can't find anyone who is interested then ask yourself, "Why did I choose this topic?" "What exactly am I trying to find?"

Building Your Research I

1. Identify an area of special interest to you and write the topic in general terms.
2. Narrow down the topic to something very specific and do-able.
3. Based on the different reasons why research is carried out, why do you want to do this particular research?
   Note: The answer to #3 becomes the rationale for your thesis.
4. Now, rewrite your topic in very specific terms.
5. Find at least three current journals that have information pertinent to your chosen topic.

STEP 3 ▶ Reading More About Your Research Topic

Once you have found a topic that interests you and you have narrowed it down to something that can be observed and is do-able, the next thing to do is to find out what has been done by other researchers that will be useful to you. This means reading about your topic (*and reading, and reading, and reading some more*).

Reading about your research topic is very helpful for a number of reasons:

1. It is very disheartening to think of an interesting topic for your research only to find out that this topic has been researched far too many times or that someone else has already done exactly what you were going to do! While you are reading, however, you may be able to pick out an anomaly in the previous research or realize that you can investigate it in another way.

2. Very often, previous research will help you to clarify terms or variables you will use in your research. In many cases, you can get ideas of how to actually carry out your research – a research design for collecting and analysing your data.

3. Reading will help you build on previous research so you can add to the existing literature – a major reason for carrying out research. When it is time for you to write your proposal, it will also help you build up your case for the need for your own research.

4. Reading provides a greater knowledge base that will form the foundation of your own work and will actually form the basis of your research.

5. You will be able to relate your work to what has already been done, compare your results with what others have found, and to account for the similarities and differences. This is particularly helpful when you start to write Chapter Five in your final thesis.

Do not get discouraged when you start the literature review of your topic. Although you might think that your idea for research has never been thought of before, when you start searching the literature you realise that others may have already done something quite similar. You are naturally a little disappointed but after a while you come up with another great idea. Then you find that this has also been done before. This process can be very demoralising and you may think that you will never find some area that is original. However, you will notice a trend in your ideas. As you read more about your subject, you will find that each of your rejected ideas is more modern than the one before – that is, it is a more recent idea. This trend gives you two excellent validations of your creativity. First, it shows you that the ideas you are generating are significant for your field (only someone else thought of them first!) Secondly, it shows that you are becoming more modern in your understanding. Then you realise that you are finally on the right track.

What to Do While Reading

Don't waste what you read. Always note why it is relevant or useful and how you might be able to use it in your final paper. While you are reading, keep the following in mind:

- See how other authors have defined the variables you are including in your research. This will help you further define (format operational definitions) and validate the variables you will be using in your own research. You can cite the authors as 'proof' that you have defined the variables appropriately.
- Write down important aspects of the research such as definitions of the variables, the findings, interesting quotes, important data, etc.
- Most importantly, writing down quotes might prevent plagiarism. Sometimes students find it difficult to explain a part of their research so they 'borrow' bits and pieces of what others have written and try to pass it off as their own. Plagiarism is a big NO NO! You must give credit where credit is due.

Above all....keep notes that are well referenced. Make sure that you have the author's full name, the title of the book or article, the date of publication, the city of the publishers and the publisher's name. If the reference is from an article, make sure that you note the volume number and all the page numbers.

The habit of keeping concise references will save you a lot of time when you finally reach the stage of writing your research paper. By making detailed notes when you first start your research, you won't have to think where you got that piece of information and go back and do your preliminary research all over again! If you can, make notes on how you intend to use each reference as this will also help clarify what is important to you.

Organising Your References

There are two main methods for organising references – cards and computers. If you are aiming for a PhD or intend to do lifelong research then get into current bibliographic software, such as Endnote, right at the start. If the university does not licence the software you need, then your supervisor may be able to help you get a grant to buy it. For long-term research, where you will need to use the same references for published papers and other projects, you will need to keep full citation information so that you can write in any of the standard styles – for example, APA does not require first names but MLA does! This means that if you only collected information for writing in the APA style, you will find it very time consuming trying to get first names if you later have to write in the MLA style. Bibliographic software allows you to change the styles in which you can output your reports at a click of the mouse. If you are going to be a researcher, then you can code your references and include the code with other observations, video, audio, scans, etc., using integrated software such as Atlas or artificial intelligence Qualitative Data Analysis (QDA) or packages such as Qualrus for coding, tracking, and analysing your knowledge base.

However, if this is a one-time piece of research, then you don't need to invest time and energy in learning a programme and you can put your reference notes on cards. Traditional texts on research writing tell you to put the references on 3" x 5" cards. This is about the smartest thing you can do and it is very worthwhile to invest in a pack of these cards before you start your serious reading. On the front of the card, you write the name, title of the text, the author's name, the publisher's name, city and state of publication and the date of publication. For citations from a periodical, remember to add the volume number and the page numbers of the article. Then, if there is enough space on the back of the card, or in a notebook with pages that will not fall out, you write the information you think is important – the direct quotation that you think you might use, (along with the page number) or any other important information that you think will be useful. Figure 1.1 gives an example of how to make a reference on one side of a note card and a quotation on the other side.

When you finally get to the stage of writing the references section, you just shuffle the cards into alphabetical order according to the last name of the author (for APA referencing)!

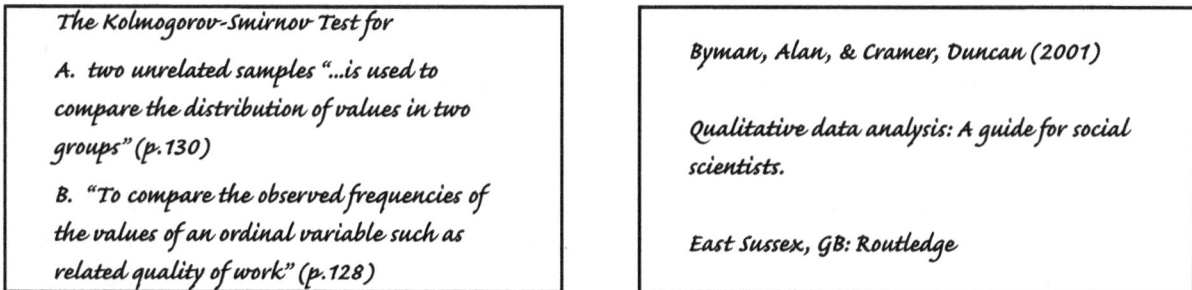

<table>
<tr>
<td>

The Kolmogorov-Smirnov Test for

A. two unrelated samples "…is used to compare the distribution of values in two groups" (p.130)

B. "To compare the observed frequencies of the values of an ordinal variable such as related quality of work" (p.128)

</td>
<td>

Byman, Alan, & Cramer, Duncan (2001)

Qualitative data analysis: A guide for social scientists.

East Sussex, GB: Routledge

</td>
</tr>
</table>

Figure 1.1: An example of reference notes written on a 3 x 5 card

Where to Find Information

At the beginning, when you start to define (operationalise) some of the variables you want to study, you can always get definitions from a dictionary or text books. The reference sections of text books and journal articles, particularly if they are up-to-date, will also give you some clues where you can start looking for more references about your research. Most text books and dictionaries, however, are very general sources of information and only start you off in the right direction.

Next, visit your 'Doc Centre' and see what other students have done. Looking at the topics that other students have chosen to research is particularly important in Caribbean countries. A lot of information already exists but has never been published and so students miss out on the advantage of building on someone else's work, of refuting the findings of other students, or of thinking you are original and then being told someone else has just already done it!

The university library is still the best place to start serious research! Use the library's reference section and ask the librarian for help if you need to. To be effective, first get a list of the current periodicals in the library and give this preference in your initial search. Do this first because you can photocopy information immediately. Remember that in the Caribbean, it can be costly and take months to get a copy of something that is not in the library. In many universities, supervisors usually insist that their PhD students join professional societies and develop personal international contacts. These help with conference information, funding and awards and, importantly, other students can e-mail references from their libraries that could take you months to get!

While looking through journals and periodicals, most students complain that they can't find anything that is pertinent to the Caribbean population and feel that all the information they read about is from 'foreign' and of no use to researchers in the Caribbean. Actually, it isn't! When one of the authors of this text was investigating learned helplessness behaviours in Jamaican children, there appeared to be no previous research that was Caribbean-based on the learned helplessness phenomena. She did, however, find some very interesting articles about learned helplessness behaviours of children living in Palestinian camps and North American Indian children that she was able to use as comparisons in her study.

Next, look to see what other print and electronic resources are available. In the university library, the librarian may be able to help by ordering specific articles for you – but remember, this can take some time. There are also many web sites that you can use. When you use electronic media, for general information, start off by using one of the large web servers and then go to different search engines, such as "*metacrawler.com*" or "*google.com*." The *Internet Public Library* (ipl.org) and "*findarticles.com*" are other very useful places to start a search.

There are also specialist data bases in your area of interest, for example, *EBSCO* Information Services, *Psych Info*, *ERIC* and *ISI* web of knowledge, including social science citations. Your university or institution will subscribe to many of these databases and your librarians will help you to use them. These data bases have exquisite search facilities that enable you to get a feeling for how the popularity of research topics changes. Start by browsing and playing with these searchers so you get to know the standard keywords and descriptors for your topic. Without these, you can spend days in university libraries and end up with very little valid information – you could search for ages and never be aware of relevant citations that are available!

There is a whole world of information out there in cyberspace. BUT, once you get into these search engines, you must start to narrow down your search for information. For example, when we needed some information on statistics, we received over one million pieces of information! There was no way we could search through all this and we quickly learned to be more specific in stating exactly what we were looking for! One of the tips given by the web site *Yahoo* is not to write "car" but to write the name of a "specific make" of car. This also holds true for research topics!

When you are looking for references, remember the different authoritative academic statuses of different sources. Some of the least valid sources are newspaper articles that are not authenticated by a reputable agency such as Reuters. These 'clippings' have little validity as scientific evidence but students often use them as references. Similarly, there is little point in listing authors referring to whole books because no one will read the whole book to look for the concept or fact that you might be citing. You must have the actual quotation and page number – even if it is only in a footnote or endnote, or in your own data base, for your supervisor to validate that you have written the correct citation.

Think about this...

Citing textbooks and dictionaries indicates lack of specificity and should be minimised. Remember that recent studies in peer-reviewed journals carry much more academic weight than newspaper clippings or sections of text books. Always try for the most recent articles first!

Because so many students now have access to the world wide web, it is no longer acceptable to use references that are out of date (unless, of course, you are referring to changes in theories, citing classic works or something that took place many years ago). Too often, the reference section of a thesis submitted by students consists only of references that are obsolete or refer to entire text books (with no page numbers!) External examiners who read research papers often complain about this. Needless to say, the use of obsolete or invalid references does reduce your grade or can lead to a reject slip from an editor of a journal.

Building Your Research II

1. Write down your narrowed-down and do-able topic.
2. Write the key words of your topic. Remember to be specific.
3. Do a computer search using the key words.
4. Visit the library and make reference notes (using your 3 x 5 reference cards) on the journal articles that focus on your specific topic.

STEP 4 ▶ Beginning to Form Your Hypotheses

Using the Statement of Purpose

All the examples we presented in how to narrow down your topic were in the form of questions and these questions are considered your 'draft' research questions. From all of these questions, you make one grand statement that turns into your *Statement of Purpose.* Your Statement of Purpose is the *big picture* of your research topic (such as "An investigation into why students drop out of college before finishing their master's thesis" or "An examination of the amount of aggression exhibited in primary schools"). This is what you write in the introduction of your thesis when you state, "The major purpose of this study was to investigate (examine, determine whether....) This actually turns into your thesis statement – the stand you are taking in your study and this statement develops as you develop the rationale for coming up with the statement of the problem.

Now, look at your questions. These are actually the problems that you want solved Take each question, one at a time, and turn it into a hypothesis which then can be tested. Note how we are narrowing down what you have to do – from the overall *big picture* to several smaller ones.

In practice, this should be how your research works: thinking of research questions, formulating a statement of the purpose of your research, and making a hypothesis for each question – a 'top-down' approach. The top-down logic entails that you make your thesis statement (the stand you are taking) which can be tested by answering your research questions. You answer these questions by testing the hypotheses derived from them. At the same time, you must realise that you *empirically justify* your research through the 'bottom-up' approach. This means that you have to first test your hypotheses. By rejecting (or failing to reject) it, you answer the research questions which in turns supports (or does not support) your thesis statement.

These two approaches must be considered when you write your final thesis statement.

How Research Works

An example of top-down (#1 – 4) and bottom-up (#5 -8) approach to research:

1. Think of a problem that you feel needs investigating or examining (the statement of the problem).
2. Make a list of research questions that you feel need answering as they pertain directly to the thesis statement (the stand you are taking).
3. Based on each research question, replace each one by at least one testable hypothesis.
4. State each hypothesis in terms of the variables under investigation, the conditions being studied and of the results you expect to get.
5. Test each hypothesis by collecting and analysing data.
6. Obtain results through suitable analysis of your measures.
7. By testing these hypotheses, you can reject (or fail to reject) your hypothesis and answer your questions.
8. By answering the questions, you support (or fail to support) your thesis statement.

A Tip When Writing Research Questions

When you start to make up your research questions, be aware that it is better to have simple, single issue questions because each of these simple questions can be replaced with just one or two hypotheses. Ideally, you should try to phrase each question in a simple testable form so that it can be replaced with just one hypothesis. Sometimes the questions are complex and then you should rewrite them as a set of simpler questions because you may end up with a general hypothesis that is not directly testable – one that either doesn't mention the variables that will be used or ignores the relationship between the variables that have to be tested. In such a case, each of these complex questions must be written as several simpler questions leading to specific testable hypotheses.

Forming Your Hypothesis

Formulating your hypothesis is an important step in your research because it specifically defines and limits the research problem. In fact, without a hypothesis, it becomes very difficult to accomplish valid research! The hypothesis is stated in terms of the variables being studied and contains operational definitions and conditions. This means that you should know what you are going to measure before you set up your research hypothesis (see **Chapter 2: Knowing What Your Variables Are** and **Operationally Defining Your Terms**).

---

hypothesis (plural = hypotheses)
A predictive statement or assumption about the outcome of your analysis.

A hypothesis is a predictive statement or assumption about the outcome of your research. Once you have decided on the problem that you want to solve and the question(s) you want answered (your research topic), you usually make an "educated guess" (the predictive statement) about what you think you will find when you start to analyse the data. The predicted outcome is based on what you have already read or observed – on findings from previous research and/or personal observations that you have made while thinking about your research topic. This predictive statement about the outcome is the hypothesis and serves as the basis for your data gathering.

Steps in Formulating Your Hypothesis

First: Once you have decided on your research topic, narrowed the topic down to something that is do-able, you then formulate your thesis statement or problem.[5] Remember that you have already thought of the major questions that you wanted your research to answer. These are the questions (usually two or more of them), that if answered, will resolve the main issues that motivated you to think about this topic in the first place. When you are framing your questions, make sure that you ask *only the questions necessary to support* your thesis statement. The questions should not overlap and have only one possible answer.

Second: Replace each question with one (or more) hypothesis that can be tested to answer the question. Each question must be replaced with at least one hypothesis. Everything you do in your research will be based on finding out whether you will reject or fail to reject your hypothesis. You may have to have more than one hypothesis for each question, but again, have all the hypotheses that are necessary and *they must not overlap*.

Third: Your hypothesis should state exactly who or what you are examining, measuring or investigating (your variables) *and* what you expect to find (your results). Look at page 18 for a concrete example on the formulation of a null hypothesis.

H_0 or H_1?

There are two different forms in which a hypothesis can be stated: the null hypothesis (H_0) or the alternative hypothesis (H_1 or H_A)[6]. The H_1 is also called a directional hypothesis because it is predicting the direction of the results of the hypothesis. When you start to write up your research, however, you should only use one form. (Yes, we have seen students who put both forms of hypotheses in their Chapter One! *and* add the questions! This tends to confuse both the researcher and the reader.)

The Null Hypothesis (H_0)

The null hypothesis (H_0) is a statement that assumes that any effect, contrast, or difference that you are looking for *does not exist* in the population as a whole – that there is a null (or no) effect. To put it another way, the null hypothesis states that there is *no difference* between means, correlations, etc., of scores, variables, treatments, conditions, obtained from the population you are sampling. Using the H_0 does not have to reflect what you expect.

---

5 Remember that the thesis statement is the "reason" for your research.
6 Note that in this text, we use H_1, but both forms are acceptable.

It is used because the purpose of hypothesis testing is to test the validity of the null hypothesis according to the data collected. For example, if a researcher wanted to find out if one method to teach reading was better than another and secretly thought that Method A would be better than Method B, an example of the H_0 would be "Mean scores of reading tests do not differ regardless of the method used to teach reading." Then the researcher would hope that statistical analyses of the reading scores would allow him or her to reject the null hypothesis.

If you are confused about the concept of using the null hypothesis, remember that the idea of statistical testing is to *disprove or reject the hypothesis*. It's a double negative effect. Remember from school that two negatives make a positive, -(-1) = +1. To show there is an effect, you have to first prove there is no null effect – oh, that double negative! Very frequently, researchers want their null hypotheses to be false in order to answer 'yes' to their questions and so support their research thesis that a difference actually exists. This means that when they hypothesise that there is no difference or effect in the population (by using the H_0), they really hope to find that there is a difference or effect!

By assuming that there is no null effect, they prove that there is an effect in the population – these double negatives, again! Unfortunately, results will **never** allow us to say "We accept the null hypothesis," we have to say, "We reject the null hypothesis at the chosen significance level" or that "We cannot reject the null hypothesis at the chosen significance level." The reason given for this is that we can generally prove that something is false but it is almost impossible to prove that something is always true.

An Example of Formulating a Null Hypothesis

You may have observed that, in general, males are taller than females and you want to investigate this issue. This would give rise to the research question "Is the average height of males the same as the average height of females?" Now you have to replace the question with a null hypothesis whose testing must logically answer the question. In this example, the null hypothesis would be "There is no difference between the average height of males and the average height of females." Note that the question and the hypothesis are close in meaning so that if the null hypothesis is rejected, then there must be a difference in the average height of males and females. This would answer your research question.

In forming this question you were probably thinking of measuring the height of many males and females (chosen at random from a random sample), then noting each person's height and gender. Your intended analysis would be to separate the numbers for the heights of males from the numbers for the heights of females so that you could calculate the average height of both groups. Then you would compare these average heights by taking one average from the other to find the difference in the average height of each gender. Thinking that you could do this data collection and analysis convinces you that the question is answerable and that the research is do-able.

Test Yourself 1

Stop a minute....Can you see the logical fault in assuming that this null hypothesis will answer the research question:"Are there any differences in the average height of males and the average height of females?

See the answer at the end of the text.

The Alternate Hypothesis (H₁)

The alternate hypothesis (H$_1$) states that there *is a difference* and determines the directionality of that difference. This is the result that the researcher generally wants to find and where your 'educated guess' fits in. If you use the H$_1$, you should base it on the *differences* that you have observed, experienced and concluded while thinking and talking about your research topic and what you have read on published findings from previous research. In the height example given above, the H$_1$ would be "Males are taller than females" because this is what you have observed. You expect your educated guess to be proved correct and are stating the direction of the difference – that males are taller than females.

Cheer Up!

Many researchers prefer to use the null hypothesis that is then rejected or not rejected and if you haven't a clue what you will find, then you must write your hypothesis as the H$_0$. This is known as a *non-directional hypothesis* – things can go one way or the other. If you are fairly sure that you know the outcome of your research, you can frame your hypothesis to reflect your expectations and use the H$_1$ – particularly if your background research provides you with evidence that the answer will be 'yes.' This is called a *directional hypothesis* and means that you are predicting (*hypothesising*) that the outcome will go in one direction only – either higher *or* lower, more *or* less.

We have found that many of our students only ask research questions and do not bother trying to formulate any hypotheses, (e.g., "Do more male than female undergraduate students drop out of university?"). Once you have thought of the questions, it becomes much easier to think about the answers to your research questions if the questions are changed into statistical hypotheses that can be tested. The null hypothesis for the question asked at the beginning of this paragraph would then be: H$_0$: "An equal number of female and male undergraduate students are likely to drop out of university."

Building Your Research III

1. Write your thesis statement.
2. Turn your thesis statement into a series of questions.
3. Replace each question with a hypothesis.
   Remember....be **very** specific.
4. State whether it is written as H$_0$ or H$_1$.
5. Based on your library search, your own experiences and/or observations, what do you expect to find for each hypothesis?

Test Yourself 2

This hypothesis is written as H_1: Children who are given solvable tasks will display less perseverance than children given insolvable tasks.

Write the H_0:

Write both the null hypothesis and the alternate hypothesis for:
1. Research investigating parental interest in school and academic success in high school students.
2. Research investigating the difference between two different methods (computer assisted or lecture) of teaching math to Grade 3 students.

See the answers at the end of this text.

2
Learning About Variables

Knowing What Your Variables Are

We have mentioned variables many times when discussing the hypothesis. Variables vary! Hence their name. They are defined as "...the part (property, characteristic) of your research that may have different values at different times depending on the conditions."[1] Variables are the 'things' you are going to study and the type of variable you use depends on the role it plays in the research design. In experimental and quasi-experimental research, we investigate differences between two or more variables by deliberately varying, changing or grouping one variable (e.g., according to age or gender) and then looking to see whether there are any differences in the measures (e.g., the scores) obtained from the other variable.

In correlational research, we use two variables and examine at the relationship between the numbers associated with each of them. For example, if you wanted to find the relationship between the number of hours that children study and their academic scores, your two variables would be a list of the number of hours that each child spent studying and a second list of each child's score on a specific test.

Qualitative and Quantitative Variables

Qualitative variables are categories of variables that may also be called categorical, nominal, demographic or organismic variables. These variables are generally the *names* we give to groups, levels, areas, categories, etc. When you start to analyse your data, qualitative variables are generally coded according to some underlying structure (for example, to indicate the category 'gender:' you might code: males = 1 and females = 2; levels of dosage: no dosage = 0, low dosage = 1, medium dosage = 2, high dosage = 3; level of salary: shop assistant = 1, teacher = 2, lawyer = 3, company director = 4). When you code qualitative variables, data analysis becomes easier to manage.

Even though we assign a numeric value to these variables, remember that the numbers only stand for the names of the categories being used and do not denote size. This can be compared to coding busses by using numbers: a Number 10 bus and a Number 20 bus. In this example, bus Number 20 is not twice the size of bus Number 10. However, by coding these qualitative variables according to some predetermined structure, further exploratory analysis is possible.

Quantitative variables are usually some form of calculations or scores that are measured using nominal, ordinal, interval or ratio scales. They are expressed in numbers such as scores on a test, a specific amount of time, the number of hours watching TV, the number of Yes and No responses. Generally, they consist of a list of numbers – one number for each person or thing measured. For example, if you have a sample of 20 people, the variable "math scores" would consist of 20 numbers, one number for each person.

---

1. Pagano, 1999, p. 6.

A Word (or Two) About Measurements

Many students use nominal data, intervals, and rank-orderings as the basis for collecting data. We felt that you should have an idea of what is meant when words such as 'nominal data' or 'intervals' are used and thought that an understanding of how you come up with the frequencies, rank-orderings or nominal data would be beneficial here.

Nominal: Two or more named categories that must be different from each other. Examples of variables using nominal measurements include such categories as: grades, nationality, religious affiliation, political party, colour, make of car, gender, socioeconomic status (SES), pass/fail, true/false, etc. You can then use these different types of categories to try to determine some other characteristic such as reaction time, personality types, reaction to alcohol, etc., according to the category selected.

> Much experimental research uses nominal (qualitative) data to place participants into categories or groups before assigning an experimental or treatment condition (e.g., females, males; participants who are receiving placebos versus those who are receiving low, medium or high doses of a medication, etc.) or before analysing data from scales, questionnaires, conditions or treatments.

Nominal categories can be assigned numbers for coding purposes when doing statistical analyses but there is no order of relationship between the numbers assigned (for example: males = 1; females = 2). Remember, these are just numbers assigned to make the statistical analyses easier.

Ordinal: Defines the *relative position* (gives a numerical order – hence its name) of objects or individuals with respect to different characteristics, attributes, perceptions or attitudes. The main idea is that, for each item, individual or object being measured, the scale must be able to determine the *order* of position. The scale positions as indicated by the numbers are placed in a clearly defined order but the numbers do not indicate a definite distance between the points. Teachers often use an ordinal scale when ranking students in a classroom, e.g., Tommy is #1 but that does not mean he is twice as good academically as Sue who is ranked #2. When looking at SES, job positions may be ranked from lowest (i.e., unemployed = 1) to highest (company director = 5).

> An ordinal scale reflects only the order of positions and not the distances between them.

Interval: An interval scale is one in which the positions are arranged in terms of greater, equal or less. It looks similar to an ordinal scale and it does not have an absolute zero. Unlike the units of the ordinal scale, however, it is assumed that the differences between categories or intervals are equal. Thus, by using an interval scale, you obtain a higher level of measurement than if you used an ordinal scale. For example, the intervals marked on a thermometer have equal intervals – the interval between 1° and 2° is the same interval as between 50° and 51°. Although each unit is equal, you cannot say that a measure obtained on this scale (as for example, on a Fahrenheit Scale) that 100°F, is twice as hot as 50°F. However, one can state that greater differences in the numbers on the scale reflect greater differences in the variable being measured as, for example, 100°F is a lot hotter than 50°F!

> Realise that unless a scale has an absolute zero, numbers cannot be compared. The numbers show degree only and not strength. On nominal, ordinal and interval scales, for example, a measurement of 4 does not mean that it is twice as strong as a measurement of 2.
>
> The scale positions only indicate the order of position as, for example, responses to an item in a questionnaire: (1) favourably inclined (2) neutral or (3) hostile towards a particular characteristic, attribute or attitude. In this example, a person who put a 3 beside a statement would only indicate that he is more hostile towards something than if he had put a 1 or a 2 – not that he is three times as hostile!

Ratio: A ratio scale has the characteristics of an interval scale but also contains a fixed zero (for example, test scores, measures of weight, time intervals, volume, areas, magnitude, angles, etc.) This means that you can make comparisons and state that Jane took twice as long as John to finish the examination or that a pound of potatoes costs twice as much money as a dozen oranges.

It is important to note here that there are only a few measures relating to people that are truly ratio scales. You can say that if Bob weighs 180 pounds, he is twice as heavy as Jane who weighs 90 pounds, but you cannot say that a person with an IQ score of 160 is twice as intelligent as a person with an IQ score of 80 because an IQ score of zero does not mean that a person has no intelligence whatsoever!

> ## Test Yourself 3
>
> Identify the rating scale that would be most appropriate for measuring each of the following variables:
> 1. The number of taxies that enter the university campus each day.
> 2. The gender of teachers responding to a questionnaire.
> 3. The rating of university lecturers based on a 5-point scale. There is insufficient basis for assuming equal intervals between adjacent units.
> 4. The difference in heights of boys and girls in a Grade One Class.
> 5. Proficiency in literacy is scored on a scale of 0 - 50. The scale is well standardised and can be thought of as having equal intervals between adjacent units.

Answers can be found at the end of the text.

Helpful Hint
The important thing to remember when you start to analyse your data and put qualitative data into codes, is to create a 'code book.' Write down your codes or in a bound notebook. Keep this code book in a safe place so that you will not forget what each code stands for.

Continuous, Discrete and Dichotomous Measurements

There are three qualities of measurement. The best is *continuous*, like a long continuous line, because you can obtain total information about the variable. You can measure at every point along the line and your measurement is limited only by your time and the accuracy of your measuring instrument. An example of a continuous variable is age and you can measure very close to any 'exact' age in years, months, weeks, days, hours, and seconds.

The second best quality of measurement is *discrete*. This is where you only measure some given points. In the age example, perhaps we only measured age in to the nearest year so all the people who were between 19^1/$_2$ and 20^1/$_2$ years were recorded as 20 year-olds. By doing this, we have lost some information because now, we only know each person's approximate age. We would throw away even more information if, for some reason, we had decided to use only three discrete categories, such as (a) below 20 years, (b) from 20 to 30 years, and (c) older than 30 years.

The lowest quality of measurement is *dichotomous*. This is a special case when, for some reason, the number of discrete points is reduced to only 2. An example of this would be coding 1 for all people under 30 years and 2 for people for 31 years and older. Can you see how much information is lost?

The bad thing about reducing the quality of measurement is that by measuring only some points of a variable, we are throwing away information about that variable – we are ignoring how much the variable varies! In the example using age as a variable, if we measure it by using a discrete or dichotomous category, we are ignoring variations in age and so may not find out whether age is an important variable in our study, whether it is a confounding variable or, indeed, whether it should be measured at all!

Variables such as age or weight can be measured along a continuous line using many points but some variables exist only as ordered points along a line. Examples of these types of variables include the number of children in a family (you can have 2 or 3 children but not 2^1/$_2$ children!), the number of phone calls (you can have 6 or 7 phone calls but not 6^1/$_2$ phone calls!), the order or ranking in a class or subject (you can come 1st or 2nd but not 1^1/$_2$), points on a Likert scale and so on. These variables are called *ordered discrete* variables because intermediate points do not exist for these types of variables.

When a variable has only unordered, discrete categories that are not in any natural order, such as colours, names, makes of cars, gender or 'yes' or 'no' answers, then we have an *unordered dichotomous* variable. Use these variables only when necessary because you can only count occurrences in each category to see how popular each category is.

Independent Variables (IV) and Dependent Variables (DV)

If you are carrying out research to investigate *differences* among groups, treatments, conditions, etc., then there are names of two variables with which you must become very familiar: the independent variable (IV) and the dependent variable (DV). It is important that you understand the roles they play in your research. When you start analysing your data that you have so painstakingly collected, you will need to put the right variables in the right places in the statistical programmes. Remember that the computer doesn't have a clue whether the variables are IVs or DVs, so you have to tell it!

Independent Variables (IV)

These are the things (remember the definition...the property or characteristic of some event or person) that experimenters systematically control, vary or manipulate. They generally function as hypothetical 'causes' of some effect. In both experimental and non-experimental research, independent variables can consist of almost anything that can be manipulated, controlled, varied or grouped. Usually, researchers want to determine whether one variable has any effect on another variable, so they change the levels, difficulty, times, dosage amounts, groups of people, or whatever, of the independent variable and measure the effects of the manipulation or grouping on the other variables (the dependent variables).

In experimental and survey research, independent variables are what you think might be 'doing the influencing:' groups of people (college students and high school students); gender (males and females); age groups (young and old); material used (hard and easy); type of reading programme (Programme A and Programme B); school types (private and government; rural and urban; traditional high school and all-age schools); changes in time (morning and night); changes in experience (e.g., working under varying levels of noise such as high, medium or low); changes in stimulus materials (brightness of lights, time of exposure to materials; dull versus interesting); levels of drug dosages, and so on. Again, the list is seemingly endless.

Dependent Variables (DV)

Dependent variables consist of some aspect of a behaviour or performance (for example, scores on tests, responses to questionnaires, amount of time taken to complete a task, number of responses, reaction time, etc.) that are given by the participants in a research study according to the type of tasks or materials given. These are the outcomes (usually scores) of measurements used to determine whether variations, manipulations or treatments have produced any effect. They are called dependent because the results or scores *depend* on what you have done with the independent variables. The researcher has varied, grouped or manipulated the independent variable and wants to find out if this has produced any effect on the dependent variable. The easiest way to remember it is that changes in the dependent variable are *dependent* on what happens to the other, independent, variables.

> In a survey study, ratings given to question items would be the dependent variable and characteristics of the population to whom the questionnaire was given (qualitative variables such as gender, age, experience, etc.) would be the independent variables.

An Example of IVs and DVs

One of the authors wanted to determine whether exposure to failure affected the amount of time children spent on a subsequent task ('perseverance at a task'). Exposure to failure was manipulated by giving one group of children a problem that could not be solved and giving a second group a problem that could be solved. In this example, the researcher generated an 'exposure to failure' group and an 'exposure to success' group by manipulating the type of problem given to the children to solve. Following the experimental condition of success or failure, she then measured the amount of time the children in the two groups took to complete a subsequent task. The experimental condition (type of problem to solve) was the *independent variable* because it was manipulated and the amount of time spent on the other task was the *dependent variable*. It was hypothesised that the time (the dependent variable) to complete the task would depend on the type of problem (the independent variable) given to the two groups of children.

Note that you don't have to use only one variable in your research. In fact, you can use many variables in one piece of research. In the example given above, the experimental condition was only one of the independent variables. The experimental variable had two values coded as unsolvable =1 and solvable = 2, indicating the degree of 'solvability.' In the same research, other independent variables with two values were also examined: gender (coded as male students =1 and female students = 2), age (coded as 8 year-old students = 1 and 10 year-old students = 2), and school type (coded as government schools = 1 and private schools = 2). These last three independent variables (gender, age, and school type) obviously could not be manipulated – the naturally occurring variables were accepted as they were.

> Finally, when you are carrying out correlational research – investigating how two variables may be related to each other – you do not have to worry which of the numbers are IVs or DVs, the pairs of numbers are just called variables.

Perception or Prevalence Variables

It is also helpful to realise that you can have 'perception' variables and 'prevalence' variables. You should not confuse these two types of variables. If you do, it might lead you into making false claims about your research and lead you into using meaningless analysis. Being clear about this difference will help you to avoid these mistakes.

Perception variables assess judgements or opinions and there are no right or wrong answers because it is a personal judgement or opinion that belongs to the person responding to a particular question. Examples in which perception variables can be used include 'Likert-type' rating scales where the numbers 1 to 5 are assigned to "strongly agree, agree, neutral, disagree, strongly disagree" or "Very often, often, sometimes, rarely, very rarely", or scales like 'Osgood's Semantic Differential' where the respondent is asked to judge an attribute on a 7 point double anchored scale (that is, only each end of the scale is labelled) such as "unhappy 1 2 3 4 5 6 7 happy." (See Chapter 7 for an overview of scales).

An Example of Using Perception Variables

When investigating 'knowledge of giftedness' by school teachers, a researcher wanted to find out whether male and female teachers differed in their responses on a questionnaire. In this naturalistic study, gender, years of teaching and type of school were the independent variables and responses to the questionnaire were the dependent variables. In the instructions given for the giftedness research, it was stressed that there were no right or wrong answers because the researcher was investigating teachers' 'perceptions' of gifted behaviours. The resulting numbers represented the respondents' *judgements* or *perceptions* of something. They did not actually measure "how much judgement" or "how much perception" of that "something."

Prevalence variables are 'public' measures in that other people can observe and measure the same thing and get the same result (within errors of measurement). Examples are height, income, gender, telephone numbers, or the actual number of times something is done. These can also be called 'public observables' because when other members of the public observe them they will agree on their response. The defining aspect of prevalence data is that if other people could also observe it, then they would give the same response.

Building Your Research IV

Name each variable you are studying. Be specific.

If you are doing experimental or quasi-experimental research:
1. What is your experimental or treatment condition?
2. What variables are the dependent variables?
3. What variables are the independent variables?
4. Are you using perception or prevalence variables? (or a combination of both?)
5. Which variables are perception and which ones are prevalence?
6. What measurement scales are you using to measure the dependent variables?

If you are doing correlational research:
1. State the expected relationship between each set of variables.
2. Are you using perception or prevalence variables? (or a combination of both?)
3. Which variables are perception and which ones are prevalence?
4. How will you measure these variables?

Test Yourself 4

Read the two questions. Which one results in a perception response and which one in a prevalence response? Explain your answer.

Question A: How often did you read books last week?

1 rarely   2 not often   3 often   4 very often   5 frequently

_____   _____   _____   _____   _____

Question B: How many times last week did you read a book?_____

Answers can be found at end of the text.

Confounding Variables

Confounding (extraneous/contaminating) variables are just plain nuisances which is why they are also termed nuisance variables! Gall, Gall and Borg (2003) defined a confounding variable as "...any variable other than the treatment variable that, if not controlled, can affect the experimental outcome" (p. 368). These confounding variables can get in the way of what you thought was a nicely thought out piece of research and affect the validity of your results. Confounding variables may actually prove to be a valid alternate explanation of your findings which you did not think of at the beginning of your research.

Generally speaking, it is almost impossible to conduct a piece of research without including one or more confounding variables. These can be broadly identified under three major headings: organismic, environment, and task variables.

Organismic variables cover a wide range of history of the participant as in gender, age, weight, prior learning, personal biases, attitudes, cognitive ability, and so on. For example, maturation effects may contaminate the results if a participant grows older, wiser, stronger, or more test-taking-wise during the experimental or treatment conditions. This is of particular importance when carrying out research that takes place over a period of time.

Environmental variables refer to what goes on within the experimental or treatment situation. Results might not be valid or reliable because the measuring instruments might have changed, observers might be measuring different things or the results might have been obtained simply because different kinds of people have been selected to be in one group than selected for another. These types of confounding variables occur most frequently in quasi-experimental research when the researcher is not able to have full control over participant assignment.

Task variables refer to the type of task given to participants (as in easy, medium, hard), and the effect of time of day when the participant took part in your research. For example, if you are investigating differences in scores, be very careful that all participants in the research are given the same tasks or questions and, if you are comparing scores, make sure that the time of day did not vary to any great extent.

When you are planning your research, the idea is to realise that confounding variables do exist and so you try to control for them. Sometimes they can be very hard to spot.

Controlling for Confounding Variables

One way of controlling for confounding variables is to start to think of as many different explanations or interpretations of your results (before you start your research). Often, it is a good idea for beginner researchers to have someone check over the research design and discuss other possible explanations for your expected findings.

Then, you can try to contain these variables in a number of ways:

(i)   Hold these variables constant. For example, if you think that your results on reaction time will be influenced by age (you think that old people move slower!), then you could use people belonging to a certain age group. If you think that gender will influence your results, use only males or only females.

(ii) Include these variables as an integral part of your research. In the age example given above, you could build age levels in to your research design. If intelligence, age or previous experience could be interpreted as being important factors of your research, then measure them and include them as factors for analyses. If you find that these factors are unimportant, you can defend your results by stating that these factors did not affect your results and you just collapse (merge) these groups and continue with your analyses.

(iii) Randomly assign participants to a treatment or experimental condition. This will go a long way to ensure that a good majority of the confounding variables are distributed over the entire experiment.

(iv) Use regression procedures, such as partial correlations or ANCOVA[2] to control for confounding variables statistically.

Making Operational Definitions

An operational definition is your *working* definition. It assigns meanings to your variables in terms of the 'operations' that you need to use or measure them. This operational definition gives meaning to an abstract concept or construct in terms of behaviours that can be observed and measured. Many beginning research students do not see the need to operationalise their terms. They start out wanting to investigate somewhat ambiguous and hypothetical constructs, such as perception of justice, motivation in the work place, creativity, career satisfaction, locus of control, apprehension of mathematics or appreciation of reading. These are very general concepts that cannot be observed or measured so each construct must be strictly defined *as it specifically pertains to your research topic*. Then each behaviour pertaining to that concept must be further defined so that it can also be observed and measured.

For example, "aggression" can be defined as "behaviour of a person whose interest is the physical or psychological injury of another" that includes "any offensive or threatening action or procedure." You have defined what "aggression" is; now you have to define what specific behaviours can result in physical or psychological injury to another. These specific behaviours become the operational definitions of aggression that can be observed and measured.

---

2 ANCOVA is not covered in this text. It is recommended that inexperienced researchers should consult an expert before using statistical techniques such as ANCOVA (Analysis of Covariance) or MANOVA (Multivariate Analysis of Covariance).

Think About This ...

In Jamaica, we have heard the word, indicator, used to define a construct and this word is assumed to mean the same thing as operational definition. An indicator means that you have to think of all the actions or behaviours that can be measured to indicate or show that something has taken place. However, these indicators still have to be operationalised so that you can measure them.

The majority of topics involving hypothetical constructs are very worthwhile, but they quickly become very large and unwieldy. Even though you have narrowed down your research so it is do-able, by now, you should have realised that you must operationally define the constructs that you are trying to research. When you make an operational statement, you take a broad construct, such as "motivation," "aggression," "perception" and start thinking about how it can be turned into observable behaviours that are reliable and measurable. In other words, you have to ask, "What are the indicators of the construct I want to investigate?" "How do I define these specific indicators or behaviours?" "How do my definitions relate to my research topic?"

Sometimes, words that you do not think of as "constructs" still need to be operationally defined. For example, some of our students decided to look at "writing." This is a term that can mean a number of things: from holding a pencil and forming letters to making grammatical mistakes to being able to write a particular type of composition.

When forming operational definitions, think carefully
what you are going to measure
how you will be able to measure it
and the measurement scales you will be using.

Although it was suggested that you could start defining a term by looking it up in a dictionary, making the operational definitions required for your research requires a more precise definition than you would find in a dictionary. It should be a definition in terms of observable, measurable behaviours comparable to operational definitions published in other research. If your operational definitions are not objective or precise, then the measures that make up the dependent variables will probably be unreliable. Remember that future researchers might want to replicate your research to check your obtained results and this can best be done only with precisely defined variables.

Examples have already been given how to operationalise aggressive and dropout behaviours. If you are looking at the concept of motivation, the first question to ask is "Motivated to do what?" and then think of all the behaviours that indicate motivation for a particular task or situation and exactly how you will be able to measure these behaviours. Make sure that the behaviours are validated by other research or by someone familiar with your area of research.

In the study about behaviours associated with learned helplessness, one of the measurable components used to determine whether a student exhibited learned helplessness behaviours was 'lack of persistence at completing a task following failure at a prior task.' Persistence was defined as 'the total amount of time a student spent at one task before turning to another task' and the amount of time in minutes was the measurement used. Another variable was 'ability to initiate responses' and the number of responses initiated by the student was counted. Both of these behaviours could be observed and measured. By the way, did you recognise that all of these variables were dependent variables?

Test Yourself 5

Write operational definitions for the following constructs

*motivation	intelligence
*popularity	underachievement
*anxiety	social-economic status
*frustration	level of training
*giftedness	reading ability
locus of control	delinquency

The constructs marked with * may be difficult to define. Why?

Answers can be found at the end of the text

How Terms Are Used

1. In the research investigating learned helplessness behaviours, the **construct** investigated was learned helplessness behaviours.
2. The **thesis statement** was "Children who were exposed to failure exhibited a greater degree of behaviours associated with learned helplessness than children who were not exposed to failure."
3. The **experimental condition** was "Exposure to success or failure conditions" – actually, this was defined as the type of task (solvable versus unsolvable) given to the children.
4. One of the **research questions** was "Did children who are given the unsolvable task spend less time on a subsequent task than children who were given a task that they could solve?"
5. Based on this question, the **null hypothesis** (H_0) was formulated: "There was no difference in the average time spent on a subsequent task by children in Grades 2 and 4 regardless of type of task initially presented to them."

    In this example, the researcher used H_1 "Children in Grades 2 and 4 who were exposed to an unsolvable task condition exhibited less perseverance than children who were exposed to a solvable task." She **hypothesised** (made an educated guess based on previous research) that the answer would be yes.
6. Indicators of learned helplessness behaviours (the **construct**) were based on previous research and included **factors** such as lack of perseverance (**operationally defined** as the inability to spend enough time on a task to complete it, i.e., "giving up") and the time spent at a task was measured: inability to initiate responses (the number of initiated responses were counted); and lack of persistence at task (the number of hidden pictures the child was able to find before giving up). These are all **operationally defined variables** with behaviours that could be observed and measured.

Finally...

Y̶ou have chosen your research topic, narrowed it down to something that you can do, completed a fair amount of reading, made copious notes and references about your topic, and defined and operationalised your variables. Additionally, you have asked your questions and, from them, formed your hypothesis. Now, you have to decide on what type of research you need to do to fulfil your graduation requirements.

Building Your Research V

Look at your list of variables in Building Your Research IV

1. What specific behaviours are you going to observe?
2. Operationally define each variable so it can be observed and measured.
3. What are the confounding variables that might affect your research findings?
4. Indicate how you plan to control for these confounding variables if necessary (e.g., randomisation techniques, statistical methods).

❖ Deciding On a Research Design

Should you worry about a research design? The answer to this question is a resounding "Yes!" A research design is your road map to a successful research paper. When it comes to the data collection and analyses, the research design tells you where you should start, how you will get there and all the things you must do along the way so you won't get lost. By looking at and following your road map (i.e., your research design), you can avoid making many common mistakes such as not controlling for confounding variables, not collecting enough data, (even worse, collecting data that you cannot use!), using inappropriate statistical analyses, coming to faulty conclusions, or at the very worse, failing your course or having your final paper rejected.

Part Two: Get Ready is about choosing the most appropriate research design. It will help you recognise which type of research design best fits your study or investigation, which variables are important – ones that you can most easily measure and analyse – and it recommends the types of statistical analyses that would be most appropriate. This part is divided into three sections: Experimental Research Designs, Non-Experimental Research Designs and Non-parametric Research Designs.

In *Part One: On Your Mark*, you learned that there are many different reasons for carrying out research. In **Part Two: Get Ready**, you will find that there are as many different ways of actually carrying out the research as there are reasons. Fortunately, most research can be divided into a few designs that are standard "cookbook" procedures that you can follow. Once you have identified the research design that you feel comfortable with and one that is "do-able," you just follow the recipe and adapt the associated procedures. This means that you do not have to reinvent the wheel! Additionally, by examining the different types of research designs, you just might find a better alternative for what you want to do. These three sections contain the basic principals of the research process and even if you are in a hurry and want to skip to Part 3 in order to start writing your questionnaires, it is a good idea to first read about the basic assumptions underlying good research. Remember that many of you will want to discover whether groups of people differ in their responses to your questionnaire and the information provided in this section is useful and relevant.

In this section, we have outlined the "basics" required for each type of research design. If you are doing research for a Master's degree, you would probably need to use only one or two fairly basic designs but if you are doing research for a PhD, then you will most likely be using a combination of designs.

> When you use a combination of research designs, you must treat each design as if it were a separate entity then incorporate all results into an integrated whole.

Word Maps

When you are reading this section, you will see that some of the examples of research are outlined in the form of a synopsis that we call "Word Maps" for research designs. Over the years, we have found that when we require students to make a Word Map of their research, it clarifies what they are doing and how they will be doing it. The word maps help you summarise your research so that it can be integrated into the different chapters of your final thesis.

A Table of Your Research

Additionally, we will show you how to draw tables for your designs. These tables will show you how to organise your variables and give you some idea of how to figure out how many participants you will need for your research project.

3
As You Begin

When you come to think about it, there are actually only two broad categories of quantitative research designs: experimental and non-experimental. Of course, each category has many subcategories. Nothing good is ever that easy! Experimental research encompasses "true" experimental and quasi-experimental research and both of these include different designs such as the independent samples design, matched pairs design, repeated measures design, pre-test/treatment/post-test, and so on. Non-experimental research includes descriptive and relational research using correlational methods, causal-comparative methods, surveys and questionnaires (the latter is discussed in Part 3). Each subcategory is explained – the variables you can use, the type of data you should collect, and what statistics would be the most appropriate to use to analyse your data. (The methods for statistical analyses are explained in Part 5).

Parametric or Non-Parametric Research Designs?

Before you start to look at the different research designs, it is a good idea to know whether you are doing parametric or non-parametric research. The main difference between parametric and non-parametric research is that in parametric research, it is assumed that the participants are drawn randomly from a *normal* population while in non-parametric research, this is not a requirement. This knowledge is important because if you don't know the difference between the two types of research, you might just have a wrong sample size or use the wrong statistics for analysing your data. This would be a disaster and all your work would have been in vain!

What on Earth Is a Parameter? – Sampling Procedures

A parameter[1] is a measure (a number) computed from *all* the observations in a *given population*. You should be aware that the actual parameters of a population are largely unknown but are *estimated* from statistics computed from a *sample* of the population you want to study. When carrying out parametric research, an investigator is trying to find out what are the average values of a large population by gathering data from a smaller sample of that population. It would be very difficult to obtain enough data to calculate descriptive measures (the mean and standard deviation) from an entire population, so we gather information from a representative sample of the population being studied. We can then use that information from the small *representative* sample to generalise to the larger population.

---

1 If you are confused about parameters, think about a bakery producing different kinds of cakes. If you wanted to find the average weight of chocolate cakes produced by that bakery, all the chocolate cakes in that bakery would be considered the parameter. You would randomly select a few chocolate cakes to weigh and these few cakes that you have chosen to weigh are your sample. Note that you cannot generalize your findings of the average weight of chocolate cakes to the other cakes in the bakery because your parameter is chocolate cakes.

> A parameter refers to the measure of a population set of scores.
> A statistic refers to the measure of a sample of the population.

An Example of a Sample

Suppose you wanted to find out the average distance that Jamaican children (between the ages of 6 and 18) have to travel to school. You could ask every child how far they have to travel to school, but this would be extremely difficult to do because there are a lot of Jamaican school children and, besides, you could never be sure that you have found *all* the school children in Jamaica. Instead, you would ask just a representative few. This is what we call a *representative sample*. After you have collected the data (the amount in miles or kilometres that each child in your sample has to travel), then you can calculate the corresponding statistic and use it to estimate what it would be for the whole population – for all the children – if we could have obtained data from all the school children in Jamaica in the first place.

What is a Normal Population?

The basic assumption of parametric research is that the scores or data from your population make up a normal distribution. When we talk about a normal distribution, all we mean is that if you were able to obtain measures from everyone in the population to be studied, the distribution would look similar to the bell shape of the normal curve shown in Figure 3.1. Some measures would fall at one end of the curve, others at the other end, but the majority would fall somewhere in the middle.

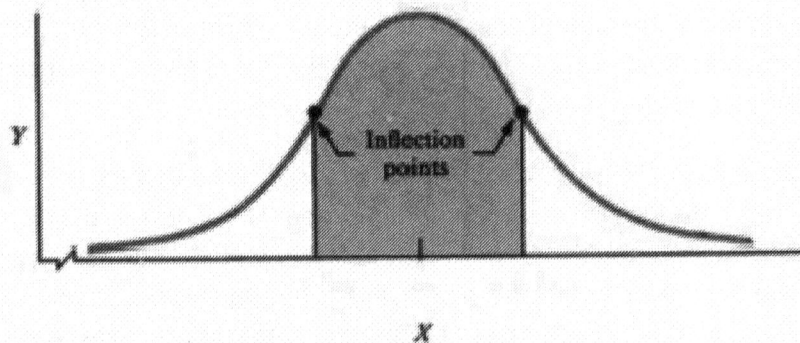

Figure 3.1: A characteristic distribution of the normal curve showing the values (scores) of X on the abscissa (the horizontal line) and Y on the ordinate (the vertical line). Y stands for the density (for a continuous variable) or probability or frequency (for a discrete variable). About $2/3$ of the population mean scores fall between the two horizontal lines.

In the travel example, the population consisted of *all* the school children in Jamaica. If you could obtain data from all the children in Jamaica and plot it, the resulting graph of the distance travelled by all the children in Jamaica (including elementary, high schools, boarding schools, special schools, private schools, etc.) might be similar to the bell-shaped curve shown in Figure 3.1.

Suppose, however, you were not very careful in selecting your sample, would you be positive that your dataset was normally distributed? What would be the result if your sample included a majority of children living in rural areas but very few from urban areas? You might also come up with very wrong statistics if you chose a lot of children who had to travel long distances to attend special schools and those who went away to boarding schools but only a few of the children who attended regular school. This is where randomisation techniques come in useful.

In such a large survey, it might also be necessary to think of grouping the children according to different categories: urban, rural, private schools, special schools, etc. This is called *stratified sampling* – to make sure that subgroups of a population are adequately identified – then you would draw a random sample from each subgroup. The norms given for IQ tests, for example, are based on stratified samples of the population.

How Many People (or Things) in a Sample?

If your random sample is too small, you will not be able to tell if your research results reflect real effects in the population or if the results are only due to the individual characteristics of the few who make up the one particular sample you chose. In fact, if you had the time and resources to do exactly the same research again and again, using different samples of the same inadequate size, you would likely get very different results each time. Some of these small samples might give 'true' results but many would give results that were biased by the peculiarities of the few individual cases that made up that particular sample. However, you usually only do the research once, so you have no way of knowing if the result from your small sample was one of the 'true' results or not. The art is to get a sample that is not too large and not too small but just the right size.

The ideal sample size depends on whether or not:
- you are using random sampling and how certain you want to be that you don't reject the truth (that is, make a Type 1 error).
- how certain you want to be that you don't accept errors as true (a Type 2 error).
- the smallest effect you want to be able to detect (effect size).
- the amount of 'wastage' you expect (sample attenuation).

Clever experimental designs for reducing error variance (e.g., using block designs or paired rather than independent *t*-tests) can also markedly reduce the size of sample you need. That is, a small increase on a small sample is usually worth more than adding large numbers to an already large sample.

As a rule of thumb, using the commonly accepted $\alpha = 0.05$ sampling and ensuring that all statistical assumptions have been met for each statistical technique used, for a Master's Thesis or project, we suggest a *minimum* of 15 participants per group for *t*-tests and *F*-tests, 30 participants for correlation research, and 8 expected-per-cell for Chi-square tests. On top of this, you should add extra numbers to allow for 'wastage' due to dropouts and un-usable or missing data. For survey research, it is suggested that there should be a minimum of 100 participants and, if you are dividing your participants into different groups, then there should be between 15 to 20 participants in each subgroup.[2]

---

2. For more advanced researchers who need to be accurate about the sample size, Pagano (1994, pp 298-305) gives a very good description of using the relationship between power and alpha level to estimate sample size.

In practical situations, such as classroom research, it is better to use affordable intact groups that are above the minimum requirement, rather than risking disruptions by reducing numbers to an ideal sample size. If you intend to use different statistical techniques, e.g., for answering different research questions, then choose the largest of the sample sizes needed. For example, if you wanted to use a Chi-square test for comparing effectiveness for boys and girls of two teaching methods in one class, you would have a 2 X 2 table (boys and girls by Method 1 and boys and girls by Method 2) which gives 4 cells. Providing you have at least 8 participants in each cell, you would have 32 participants – above the minimum sample size. As there will probably be a little more than this number of boys and girls in the whole class, you can use the intact class at little extra resource cost, assigning at least 8 boys and 8 girls at random to each method, which will allow some leeway for 'wastage' and cause minimum disruption in the school. Note that using all the children from one class (i.e., blocking by class and teacher), rather than using one class and one teacher for each method, reduces unwanted variation due to different classes and different teachers, and so will make your sample size even more effective.

Randomisation Techniques

In order to be able to generalise our results from our sample population, we need to ensure that the measures we obtain from the participants in our sample are similar to what we would get if we were able to test the entire population. This means that we need a representative sample. To do this, it is necessary to use randomisation techniques. Random selection means (i) that you cannot know beforehand which members of the population will be selected to be in the sample and (ii) that each member of the population under consideration has an equal chance of being selected.

If you have ever watched raffle tickets being drawn or played Bingo, you will have a good idea of randomisation –no one knows which number will be chosen. By putting in only one of each number or letter, each number or letter has an equal chance of being drawn. Note that if there were many more number 10's than other numbers, then there is much more chance of choosing more tickets with 10 on it, but the selection is still random because you cannot tell beforehand if a 10 or some other number will be chosen.

Randomisation techniques should be used because people usually choose for a reason. It may be a subconscious reason; they may not even know what the reason is and think that they are being completely unbiased in their sample selection. It has been found, however, that when people choose, there is usually a pattern in their choices and the patterns are even more obvious when people try their hardest to choose at random! The important thing to remember is that everyone in a population should have an equal chance of being selected for your sample. If the ticket is not in the bowl then it can't be selected!

Randomisation techniques can be as simple as tossing a coin, drawing out names from a bowl, or by using a table of random numbers (found in the appendix of most statistic texts). You use randomisation techniques for two different reasons: (i) to select people to take part in your research (called a *random sample*) and (ii) to ensure that the people in your sample are randomly assigned to one condition or another (called *random assignment*).

Generally speaking, you should always try to use random sampling and random assignment to avoid biased selections that might weaken your research. Once you have a true random sample selection, you can use the information obtained from this random sample to compute descriptive measures (the means and standard deviation) and use these for further statistical analyses. You can also use the data to make assumptions about the parameters of the entire population.

An Example of a Population Sample Based on the Assumption of Normal Distribution

A researcher wanted to find out if elementary school teachers in Jamaica were aware of the characteristics of students who were gifted. He randomly selected 400 male and female elementary school teachers in both rural and urban areas (see Table 3.1 for an example of his final selection) and, using a questionnaire, asked them to rate different attributes of giftedness on a scale of 1 to 7. After he received their responses, he analysed the results and was able to generalise his findings to all elementary school teachers in Jamaica.

He had to use a random sample of teachers because it would have been almost impossible (as well as time consuming) to ask <u>all</u> the elementary school teachers in Jamaica to respond to his questionnaire. Because of his method of randomly selecting his sample from the larger population, his sample could be considered representative of all elementary school teachers in Jamaica. Actually, this researcher had a very difficult time ensuring that his sample of male teachers was randomly selected – something for future researchers to think about!

Table 3.1: *An Example of a Table Showing a 2 X 2 Research Design.*

SCHOOL TYPE	URBAN		RURAL	
GENDER	FEMALE	MALE	FEMALE	MALE
NUMBER	100	100	100	100

Note: N = 400

In this example, all elementary school teachers in Jamaica were his population parameter and teachers were randomly selected (his sample) to be asked to respond to his questionnaire. The researcher sent his questionnaire to both male and female teachers in rural and urban areas because this can be thought of as a 'scaled-down model' of the total population and means that he can generalise his findings to all elementary school teachers in Jamaica. Note that he could NOT generalise his findings to high school teachers, special-education teachers, teachers in New York City, etc., because they were not included in his sample and could not be considered a part of his population parameter.

Non-Parametric Research

$\mathbf{N}$on-parametric (also called "distribution-free") research requires only minimal knowledge about the distribution of population being investigated and, unlike parametric research, assumptions about the "normal" shape of the population distribution are not required. This only means that the population under study may not have a similar shape or be as symmetric as the assumption of the normal population required for parametric research. In the social sciences, often measurements of attributes, traits and characteristics are not normally distributed and may be skewed to the high or low end of the measurement scale.

When you use a non-parametric research design, you **cannot** use statistical analyses based on the assumptions of a normal population. It is important, however, to realise that all other aspects of a good research design are necessary: a random selection of the population being studied to make sure that your sample is a scaled-down model of the population distribution – even though it may be an unknown distribution – and ensuring that you obtain independent observations[3] when collecting data. Without these precautions, you cannot ensure generalisation of your findings to whatever population you are trying to study.

Non-parametric research designs are also appropriate when variables consist of categories that do not follow a natural order, as for example when data is collected in the form of frequencies, orderings, and/or rankings. The important thing to note is that these variables being measured are qualitative in nature and that any of the nominal categories that make up your variables do not occur in any specific order.

The two examples that follow are examples of non-parametric research because the population under study was not necessarily normally distributed. In the first example, the researchers chose Grade Nine students at one school only and in the second example, the participants were patients at one local hospital. In both examples, it could not be assumed that the participants were from a normal distribution. Consequently, non-parametric statistics had to be used for analysis.

An Example of Non-Parametric Research – I

A pilot study was conducted in a school to see if an HIV information seminar was effective in conveying new information about HIV to Grade 9 students. The H_0 was: "Presenting a seminar on HIV increased Grade Nine students' level of knowledge of HIV." The researchers theorised that if this method of presenting information on HIV was effective for these students, then this method could be used with students in other grades and in other high schools. Pre- and post-tests were administered to a small sample of students who had been randomly drawn from all the Grade 9 classes in that school. The pretest regarding the students' knowledge of HIV was given before the information was presented and the post-test was given directly after the new information was presented. In this study, although the researchers collected actual number scores from the two tests, these scores were converted into rank differences and analysed using the Wilcoxon Matched-Pairs Signed-Ranks test.

---

3. This means that making one observation (collecting one set of responses) does not affect the making of another observation. For example, focus group discussions are not considered independent.

An Example of Non-Parametric Research– II

A researcher wanted to find if there were differences in the number of stressful life events as reported by cardiac patients and by orthopaedic patients in a local hospital. The null hypothesis (H_0) was: "Cardiac patients and orthopaedic patients in a local hospital reported similar stressful life events." To carry out his research, he asked each patient to put a check mark beside each stressful life event that he/she had experienced in the last year and then the responses for each group were ranked from lowest to highest. He then analysed the responses using the Wilcoxon Rank-Sum Test – a good non-parametric test to use when the sample population is equal to or less than 25.

Conclusion: Parametric or Non-Parametric Research?

The practical importance of assuming that population scores rely on parameter estimation and follow a normal distribution is that you are able to assume a lot of information without having to collect a lot of data –the more information you have then the more significant your results are likely to be for the same sized samples.

You can also use approximate responses resulting in discrete or categorical variables, but then you must use less powerful non-parametric tests to reflect the loss of information caused by the approximations. For example, if you analyse data using the rank order of children's scores on two tests instead of the actual scores themselves, then you have to use Spearman's *rho* which is a less powerful version of Pearson *r*. If you only count *how often* the observations fall into different categories (when categories have no natural order, such as the number of "yes" or "no" answers), these categories cannot be ordered like the numbers on a ruler, and you will have to use non-parametric tests.

If you are designing a questionnaire, rephrase your questions to get high quality ratio data. For example, instead of asking a question that requires a simple yes/no answer, ask how many times. Rather than "Have you been to the cinema in the last month?" use "How many times have you been to the cinema in the last month?" If you want to waste information (and some times for cultural acceptability you have to, as for example, in the question: "How much do you earn?" or "What is your age?"), you can always later classify your data into groups or rank it, but you cannot go the other way – that is collect low information data such as yes/no counts and later convert it into high information measures.

We feel that it is best to try to use a parametric research design because it requires smaller sample sizes for the same levels of significance and these results may prove of interest to a wider reading audience. When you are thinking about your research design, try, if you can, to form hypotheses that require the collection of data from a normally distributed population.

Unfortunately, you can't just assume that the scores will be normally distributed just to make your life easier by using a smaller sample. You should be able to justify this assumption on theoretical grounds. But, don't worry about this because you can always check for normality of data sets within a population by doing a simple test – the Kolmogorov-Smirnov One-Sample test – on your scores to ensure that they do meet the assumption of normality. Although this test has a long and difficult sounding name, it is actually very easy to do and "how to do it" is explained in Section 3.

Time for a Decision!

Once you have most of the basic work done and are ready to write your research proposal, there is only one important thing left to do – figure out how you are going to analyse your data by using the most appropriate statistical tests. This is an important part of your proposal because it tells the reader that you honestly have an idea of the type of data you will be collecting and how you will be analysing it.

The easiest way to decide on the different types of statistics needed is to look at the Decision Chart on page 46. The major idea of using the Decision Chart is that you have to keep answering questions about your research hypothesis and data collection until you finally arrive at the statistic(s) you need to answer your hypothesis.

Some of the questions that you need to ask are:

- What is your research hypothesis?
- Who or what was involved?
- What type of data did you collect?
- Are you looking for relationships among scores?
- Are you looking for differences between scores?
- Is your research parametric or non-parametric?
- If you gave more than one test or questionnaire or used more than one experimental condition, did the same participants provide the scores (as in scores from pre- and post- tests) or did different participants provide the data (as in the experiment using different seeds and experimental conditions)?

When we discussed sampling procedures, you learned (along with some basic assumptions such as random sampling and independent responses) that one of the differences between parametric and non-parametric research was which statistical procedure would be most appropriate. Figure 3.2 gives a brief overview of the assumptions and measures required for the different methods.

You should use parametric statistical methods when
1. the distribution of scores in the population is normal.
2. the population variances about the mean are fairly equal.
3. the measures yield ordinal or ratio scores or have equal intervals.

You should use non-parametric statistical methods when
1. there are large deviations from assumptions about the normal distribution of the data set.
2. there are large deviations in equality of population variances of the groups.
3. the measures yield categorical or rank scores or do not have equal intervals.

Figure 3.2: Assumptions and measurements required for parametric and nonparametric statistical tests.

To determine whether you will use parametric or non-parametric statistical tests[4], it is recommended that you first:

- Use the Kolmogorov-Smirnov to check for normality of the distribution of scores.
- Use the Levene's Test for Equality of Variances to check whether the variances for two groups (as in the *t*-test) or for more than two groups (as in the ANOVA) can be assumed.

If the assumptions for using parametric statistics are not met, then you use the non-parametric statistics. Figure 3.3 is a list of some of the types of the basic research designs with matching parametric tests and their equivalent non-parametric tests.

Type of Research	Parametric Tests	Non-parametric Tests
Correlation/Relationships	Pearson *r*	Spearman's *rho*
Partial correlation	Pearson *r*	
Independent-Samples	*t*-test (independent samples)	Mann-Whitney Test
Paired-samples	*t*-test (paired samples)	Wilcoxon Signed Rank Test
One-way between groups	one-way ANOVA (with comparisons)	Kruskal-Wallis
One-way repeated measures	one-way ANOVA (with comparisons)	Friedman Test
Two-way between groups (with interactions)	two-way ANOVA	
Frequencies		Chi-square for independence

Figure 3.3: Basic types of research and equivalent parametric and non-parametric tests.

Using the Decision Chart

To get the most information out of the Decision Chart, start at the top with your hypothesis. Note that answering questions regarding relations and frequencies are fairly straightforward and only require one or two questions. When you get to finding differences between scores, then you have to really settle down and think about your hypotheses. You start out by asking, "What is my research hypothesis?" Look along the top line and start answering the questions to end up with all the correct statistics you can use.

A. To find out if two sets of scores are related: If your hypothesis concerns some form of relations between Variable X and Variable Y, then you will look at the oval marked **correlations?** Next ask: "Is my research parametric or non-parametric?" Follow the arrow to the right and if it is parametric, the correct statistical test to use is Pearson *r* and if it is non-parametric, then the correct statistical test to use is Spearman's *rho*.

4. All of these statistical tests are explained in Part 5. Do not worry about them now, just make a note of when they may be best used.

B. To find out whether observed frequencies (using nominal data) differ or are similar to expected frequencies: If your null hypothesis states that there will be no differences between participants allocated to *different categories*, then you would look at the oval marked **categories**? Follow the arrow to the left and you will find that you have to use Chi Square.

C. Finding out whether there are differences between conditions: If your hypothesis is concerned about differences between conditions or responses to questions, then you go to the oval marked **differences**? Now follow the arrow down and ask the next question: one variable or two? If you are using only one variable, then follow the arrow to the left and if you are using two (or more), follow the arrow to the right. Continue following the arrows and asking questions (found in the ovals) and answering them (found in the boxes) until you arrive at the final statistical method that would be most appropriate for your research

For example, if you are using only one variable, then your next question would be "How many conditions are in my research?" This question is in the oval marked **how many conditions**? If you answered **three or more** (found in the square to the right), then your next question would be "Are the participants same or different in each group?" (found in the oval marked **same or different**?). If you answered same (in the box marked **same**), then you follow the arrow to the final box where it says **Par? ANOVA (related) or Non-Par? Friedman**. As there was not enough space to ask the final question about whether your research was parametric or non-parametric, you have to decide which test is the correct one to use. But, frankly speaking, this is a decision that should have been made long ago!

An Example of Using the Decision Chart

To give you a practical example of using the Decision Chart, refer to the research investigating learned helplessness behaviours described in Part One. One of the null hypotheses was: "There was no difference in the average time spent on a subsequent task by children regardless of previous exposure to a solvable or unsolvable task."

Starting at the top line, the first question to be asked is "What are we trying to find?" and the answer is: "Differences between the one condition of success or failure." Remember that we wanted to find out if the scores of children differed when one group of children were given a problem they could solve and the second group were given a problem that they couldn't solve.

1. Starting from this oval, follow the arrow to the next question: **one variable or two?** The answer would be one (only one condition is being analysed) and we would follow the arrow to the right.

2. The next question to be answered is: **same or different participants?** And the answer to this question is **different** because we used scores from two different groups of children.

3. This means that we now follow the arrow to the right and finish up with **Par *t*-test (unrelated)** or **Non-Par Mann-Whitney**. Because of the research design – the students were randomly chosen and randomly assigned to groups, and the K-S results showed that the scores came from a normal distribution, the research was definitely parametric and so the correct test to use would be the *t*-test.

Related or Non-Related?

The only thing that might present a problem to researchers new to statistics could be "What is the difference between related and non-related?" If you look at the decision chart, you can see that towards the end of each decision are the questions **same?** and **different?** Remember that this question refers to the participants in your research. If you obtained scores from the same participants – maybe after a time interval (as on a pretest and post-test) or under two different conditions (to find out if there are any differences between GSAT scores and grades by the same students when they are in Grade Nine, or to investigate whether the same individuals would react differently when they are placed in different conditions), then this would require a related test because even though the conditions or tests may be different, the two or more sets of scores were obtained from the same group of people.

In non-related tests, you want to see if there are any differences between conditions or scores, but this time you are using scores from two or more different sets of participants, as for example scores of tests written by males and scores of tests written by females.

Finally, one question that we have often been asked is, "How many statistical tests can you use in one study?" The answer to this is easy:

USE AS MANY AS YOU NEED TO ANSWER ALL YOUR HYPOTHESES.

For example, one of your hypotheses might have been to find out if two variables are related and you would use Pearson r (or Spearman's rho) to determine whether there was, in fact, a relationship between the two variables. An additional hypothesis might have asked if there was a gender or age difference and then you would use either a t-test (for gender or age) to determine differences between the mean scores of two groups or an ANOVA if there were three or more groups.

Don't be afraid of using statistics. As you will see in the Part 4, analysing your data is interesting and relatively simple because the computer programmes that are available are very researcher-user friendly! This might sound difficult but, as we shall see in Part 4, it is actually very easy!

A Decision Chart for Testing your Hypothesis

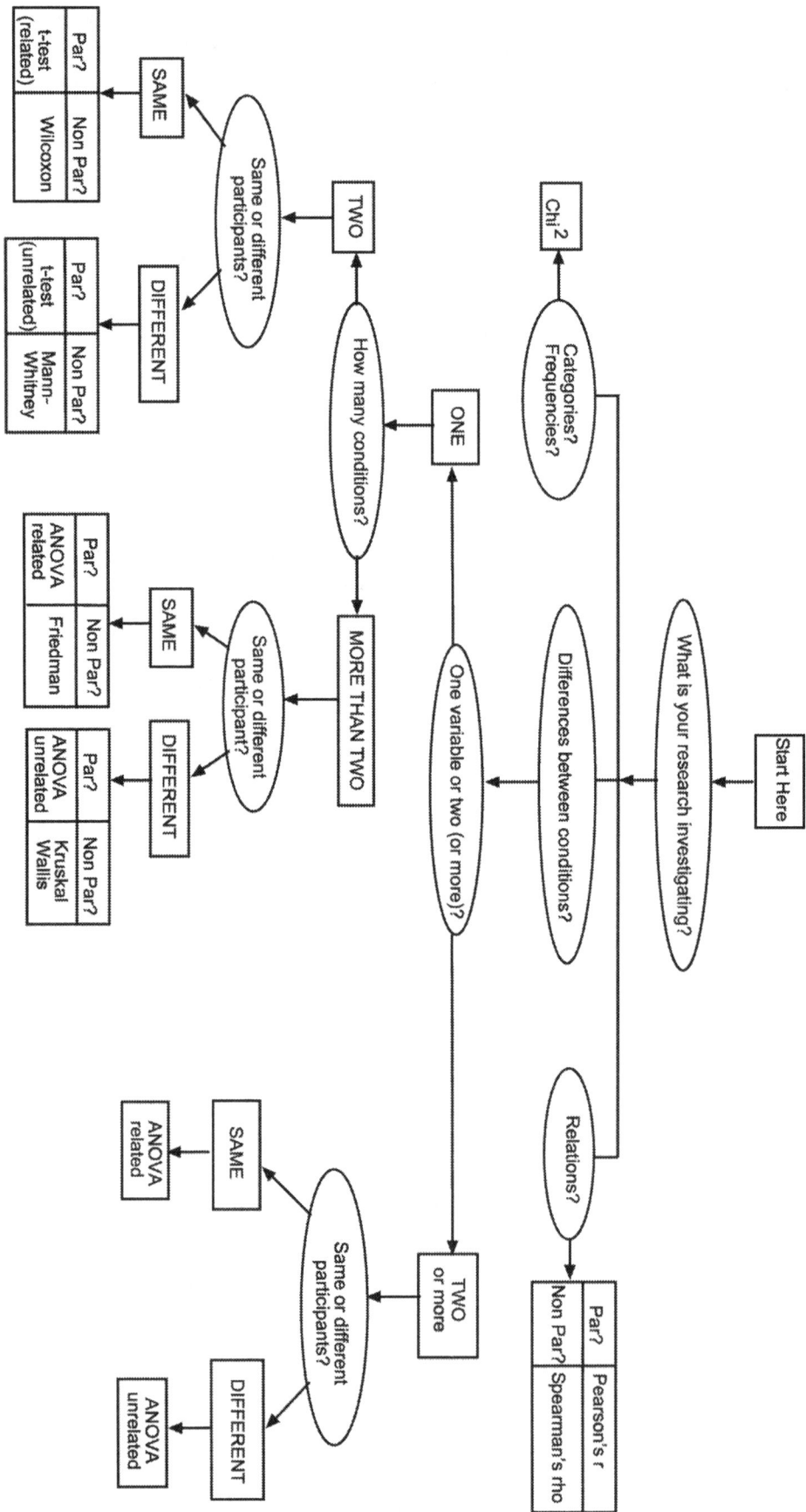

Start Here → What is your research investigating?

What is your research investigating? → Differences between conditions?

Differences between conditions? → One variable or two (or more)?

One variable or two (or more)? → Categories? Frequencies?

Categories? Frequencies? → Chi 2

One variable or two (or more)? → How many conditions?

How many conditions? → ONE → How many conditions?

How many conditions? → TWO → Same or different participants?

Same or different participants? → SAME → Par? t-test (related) | Non Par? Wilcoxon

Same or different participants? → DIFFERENT → Par? t-test (unrelated) | Non Par? Mann-Whitney

How many conditions? → MORE THAN TWO → Same or different participant?

Same or different participant? → SAME → Par? ANOVA related | Non Par? Friedman

Same or different participant? → DIFFERENT → Par? ANOVA unrelated | Non Par? Kruskal Wallis

Differences between conditions? → Relations? → Par? Pearson's r | Non Par? Spearman's rho

One variable or two (or more)? → TWO or more → Same or different participants?

Same or different participants? → SAME → ANOVA related

Same or different participants? → DIFFERENT → ANOVA unrelated

Note:
Par = parametric tests
Non Par = non parametric tests

4
Parametric Research Designs

We start this chapter by describing some basic experimental research designs showing you what is involved in preparing well thought-out research. Even if you have no desire to conduct experimental research, it is still a good idea to read through this chapter because almost everything about experimental research designs can be applied to non-experimental research! We also introduce you to the concept of drawing "word maps". By making a synopsis of your research in the form of a word map, you get a clear understanding of what your research involves.

"True" Experimental Research Designs

A definition of a "true" experiment is: "An experiment is a research situation in which at least one independent variable, called the experimental variable, is deliberately manipulated[1] or varied by the researcher."[1] An experiment is actually a form of controlled and disciplined observation. In a true experiment, after one (or more) variable(s) has been manipulated[2] or varied, the researcher carefully observes and notes the outcome of the manipulations. The measurements of the observations are the dependent variables – they depend on what is happening in the treatment or experimental condition. The data are then analysed to determine whether the treatment (or experimental) condition really did make a difference or whether the differences were likely to have occurred only by chance.

> The dependent variable is usually referred to as "X
> The independent variable is usually referred to as "Y"
> The experimental condition is usually referred to as the "treatment variable"

Experiments take place far more often in everyday life than you would think! As a very simple example of an experiment, a person might say: "What would happen if I added sugar to my black coffee?" The person would then add a teaspoon of sugar to his coffee and discover that it tasted sweeter than coffee without sugar. You are even experimenting when you change the colour of a belt to see if it looks better with the new trousers you just bought. The main idea of an experiment for research purposes is this: a researcher takes "X" (a situation or event) and does something to it or some part of it – gives it the treatment. In an experiment, the researcher generally wants to find out "What will happen if I take a condition and if I change, control for, vary, or manipulate it?"

---

1. Wiersma, 1999, p. 107.
2. One of the things that scare off many beginning researchers is the word "manipulate." This only means that you take a certain setting or a particular event and vary what happens in it.

The *experimental (or treatment) condition* refers to the condition that exposes participants taking part in the research to the independent variable. It is the condition that is planned in advance by the researcher. You can alter, control for or manipulate most types of experimental conditions: the type of material given to participants, changing the brightness of lights, levels of noise, and so on. In the example of behaviours associated with learned helplessness, the type of problem (solvable vs. insolvable) given to the children was the experimental condition. In medical research, the experimental condition is often the level of drug dosage given to participants. Edison used different types of filaments (experimental condition) to determine which type lasted the longest when he was experimenting with the manufacture of light bulbs.

An Introduction to "Word Maps" of Your Research

In this section, we show you how to write "word maps." We have found that when beginning researchers have to write a synopsis of their research design in the format of a "Word Map," it gives them direction and helps clarify what they want to do. Each word map is written in a simple format:

- Problem (thesis) statement
- Hypothesis (either non-directional H_0 or directional H_1)
- Operational definitions of key terms
- Independent variables
- Dependent variable(s)
- Confounding variables
- What statistics are to be used for the analysis

Examples of Word Maps are scattered throughout this section.

An Example of a Simple Experiment

High school students were given the task of finding out whether exposure to different coloured lights (either blue or green) affected the growth of plants. The students randomly divided a packet of seeds into two groups and planted the seeds in one of two boxes each containing identical soil mixture. One box was placed under a blue light while the other was placed under a green light. The seeds were given equal amount of watering and an equal exposure time to the light assigned to each box. At the end of two months, the plants in each box were measured and the height of each plant recorded. This research can been written as a word-map shown in Word Map 1.

In this experiment, many possible confounding variables, such as difference in the amount of water, time of exposure to the light, differences in seed quality and soil quality, were controlled so that difference in plant growth could be attributed only to the difference in colour of light. The data was analysed using a *t*-test because there were only two groups (seeds growing under blue light versus those growing under green light). A *t*-test was appropriate because the null hypothesis stated that there was no difference between two conditions. This means that average heights of plants in Group 1 must not be significantly taller than, or shorter than the plants in Group 2.

WORD MAP 1

Problem Statement: An experiment investigating the effect of green or blue lights on plant growth

Null Hypothesis: There was no difference in plant growth under blue or green lights.

Operational Definitions

   plants: seeds from a package randomly divided into two equal groups

   Treatment A: exposure to blue light only

   Treatment B: exposure to green light only

Independent Variable	***Dependent Variable***
Treatment A or B	Height of each plant measured by a wooden ruler

Analysis: *t*-test (to determine differences between plant growth of the two groups)

A Pretest/Treatment/Post-test Research Design

Figure 4.1 shows the four stages of a simple experiment to find out if a treatment or experimental condition works. The condition could be any of a number of things: a special method of teaching, using different medications, growing plants under green or blue lights, or giving children solvable or unsolvable tasks to do. In this example, we have included a control group so that the results of those in the treatment group could be compared with the results of those in the control group.

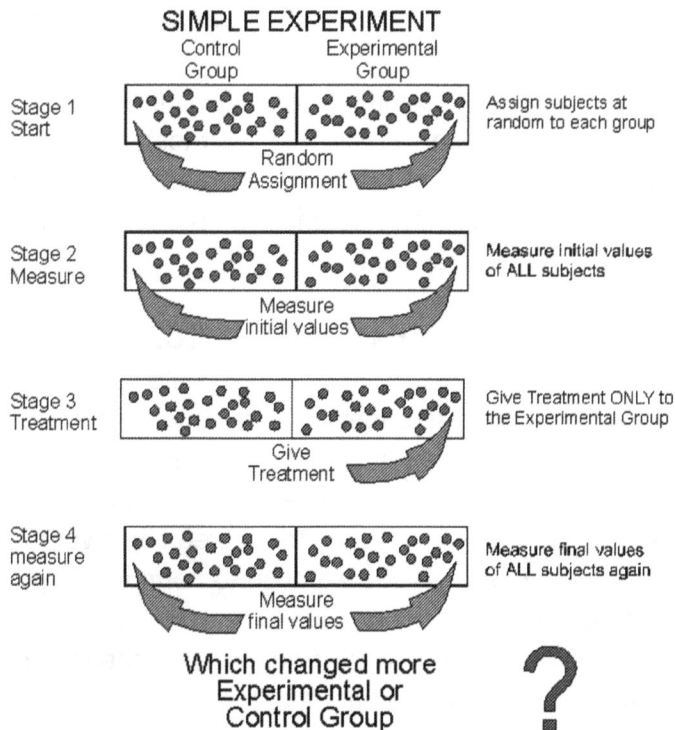

Figure 4.1: Four stages of an experiment with two groups.

Examine what happens at each of the different stages in Figure 4.1.

Stage 1: Randomly selected participants are randomly assigned to one of two groups.

Stage 2: The initial level of the dependent variable is measured by means of a pretest. This acts as a check on your random assignment. If you have assigned the participants at random to each group, then you would expect to get an equal number of participants in each group who score high, medium or low on your measure. This means that, on average, there should be no initial difference between the two groups on your dependent measure. (This randomisation process also protects you from getting participants in one group who are very different from participants in the other group on other measures that you might not have considered).

Stage 3: You "do your thing" – give the special treatment, but only to the experimental group. The control group will carry on doing what they usually do and no special treatment is given to them.

Now, you want to know if your treatment had any effect – that is "Did the scores of the participants in the treatment group differ significantly from the scores of the participants who did not receive any treatment?" You find this out in Stage 4.

Stage 4: You measure the dependent variable through a post-test given to all participants to see if scores from the experimental group, that is the treatment group, differed significantly from those of the control group.

As numerical data has been collected, you can find the means and standard deviations (measures of central tendency and variation) and analyse these scores using a *t*-test because there are only two groups. Scores from the pretest would show (hopefully) that there was no significant difference between the mean scores of the two groups and that your random assignment of participants to the different groups controlled for systematic differences. Scores from the post-test would be analysed in a similar manner, but this time, there might be a difference between the mean scores of the two groups. If there was a significant difference, then you can say that your condition or treatment most likely did have an effect.

Participants, Treatment Conditions and Time Constraints

Simple two-condition experiments can be elaborated to test more than one treatment. As in most experimental research, there can be any number and types of experimental or treatment conditions, it just depends on the amount of time you have to complete the research. For example, in the plant growth experiment, the students could have used the same two experimental conditions (exposure to green light versus exposure to blue light) and added a "control" group of seeds exposed to normal sunlight. Then the plant height of the two experimental groups could have been compared to that of the control group. Because the students only added an extra light source, the total research would not have required any extra time. This also meant that they would have had to use an *analysis of variance* (ANOVA) because there would have been more than two groups in their study

How many treatments you explore also depends on what your research is being used for: a Master's Degree, a PhD. or a journal article. If you have to do a research thesis in order to graduate, you do not want to have to spend years collecting data and hopefully, the research will be completed and written up within a year. For a PhD degree, however, you will have to spend a much longer time. When looking at the time element, the research involving plant growth was for a high school project and was completed within eight weeks, the stress research (described below) was for a Master's degree and took six months before all the treatments were given and the data collected. With the help of five research assistants, data collection for the learned helplessness research was completed in one year for a PhD.

An Example of a Simple Experiment Using Five Groups

For a more elaborate research design, suppose we had five treatments. In Figure 4.1, we showed a simple experiment by only using two groups but we could have started by randomly assigning our participants to any one of five groups as shown in Figure 4.2. What happens during the first two stages are similar. Then, in Stage 3, each different group is given a different treatment.

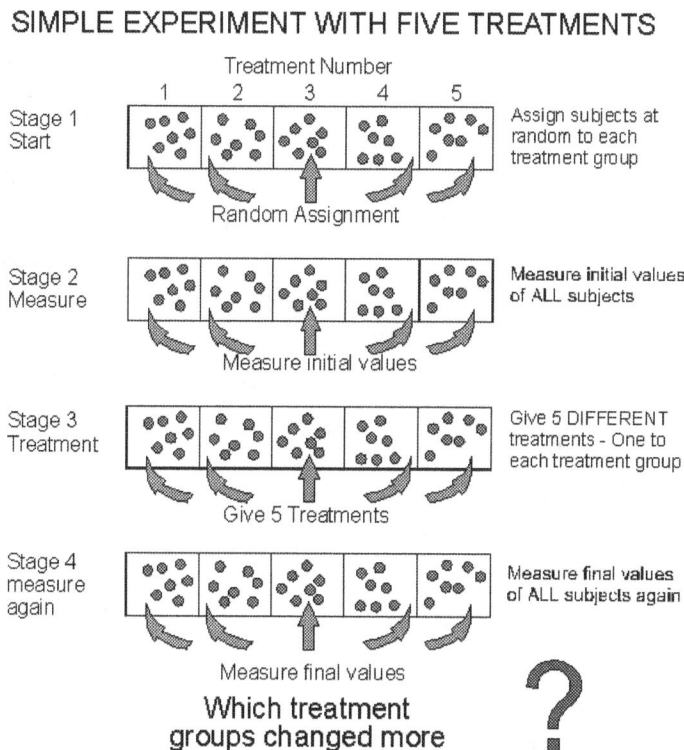

SIMPLE EXPERIMENT WITH FIVE TREATMENTS

Figure 4.2: Four stages of an experiment with five groups.

At the end, in Stage 4, we could see which scores of the five treatment groups changed most. This will tell us if the different treatments had different effects and, if so, which treatment was the most effective. In this case, you would have to use an analysis of variance (ANOVA) because *t*-tests can only be used when there are two groups and the ANOVA should be used for three or more groups. In addition, you can also use a statistical programme to compare the scores of the different groups – but more about this in Part 5.

Notice that in these two experiments, the researcher used a control group which is considered an integral aspect of many experimental procedures. The participants in a control group do not receive experimental treatment at all or, in educational research, may receive a different treatment of some sort that is not related to the programme under study (e.g., teaching a class using a new method and teaching a second class in the usual manner). The purpose of including a control group into the experimental design is that scores from this group provide a basis for purposes of comparison.

Factorial Research Designs

Factorial designs are used when two or more independent variables with at least two levels of each variable are included in the same research design. Each independent variable is called a "factor", hence its name. Often, when reading about research that has been done, you may see something like "2 X 2" (read the X as "by") describing a research design. This simply means that there were two independent factors each with two levels. There can be any number of factors and each factor can have any number of levels. For example, the research investigating learned helplessness behaviours was actually a five factor research design with each factor having two levels (2 X 2 X 2 X 2 X 2). The factors were experimental condition (success and failure) X grade level (Grade 1 and Grade 4) X achievement ranking (low and high) X gender (boys and girls) X school type (private and government).

Be warned! The number of different groups and consequently how many participants you would need for each group increases dramatically if you add too many factors with too many different levels! Using numbers to describe a factorial design shows you how many different groups you must have for your research design. In a 2 X 2 factorial design, you need 2 X 2 = 4 different groups and might be able to get by with as few as n = 10 (n stands for participants in each group) or N = 40 (N stands for the total number of participants). In the five factorial design, 2 X 2 X 2 X 2 X 2, 32 different groups were needed. (You just keep multiplying!) If you wanted 10 participants in each group, you would need a larger number of participants (N = 320). If the researcher had used one more level of achievement and made the design a 2 X 2 X 3 X 2 X 2, she would have needed 48 groups and, consequently, many more participants – 480 to be exact!

One advantage of a factorial design is that it is many experiments in one so that the many different conditions and levels as well as the interactions can all be compared. This enables the researcher to find out if the treatments, when given together, interact to reinforce each other or interact to cancel out each other's effect or if a group of treatments might be better than some other group of treatments.

About Interaction Effects[3]

When discussing the use of ANOVA for analysing data, we have also introduced a new term, the *interaction effect*. This is an important term to know when you are doing research using a factorial design. Remember that a factorial research design is one in which two or more factors (independent variables) with at least two levels of each factor

---

3. Do not worry about interactions as this stage. When you get to Chapter 17, you will be shown how to draw interactions and how to interpret them.

are included in the same research design and the treatments or conditions used are combinations of the factors. This means that you can test two or three hypotheses simply by using a two-way ANOVA.

For example, look back at the discussion of the learned helplessness research. One factor was school type with two levels (private and government), another was gender with two levels (boys and girls), a third was grade with two levels (Grade 1 and Grade 4) and the dependent variable was scores on a test. If we wanted to find out whether the scores differed according to school type, gender and grade, then we could do a one-way ANOVA and that would tell us that the scores were different or the same for each of the factors. This is called the **main effects** (another important term). This is not as difficult as it sounds. Main effects give the results for the variables being measured *without* considering the different factors (or levels that were a part of that factor). An **interaction effect** will occur if scores are not the same at different levels of the factor being measured.

If we want to find out whether there is an interaction effect among factors, then we would have to use the **two-way ANOVA**. This would tell us that the scores might be high for boys in Grade 4 but not for girls in Grade 4, or that scores might be high for all children in Grade 1 but not for all children in Grade 4, or that the scores might be high for children attending government schools and low for children attending private schools – that the scores differ according to the different levels of the factors.

When we do a simple or one-way ANOVA, we are just investigating whether the treatment or experimental condition (the IV) has any effect on the criterion (the DV) and looking at the main effects.

When we use a two-way ANOVA, we are looking for interactions, and looking to see if the effect of one factor is the same or different at all of the levels of the other factor.

For example, suppose you were measuring levels of motivation on math scores. You also wanted to find out if there were (a) gender differences and (b) grade differences. Your three factors (independent variables) would be (1) two levels of motivation (high and low), (2) gender (males or females) and (3) two levels of grade (Grade 1 and Grade 5). This would make your research a 2 X 2 X 2 factorial design. If you wanted to look at three levels of motivation, then you would have a 3 X 2 X 2 factorial design and you would need more participants to take part in your research.

When you analysed your findings, you might find that math scores were significantly different according to levels of motivation but not for grade level. If you only looked at the main effects, you might lose some important information because once you examine the interactions between grade level, motivation and math scores, you might find that level of motivation for students in Grade 1 did not affect math scores but that it did for students in Grade 5. The interaction might similar to that pictured in Figure 4.3. More about interaction effects when you learn about the two-way ANOVA in Part 5.

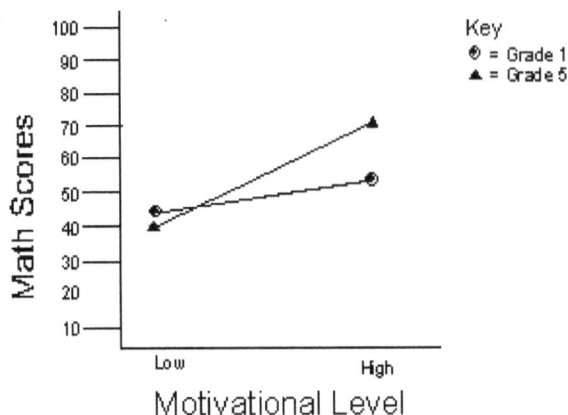

Figure 4.3: An example of the interaction effect showing that levels of motivation have a greater impact on mathematic scores of Grade 5 students than of Grade 1 students. The lines are not parallel showing an interaction effect.

An Example of a Simple Factorial Design

A researcher wanted to find out if relaxation therapy would relieve pre-examination stress for female students attending teachers' colleges (see Word Map 2). She also wanted to know if teaching the students how to study would improve their examination results – these were her two treatment conditions. She naturally wondered what would happen if she gave both these treatments together. Would they interact to cancel each out – that is, would the students become so relaxed that they might lose the motivation to use their study training? Or, would the two treatments together interact to reinforce each other and improve exam results more than if only one or the other treatment was given on its own?

Stage 1:   She randomly assigned her participants into four groups (Figure 4.4.)

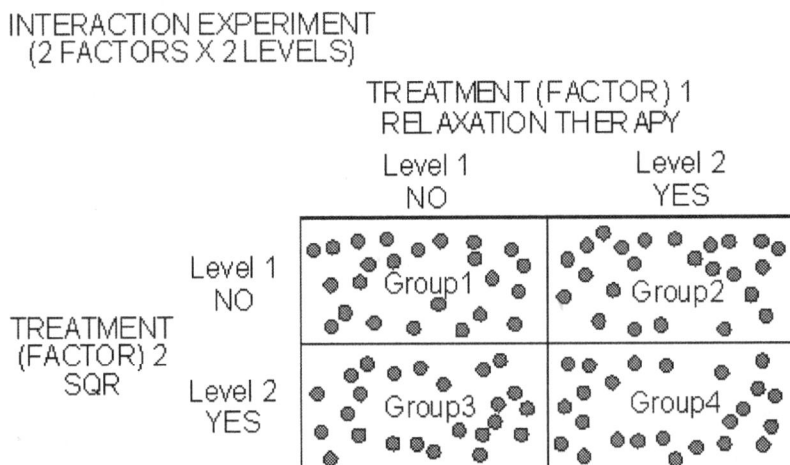

Figure 4.4: A diagram of an experiment involving an interaction.

Stage 2: She measured the students' pre-exam stress just before a major examination. Measures obtained from her "pre-exam stress questionnaire" and final marks from the first examination written by these students were her two pretests – they were both given prior to the treatments.

Stage 3: She gave her treatments: Participants in Group 1 received no instruction in relaxation therapy or in how to study (NO NO group) and were considered her control group. Participants in Group 2 received instruction in relaxation therapy only (NO YES group). Participants in Group 3 only received instruction in SQR³ (the 'how to study' method) only (YES NO group), and the participants in Group 4 received instruction in both relaxation therapy and instruction in SQR³ (YES YES group).

As the participants in Group 4 were to receive BOTH treatments, she planned to use this group to test for any interaction between the treatments. Also, because Group One (her control group) was receiving no treatment at all, she could use the results of this group as 'base data' against which she could compare the advantages of any of her treatments.

Stage 4: Immediately prior to the participants writing their final examination, she again measured the amount of stress they reported feeling. These second measures were considered the 'post-test' as they were given following the treatment(s). When she analysed the results for all four groups, she found that the participants in Group 4 (the ones given both relaxation therapy and SQR³ (the YES YES group) reported a greater reduction in stress prior to taking examinations. In addition, she also found that the examination results of the participants in Group 4 improved significantly when compared to scores on the examination written prior to the treatment and when compared to the examination results of the participants in the other three groups.

In this experiment, the researcher had chosen her participants (the population sample) at random to represent female students attending teachers' colleges. She also randomly assigned the participants into one of four groups to administer the four treatments. She had two outcome measures or dependent variables (i) a measure of pre-examination stress as shown by responses on her questionnaire and (ii) the examination results. She also had four 'treatments', which were the relaxation therapy, the SQR³, a combination of the relaxation therapy and SQR³, and the fourth treatment was "nothing" – the participants in this treatment were her control group.

To analyse the data collected in this research, the investigator used the Pearson *r* (correlational statistics) to look for any relationship between reported stress levels and examination results and a two-way ANOVA because this was a 2 X 2 factorial analysis (2 treatments and 2 levels). She used the ANOVA to determine whether results from her pretest stress questionnaire were similar or different across all four groups and to analyse whether there were significant differences in the examination results.

She used the Pearson *r* to find out if the amount of stress that the students reported was related to their examination results and found that students who had high pretest anxiety also scored lower marks on the examination. In her initial testing, she had found no significant differences among the four groups on the pre-examination stress questionnaire and for the first examination results. She was happy at finding this because this confirmed that the participants in the four groups were randomly assigned.

WORD MAP 2

Problem statement: A study of the effects of relaxation training and how to study (SQR^3) training programme upon amount of stress and examination results of female students attending teachers' colleges.

Hypotheses:

1. There was no relationship between reported levels of stress and scores on final examinations.
2. Reported levels of stress (measured by pretest and post-test) did not differ significantly among students following six weeks of relaxation training.
3. Reported levels of stress (measured by pretest and post-test) did not differ significantly among students following six weeks of how to study (SQR^3) training programme.
4. Reported levels of stress (measured by pretest and post-test) did not differ significantly among students following six weeks of both the relaxation and how to study (SQR^3) training programme.
5. There was no difference between final examination results of students in each of the three conditions: (a) relaxation training, (b) how to study (SQR^3) training, and (c) both relaxation and how to study training.
6. Scores of students for both the stress questionnaire and the final examination were similar regardless of the treatment condition.

Operational Definitions:

Individuals included in the study: 100 female students attending teachers' colleges randomly selected and randomly assigned to one of four groups

Stress questionnaires: Pretest/Post-test (based upon a standardised test purchased from Publisher A)

Treatment A: relaxation techniques for Groups 2 and 4

Treatment B: SQR^3 training for Groups 3 and 4

Independent Variables	*Dependent Variables*
Treatment A	Scores of pretest stress questionnaire
Treatment B	Scores of first examination
Treatments A and B	Scores of post-test stress questionnaire
Control Group (no treatment)	Scores of second examination

Possible Confounding Variables

Motivation of students

Intellectual ability of students

Note: These may have been controlled for by randomly assigning students to the different treatment groups.

Analyses: Pearson *r* and ANOVA

For the post-test data, she used responses from her second pre-examination stress questionnaire and the scores from the final examination. A two-way ANOVA was used to determine if scores of each group differed significantly on the two measures and the Pearson r to determine relations between the amount of pre-examination stress and the final examination results. The two-way ANOVA was also used to determine whether there was an interaction between the two methods (but there was not, the combination of the two methods proved to be the most effective at easing stress and improving exam results).

By carefully controlling the treatment conditions, she was able to discover that relaxation therapy combined with learning how to study produced less feelings of pre-examination stress and increased examination results for female students attending teachers' colleges – a useful piece of information.

Making a Table of Your Research Design

When you are planning experimental research – actually, almost any form of research– it is a good idea to make a table of your research design (different from writing a Word Map) to see exactly what is involved. There are many standard ways of making a table: '+ – -' tables and 'X – 0' (YES – No) treatment tables are common (as shown in Figure 4.4).

We first look at table that clearly shows the number of participants in each treatment as well as the different independent variables. The table for the experimental design used in the research about learned helplessness behaviours is shown in Tables 4.1a and 4.1b. The first heading is the experimental condition, the independent variables/factors are (1) gender, (2) age of participants, and (3) school type. The numbers at the bottom represent the number of participants used in the research. Note that none of these variables are the dependent variable – the DV will be the total score obtained by each of the students on each the five tasks following the experimental condition.

Table 4.1a: An Example of "Making a Table" of a Research Design for Experimental Condition 1: Unsolvable Problems

EXPERIMENTAL CONDITION 1	MALES		FEMALES	
Age Group	8 years old	12 years old	8 years old	12 years old
School Type	gov priv	gov priv	gov priv	gov priv
No.of subjects	20 20	20 20	20 20	20 20

n = 160; 1 = unsolvable problems; gov = government schools; pri = private schools

Table 4.1b: *An Example of "Making a Table" of a Research Design for Experimental Condition 2: Solvable Problems*

EXPERIMENTAL CONDITION 1	MALES		FEMALES	
Age Group	8 years old	12 years old	8 years old	12 years old
School Type	gov priv	gov priv	gov priv	gov priv
No.of subjects	20 20	20 20	20 20	20 20

n = 160; 2 = solvable problems; gov = government schools; pri = private schools

Note that each table has its own key for all the abbreviations you have used. Readers do not want to have to read through different pages to find out exactly what the abbreviations mean.

If you decide to do a study with many different independent variables, it is usually a good idea to draw out your research design this way to ensure that you will have enough participants for your study. For example, a student-researcher wanted to look at the value of a particular course taught in college from the perspective of both students and tutors and to discover whether there was a gender bias towards this course. When he drew a table for his research design (see Table 4.2), he realised that there were just not enough male tutors teaching this course to randomly select his participants or to determine whether there was a gender bias about the course. Consequently, he had to revise his ideas somewhat. It was better that he realised that this would be a problem before he started collecting his data.

Table 4.2: *A Research Design to Investigate Value and Gender Bias Toward Course Y*

TUTORS OF COURSE Y		STUDENTS TAKING COURSE Y	
MALES	FEMALES	MALES	FEMALES
15	15	30	30

Another way of drawing a research design is shown in Table 4.3. In this table, the researcher drew boxes and labelled them "Yes" and "No." He then placed the number of participants in each box according to which treatment they would receive. Notice that there is a NO-NO treatment group meaning that no-one in this group would receive any treatment at all (the control group), a YES-YES treatment group meaning that everyone in this group would receive both treatments, the participants in the YES-NO group would receive Treatment 1 but not Treatment 2 and the participants in the NO-YES group would not receive Treatment 1 but would receive Treatment 2. This method of drawing a research design also shows how many participants in each condition and the type of treatment each group would receive.

Table 4.3: *An Example of "Making a Table" of the Experimental Design for the Experiment on Reducing Stress*

	NO TREATMENT 1	YES TREATMENT 1
NO TREATMENT 2	Group 1 (n = 25) (Control)	Group 2 (n = 25) (Relax only)
YES TREATMENT 2	Group 2 (n = 25) (SQR^3 only)	Group 4 (n = 25) (both SQR^3 &Relax only)

Note: N = 100; relax = relaxation training

It doesn't matter how you draw your research design but it is a good idea to always start with some form of drawing out of your design so you have a good idea of the total number of participants your research will require before you start collecting data.

More Types of Research Designs

Independent Samples Design

The independent samples design can also be called between-participants unrelated design. It simply means that individuals are first randomly selected and then randomly assigned to any one of a number of different conditions. Most of the research described thus far have been independent samples design. Note that there can be more than one condition, but the main idea is that a participant (individual, plant seed, or machine part) must be randomly assigned to only one condition. Needless to say, this is the easiest type of experimental research. The data is fairly easy to analyse: independent *t*-tests for two experimental conditions and one-way ANOVA (unrelated) for three or more experimental conditions – because no person gets more than one condition or treatment, you can not look for interactions in this type of design.

You use the independent samples design when differences between natural groups are being investigated, for example, different ages, gender, religious preference, etc. because you simply cannot manipulate these variables. The major disadvantage is that sometimes the use of different individuals may produce individual differences (for example, someone with unusually high intelligence can give some lop-sided scores) but this can usually be offset by ensuring that participants are (i) randomly selected for the research and (ii) randomly assigned to the experimental or treatment condition.

Matched Pairs Design

In matched pairs designs, participants are matched in pairs (or blocks of two) on the basis of a particular characteristic and then each one of the pair is randomly assigned to one of the experimental or treatment conditions. This means that there will always be an equal number of participants in each treatment condition. The most obvious way of ensuring that each pair is evenly matched is by using identical twins! However, finding enough pairs of identical twins for an adequate study is almost impossible for most researchers, so other ways have to be thought of. Some ways of matching pairs are by using IQ scores, academic marks, height, weight, verbal ability, some form of health history such as number of previous heart attacks, and so on. It is important to discover whether we truly have a matched pair design by looking at the correlations between the measures of the two pairs and a correlation greater than 0.50 is considered acceptable.

A matched pairs design would also be useful if we want to compare the 'desirability' of any two products and we can ask one person to rate two different products. In this case we are considering one person as a "block" and giving two treatments to that one person. We see many examples of this on television when companies show that one brand of hand cream is 'superior' to another and the commercials show a person who has used Brand A on the right arm and Brand B on the left arm. This form of research is much better than asking different participants to rate each product, because people can vary in their values. In this way, each pair of ratings is given from the perspective (values) of one person and the matching pairs design would help to reduce this unwanted variation between raters. It is also important to know that each participant is consistent in how he or she rates each product and this consistency must be carefully built into your research design.

Matched pairs design are useful for reducing one unwanted source of variation – that of individual differences between the control and experimental groups. This means that we get rid of the unwanted variation that would have been there if we hadn't taken account of the matching variable.

Some of the problems with this design are that (i) inference from the results might be restricted because by using matched pairs, you are limiting your sample and you can never be sure that the participants are matched on all the variables that are likely to affect their performance, (ii) knowledge of the matching condition might make participants behave differently and so reduce the validity of your experiment, (iii) although more than two groups may be used, it becomes very difficult to find enough participants who can be randomly selected and matched for three or more groups and (iv) it can not be used when participants **have** to be different as, for example, when you want to investigate gender differences.

An example of using matched pairs design would be to match children according to their mental age, keeping chronological age and gender constant. This means that a boy of a certain age would be matched with another boy of the same age and both would have a similar mental age or IQ score. Girls would be matched in the same way. Then each one of the pairs (blocks) would be randomly assigned to a group. Next you would have to give each child in both groups some form of pretest and check to see that there was no significant difference between the mean scores of each group of students. This shouldn't be a problem because you matched each pair of students on mental age, gender and chronological age and then randomly them into different groups.

If you wanted to examine, for example, the effects of a special method of teaching reading using the matched pairs design, then you would match the children as above and assign one of each pair to either the special method group or to the control group. Then you would have to give all the children a pretest measuring their reading ability, give one group the treatment condition (the control group would just be taught in the same old way) and then both groups a post-test to see the effects of the treatment. If the researcher found that the children who had been taught the special method of reading scored higher on the post-test than the children who had not been given the treatment (using a paired *t*-test), the researcher could say that the special method of teaching children to read was effective. Note that the researcher has controlled for variations in age, gender and mental ability (but of course, there are other confounding variables, such as motivation and parental concern, that could also have accounted for this effect).

> **WARNING** – most experimental versus control group experiments in education show that the experimental group scores are better. This is not because of the 'new special method' that was used, but because of other uncontrolled variables such as the enthusiasm of the teachers for something new, or the interest roused in the children by something new.

Repeated Measures Design

This design is also called the **within-participants design** and means that the same participants are in all experimental conditions. This does eliminate individual differences between experimental conditions but the major problem is that sometimes there will be an order effect (a confounding variable) that will affect the outcome and, consequently, your research. For example, if a person becomes increasingly familiar with the experimental condition, scores might increase just because there has been that much extra practice time. Or, a person just might get tired and thus show a decrease in scores.

The way to counterbalance this is to vary how the same person is presented with the treatment conditions: randomly assign one half of the participants to half of Condition A first and then half of Condition B second, and the other half to Condition B first followed by Condition A second, until all conditions have been done by all participants. This is a counterbalanced design – a 2 X 2 factorial design analyses using ANOVA and is similar to the stress research (described in Figure 4.4 on p. 54). The main effects are treatments and counterbalancing. However, here the interaction is the **order effect**. In other words, we are asking, "Does it matter which treatment came first?"

There are many problems with the counterbalance design – practice and fatigue effects, sensitisation and carry over effects from one treatment to another. Unless you are particularly interested in the order effect then it may be better to just get a larger sample so that you can give different treatments to different groups and then you won't have to worry about the order in which you give the treatments.

Quasi-Experimental Designs

Very often, researchers cannot randomly select their participants but have to use intact groups – this is why it is called *quasi*-experimental. (Quasi means "resembling.") All the things you need to think of and do for experimental research are the same for quasi-experimental research, except, of course, you don't randomly select participants, you use intact groups but remember that you can still randomly assign these intact groups to the experimental or treatment conditions.

Quasi-experimental research is very common in areas in which it is difficult or unethical to randomly assign individual participants to any one specific group and is used in businesses with many workers in one area (such as offices, factories, hospitals, wards, clinics), and in educational settings (such as school districts, schools, classrooms).

Example 1

A company wanted to find out if workers at a complex task worked better in quiet or noisy surroundings. They varied the noise levels in the work place over specified periods of time and counted the numbers of errors made by the workers at each noise level. This is a quasi-experiment because an intact group of workers (all the workers in the company) were the participants. This research is also an example of a repeated-measures design because the mistakes each worker made were measured at each of the three noise levels. The numbers of errors made by the workers were counted under each experimental condition and an ANOVA was used to determine whether there were any significant differences between the mean numbers of errors made by the workers at each level.

Example 2

An educator wanted to find out whether phonic or the whole-word method of teaching reading led to greater improved reading ability for students in Grade One. In four Grade One classes, students were taught to read using only the phonic approach while in four other Grade One classes, students were taught to read using the only whole word approach. Prior to the experimental condition (method of teaching reading), all Grade One students were given a pretest to determine their ability to read and, at the end of the school year, all students were given a post-test to determine which group of students improved the most in reading ability. This is a quasi-experiment because intact classes of students were used. It would have been impossible to randomly select students for each teaching method, although the intact classes were randomly assigned to each method. However, it might be possible to randomly select whole classes so that the sample of classes represents classes in general, e.g., some from rural and urban areas, some from high and low SES districts, etc. (See Word Map 3).

As If This Wasn't Enough......

Cross-Sectional Research

Cross-sectional research is often carried out when time is an important factor in your research. In a cross-sectional research design, you figuratively take "...a slice of time and compare participants of different ages on some variable."[4] Participants are placed into groups according to age, as for example, young adolescents (13-14 years old) and older adolescents (16-17 years old) or by school grades (students in the first grade and students in the third grade). The research would be carried out as any other research except that you have added an extra variable but the results would be reported according to age, school grade, etc. The learned helpless research is an example of cross sectional research because the participants in this research were children attending Grades 1 and 4 and the data for this research were collected at one point in time.

---

4. Kerlinger, 1996, p. 98.

WORD MAP 3

Problem Statement: A study of the effects of two reading programmes (phonic versus whole word) on the reading achievement of students in inner city Grade One classes

Hypothesis: Scores of reading ability of Grade One students following three semesters of teaching were similar regardless of the reading programme taught.

Operational Definitions

Participants in the study: Intact classes of Grade One students attending eight randomly selected government inner-city primary schools.

Reading Programme A: phonic method with a set of reading materials and suggested activities purchased from Publisher A.

Reading Programme B: whole word method with a set of reading materials and suggested activities purchased by Publisher B.

Independent Variables	***Dependent Variable***
Reading Programmes A and B	Scores of reading achievement (as measured by the difference of scores on a standardised reading achievement test – one form given prior to the treatment and one form given after the treatment)

Possible Confounding Variables	***Possible Control Variables***
Teacher and Teaching Style	Gender of students
Students' learning style	Prior reading achievement
Students' scholastic ability	
Number of students in each class	
Motivation by parents	

Note: By randomly assigning each intact class to one of two groups, some of these confounding variables may be controlled.

Analyses: ANOVA, regression techniques

Longitudinal Research

Longitudinal research entails observations of the same participants taking part in a research project over a period of time that can last from a few weeks to many years. The data is collected at different points in time but from the same person. This type of research is useful when investigating whether attitudes towards some form of change over time or looking at trends or opinions over time. In a recent study carried out by a PhD candidate, the researcher investigated (among other things) the relationship between academic achievement and IQ scores of school children over a period of five years.

The Solomon Four-Group Design

On some occasions, a pretest might serve to sensitise (increase the knowledge of) the participants to what is being tested and so influence the results, as for example, with research investigating knowledge of a particular concept before and after a specific treatment condition. When researchers wanted to determine the extent of college students' knowledge of HIV, they decided to give all the first-year students a pretest, then randomly selected half of the students to view a film about HIV. This was to be followed one week later with a post-test given to all the students to determine whether viewing the film had led to increased knowledge (see Word Map 4).

It was thought, however, that maybe the students who did not view the film but had taken the pretest might want to learn more about the participant and do some independent study on their own. Then, when a post-test is given, they also might show an increase of knowledge about HIV even though they were not shown the film. This increased knowledge might lead to the false rejection of their alternate hypothesis: "When college students view a film about HIV, this leads to an increased awareness of the disease."

In cases such as this, when it is believed that a pretest might have some effect on the final results, it is possible to control for the pretest effects by using a Solomon Four-Group design. In the HIV example given above, the researchers had to worry that the pretest might interest the students who were in the pretest/post-test control group and that this interest might influence the results. They decided that the Solomon Four-Group design would be the most appropriate means to analyse the data.

WORD MAP 4

Problem Statement: A study on the effect of viewing a film about HIV on increased knowledge about this disease.

Hypothesis: Students who have viewed the film about HIV were better informed about HIV than students who did not view the film.

Operational Definitions
Participants in the study: All first year college students attending one college
Film about HIV (donated by WHO)

Independent Variable	**Dependent Variable**
Film about HIV	Gain in scores of HIV awareness (as measured by the difference of scores on a questionnaire published by WHO – one form given prior to the treatment and one form given after the treatment)

Possible Confounding Variables	**Possible Control Variables**
Prior knowledge of HIV	Gender of students
Motivation to learn more about HIV	Age of students

Analyses: Solomon Four-Group

Statistical Analysis of the Solomon Four Group Design

In this type of research design (a non-parametric research design because they used an intact group of first-year students at one college), the experimental group and the control group are split in half to give four groups and only one of the experimental groups and one of the control groups are given the pretest. The drawing of the research design for the four groups would look like that shown in Table 4.4.

Table 4.4: *An Example of a Table Drawn for the Solomon Four-Group Research Design*

PROCEDURE	TREATMENT CONDITION	
	Film	No Film
PRETESTING	Group I	Group III
NO PRETESTING	Group II	Group IV

It can also be drawn out as shown in Table 4.5. This drawing shows very clearly what the participants in each group will be doing. Remember that all the participants have been randomly assigned to one of the four groups.

Table 4.5: *An Alternate Method of Drawing a Table for a Solomon Four-Group Research Design*

	PRETEST	FILM	POST-TEST
GROUP 1	O	X	O
GROUP 2		X	O
GROUP 3	O		O
GROUP 4			O

Note: O means Pre- and Post- Tests were given, X means Film shown

An Explanation of How the Solomon Four-Group Design Works

Don't worry about the actual calculations. This just explains what is happening and although it looks very confusing, remember that the computer does all the calculations for you and you just have to remember what group is doing what. Hence the need for your research design.

1. The scores on the pretests by Groups I (pretest, treatment, post-test) and III (pretest, no treatment, post-test) are averaged and an assumption is made that these scores will be similar for Groups II (no pretest, treatment, post-test) and IV (no pretest, no treatment, post-test only) if they had been pretested. (This is because the participants were randomly assigned to groups.)
2. The scores on the post-test from Group II are analysed (no pretest, treatment, post-test). You can assume that the analyses is not contaminated by the pretesting procedures. Compare the estimated pretest scores and the actual post-test scores of Group II (treatment, post-test) to show whether the treatment is effective, is not effective or has no obvious effect.
3. Compare this effect with that obtained in Group IV (no pretest, no treatment).
4. Compare the differences in post-test scores between Groups I and III with those

found in Groups II and IV to calculate the effects of pretesting on the treatment conditions. If the results are positive, it indicates that the pretest did influence the results and if negative, the pretest did not influence the results.

Many researchers never use this design because the Solomon-Four group design requires twice as many participants just to test if there is a pretest by treatment effect. That's twice the work and twice the cost, so it is not the favourite choice of overworked researchers!

A Checklist When Planning an Experimental/Quasi-Experimental Research Design

1. First make sure that you have a definite hypothesis (or hypotheses) and that your experimental conditions will test each hypothesis. Remember that the whole purpose of your research and statistical analyses is to impartially decide whether your hypothesis can or cannot be rejected – never say 'accepted.'

2. Next and probably the most important, you must make sure that the participants[5] in your research are randomly selected and assigned. If you randomly choose your participants in an unbiased way so that they can be considered representative of the larger population (the normal population), and randomly assign them to treatment groups then you can generalise your findings to that larger population (something most researchers want to do). You also must realise that all parametric research is based on the assumption that participants have been randomly selected from a normal population.

> In the stress research, the researcher could not generalise her findings to all students because she only used female students as her participants. If she had wanted to generalise her findings to all students attending teachers' colleges, she would have had to find enough male students who were willing to take part in her experiment.

3. Make sure that you have carefully defined your independent variables and your experimental/treatment conditions so that you know exactly what you and the participants will be doing. (Actually, by the time you get this far into your research, this should have already been done when you spent all that time making operational definitions for each of your variables.) Now, you should see why it is so important to operationalise all your variables so they can be observed and measured.

4. Make sure that your measuring instruments are reliable and valid. This is done by carefully defining what you are going to measure and how you are going to measure it. If you are using different research assistants to obtain your data, you will have to train your researchers and ensure that there is agreement as to exactly what they will be observing and measuring.

---

5. Nowadays, the term "subjects" is replaced by "participants" because these are people who are participating in your research. At the same time, if you are referring to people who responded to a questionnaire, use the term "respondents."

> If you are using some form of measuring instrument, make sure that it does not vary from condition to condition as, for example, a cloth tape measure will stretch over time, scales should be calibrated prior to each use. If you will be using a questionnaire, as in the stress research, the questions must be directly related to the construct being studied (see **Chapter 7, Why USe Questionnaires?**).

5. Make sure that you have not only controlled the independent variable but have tried to control for other confounding variables that might "muddy" your findings. A confounding variable is something that might change your results because it is an unwanted but inseparable part of the treatments you are interested in. For instance, if you are looking at the effect of something on young children (a teaching method, for example), the time of day when you measure the effect might affect the outcome – in the mornings, young children might be willing to work hard but by the evening, they just might be too tired to answer or respond correctly. In the stress research, the participants were asked not to talk to each other about what they were doing in each group. In the matched pairs example, a possible confounding variable of differences in mental ability along with order of presentation of materials were built into the design.

Test yourself 6

Read the proposed research carefully and then answer the questions that follow.

1. A company director of a large garment manufacturing plant wanted to find out if employees would produce more garments if they were hired on a piece-work basis rather than being paid by the week.

2. A scientist was interested in the effect of a drug on reaction time. He gave the drug and then measured reaction time in a driving task.
   (a) Decide whether the research is experimental or quasi-experimental and state why you think so.
   (b) State the experimental condition and the independent variable(s)
   (c) Draw out a word map for each research design.
   (d) What statistical analysis would you use and why?

Answers can be found at the end of the text.

5
Non-Experimental Research

Very often, investigators need to find answers to problems they have observed by carrying out research that is non-experimental. In truth, finding answers to many research questions does not require experimental manipulations or treatment conditions. In some situations, independent variables simply cannot be manipulated but, instead, must be placed into categories. When organismic variables (as for example, intelligence, social economic background, teaching style, attitudes, etc.) under investigation cannot be manipulated, or when it is unethical to manipulate variables, then non-experimental research is the answer.

In the section on experimental research, you were shown how to investigate differences (or similarities) between two or more variables by deliberately changing one variable and then looking to see whether there were differences in the other variable(s). In non-experimental research, we are more interested in investigating variations or relationships in existing groups or relationships between existing groups rather than actively making changes that might alter the degree to which things vary. Note, however, even though you can not manipulate many variables, you can still check for differences between them using statistical analyses such as *t*-tests or ANOVAs.

> Non-experimental research looks at the magnitude and direction of relations between two sets of variables and examines them in their natural settings.

Correlational Research Designs

A major method of investigating whether two variables are associated is through the use of the correlational research design. Correlational relationships are also known as bi-variate relationships because the research involves two variables (the "bi-" of bi-variate). In this type of design, variables are not called independent or dependent but simply "variables." Unlike experimental research in which scores obtained from the dependent variables provide the data to be analysed, in correlational research, data are collected on two sets of variables, X and Y, and the two sets of data are then analysed to determine the relationship between them.

The main functions of correlational research are to try to uncover relationships between two variables and to discover the direction and magnitude of these relationships – whether a set of scores from one variable is similar to the set of scores from another variable. When you first look at the two set of scores, you may be able to guess that there is some sort of relationship, but by using correlational statistics to analyse your data, you can precisely define the relationship through a mathematical expression called the *coefficient of correlation*.

Although we feel that most students have a good understanding of the concept of correlation, we will give a brief description for those who may be a little confused. To put it simplistically, in a perfect positive linear relationship (r = +1.00), high scores of variable X go with high scores of variable Y and low scores of variable X go with low scores of variable Y. Think of this as "HIGH/HIGH – LOW/LOW." This is shown in Figure 5.1(a).

In a perfect negative linear relationship, (r = - 1.00), then high scores of variable X go with low scores of variable Y and low scores of variable X to go with the high scores of variable Y. Think of this as "HIGH/LOW – LOW/HIGH." This is shown in Figure 5.1(b).

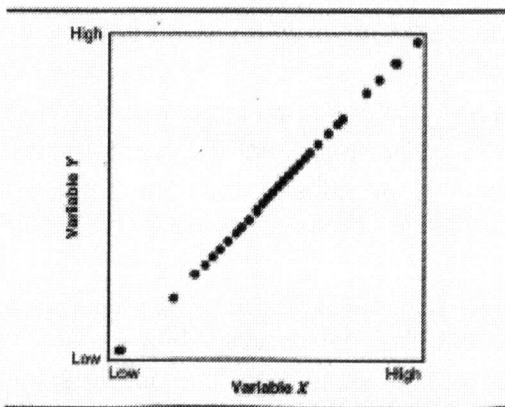

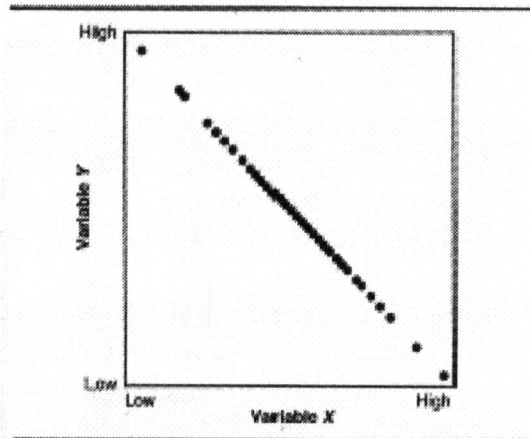

Figures 5.1 (a) and (b): Illustrations of (a) a perfect positive linear relationship and (b) a perfect negative linear relationship. In both cases, the two sets of points or scores fall on a straight line.

Correlations can vary between +1.0 and -1.0 and if the correlation is "0", this means that there is no relationship at all. Obviously, the closer the correlations are to +1.0 or -1.0, the more significant will be the correlation. If r or *rho* (r = Pearson r; *rho* = Spearman's *rho* – both are types of correlational statistics) are significant, this tells you that the chances are that the relationship between scores were *not* due to chance fluctuations.

> You must realise that in the majority of research, perfect linear relationships are rarely found. But do not panic, because when you start using the computer programmes for data analyses, the printout will tell you which correlations are statistically significant and which ones are not.

Planning Correlational Research

When you are planning correlational research, you start with the same first steps as when you plan to carry out experimental research. You start with questions, you formulate the hypothesis (or any number of hypotheses) and operationally define the variables that possess the characteristics that you wish to study, (e.g., smokers and non-smokers, males and females, internal locus of control and external locus of control, underachievers and overachievers, IQ scores and academic scores, fluoride in drinking water and tooth decay.) As with most research, the list of variables that can be used to examine relationships can be almost endless.

It is also important for you to know that, similar to experimental research, you can also formulate many different hypotheses. Remember that the H_0 predicts that the correlation can go any way and the H_1 predicts a correlation in one direction – either positive or negative.

Next, check whether the variables being studied form homogeneous groups or whether they might have to be divided into further subgroups. Look for types of subgroups (e.g., school types might have to be divided into rural and suburban, or private and government schools; students might be subdivided according to grade as in Grade 1 students and Grade 4 students, the general population might be divided according to gender, age, religious affiliation, SES, and so on.)

Finally, decide on how you will collect the data. Again, there is no limit as to the method of data collection – responses to questionnaires, standardised tests, researcher-made tests, interviews, observations, pretests and post-tests, and so on. Just remember that the type of measurement data you plan to collect will direct the type of statistical analyses you can use. (Look at the Decision Chart to see the different types of techniques that are most commonly used.)

Example 1 of a Correlational Research Design

An example of a research design using correlational analysis has already been described in the stress experiment. The researcher wanted to find out whether the reported amount of stress prior to writing an examination was related to scores on examinations. She gave the students a questionnaire asking them about their perceived level of stress and correlated the scores from the questionnaire (one variable) with scores from their examination (a second variable). She did the same thing following the treatment. She was able to analyse her data using the parametric test, Pearson *r*, because she randomly selected her participants and randomly assigned each student to different treatment groups.

Example 2 of a Correlational Research Design

A researcher was interested in determining whether there was a correlation between the amount of hours that adolescents view television and their grades in school. Although he secretly thought there would be a negative correlation between the two variables (that is, he hypothesised that students who watched TV for long hours would receive lower grades), he was not positive. To play it safe, he used the null hypothesis: "The amount of hours watching television had no effect on school grade percentages." He randomly selected a group of Grade Nine students (males and females) from high schools in a large urban area and asked them how many hours per week they spent watching television. Next, he was able to look at their academic records and determine their average grade percentages. Because he randomly selected his participants, checked the normality of his data and did not use nominal or interval measurements, he was able to use Pearson *r* for analysing his data. (His research design is drawn out in Word Map 5.)

WORD MAP 5

Problem Statement: A study investigating whether the amount of hours that teenagers watch television was related to school grades.

Null Hypothesis: There was no relation between the amount of hours that teenagers watched television and their academic grades.

Operational Definitions

participants: Male and female Grade Nine students randomly drawn from randomly selected high schools in an urban area

television watching: Average number of hours between Monday and Friday spent watching TV

academic grades: Average of final academic grade in percentages (all non-academic subjects such as music, art, PT., etc., excluded) of one semester

Variables

Variable 1: hours of TV watching

Variable 2: academic grades

Analysis: Pearson *r*

Read "Think About This" to discover how the researcher could add a *t*-test to analyse his data collection.

Think About This...

Do you remember that at the beginning of this section, we stated that more than one research design can be used? If you think ahead and collect the right data, you can do more than one type of analysis to answer other questions with your data.

Note that the use of different research designs also leads to a stronger and well-received thesis! Suppose, before collecting the data, the researcher suspected that boys tended to watch television more often than girls and that their academic grades seemed to be lower. He could test for this if he asked his respondents to place a check in one of the boxes marked male ( ) or female ( ).

Just by doing this, he could determine whether there were any gender differences for TV watching and academic grades and use a *t*-test to determine whether the number of hours that boys watched TV differed significantly from the number of hours that girls watched TV. He could also to use a *t*-test to analyse gender differences between academic grades.

> For data measured using interval or ratio measurements and meeting all the parametric assumptions, use Pearson *r* – also called the product-moment coefficient of correlation.
>
> For data using ordinal measurements and/or when the assumptions for parametric testing are not met, use Spearman's *rho*.

Causal/Comparative Research Designs

Causal/comparative research designs allow the study of possible cause-and-effect relationships under conditions in which experimental manipulations are difficult, impossible or unethical. For example, giving a life-saving drug to one group and a placebo to the second group would certainly be considered unethical. It would be impossible to force a group of people to smoke to investigate the effect of smoking on the lungs. Investigating the effect of adding fluoride to drinking water on tooth decay, however, would be both possible and ethical. In all three examples, a causal/comparative research design could be used but could you just imagine the hue and cry if a researcher published his study showing that a life saving drug was not given to certain people or, if certain people were requested to smoke a lot of cigarettes to show the effect of smoking?

All causal/comparative research designs must be very carefully thought out. The hypothesis for causal research is that a particular variable (characteristic, occurrence or event) (X)[1] is one of the factors that may determine or could be the possible cause of the characteristic, occurrence or event of another variable (Y). As stated in Part 1, finding "causes" of something is a very difficult thing to demonstrate. Very few studies, other than those used in medical and other physical science research, can state that one variable has positively caused a change in the other. Even the studies showing that adding fluoride to drinking water (X) led to a decrease in tooth decay (Y), also showed that brushing the teeth regularly was another necessary factor in preventing tooth decay.

Often, when relationships are found between two variables, naive thinkers find it very tempting to state that one variable has "caused" the observed change in the other variable. Usually, however, we can not tell whether Variable X was the cause of the change in Variable Y, Variable Y was the cause for the change in Variable X, or whether the cause of some change could be explained by other variables (Variables A, B, C, and so on) that were not taken into consideration. In other words, you may find a spurious relationship.

When planning this type of research, you must be certain that (i) the two variables are linked in some way – that is, X and Y vary together; (ii) Y does not precede X in time – the variable thought to be the cause of the change must precede the second variable, as was found in the case of putting fluoride in drinking water (X) and fewer incidences of tooth decay (Y); and (iii) realise that there can be many other contributing, concomitant, and/or alternative conditions that also may be operating to make the occurrence of an event probable. Also, (iv) your research must prove that the change observed in Y could not possibly have occurred without the presence of X.

---

1. See also *Introduction to Partial Correlations*, Chapter 14.

There are many examples of (i) in which X and Y vary together and (ii) X precedes Y. In Jamaica about 25 years ago, it was found that there was a high incidence of children entering school for the first time at age 5 who suffered from slight mental retardation, and/or visual or hearing impairments (Y). Research showed that this (the Y) was caused by an outbreak of measles among pregnant mothers about 5 years earlier (X). In another case, children living in an area that had high lead content (X) (it was built on an old battery factory) also suffered from mental retardation (Y). Both of these research studies were able to prove conclusively the X had caused Y and both led to important reforms.[2]

Simple Linear Regression Designs

Regression and correlation are closely related. While correlational research designs are used to determine the magnitude and direction of the relationship between two variables, linear regression is used to predict the value of one variable (Y) from the value of another variable (X). For example, many universities base their admittance on scores that students obtained when writing the Standard Achievement Tests (SATs) as it has been found that high scores on the SATs (X) are highly related to students doing well in university (Y). Thus, it was predicted that students who obtained high marks on their SATs would also do well in university and students were accepted or rejected by some universities based on this prediction. Based on a similar expectation, scores from the Common Examination that children in Jamaica used to have to sit (X) were used to determine which schools the children would be allowed to enter (Y).

As in other research designs, there are certain things to consider while planning a research design using linear regression.

- The relationship must be linear. This means that the relationship between the two variables is most accurately represented by a straight line. If the relationship is nonlinear, then the value of r or the *rho* will not be very accurate.
- The most common use of the regression line is to predict scores for people (or things) who were not in the group used to obtain the regression line. Why would you want to predict something you already know?
- Remember that the regression line is considered only as the best estimate of Y scores and that you will rarely see a perfect relationship. This means that if you are using X to predict Y, the prediction will not be exact.
- If you are planning to use a linear regression design to predict Y from X, then it is most important to make sure that the regression line is computed from scores of a similar population. The predictor variable must be related in some way to the population under study. To explain this last point, it would be useless to use SAT scores to predict success in a ballet company. This does not imply that ballet dancers could not achieve high SAT scores, it only means that there are other variables that could predict success in a ballet company – such as being musical and agile!

---

2. The first one led to a requirement that all children be immunised with the measles vaccine and the second one led to the cleaning up of the community and ensuring that extra vitamins were given to the children to combat the effects of lead poisoning.

Incorporating Correlational Research Designs into the "Big Picture"

Students often do not realise that correlational analysis is a very useful tool to use to establish the *validity of constructs* being measured. These constructs are often abstract terms that can be corroborated by looking at a participant's performance in a variety of situations that pertain to the construct and seeing if these performances are significantly related. In addition to establishing the validity of a construct, correlational analyses are used to check for *internal validity of items* in a test or questionnaire. This simply means finding out whether individual items of a test or questionnaire are actually related to the construct or concept being studied. You must be careful that all items/sub-tests are measuring the same unidimensional construct before you can add them.

An Example of Looking at the Internal Validity of a Sub-Test

A master student designed a diagnostic test for written comprehension for Grade Four students. Her test, called the *Written Comprehension Test*, consisted of six sub-tests with ten items in each sub-test and the scores of each sub-test were added to give a total comprehension score. First, she had to determine whether each item in the sub-test really contributed to the total. Using Pearson *r* to analyse the items according to teach sub-test, she was able to state that correlations were significantly different from zero with correlations ranging from .42 to .83 (all significant at $p < .01$) and that this indicated a measure of internal consistency among the items in the sub-tests.

Commonly Made Mistakes in Correlational Designs

Many naive researchers:

- believe that significant relationships in a correlational research design are proof of a cause-and-effect relationship. THEY ARE NOT!
- do not control for initial differences between groups that might otherwise explain effects that have been found.
- do not start their research with homogeneous groups. For example, they do not form sub-groups based on age, gender, SES, or other variables that might confound the findings.
- when comparing several means, neglect to use a statistical test (e.g., *t*-test) prior to determining which group means differ from the other.
- use wrong sampling distributions or inappropriate statistical tests when testing for significance of data obtained from small sample sizes.
- fail to use a non-parametric test of significance when the population grossly violates the assumptions of parametric statistical tests.
- use a large number of variables that are not related and lump them all together in the hopes of finding "something" when some variables may only be related to other variables by chance – a "shot-gun" approach.

6
Non- Parametric Research Designs

Suppose that after you collected data and created a histogram of that data, it did not have the bell-shaped curve (discussed in Chapter 3). This means that you can not make the assumption of normal distribution of data. When your measurements consist of counts, classifications and/or ratings or you have a non-normal data distribution, you can use a variety of non-parametric tests.

Spearman's rho

You use the non-parametric statistic, Spearman's *rho*, to analyse data when it is measured using rank ordering (or when the data does not otherwise meet the assumptions for parametric testing).

*For example....*A department head wanted to find out if students on teaching practice would receive similar rankings for their teaching ability while they were on teaching practice from external examiners and college tutors of the student teachers. Each external examiner and college tutor was asked to rate the student's teaching ability on a scale of 1 to 6 (with 1 indicating extremely poor teaching ability and 6 indicating exceptional ability.) The ratings each student received from the external examiners were added to give each student a total examiners' score. Each student also received another ranking based on the total score received from the college tutors. The data from both variables (external examiners and college examiners) were converted to rank orders so they could be analysed using Spearman's *rho* to see if students were given similar rankings by the external examiners and college tutors. Word Map 6 shows how the research was organised.

WORD MAP 6

Problem Statement: A study investigating whether college tutors and external examiners agreed in their rankings of student-teachers.

Null Hypothesis: The rankings of student-teachers were similar by both college tutors and external-examiners.

Operational Definitions

College tutors: all male and female college tutors who observed and rated student-teachers during their teaching practice.

External examiners: all external examiners who had been appointed to observe and rate student-teachers during their teaching practice.

Rating-scales: a prepared rating scale measuring the teaching ability of student-teachers. This scale gave a final score between 1 - 6 (1 = poor teaching ability; 6 = excellent teaching ability)

Variables

Variable 1: ranks of students based on the total scores on the rating scale given by college tutors

Variable 2: ranks of students based on the total scores on the rating scale given by external examiners

Analysis: Spearman's *rho*

The Chi-Square Design

One of the more commonly used designs for frequency distributions is the chi-square (χ^2) (pronounced kai – it rhymes with why) design. The chi-square design uses nominal data only. When collecting data using this design, you do not use raw scores from a test or raw responses to a questionnaire but you determine at how many people (or things) will fall into a specific category or group. The data involves *counting the frequency* (the number of times) that a particular event occurred for a particular group or category. In the statistical analysis, observed frequencies are compared with expected frequencies for each group. When using the χ^2, it is important to understand that observations must be grouped into mutually exclusive categories such as yes/no; old/young; achievers/non-achievers; low motivation/high motivation.

The chi-square (χ^2) is a measurement of how statistically significant is the difference between observed frequency counts (your data) and the expected frequency. When designing research to use the chi-square design, you must understand that you are testing the null hypothesis that there is no difference between the observed frequencies and the expected frequencies for each group. Results of the analysis will show you whether your observed frequencies are less than, equal to, or greater than the expected frequencies.

As a very simple example of a chi-square design, you can just count the number people who answer yes or no to a question – the *frequencies* of yes/no responses. A researcher just wanted to find out if teachers were happy or unhappy at their school and whether teachers in elementary or secondary schools differed in their feeling. She asked a random sample of teachers if they were happy in their jobs and asked them only to state "Yes" or "No." She then counted up the number of yes and no responses according to type of school. In Table 6.1, you can see the results of her survey. Note that each cell contains the number of people who replied yes or no (i.e., the frequency of each answer).

Table 6.1: *A Contingency Table Showing Results of a Survey Asking Elementary and Secondary Teachers Whether They Were Happy*

	HAPPY		
	YES	NO	TOTALS
PRIMARY	100	10	110
SECONDARY	5	56	61
TOTALS	105	66	171

TYPE OF SCHOOL

The total numbers in the boxes show the results of her counting. The numbers at the side of the table are row totals – you can see she asked 110 primary school teachers and 61 secondary teachers (171 teachers altogether). You can also see that many more of the primary teachers answered yes than no (10 times as many said yes). However, about 5 times as many secondary teachers answered no rather than yes. The numbers at the bottom of the table give the column totals. This shows that 105 said yes and that 66 said no. The conclusion is obvious even without using a Chi-square test. The larger numbers on the diagonal that goes from top-left Cell 1 to lower-right Cell 4 show that primary teachers appeared to be happier at work than secondary school teachers.

It is to be noted that chi-square tests should **not** be used when the expected frequencies for any cell falls below 5 (the rule of thumb is that it should be 8). This is a rule-of-thumb to help compensate for the fact that in practice we are using categories to calculate χ^2 but the distribution we use is continuous rather than discrete. Later, in Chapter 18, you will notice that the calculation of the expected number in each cell depends on the row and column numbers, not just the grand total.

As the χ^2 distribution is closely related to the normal distribution, you can also use it to test the difference between observed and expected distribution outcomes. This means that it can also be used to test a hypothesis about how well a sample distribution fits some theoretical or hypothesised distribution (so, it is also called a *goodness-of-fit* test.) The goodness of fit test can be used to test the null hypothesis that there was no difference between the population distribution and the normal distribution.

An Example of a Chi-Square Research Design

We wanted to investigate the possibility of whether teenagers who smoked marijuana tended to develop into users of hard drugs (e.g., cocaine, crack). In this study, there were 1425 teenagers who participated, 695 were smokers and 730 were non smokers. Of the smokers, 230 had gone on to using cocaine or some other heavy drug and 465 were not using any drugs. Of the non-smokers, 78 had started using heavy drugs while 652 reported they did not use any drugs. These findings are drawn out in a 2 X 2 contingency table shown in Table 6.2.

Table 6.2: *A 2 X 2 Contingency Table Showing Smokers and Non-Smokers Who Are Using Drugs or Not Using Drugs*

	SMOKERS	NON-SMOKERS	ROW TOTALS
HEAVY DRUG USE	230	78	308
NO DRUG USE	465	652	1117
COLUMN TOTAL	695	730	1425

Other Methods of Testing Hypotheses Using Non-Parametric Statistics

The descriptions of some of the non-parametric tests that follow are not really research designs, but methods of testing hypotheses. Each method of hypothesis testing has different requirements that you should understand and we felt that you should be aware of these differences before you start to write your proposal.

Research Design Using the Wilcoxon Matched-Pairs Signed Ranks Test

The Wilcoxon Matched-Pairs Signed Ranks Test is the non-parametric counterpart of the related *t*-test and considers both the magnitude and direction of the difference between scores. This method of analysing data uses ordinal measures to collect data and is appropriate for use with the matched-subjects or repeated measures designs. When you collect data using ordinal measures, you must be able to *put the scores into rank order.* The Wilcoxon test is used when the same subjects or matched subjects perform under two conditions and the performance of each subject (or pairs of subjects) are compared to find out whether there are differences between their scores under the two conditions. Now, you can understand why the test has such a long title!

An example of a research design using the Wilcoxon Matched-Pairs Signed Ranks test was given by Greene and D'Oliveira (1986, pp. 49-52). They described a study designed to determine whether children who went to nursery school had a larger vocabulary than children who stayed home. According to the authors, the children were matched for age, gender and intelligence and "...any other variables we think we may need to control for" (Greene & D'Oliveira, p. 49) so the only difference in the amount of children's vocabulary would be due to the children's attendance at nursery school or staying at home.

Analysis required matched-pairs because the authors stated that matched pairs had to be used "...since no one child can both stay home and go to nursery school" (p. 49) and obviously, children could not be chosen at random for the research. The researchers had to find children who attended nursery school and those who did not.

Research Design Using the Friedman Test

The Friedman Test is an extension of the Wilcoxon Matched-Pairs test and is the non-parametric equivalent of the ANOVA. It is used when the same subjects (or matched subjects) are performing under three or more conditions. Although it does have its use (for example, comparing the ranking of three or more people on the value/desirability of three or more "things"), this test is very rarely used in the social sciences because, as noted earlier, it is very difficult to try to match three sets of a population.

Research Design Using the Mann-Whitney U Test

Mann-Whitney U Test is the non-parametric counterpart of the t-test for equality of means that can be used with independent subject designs. Similar to research designs that require the *t*-test as the method for analysis, there are two conditions – an experimental condition and a control group – subjects are randomly divided into the two groups and each subject is tested only once. Note that the major difference between using the Wilcoxon and the Mann-Whitney is that measures from the *same or matched subjects* are used as data in the former and measures from *different subjects* as data in the latter. In this design, there can be no comparisons between pairs of scores so scores are ranked in both conditions as if they were a single set of scores.

Another example given by Greene and D'Oliveira (1989) explains a research design using the Mann-Whitney test as follows: Students were randomly divided into two groups and asked to remember words flashed on to a screen. Students in Group 1 were shown words that appeared on the right side while students in Group 2 were shown words that flashed on to the left side. The measurements consisted of how many words each member of each group could recall. All of the scores were then placed in rank order and then divided according to the condition under which each person performed (pp. 48-50).

Because this concept is a bit tricky, an example of how this is done is shown in Table 6.3 (with data taken from p. 53). The scores were ranked according to the number of words recalled and then the rank given to each student was placed under the appropriate column. Hence, as you can see, a student was ranked as 7.5 in Condition 1 while another student was ranked as 5.5 in Condition 2.

Table 6.3: *Number of Remembered Words by Students in Each Condition*

CONDITION	RANK (1)	CONDITION 2	RANK (2)
Student 3	3	Student 9	11
Student 4	4	Student 7	9
Student 2	1.5	Student 11	5.5
Student 6	7.5	Student 10	12
Student 1	1.5	Student 12	7.5
Student 5	5.5	Student 8	10

Research Design Using the Kruskal-Wallis Test

This test is an extension of the Mann-Whitney test and is used when you have three or more conditions and different subjects in each of the experimental conditions. The Kruskal-Wallis test is considered the non-parametric equivalent of ANOVA. The major use of this test is to determine whether scores from three or more groups differ significantly from each other. Similar to the Mann-Whitney test, the scores are first ranked and then put into the three or more different groups. Note that we are not looking at the rank order of all the scores but at the different rank order in each group.

In some educational settings, it can be difficult – and some times impossible – to randomly select and assign students when a researcher wants to determine whether a particular method of teaching or a set of instructional material would be useful. This lack of randomisation threatens the validity of the research.

If an intact group of students is to be used, try to have a control group in which the participants are similar on relevant variables. To carry out the research, you would give a pre-test to all groups (the control group and the groups with which you will be using the special methods or materials), teach the method or use the selected material and then give a post-test to the three groups. During the time that you were using the special methods or set of materials, you would have to try to ensure that the control group did not receive any special intervention.

Because you can not assume that your population was normal, you would have to analyse your data using one of the non-parametric tests. Hopefully, the results of correlational analysis using scores from the pre-tests would show that the groups were similar on the relevant variables (e.g., scores on a reading, science or math test). Then, you can analyse the scores to see if the "experimental" groups of students scored higher on the post-test scores than on their pre-test scores (using the Wilcoxon Matched-Pairs – because the two sets of scores come from the same students). Finally, any differences between the three sets of post-test scores would show you whether this method was effective for the students in this particular group (using the Kruskal-Wallis Test).

❖ Questionnaire Survey Design

Questionnaires are the most widely used of all methods of data collection. Over the years of advising students, we have found that a large majority of our undergraduate and master students use questionnaires to form the backbone of their research theses. Thus, we have given "Questionnaire Survey Designs" its own special section.[1] In this part, we explain some of the basic principals and applications of questionnaire designs and the 'nitty-gritty' of writing items. Then, we give some pointers on the psychology of the questionnaire design and include specific tips on how to get your respondents to respond – using GAMTEAP principles.

Throughout Part 3, ideas and suggestions concerning the psychology of questionnaire design, how to write items and how to administer your questionnaire have been integrated with the basic principles of survey design to show the applications and administrative function of many of the tips. Our purpose is to ensure that you do not make basic mistakes that will invalidate your research. If you understand these basic principals and applications and try to apply the suggestions we have presented, you can improve on what we have explained and extend the effectiveness of your own research design.

---

1. In this section, we concentrate mainly on questionnaire designs rather than on surveys and guided interviews. Note that all the principles given in this section for questionnaire designs should be applied to surveys and guided interviews.

7

Why Use Questionnaires?

A questionnaire is simply a list of questions. This can be a list of questions for you to ask, as in a survey, a guided interview, or a list of questions given to respondents to answer – called a self-administered questionnaire. Guided or personal interviews that allow the researcher to probe for greater in-depth responses to their questions are useful in qualitative research. Self-administered questionnaires are preferred for quantitative research because:

    i   they are less expensive to administer than personal interviews.

    ii   they require less skill to administer than personal interviews.

    iii they can be administered to a large number of participants simultaneously.

    iv in many cases, respondents may have greater confidence in anonymity and may feel more confident that their replies will not get them into trouble. In this case, you might get some very truthful answers!

    v   responses to personal interviews may be not be reliable because the person being interviewed may try to give "socially correct" responses or the interviewer may only "hear" responses that he or she wants to hear.

    vi by using the self-administered questionnaire, everyone receives the same instructions and looks at the same wording of the items. This creates some uniformity from one situation to another.

Self-administered questionnaires are most commonly used because they can be posted to the respondents, you can arrange for someone else to distribute the questionnaires to respondents to answer, or you can arrange to give the respondents the questionnaire and be there when they answer it. Actually, the most efficient method of data collection using questionnaires is to have a group of people collected in one place and administer the questionnaire to them all at the same time.

The reasons for personally distributing the questionnaire and collecting the answers are practical. We have often heard our students complain that they were not able to get back the majority of the questionnaires that they had distributed and this lack of return weakens their study. Hence, the major reason for personally distributing your questionnaires is that once you have given them out, you know you will be able to collect them! In fact, to have non-biased results, you should aim for about a minimum of a 70% return rate.[2]

Other practical reasons include (i) if you are present when the respondents are answering your questions, you can give extra explanations if required, (ii) you know that the whole group answered the questionnaire under the same conditions and (iii) peer pressure helps to keep everyone focussed on answering the questions for as long as possible. This last point is very important because you must try to have the respondents answer all the questions.

---

2. Wiersma, 1999, p. 187.

The Many Uses of Questionnaires

Researchers design questionnaires to examine people's perceptions of events, objects, characteristics, attitudes, in fact, all sorts of things, in a systematic fashion. Before starting right away to write items for your questionnaire, first look at the different reasons for using questionnaires. These reasons are divided according to the type of information required by the researcher to test his or her hypotheses.

To Ascertain Facts: Questions are based on the assumption that a person knows about what is being asked (for example, asking people about crime in their community; testing knowledge about a specific subject) or to determine whether people being interviewed or responding to written questionnaires really do know what the facts are.

Often the first part of a questionnaire has a fact-finding content and is used mainly to obtain demographic or organismic data such as age, income, marital status, number of children, etc. These items requiring basic facts can be written as fixed-format items. The data obtained from this section can then be used to place respondents into specific categories and analyses can be carried out on the responses to the rest of the questionnaire according to the different categories stated in your hypothesis.

To Ascertain Beliefs: Questions are formulated to find out information about what people believe that the facts are. Responses to these questions can provide a picture about beliefs held by individuals that may or may not be correct.

The questionnaire used by the researcher investigating teachers' knowledge of the characteristics of giftedness is a good example of a questionnaire containing these first two categories. The first part of the questionnaire was to ascertain basic facts: gender, level of training, school type and years of teaching so he could group responses according to these research questions. The second part of his questionnaire consisted of items to determine the degree that teachers perceived the characteristics of giftedness to be true. He was able to validate the degree of the teachers' knowledge of giftedness by including certain items that were not correct but generally accepted as true (see **Lie Scales and Consistency Questions; Reverse Scoring**).

To Ascertain Feelings: Questions may be phrased in forms of different degrees of emotional reactions such as fear, distrust, contempt, envy, hate, admiration, love, etc. If, however, you are examining deep feelings, it might be preferable to use open-ended questions or invest in standardised tests that professional researchers have spent years perfecting.

To Discover Standards of Action: Questions have traditionally taken the form of using two components: 1) consideration of the ethical standards of what should be done and 2) practical considerations of what it is feasible to do. You can use "ought to" scenarios in which the individual shows he knows what is the right thing to do and then present a realistic scenario to guide the individuals' actions in a specific case in which the individual states what he would actually do in this particular instance.

An example of this type of questionnaire can be found in a classic study by Stouffer (1949). He asked students to imagine they were proctoring an exam and saw a student cheating. He first gave a series of possible responses that ranged from not doing anything at all to removing the examination book and reporting the student. Then he presented the students with a number of different situations such as: "The student who was cheating was a close friend;" "The student who was cheating was a well-known cheat;" "The authorities would find out;" and so on. The students were asked how they would respond in these different situations.

To find the answers for some research questions, you may need to ask questions that may pose a threat to a respondent's social image, as for example those asking "How often have you stolen from a shop" "How much crack do you use per week?" These questions will probably interact with a perceived respondent/experimenter threat – the respondent might feel that truthful answers will get him/her into trouble. This threat can be reduced by offering anonymity or by techniques that build respondent/experimenter trust – such as ensuring confidentiality (see Chapter 10: **Ethics**).

To Investigate Present or Past Behaviour: These questions are used mainly in surveys and polls and ask specific questions requiring specific answers. For example, "What brand of coffee do you buy?" "Do you prefer shopping at Store X or Store Y?" "Will you be voting this next election?" These questions may form the "lead in" to a number of other, more searching questions.

To Determine the Reasons for Beliefs, Feelings, Policies or Behaviour: These are mostly "Why" questions and may be the follow-up from questions investigating present or past behaviour. Although a "why" question sounds simple, it is not. Remember that you are trying to find out the reasons offered and you will get more information by first thinking about the many different factors that may influence the belief, feeling, or behaviour and then asking a number of searching questions. You also might need to first interview some people who are familiar with the situation you want to investigate and ask them the "why" questions. Their reasons can form the basis of your questionnaire. For example, if you ask the question, "What made you choose this university?" you might also need to find out whether the respondents had considered other universities, who helped in the decision, and what other considerations there were in the choice.

In a questionnaire looking for reasons for something, you could make a list of possible "why" reasons and ask the respondent to indicate the degree to which he/she agrees or disagrees with each item. You could also ask "why" with an open-ended question but as you will find out, this might require too much effort on the part of the respondent and you might not receive valid or truthful answers (a GAMTEAP principle). If you have a lot of time or can afford to hire extra interviewers, you can also interview people individually to find out their reasons. This, however, requires a lot of extra effort, time and perhaps money. For example, you have to train the interviewers to ensure that there is consistency of recording the data and you may also have to pay them to do the interviews. Finally, it takes time to put the different answers into codes so the responses can be analysed.

Questionnaire Items

In Part One, as an example of "narrowing down" your research, we discussed a researcher who wanted to investigate why students dropped out of college. The major thrust of her final research centred around five questions:

1. How many students drop out of the university before they graduate?
2. What reasons do students give for dropping out of university?
3. In which departments are there more drop-outs than others?
4. Are there more male than female drop-outs?
5. Do the reasons differ by department and/or gender?

Note that these questions are not just 'yes' or 'no' questions. The first question asks 'how many?' and the second question asks 'why?' The next problem was how to process the reasons respondents gave in Question 2. She could have interviewed each "drop out" and asked them open-ended questions – but why go to all that bother? The amount of work to personally interview each person and then code and analyse all the replies would be an enormous task (even though she might also get some unexpected insights!)

Now look at the practicalities of asking Questions 3 and 4. This would mean some serious research within the different faculties to find out how many students dropped out in each department and how many were males or females. Once she found out who the drop outs were, she could track them down and find out the reasons they gave for dropping out of college (Answers to Question 2 form the basis for the answer to Question 5).

Question 2 is the part of her research that would most effectively be answered by a self-administered questionnaire. She did some pre-interviewing to find as many reasons as possible for "dropping out" of college and presented these reasons as a checklist to be rated for importance – plus she also added the 'other' category for the (hopefully) very few reasons she did not know about. Then, to answer Question 5 and by knowing which group each "reason" came from, she could compare the reasons given by each group by faculty, or by gender, or by both faculty and gender.

> When using a questionnaire to obtain information, the information is often limited to asking the respondent to write their responses to prearranged questions. This is why many questionnaires have the option "other" written in them. We have found that when people fill in this option, it is still fairly easy to code the answer and you can pick up useful pieces of information.
>
> On the other hand, using interviews to collect information gives greater opportunity for flexibility of questions but, remember the interview questions have to be as carefully formatted as the questionnaire items.

Item Types

The questions asked in the research described above show the need to incorporate different types of items or questions into a single questionnaire. For example, the first question asked "how many?" The answer to this question requires a single number and so the item can be written as a *open-ended question*. The second question is a "why" question and requires many different items probing for the different reasons people gave for dropping out of university.

The researcher could have used a series of *forced-choice* (or *forced-alternative*) items in which respondents are asked to put a tick beside the alternative that the respondents felt was the most correct reason (see Chapter 8: **Space Saving**). She decided, however, to use a *rating scale* for these questions. In her rating scale, she listed a number of possible reasons for dropping out and the respondents were asked to demonstrate the degree to which they felt that reasons given in the questionnaire reflected their own reasons for dropping out. These items can be written so that the responses can be measured as a scale. In this questionnaire, the researcher included "other" as an added item and this is an *open-ended question*. Examples of these types of questions are given throughout the rest of this section.

Think about this ...

Writing appropriate items for the questionnaire and then scoring the responses can be tricky. Naive researchers might think that they are taking the "easy way out" by using a questionnaire only to find that they have spent a lot of time and effort writing items, collecting responses and scoring something that turns out to be comparatively trivial and useless! In order to ask questions that can be answered you must (i) remember your hypothesis and what you what to find out, (ii) think carefully about the types of questions to ask and (iii) how you are going to collect, code and analyse the data.

Perception Responses Versus Prevalence Responses

Although we have already mentioned two main types of questions – perception and prevalence questions requiring perception and prevalent responses – we feel that we cannot overemphasise the importance of knowing the difference between the two concepts when writing items for your questionnaire. An example of what we call a *perception response* is a quantified opinion, as for example: "How expensive was your car on a scale from 0 to 10, 0 meaning not expensive at all and 10 meaning very expensive indeed." An example of what we call a *prevalence response* is the recall of the frequency or amount of an event that is potentially publicly verifiable as for example asking "How much did your car cost?"

The advantage of collecting prevalence data is that we can directly compare the responses from different respondents. For example, if we know how much each car cost, then we could tell if Miss Jones' car was more expensive than Mr. Brown's car. We can even add the dollar values and work out the average cost of their cars. We cannot do this, however, with perception data. We have found that many researchers make this elementary mistake. They mistakenly add, average and even correlate data from Likert-type scales that ask for perception data.

The Likert-type scale perception rating is **not** a measure of a public event. It is, at best, a measure using the respondent's *personal values* as the assessment. Respondents measure in their own unseen units so you cannot compare final numbers. For example, if a very wealthy person were asked to rate how expensive his car was and if it represented only a small outlay in relation to his normal expenses, he would say it cost maybe only 2 on a 5-point scale. Yet if the same car was bought by a poor man who had to go without many other things for many years to pay for it, then he is going to rate the same car as very expensive – perhaps 5 on a 5-point scale. This means that if we erroneously compared their ratings, we would think that the poor man who rated the expense of his car as "5" actually paid more than what the rich man paid because the rich man only rated the expense of his car as "2."

Try this simple experiment to illustrate why it is wrong to compare perception responses between different respondents. For this experiment, you don't need to have a scale because you are looking at perception responses (how people perceive their weight) and not prevalence responses (the actual weight of the people you ask). Ask a group of people to rate how heavy they are on a five point Likert-type scale:

1	2	3	4	5
very light	light	medium	heavy	very heavy

Some people are very weight conscious and will consider themselves over-weight and rate themselves as 4 or 5 even though they may actually weigh less than average. You may have slim men who in comparing themselves to a Rambo-type man, rate themselves as a 2. You will find people with the same ratings who are obviously very different weights. You will even find people with high ratings who obviously weigh a lot less than people with low ratings. So the ratings are not the actual weights of the people (the prevalence response) but perception responses. The actual weight of a person can be added and averaged but a person's perception of weight cannot.

The more highly valued the attribute, then the more in error is this misuse of the Likert-type scale perception ratings. For example, money is highly valued in many societies so if you ask, on a five point scale if your respondent earns:

1	2	3	4	5
hardly anything	a little	average	a lot	a great deal

You might get a person who earns $1million each day saying that he or she earns "hardly anything" because he or she has expenses of $2 million a day and is getting into debt at an alarming rate. Yet a man who earns only $500 a day and can easily live on that may say "a lot." In this case, the Likert-type scale is measuring $1 million a day as "hardly anything" and $500 a day as "a great deal."

High or Low Discriminating Response Formats?

An example of a low discriminating response format:

"Do you worry that you will be injured in a driving accident?" Yes No

This is a low discriminating response format because the respondent only has to discriminate between two very different choices.

An example of a highly discriminating response format for the same construct would be:

"Remember a typical car journey you have recently taken. For this journey rate on a 0 to 10 scale, how worried you were that you would be injured in a driving accident? 0 means no worry, up to 10 which means maximum worry."

This response format uses a higher discrimination because the subject must choose between 11 very similar choices. You can clearly see that the more discriminating the response then the more response effort it will require. Hence, your questionnaire should have fewer such questions. On the other hand, the lower the discrimination of the response then the more questions you can ask for a given respondent effort.

A Low Response Discrimination Format for Young Children

When asking young children (or individuals who are mentally challenged) to respond to perception items on a questionnaire, you should not expect them to define precisely how they feel, as for example, on a ten point scale, or even expect that they can respond to five bipolar adjectives. For these sets of population, you can still use a scale, but instead of using sets of adjectives, you can use symbols. We term this a low response discrimination because we are only using three faces: a "happy" face, a "neutral" face and a "sad" one as shown in Figure 7.1. If you feel, however, that you need to obtain a greater degree of feeling, you could always add "faces" that are less happy (only a slightly curved line instead of the big smile) or you could add tears to the sad face to signify "very sad."

Figure 7.1: Symbols showing "happy," "neutral" and "sad" faces.

When administering a questionnaire to young children, the researcher would read a statement to the children and immediately ask "...and how does this make you feel?" The child can then touch, circle or place a tick (√) beside one of the symbols shown in Figure 7.1. Note that in some countries, and indeed, in some country areas, children may not be familiar with the symbols you may want to use, so this must be checked before you start asking your questions. You may have to give some examples of what each symbol means.

Well....What should you use?

The answer to the question of whether you should or should not use high or low discrimination response formats is: *"For some parts yes and for other parts no."* Generally, the first part of the questionnaire is fact finding and requires little effort on the part of the respondent to answer the items with a low discrimination response. The second part of the questionnaire should contain items requiring high discriminatory responses.

You will rarely get in-depth, useful data from responses to your questionnaire by designing a questionnaire that contains all items with a low discrimination format, unless, of course, you are conducting a simple survey research or only interested in obtaining "yes/no" responses. In these cases, your questionnaire format should be relatively brief. The use of items on a questionnaire with low discrimination response formats is considered a "shot-gun" approach – the questionnaire only requires respondents to answer versions of "yes" or "no" – and implies that you have not sufficiently narrowed down your research through literature review and preliminary study – a bad sign. Not only that, but according to the GAMTEAP Principle, your respondents may get tired of having to answer these simple, low discriminatory questions and not complete your questionnaire – another bad sign!

Generally speaking, the degree of discrimination required by your questions should be at the limit of which the respondents are capable. For example, you can ask more questions requiring more discriminating responses of university students and professionals than you can of primary school children.

> It is better to err over than err under.
> We have found that usually respondent effort also increases with respondent discrimination.

The advantage of asking many questions requiring high discrimination responses on the part of the respondent is that you can ask many similar questions that are phrased differently within a narrow area. This "repeat-within-subject" design allows for more reliability, that is, more questions from different perspectives within the same area of study.

Reverse Scoring Items

Using just a few special response items can introduce an interesting response variation to motivate the respondent. The major problem with using many similar special response items together on the same questionnaire is that they create a spatial response set in which the respondent tends to make patterns by positioning his or her crosses or check marks. For example, once respondents put a few crosses on one side of the line, then there is a tendency for them to stay on that side of the line for the next few questions.

> One way to try to counter the response set is to use reverse scored items. That is you change around a question so that a respondent's usual response would also be changed.

An effective technique for reverse scoring items is shown in the following example: You are asking questions about the value of being tall. For this example, the values on the scale range from 0 - 10. In this questionnaire, people with a positive value for being tall would answer "yes," or indicate some form of high value. To reverse score, you would then intersperse questions for which that person should answer "no," or indicate some form of low value. An example of an item that is reversed scored is shown in the last question in Figure 7.2. To code this question you would subtract the actual response from the maximum 10, giving 10 - 1 = 9. So that 9 would most likely have been the respondent's answer if the question had been positively stated. "Do people show **more** respect to tall people?" The key adjective, less, in Question C has also been underlined so that you can see what words to change to make a question that can be reversed scored.

An Example of a Questionnaire Using Reverse Scoring

Instructions:
On a scale of 0 to 10, with 10 being the highest value and 0 being the lowest value, state how you feel about tall people. Put a number from 0 to 10 in the space provided beside each question.

A.   Is being tall an advantage? _____ (The respondent might give an 8 value)

B.   Would you like to be tall? _____(The respondent might give a 9 value)

C.   Do people show **less** respect to tall people? _____ (The respondent might give a 1 value)

Figure 7.2: An example of an item in a questionnaire (C) that can be reversed scored.

Reversed scored items can consist of changing adjectives as shown in Figure 7.2 or presenting statements to respondents that are "false." An example of this type of reverse scoring is shown in Item 2 of the Likert-type scale in Figure 7.3 – if respondents recognised that this statement was false, they would have to change their "mind set."

Note that studies have shown that the mean scores on reverse scored questions tend to be lower than on positively scored questions. This may be because some respondents are stuck in their response set or it could mean that the effort of changing mental set was interacting with the rating. This is another interesting experimental problem to solve, but check the literature first to see what other researchers have done.

Lie Scales, Consistency Questions and T/F Combination Questions

Some respondents may not answer your questions as accurately as you would like them to do so. This can happen for many reasons: (i) They may not really want to answer your questionnaire but don't want to tell you so they rush through putting in almost random type answers. (ii) They may not be able to give the effort it requires to answer accurately because they have other things on their mind. (iii) Maybe, they simply cannot concentrate on the task. (iv) They may maliciously want to deceive you. (v) They may want try to present a false image of themselves or the situation you are researching. (vi) They may simply be the wrong people to ask because they genuinely do not know and so they guess to please you. If you accept all this inaccurate data at face value it will add so much "noise" that it will hide any true results given by the respondents who have accurately replied to your questions. How can you identify the inaccurate answers and discard them? You need to prepare *lie scales* and *consistency checking* questions.

Lie scales usually consist of a series of questions that invite unusual answers on a particular theme – usually a valued construct such as honesty. For example, you could include in a questionnaire for secondary students several items such as: "Have you ever returned a book late to a library?" "Do you dislike any teachers in your school?" "Have you ever wanted to get back at people who are nasty to you?" "Have you ever told a little fib to get yourself out of trouble?" When you look at the responses, you make a total of the responses given to see if the respondent appears to be unbelievably honest. It is possible that a student could answer "no" (a low degree) on any one question, but very unlikely that a student would be able to honestly answer to such a low degree on all such questions. A combination of many low degree answers implies that it is very likely he/she is giving dishonest responses.

Different cultures refer to this by different names. Some US commercial questionnaires call this type of lie scale score an "Image Management" score and many commercial questionnaires also have "Acquiescence scales." These identify respondents who prefer to answer yes when they have no preference one way or the other. From your ethnographic exploration you should be aware of any political, social and cultural pressures there are on respondents to respond in biased ways. You should consider, at an early stage when you are informally interviewing your population, the types of questions you would need to identify such biased respondents. A practical disadvantage of using lie scales is that, because you need many questions for greater reliability, they take up your valuable space and the respondent's valuable effort.

Using *consistency questions* is an alternative procedure for checking for perception responses. You ask essentially the same question twice but in a different form, preferable on opposite sides of the question paper so that the respondent is less likely to realise what you are doing. You can use two questions for each of your key constructs and then it is easy for you to check whether the two answers are comparable. If the answers to any pair are very different then the respondent is not answering consistently on that construct. You will have to consider discarding at least the responses he/she gave for that construct – maybe the whole questionnaire.

Look at the items in the questionnaire investigating perception of knowledge of giftedness in Figure 7.3. The second item can be considered an example of a lie scale item but it can also function as a consistency question. In this researcher's questionnaire, his items consisted mostly of "true" characteristics of giftedness mixed with a few "untrue" statements. He was easily able to check the responses for inconsistency of responses.

A simple method of identifying "careless" respondents using prevalence questions is to use a combination of T/F questions. You simply check for combinations of answers that are impossible. For example, if when asked "How old are you?" and the respondent answers "10 years" and this is followed by "How many children do you have?" and the respondent answers "5", obviously, one or both of these answers are wrong. Although this is a very simple example of asking T/F questions, if you feel that this is needed, you can try to make more complex combinations to use in your questionnaire.

These reliability and validity checking methods need to be planned well in advance so you do not "waste" questions. By planning in advance, you can use the questions you actually need to ask (also the T/F combination checks), rather than having to introduce extra questions specially for checking. When you discard the inaccurate responses, you will end up with a smaller population in your sample. Plan for this "wastage" by having a larger sample at the start.

Coding for Missing Values

When you start entering the responses to your questionnaire, remember to code for different missing values. For example, if any questions were left blank you could code them as -99. Then you can count the number of -99s in the questionnaire. This is a type of missing values analysis. If a respondent left many questions unanswered, then the ones he/she did answer might be inaccurate and probably the entire questionnaire should be discarded. In the end, after you have given your questionnaires, coded the responses and put them into the computer, you will be able to see how successful you have been in discarding inaccurate responses. You can calculate reliability statistics like C-alpha that measure your success.

Rating Scales

The types of questionnaires most commonly used in the social sciences are those that ask people to make a distinction of degree rather than of quality. The need to measure the degree of a belief, feeling or emotion influences the form in which the data is to be collected. As you should now have a good idea of what you need to think of when you write your questions or questionnaire items, examine the different types of rating scales that may be used.

The Likert-type Scale

Likert-type scales describes people's evaluations on a unidimensional scale and responses indicate the degree of positive or negative attitudes, perceptions, feelings or emotions about something the researcher wants to investigate. The degrees are assigned numerical positions in order to make the distinction of the degree possible. In a Likert-type Scale, the respondents are asked to respond to each item on a questionnaire in terms of five different degrees of agreement or disagreement. They may be asked to circle the number or put an x or ✓ in the box that best represents their opinion.

Likert-type scales measure *perception* responses.
Likert-type scales do not provide the basis for saying how much *more* favourable or unfavourable one response is to another.

The items making up the scale are generally written so that the higher the numeric value, the more the person shows agreement with the statement. In its most simple form, if a questionnaire consisted of a total of 20 questions, and the person "agreed" with all the items, the highest possible score would be 100. If the person "disagreed" with all the items, the lowest possible score would be 20. In a well written questionnaire, a few of the items should be written so they can be reversed scored. These items are also called "consistency questions" and check for accuracy and consistency in answering the items.

The two items shown in Figure 7.3 were taken from a questionnaire written by a Master's student to determine the degree of what teachers believed as true about characteristics of gifted students.

Item 1: A major characteristic of a gifted student is high cognitive ability.

strongly agree	agree	undecided	disagree	strongly disagree
(5)	(4)	(3)	(2)	(1)

Item 2: Gifted students enjoy drills and routines.

strongly agree	agree	undecided	disagree	strongly disagree
(1)	(2)	(3)	(4)	(5)

Figure 7.3: Examples of two items on a rating scale. Note the reverse scoring for the second item.

In this example, the first item is a high indicator of a characteristic of giftedness and the high score is "5". As the second item is false and not considered a characteristic of giftedness, the values are reversed so that strongly disagree would also give a high score of "5." If a person really knew about the characteristics of giftedness, then that person would get a total score of 10 out of 10 on these two items. This high total score would reflect a high degree of knowledge about the characteristics of giftedness.

Although, we have put the actual scoring under each degree, this would **not** be on the questionnaire given to the participants in your research. This is only an example to show you how the scoring should be done and to make the point that the scoring must be consistent. The actual format of the questionnaire would look something similar to that in Figure 7.4.

Please put a ✓ in the box that indicates how you feel about the truth of each item.	strongly agree	agree	undecided	disagree	strongly disagree
A major characteristic of a gifted student is high cognitive ability.					
Gifted students enjoy drills and routines.					

Figure 7.4: An example of two items on a Likert-type scale designed for a Master's thesis.

Notice the symmetry of the descriptions on the Likert-type scales. Working from the ends towards the middle, you start with the two extremes, then two normal descriptors and finish up with "medium" in the middle. Some examples of sets of responses that are typically used in Likert-type scales include:

Very satisfactory	Very good	Very supportive	Very happy
Satisfactory	Good	Supportive	Happy
Undecided	No opinion	Neutral	Neutral
Unsatisfactory	Poor	Unsupportive	Sad
Very unsatisfactory	Very poor	Very unsupportive	Very sad

Likert-type scales are the most commonly used questionnaire design (and probably the easiest to design) but you should be aware that other methods of scaling techniques are also used in the social sciences. These are not as widely used as the Likert-type scales so we are only giving a brief overview of each.

Semantic Differential (Charles Osgood)

Measurements are based on a 7-point bipolar scale and the scale is designed to measure subjective or connotative meanings of a concept. The scale is anchored at each end by pairs of opposite adjectives – an example of which is shown in Figure 7.5. This is why it is called "bipolar." Respondents are asked to mark a cross on the line in a position that best describes how they feel about an object or concept on the bipolar dimension. You can use several of these lines, each with a bipolar dimension to cover a wider description of the object. This scale provides an effective method of measuring an individual's concept of:

* *evaluative dimensions:* negative/positive; bad/good; worthless/valuable
* *potentency dimensions:* weak/strong; small/large; light/heavy
* *activity dimensions:* slow/fast; active/passive; hot/cold

The 100mm Line

The 100 mm line is yet another method of measuring subjective or connotative meanings of an object, event or construct and consists simply of a 100 mm line anchored at each end by bipolar descriptions. It is similar to the Semantic Differential Scale except the line MUST be 100 mm long. The co-author of this text, T. Bastick, noted that he had not seen this used elsewhere but uses this technique in his own research because there are no distracting numbers that can impose an evaluation on the response. The respondent can concentrate on the dimensions and put an X in the appropriate place. For data analysis, the researcher measures the position of the X simply by holding a 100mm ruler against the line and noting the position or distance of the X from one end of the line.

This gives a 100-point discrimination and has the advantage of requiring little effort from the respondent. Leaving out the markings encourages the respondent to use an intuitive mode of responding rather than an analytic mode of responding. An example of the 100mm scale is shown in Figure 7.5.

Likert-type scale	Disagree 1	2	3	4	5	Agree
Osgood Semantic Differential	Negative					Positive
100mm Line	Light					Dark

Figure 7.5: A comparison of measurements: the Likert-type Scale, the Osgood Semantic Differential Scale and the 100mm Line Scale. These three scales are similar spatial-response formats offering increasing response discrimination.

Although the illustration of the Likert-type scale measurement in Figure 7.5 shows a range of 5 points, occasionally an even 4 point scale may be used, and in fact, may be necessary because it doesn't allow the respondent to opt-out of deciding by choosing the middle number. In some cases, when the alternatives are presented on a straight line, a respondent may choose a point between two digits, for example, about 3.5. This doesn't matter because you can still use this number. Note that it is also possible to use a 100-point rating scale with respondents who are familiar with percentages. They would be asked, for example, for their percentage agreement or disagreement about a certain concept.

Some critics of using scales of 10 or higher say that respondents are unable to accurately make such fine discriminations as offered by a 100-point scale or even a 10-point scale and many advise using a maximum of 5 points or less. They offer recommendations that the intervening points should be anchored by their descriptions to help make the rating more accurate and point out that it is unreasonable to name each point on a 10-point scale and, perhaps, impossible to name every point on a 100-point scale. They use this as an argument against the reliability of large rating scales.

The greater reliability of longer, more discriminatory scales, however, has been demonstrated by Bastick and Cook (2002). They point out that when the number of points is very large, then respondents use a holistic method of estimating their response rather than an analytical point-by-point comparison. If the method of rating analytic versus holistic is of no concern then you are unlikely to be losing respondent discrimination if you use a 10-point rather than a 100-point scale.

Whatever scale you plan to use, make sure that you decide how you will score the responses and that you know exactly how many points are allotted to each response category BEFORE you print out your final version of your questionnaire.

8
GAMTEAP
The Psychology of Questionnaire Responding

The number one design principle for questionnaires is to **G**et **A**s **M**uch **T**argeted **E**ffort **A**s **P**ossible (GAMTEAP) from your respondents. Targeted effort means that respondents spend their energy by giving you relevant information and not wasting their effort trying to figure out what a question means, how to answer it, or what part of the questionnaire to answer next.

This section shows you some of the ways that you can apply GAMTEAP principles to your questionnaire. We have already stated that a respondent will only put a certain amount of effort into answering a questionnaire. You should try to design your questionnaire to increase that effort. For example, you can use the "white space technique" to make it easier for a person to respond so that you can elicit more targeted effort and you can even use interest and reward incentives to motivate your respondents.

To Group or Not to Group? That Is the Question!

Do you put similar questions together or not? It takes effort to change mental set and so, theoretically, for minimum response effort you should put questions about the same topic together in one section. This is done so that the respondent can stay in one frame of mind to answer questions on the same topic – which is less wasted effort (GAMTEAP). However, a statistical requirement for your analyses is that each response has to be independent of other responses. This means that you should scatter questions on the same topic randomly throughout your questionnaire so that each response is not influenced by the one preceding it. This scattering of questions requires frequent changes of mental set and entails extra effort on the part of the respondent. So what do you do? Keep similar questions together or separate them?

The answer depends on whether you are asking perception questions or prevalence questions. When you ask the respondent to recall numerical descriptions of a context – prevalence questions such as how many times did he do this, did she do that, how much did it weigh, how long did it last, how much did it cost, etc., then you keep the questions together. This triangulation helps the respondent build up a more detailed and accurate recall of the context. If, however, you are asking for judgmental, evaluative, and/or rated perceptions of an object, context, or construct (perception questions), then scatter those throughout your questionnaire. You can even reverse score some of them to break up a mental set. Doing this will ensure that the respondent is not creating a "mood picture" of the context that is more influenced by the respondent's current state than by his or her more usual traits.

A Word About Space Saving

When designing the self-administered questionnaire, you will need a space – usually beside each item – in which the respondents can write their answers. One method of using space was shown in Figure 7.4 and as you can see, it requires a fair amount of space. A more effective space-saving alternative to response formats is to leave only one space in which the respondent writes a single rating. This was shown in the example for reverse scoring items (Figure 7.2 – only, of course, without the scores written beside the blank spaces). Example of a space saving technique is shown in the example of another questionnaire format in Figure 8.1.

Instructions

On a scale of 0 to 10, with 10 being the highest value and 0 being the lowest value, state how you feel about being tall. Put a number from 0 to 10 in the space provided beside each question.

1. Is being tall an advantage? _____
2. Would you like to be tall? _____
3. Do people show less respect to tall people? _____

Figure 8.1: An example of a "space saving" questionnaire format.

Language Style and Meanings

If you administer your questionnaire to groups and you will be there to answer any questions, you should still design your instructions to be so clear that you will not need to give any extra explanations. How your respondents will understand these instructions and interpret the words you choose for your questions should all have been tried out on some typical respondents in the preparation stage (test-piloting stage) of designing your questionnaire. It is during the test-piloting stage that you should make sure that you can interpret the answers in the way respondents intend. This is the qualitative ethnographic groundwork that helps to ensure the validity of your quantitative research.

Understanding the questions should take minimum respondent effort – an application of a GAMTEAP Principle. A general guideline is that it should take very much less effort to understand the language than to answer the question. This is to ensure that the respondent's language ability has a minimal influence on what you are measuring. For children, a rule of thumb is to use language appropriate to a developmental level of about three years younger than the respondent's age.

Never use a questionnaire for other purposes – such as an "esoteric register." This means using unusual words to show off your mastery of the English language. It also means that you should keep away from convoluted conditional and/or too many negative statements.

You have not designed your questionnaire to impress respondents with your vast knowledge. You have written your items to obtain information from the respondents.

Applying the GAMTEAP Principles to writing questionnaires means that your questionnaire must fit the requirements of your respondents. Write items in the language spoken by the respondents. If they are Spanish speakers, then you write in Spanish and if they are French, then you write in French. This is just common sense! There is a problem in the Caribbean, however, because the majority of the people speak Creole (patois) and some research students are reluctant to use Creole when this is the most acceptable language of their respondents.

There are many reasons for this. Research students may have been taught that patois is "bad English" and may think that they will be penalised for writing their questionnaires using bad English. In many cases, however, the use of Creole is sometimes the more effective way to communicate. When effective communication is your goal, then you should use it. On the other hand, your respondents may also have been taught that Creole has a lower status than Standard English and if you write your entire questionnaire in Creole, then your questionnaire may loose its authority because respondents might feel insulted because you have insinuated that they do not understand English. A further problem is that there is very little agreement on how to spell Creole words and words spelled phonetically may not be understood by all respondents.

As you consider these points you might decide to (i) use Creole when the English would not be understood, (ii) use English for instructions – to add authority to your instructions, (iii) make sure that your respondents understand what they are to do by "translating" your instructions into Creole and be there to "translate" statements into Creole if necessary, (iv) use Creole appropriately to make your questionnaire more culturally acceptable to your respondents. We recommend giving instructions in Creole if necessary but writing your questionnaire items in Standard English.

Formatting Your Questionnaire

The "look" of the first part of your questionnaire sets the tone for how respondents will interact with your questionnaire. This look is most important because you do not get a second chance to make that important first impression. If your questionnaire looks as if you hurriedly "threw it together," is poorly printed or hard to read, then your respondents will feel that it is not a questionnaire that requires a lot of effort on their part (a GAMTEAP Principle).

The Introduction

You need an introduction to your questionnaire. This introduction usually tells the respondent what the research is about and why they were chosen to answer the questionnaire. It also covers ethical issues such as confidentially/anonymity and the respondent's right to be able to withdraw from the task.[1] In many instances, we have found that it is better to put the introduction on a separate cover letter or include the introduction with the signed consent form. This is because all this extra information can add clutter to the questionnaire or make the questionnaire seem a lot longer than it is.

---

1. See *Chapter 10: Reliability, Validity, Ethics, and Cover Letter*

When you are using a covering letter and/or consent form and you are attending the session, it is also prudent to repeat the introduction, talk about confidentiality and the ability to withdraw – an application of the GAMTEAP Principles – because your respondents will feel safer, more secure and thus be able to respond more easily. This verbal information can be considered as part of the "mood setting" when you introduce a group-administered questionnaire.

When you are administering your questionnaire to a group, you should thank your respondents at the start, before they begin to look at the questionnaire, so that they feel some moral obligation to answer the questionnaire to the best of their ability. Additionally, you can explain the importance of what you are doing – similar to what you stated in your proposal to convince the research committee to allow you to do this research. If you have the backing, you can even offer a gratuity or monetary reward to your respondents. In a meta-analysis of the effects of rewards on response return, researchers in the US (Hopkins and Gullickson, 1992) found that even a small gratuity increased the non-response rate.

If you plan to offer some form of gratuity as a motivator, this should be mentioned in your cover letter or before you give out the questionnaire, provided that this will not bias responses. In group administration, you may have to mention that respondents must not influence each other's answers. This is necessary because all answers must be independent as a statistical requirement for your analysis – hence, focus group data cannot be analysed in the normal way because the responses are not independent. When respondents have completed the questionnaire, they should leave with a good feeling – remember to thank them again for their effort and remind them how they will benefit or how they have helped others in some way.

If you have explained about your research and its importance in the cover letter or consent form, then, usually, the first part of your questionnaire is used to collect organismic or demographic data – data for you to use to describe your sample and/or to compare groups (e.g., categories of age, gender, education, work experience, salary) or whatever else is considered necessary to place respondents into nominal categories to test your hypotheses. Some respondents may consider these "personal" questions to be intrusive but if they are necessary questions, the respondents must be prepared. This may be accomplished in the information that has been written in the consent form or the cover letter. If you are administering your questionnaire to a group where this might be a problem, it can be effective to prepare respondents with an acclimatisation talk before administering the questionnaire and placing a "heavy" emphasis on anonymity or confidentiality.

In this first "demographic" section, realise that instead of asking for information directly, it might be easier to obtain the required information and respondents may be more likely to respond if you group response numbers and then ask the respondent to place a check beside the most appropriate box. This type of question is referred to as a "fixed alternative" question and is used mainly for finding out the respondent's approximate age, annual salary, religion, or any other questions requesting personal information that the respondents might not want to answer.

Although you might lose some information, older respondents who are "age conscious" might be more likely to answer a fixed alternative item rather than having to answer directly: "How old are you?" An example of a fixed alternative item could be written:

For the purpose of this research, we need to have a rough estimation of
your age. Please place a ✓ beside the correct category
( ) between 20 – 25 years
( ) between 26 – 30 years
( ) between 31 – 35 years
and so on to .... ( ) over 65 years

Note that items asking personal questions should be appropriate to the population you will be using to answer your questionnaire. If, for example, you are giving the questionnaire to students, simply ask: "What is your age?" or "Age: Years _____ Months _____

Another example of an item with a fixed alternative is:
Marital Status: single ( )   married ( )   widowed ( )   divorced ( )

Ensuring that ALL Questions are Answered

It is essential that respondents answer all the questions (an important GAMTEAP Principle). If this does not happen, you will have missing values that will reduce your sample size or you might have to try to find the respondents and ask them to finish responding to the questionnaire. Finding respondents to ask them to complete the questionnaire is also resource intensive and reduces the quality of the responses because the atmosphere in which they answer will be different than when they answered the other questions.

Here are a few tips to ensure that all questions are answered. Note that this is more of an art of timing than a science. We can give you the guidelines but you have to observe and feel the actual situation to get the best timing. When giving a questionnaire to groups that might be disruptive as, for example, lower stream school children in large classes:

• Be fairly directive rather than letting them fill out the questionnaire at their own pace. You should break the questionnaire into sections. Read the instructions for each section – this asserts some control as well as making it easier for them to respond.

• Make sure that the children start each new section together as it can cause management problems if some children should finish before others. To avoid this, you can announce time guides at the beginning and near the end. You can announce, "You have 10 minutes to answer this section. You should now be halfway through. You have 2 minutes left to answer the questions."

• When you are aware that some children will answer their questionnaire earlier than others, it is a good idea to "stretch" the time at the end of each section by giving a little extra time. Also, you can add a relevant "open ended" question at the end of each section. This is mainly a time-filler question to keep the early finishers busy for a little longer so that they don't disrupt those who are still working. You can also use their answers to these open-ended questions to add some meaningful and interesting descriptions of the numerical results of your analysis.

- When you can see many have finished but some still have not finished, say, "When you have answered all questions in this section (avoid the word "finished") carefully check all your answers." This will give some more time for the slower ones to finish answering the questions without disruption from those who have finished.

- Plan to stop the whole group answering a section as soon as the last student has finished the "compulsory" questions. It doesn't matter if many students do not complete the open-ended question, because, remember, it is mainly used as a time-filler. If, at the end of the time for the whole questionnaire, the group is becoming disruptive but some students have still not finished some sections, then as a last resort to save the situation, you can stop the whole group answering and dismiss the students who have finished.

- When the finishers have left, make the ones who are left behind feel "special" rather than as though they have been kept in detention. It is important that all respondents are left with a good feeling, that is, that they should want to respond to a questionnaire again.

The "Look" of a Questionnaire

A GAMTEAP Principle
You should minimise everything that does not help the respondent to answer the questions.

In this section, we have included some examples of questionnaires that have been used so you can see the formatting principles in use and adapt them to the design of your own questionnaires. Applying GAMTEAP Principles means minimising all the things you put on the questionnaire – even the things you need for your own administrative purposes – this can even include the question numbers! The respondent doesn't need to know the number of the question in order to answer it. Only you need to know the number of the question so that you can enter the responses into your data base.

Questionnaire Design: *Example 1*

In the following example, we try to make each questionnaire appear as though it requires very little effort from the respondent (a basic GAMTEAP Principle). This is because, usually, people have other things they rather do than answer your questionnaire. If it seems that answering your questionnaire will require a lot of their effort then they will not do it, or they might do it but with little effort.

The **principle of maximizing white space** helps to make the questionnaire seem as if it contains much less for the respondent to do. Consequently, it is less likely to be rejected because it involves too much effort. Once the respondent has made a commitment by answering a few questions, then it is likely that he or she will continue to the end. This is known as the "foot in the door technique!" Hence, it is sometimes a good idea to put a few simple "dummy" questions at the start that the respondent will be attracted to answer. Although they may not be necessary for your analysis, they should seem relevant to the research area. An example for educated adults might be "What is your highest educational qualification?" Respondents are likely to be proud to remember their highest educational qualification.

You can increase the white space in many ways:

i   Leave out or minimise what does not help the respondent – question numbers, question marks at the end of each question (they are understood).

ii   Use thin line art graphics rather than heavy black printed clip art. You can easily see that —— is lighter than ▬▬ and that ☐ is lighter than ◼ . You really notice the difference when you have a whole page of them.

iii Use initials for response format choices rather than the whole word or phrase: **D** for Disagree, **A** for Agree, **Y** for Yes, **N** for No, **S** for Sometimes. If you plan to do this, then you may need to use the first few questions as a "training exercise." This means that using space for the training questions is only worthwhile if you will save space overall because you have many such responses.

iv   It is better to use a slightly smaller font (try Ariel 10 instead of Times New Roman 12) and reduced leading (or line space) than using a larger font. This way the same information takes up much less space.

v   Line up graphic elements vertically and horizontally, so the respondent's eyes do not have to jump all over the place, but are kept in the same area. I think that, subjectively, the amount of effort involved is judged by how much you have to move your eyes. (This would make an easy and interesting ANOVA experiment – use a computer screen to display the same amounts of information in different arrangements and ask the respondent to type in a rating of the complexity of each.) So, you need to do more than left align text. Use the tab as well, so that information lines up vertically.

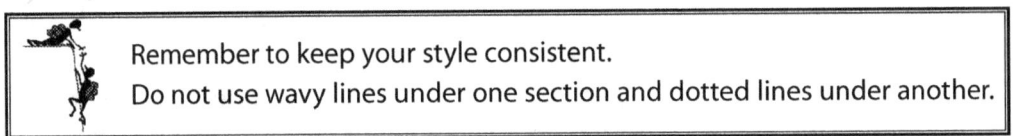

> Remember to keep your style consistent.
> Do not use wavy lines under one section and dotted lines under another.

Figure 8.2 shows the first part of a questionnaire for middle school children. Look at it carefully and read the explanations that follow to understand why the different parts have been included.

| SIDE A | YOUR QUESTIONNAIRE | A1 |

Print name: _____ ____ ____ ____ ____ ____ ____ ____ ____ ____ Date: ____ ____ ____ ____ Age: Years ____ Months ____

Name of School: ____ ____ ____ ____ ____ ____ ____ ____ ____ (tick ✔) Male ( ) or Female ( )

Figure 8.2: First part of questionnaire for middle school children.

"SIDE A" This is an "administration handle." It is a marker that is easily located by the respondents for directing their attention. Its purpose is to help with instructions from the administrator in guiding the respondent through the questionnaire. For example, you can say: "Now make sure you are looking at SIDE A of your questionnaire." These handles are essential for identifying sections in guiding respondents in group administrations but should not add unnecessarily to the amount of effort required to read the questionnaire.

Instead of using SIDE A, you could use simple graphic markers such as a thin line or an extra space between sections, or you could type sections in distinctive styles. Use anything that does not seem "extra" to what the respondent has to read in order to answer the questions.

"YOUR QUESTIONNAIRE" rather than only "QUESTIONNAIRE"

Applying a GAMTEAP Principle, the "YOUR" has been added to give a sense of ownership and hence commitment to giving more effort.

☐   The box in the top right-hand corner is a "coding box." It is for you, not for the respondent and is placed there so that you can identify each respondent by a number. If you do not need to know who the respondent is then you do not need the box. You can simply collect your questionnaires and write consecutive numbers anywhere in the top right-hand corner to uniquely identify that data. This becomes your subject ID at the input stage.

It may be essential that the data from each respondent is uniquely identified, particularly if you plan to match data about the same respondent from different sources. For example, you may need to match what a student says about him/herself with what the teacher says, for test-retest correlations, when you want to check the external validity of responses, or when you wish to use the initial responses for further respondent selection. In these cases, you make a numbered list of the respondents and put the number of the respondent in the box. Then you make sure that each respondent gets the questionnaire with their correct number. It is wise to double-check this so that you do not get your data mixed up. There are different ways of doing this but they depend on the cooperation, ability and willingness of the respondent. Because things can go wrong, we suggest that you use more than one method as a safety precaution.

Some ways of matching sets of data collected on different occasions from numbered respondents, as for example, using test-retest data.

1. Have two numbers for each name on your list of respondents. One is the natural order (the alphabetical first or last name) and the other is a code that the respondent keeps. Rather than using a completely independent code, it is wiser to choose a code derived from the list number in a way that it looks completely different. For example, you can square the list number, add 7 and reverse the digits – but remember what you have done!

Because you know the code, you can always check that the respondent has the correct coded number without exposing your list of respondents. You ask the respondent to enter his/her code in place of the name. You have to make sure they don't loose their code between the test and retest and this can be risky with many school children. The other way, and probably a safer, to do this is to write the code in the box as each student hands in his/her paper.

One way of demonstrating confidentiality is to show the respondents that although they are asked to write their name on the questionnaire at this time because you need it to compare scores, each questionnaire is also given a number. Once you have recorded the data by number, you show how the names on the questionnaire can be torn off and thrown away, so nobody, not even the researcher, can ever find out which name goes with each number. Although this might violate the principle of increasing the white space as it might require too much white space, it may be worth while if people can "see" where the names will be torn off! This method is often used when your research requires personal information or other information that may cause the respondent to lie about if he or she thought it would be used publicly. In this case, names would be placed at the top and the coding box placed to one side lower down.

2. The following is a variation of a method commonly used with password authentication. You ask for some information, not about the respondent, but associated with them, that does not change, something like the first name of the respondent's mother. Do not ask for information that might change, such as the name of a favourite film star and do not ask them about data that anyone can obtain, such as their birth date. The more such easily remembered pieces of information you ask for on a questionnaire then the more reliable will be the matching with subsequent questionnaires filled in by the same respondent. Of course, this assumes the respondent's willingness not to trick you.

"Print name" This assumes that you need the name for matching. If it is likely that you may not be able to read what the respondent has written, then ask for it to be printed. This holds true whether it is the name or anything else. It doesn't say "Print your name" because "your" will be understood by these respondents and so would unnecessarily clutter up the questionnaire.

Showing Your Respondents How to Use the Response Formats

Notice that the different response formats used in this questionnaire are first introduced at the start when the administrator can, if necessary, explain what to do to the whole group at one time, rather than disturb the group later by having to answer individual queries. There is the line for writing on _____. There is the set of brackets ( ) where the respondent can put a tick. There could also be a single space on which the respondent writes a number. Different response formats should be as few as possible and they must be consistent throughout the questionnaire.

The first few usual questions are used to subconsciously train the respondent in how to use the response format on the rest of the questionnaire without having to clutter the questionnaire with instructions on how to respond. The respondents know "Print name" followed by a line placed in the underline position means that they are expected to print their name on the line, and this is reinforced with the further examples of "Date _____ Age: Years ____ Months ____." So, when the respondent sees a question followed by an underline later in the questionnaire, they know, without being told, that they are expected to write an answer on the line. Similarly, by putting a tick and the word "Tick" or the symbol ✓ inside brackets, this is ideographically instructing the respondent to place a tick in the brackets. Hence, when they see the ( ) response format later they will know it means that they are expected to mark between two choices by putting a tick between the appropriate brackets.

The problem with ticking is that sometimes the ticks are badly placed by the respondent so that when you look through the questionnaires it is difficult to tell which choice was intended. Lines and the response brackets or boxes also take up a lot of space. For these reasons, it is better to ask the respondent to circle his/her choice from the options given. This takes less room, because only the options need to be printed and, although the circling process requires a little more effort than a tick, the cost in response effort is worth the increased accuracy of the data.

Markers Between Sections

Did you notice that there was more line space between the heading "YOUR QUESTIONNAIRE" than there was between the two lines requesting the organismic data? This is a subtle marker between sections indicating that a change in responding is required.

Numbering the Questions

As mentioned earlier, the numbers beside each question are for you and not for the respondent. They are mainly for you to correctly enter the responses into the correct column in the data matrix. The impact of these numbers on the respondent should be minimised. (i) You can make them as small and as light as possible (as long as you can read them) by choosing a fine small font size. (ii) There is no need to number every question. Just number the first and last question of each section, to check your input. Perhaps every fifth question will be sufficient to check the registration for input. (iii) Put the question numbers on the same line as the start of questions to which they refer but away from the questions, on the other side of a vertical bar if appropriate. This implicitly tells the respondent, "This is not part of the question – you don't have to pay attention to this."

Figure 8.3 shows the second side of a questionnaire that was administered to a group of Grade Nine students. Again, look at it carefully and read the explanations that follow to understand why the different parts have been included.

Questionnaire Design: *Example 2*

"SIDE B" You should be able to recognise the "administrative handle" and know its use. On this side of the questionnaire, it is so that the administrator can say something like: "Now turn to Side B of your questionnaire" and all the respondents can easily check that they have complied with these instructions.

A box placed around the instructions

The box containing the instructions separates the instructions that are to be done together from the questionnaire that the respondents are to do by themselves. Note that it also acts as partial training exercise. Having the instructions in a box enables the administrator to say: "Now look at the instructions in the box as I read them to you."

SIDE B

> The following sentences are about you. For each sentence (i) If you Agree you are like it says then circle the A. If you Disagree it is like you then circle the D. (ii) Then mark each sentence on the line, from 0 to 10, to show how strongly you agree or disagree.
>
> | | |
> |---|---|
> | *0 means 'no agreement/disagreement'* | *1-2 means 'agree/disagree a little'* |
> | *4-5 means 'mostly agree/disagree'* | *6-7 means 'strongly agree/disagree'* |
> | *3-9 means 'very strongly agree/disagree'* | *10 means 'completely agree/disagree'* |
>
> Practice questions
> A Ⓐ _7_ I am tall for my age.   A D ___ I like to play sports.   A D ___ Sometimes I stay late at school

Wait until you are told to start. There are no right or wrong answers, so give your first best answer and quickly move on to the next question.

A D ___ I like to keep moving around.

A D ___ I make friends quickly.

A D ___ I like to wrestle and to horse around.

A D ___ I like to shoot with a slingshot or catapult.

A D ___ I must admit I'm a pretty good talker.

A D ___ Whenever there's a float going someplace, I like to follow it.

A D ___ It's hard for me to finish my work if I don't like it.

A D ___ I rarely worry about looking foolish to others.

A D ___ I worry about what people will think of me even when I know it doesn't make any difference.

A D ___ I become tense and jittery if I know someone is sizing me up.

A D ___ I am concerned if I know people are forming an unfavourable impression of me.

Figure 8.3: The top of "Side B" of a questionnaire given to Grade Nine students (14-15 years old).

"The following sentences are about you."

The "you" is to add ownership and commitment, hence effort, and to focus the respondents' attention on the introspective nature of the questions. This is intended to increase the validity for responses to such self-rating questions.

*Note the capitalisation of **A**gree and **D**isagree.*

This is to match the A and D response options. It keeps the instructions intuitively consistent, which means less respondent effort is wasted in having to remember what the response codes mean (GAMTEAP).

Using A D response codes.

Using the words, "Agree" and "Disagree" increases the white space while using the letters, "A" and "D", decreases the amount of space needed, making the questionnaire seeming to require less effort.

"The rating range used is 0 to 10"

As discussed earlier, the range from 0 to 10 is considered suitable for education because teachers and students are used to marking out of ten. This means that the instructions for rating can be rephrased as "mark out of 10" – with zero intuitively meaning none and 10 as "the maximum."

Use underline very sparingly as an emphasis

When everything is underlined, nothing is emphasised. When you read out the instructions, you can verbally emphasise what is underlined.

Blocks of text (with bold, italic and different fonts giving different weights)

Notice how the blocks of text are used like graphic elements with space between them to indicate sections that punctuate response modes. All this makes it easier for the respondent to understand what is required and respond (GAMTEAP). For example, the actual questions use a small font and interline space (leading) and this allows a larger space between each question. This punctuates consecutive questions and adds white space.

Question Numbering

We have already discussed why question numbers should be small, out of the way, intermittent, or not even used at all. In this example, however, you will note that although the questions have been numbered, the sections have been have been divided into A, B, C, etc., and the numbering starts afresh for each section. This disguises how many questions you are actually asking. On this single sheet of paper there were 51 questions. If these had been numbered from 1 to 51, the respondent may have thought that 51 questions required too much effort. Numbering in natural sections avoids this problem and helps chunk data input.

"Wait until you are told to start"

This reinforces management of group-administered questionnaires.

It is important to realise that you should **never** print something on your questionnaire stating that it should be answered in a certain amount of time, as for example, "You will be allowed 30 minutes to complete this questionnaire" because groups vary greatly in the time they require to finish ALL of the questions. This matter of timing allows the administrator the flexibility of giving more time if necessary on parts of the questionnaire that do not involve timed tests.

"There are no right or wrong answers, so give your first best answer and quickly move on to the next question"

This instruction is carefully balanced between ensuring that respondents do not spend too much time considering each question so that they do not finish ("There are no right or wrong answers"), and ensuring that they do give their best effort ("so give your first best answer") and will finish in time ("and quickly move on to the next question").

The use of two columns

You will notice that this example uses two columns. The purpose of this is so that the eyes of the respondent move down the page twice as fast. This gives the illusion of more rapid progress, which is more motivating and makes it easier to respond (GAMTEAP). This same principle is used in formatting reading materials for people who find reading a great effort (e.g., newspapers and elementary textbooks as opposed to dissertations).

If the questions continue on to another page, then something similar to the following should be written on the bottom of the page: "continued on next page.." or "Please turn to the next page." This is to ensure that pages are not inadvertently left unanswered. Try, however, to keep all questions on one sheet of paper and used double-sided printing if it is necessary.

Printing on both sides of a sheet of paper means that:
  (i)   you do not have to collate sheets of paper,
  (ii) parts of the questionnaire do not get lost,
  (iii) you can put questions that you do not want seen together on opposite sides. This is because the answer to one question might influence the answer to the other – introducing local item dependence (LID),
  (iv) it seems that a questionnaire on one sheet of paper requires less effort than a questionnaire that takes up two separate sheets of paper.

This last point is important because the number of sheets of paper making up a questionnaire is initially equated with amount of effort. All else being equal, the fewer sheets the more likely it is that the respondent will answer your questionnaire. Using only one sheet of paper also saves you printing costs. A useful tip is to use legal-size paper. This gives you a lot more space on a single sheet if you need it.

At the foot of the very last page, do not write "Finish" or "End of Questionnaire" because some respondents will stop, saying that they have finished, while others are still completing their questions. Respondents with time on their hands can be disruptive. To prevent disruptions in group-administered questionnaires, you should always put a time-filling open response question at the end – one that implies a lot of writing is necessary. This will keep the early finishers busy. By making the question relevant, you can qualitatively analyse the answers that you do get and use the results to throw light on your numerical answers. This is similar to the smaller time-fillers in an administrator-paced sectioned questionnaire.

After the last open-ended question, you can put an instruction such as "Please check that you have answered every question." This will keep the early finishers busy for a little longer. If there are some respondents who have finished all this, say to them individually, "Please check very carefully the questions on the last page numbered X to X." This is to keep the extremely fast ones busy. Directing them to a particular set of consecutive questions is more motivating because it seems that these are the more important questions. Make sure you choose enough questions for them to check to allow time for the others to finish. You should never allow students who finish early to leave individually as they finish. This not only disrupts the others but it encourages the others to do what they can to leave as well. For example, they may not finish, or just might write ill-considered, quick responses just to get out. On the contrary, you should build up an expectation that no-one will disturb another person and use peer pressure to dissuade the early finishers from wanting to leave (GAMTEAP).

When everyone has finished you must then check that their identifying information is correct. Collect the papers from each person before they are allowed to leave and again check that the identifying information is there. If it is not, then ask them to fill it in. A questionnaire without identifying information can just be wasted data.

Remember "reciprocation" – respondents should be thanked again and reminded of their benefits from completing the questionnaire. When they leave, they should feel satisfied and interested in partaking in further research.

The Need to Train Your Respondents

Realise that many children (and some adults!) are not "survey smart" and may need guidance in judging the meaning of the intermediate numbers. In the example of the questionnaire, shown in Figure 8.3, the meaning has been given. In many cases, however, you will have to explain that they write **one number only**. If you do not explain this then some will copy the numbers as an ideogram – they will write *4-5* or *8-9* because they have copied these numbers from the instructions.

Generally speaking, you should use formats that are familiar to the respondents (GAMTEAP) unless, overall, you can get more targeted effort from another type of response. When the response format is not very familiar to your respondents, you may need to give practice examples. The example given in the Questionnaire design: Example 2 (Figure 8.3) is such a case. This is an interesting forced-choice rating response format that has been developed by Bastick (2003). Responses to each item are in two parts. The first part is forced-choice: Agree or Disagree. The second part is a rating of the strength of the first part of the response: "How strongly do you Agree or Disagree?"

This response format was developed for two reasons: it allows the reliability of forced-choice and rating-response formats to be compared and it doubles the discrimination of the rating response. When giving practice examples to this particular format, it is advisable to give a "worked example" first.

To continue with the explanations . . .

"The first one is done for you"

> This gives you an opportunity of role-playing the thinking processes involved in answering the question, and in reinforcing the response instructions as for example, in the forced-choice or rating-response format where the respondents have to write only one number. Make sure the first "worked example" is the most applicable and the easiest for the students to follow.

The example we gave in Figure 8.1 (about being tall) would be suitable for an administrator who is relatively short. He or she could then explain that he or she disagrees by comparing his/her height to others and thus choose to circle the D for Disagree. Then, because the administrator is very short, he or she would disagree strongly choosing "7" because it matches "strongly disagree."

Instructions and explanations should be broken down to one step at a time and REHEARSED word-for-word against the clock before you administer your questionnaire. Many research students who neglect to rehearse their instructions end up making a mess of their questionnaire administrations and invalidating all their hard design work.

Questionnaire Design: *Example 3*

The questionnaire, of which a part is shown in Figure 8.4 embodies a motivation questionnaire (Bastick, 2003). The more important aspects of the questionnaire are explained. Note the "professional" appearance of the questionnaire. It shows that the researcher had given a lot of thought to the formatting and follows the principles of GAMTEAP.

Joan Crosswell, Researcher

TEACHERS' QUESTIONNAIRE

AGE [ ]   Sheet number # [ ]

SEX [ ] male   [ ] female   YEARS OF TEACHING EXPERIENCE [ ]

WHICH AREA ARE YOU FROM   [ ] rural   [ ] urban   TODAY'S DATE [ ]

YEAR GROUP [ ] 1st Year   [ ] 2nd Year   [ ] 3rd Year   [ ] 4th/University

ARE YOU TRAINING FOR   [ ] preschool   [ ] primary   [ ] secondary

Instructions:

Each of the following statements is about you. Mark each out of 10 to indicate the extent to which you agree with it. Put the mark you give in the box.

0 for no agreement, up to
10 for maximum agreement

I CHOOSE TEACHING BECAUSE...

1. Teachers enjoy good status in the community and the society as a whole. [ ]
2. I will have enough time to earn extra money. [ ]
3. It allows me to be a manager. [ ]
4. The salary will be adequate to meet my demands. [ ]
5. Fees for Teachers' college are affordable. [ ]
6. Teaching is the profession with the most holidays with pay. [ ]

7. I see it as a life-long career. [ ]
8. I can make worthwhile contributions to the academic development of others. [ ]
9. I love children. [ ]
10. It is the profession I have always wanted. [ ]
11. It offers job security. [ ]
12. I wanted to. [ ]
13. I can make worthwhile contributions to the social development of others. [ ]

Mark how good you think you will be as teacher after this course. 0 for not good up to 10 for excellent [ ]
For how long, after this course, do you think you will continue to work as a teacher? ____ years

Figure 8.4: Questionnaire for tertiary students

Alignment

The first thing that you might notice about this questionnaire is how the response boxes are all aligned. This gives a much simpler appearance to the questionnaire for the purpose described.

Researcher's Name

It was helpful in this data collection, to build an identification between the student-teacher researcher and the student-teacher respondents (GAMTEAP). To this end, the questionnaire is "personalised" at the very start with the name of the administrator. This is noted in the administrator's introduction when administering the questionnaire.

Format

There is only one type of response format – fill in the box – and the information needed for each box is succinctly noted by a label or question close to each box. This considerably reduces non targeted respondent effort – leaving more effort for answering the questions.

Question Numbering

Because there are only 13 questions in the main part of the questionnaire, these have been numbered to "advertise" that there are only 13 questions on this questionnaire, implying little effort is needed. Actually there are 23 questions on this part of the questionnaire – nearly twice as many as the respondent is aware of. However, the question numbers used by the researcher are well out of the way, intermittent and placed in sections so as not to accentuate the total number of questions on the questionnaire.

The Undirected Response Format

The age variable is not marked in "years" to make the question more acceptable to those who may not want to state their age. This is a common reticence in ageist cultures (those who value youth more than age) and the respondent can put a range or leave it blank if preferred. In practice, respondents usually take the line of least effort when filling questionnaires and here you can use this to your advantage. It is less effort for them to enter their actual age, as you want, than for them to work out a range or entertain the idea that they are too old to give an answer. The same undirected response format can work with income and other such information.

> When you are writing a questionnaire ensure that the finished product looks "professional".

9
The "Nitty Gritty" of Pre-Planning Your Questionnaire Items

You have been given a lot of information to think about – why you are asking the questions, the different types of questions that can be used in questionnaires, the different ways to write items and how to group (or not group) them, different methods to obtain your measurement data, and of course, GAMTEAP Principles. Now, it is time to actually look at a list of what you have to do to write an effective questionnaire.

- Think of *why* you are doing this research. This means that you first have to decide exactly what you want to measure. This decision is based on your thesis statement, your initial questions and your hypotheses. All the items in your questionnaire should be designed to reject (or fail to reject) your hypotheses. All too often, researchers start to develop a questionnaire and write items before defining the constructs they want to measure or thinking seriously about the research hypotheses and data collection.

- Although you may have started out with an abstract construct, precisely define what you are going to measure. In other words, narrow down your research topic so that it is do-able within a specific time frame.

- Operationalise your variables. Determine exactly what indicators are characteristic of the construct being investigated. You have thought of a characteristic, trait, perception, attitude or some other construct that you want to measure but make sure that you have specified the behaviour that is indicative of that "something" and that these definitions are directly related to your own research. These definitions are based on findings from your literature research and/or interviews with qualified professionals in your area of research.

> When the content of the items represents the construct being investigated, the content related validity of the questionnaire increases.

- Once you have found a number of indicators, then you have to sit down and really think of the many ways in which these indicators can be measured. Assemble a large assortment of items that are directly concerned with the indicators, traits and characteristics that you want to measure.

- Make sure that each item is relevant to what you are investigating and is either clearly favourable or unfavourable. For example, if you are going to measure attitudes toward reading, try to collect a large number of items that reflect different attitudes. For such a questionnaire, two of your items might be: "I prefer to read at night instead of watching television" (considered a favourable response) or "I usually put off doing my reading homework until just before the bell rings for class" (considered an unfavourable response).

- Throw out all items that appear to be ambiguous, irrelevant, neutral or too extreme (e.g., "I hate reading"; "I love reading"), items that are very personal and items that suggest that a particular response is desirable.

- For rating items, assign a value to all remaining items. Remember: when you are designing a Likert-type scale, the value assigned to each item is not given to the subjects responding to the questionnaire.

- If you are using a forced-choice or selected-response questionnaire, then make sure that the responses to the items are appropriate. "Strongly agree" to "strongly disagree" was used when using a Likert-type scale asking about the characteristics of giftedness, but there are many other different ways that sets of responses may be worded. Look at the examples of other sets of comparison adjectives (p. 94) or try writing items appropriate for the Osgood Semantic Differential Scale or the 100mm Line using bipolar dimensions.

- When you are item writing, make sure that the wording of each item is unambiguous and that the respondents can understand what is being stated. This means that the vocabulary should be below or within the reading level of those who will be replying to the questionnaire. Do not use vague words, jargon or highly technical terms (unless the purpose of your questionnaire is meant to test knowledge of the terms).

- Finally, make sure that each item contains only one concept (as an example of two concepts: "I think that teachers deserve higher wages and longer holidays.")

Of course, a very important aspect of the entire questionnaire process is deciding on your sample. The target population must be identified before you start item writing and your sample selection is based entirely on your hypothesis. Writing questionnaire items specifically for a particular set of respondents goes a long way to ensure accuracy of responses, the rate of response and the content-validity of the questionnaire.

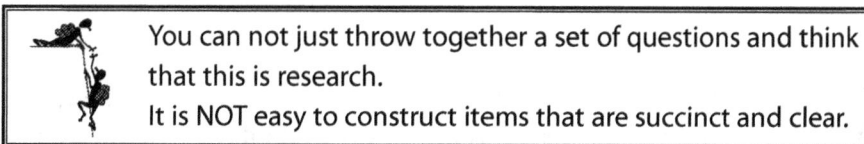

> You can not just throw together a set of questions and think that this is research.
> It is NOT easy to construct items that are succinct and clear.

Question Content

During all this time, you should be keeping a "process trail" – this is similar to an audit trail in accounting. The process trail consists of notes of:

i   Why you asked each question – this relates to your research questions, hypotheses and should be based on your previous reading;

ii   The type of responses you expect to get – this is a check on whether you are asking the questions in the best way to obtain the type of responses you expect; and

iii   What type of statistical technique(s) you expect to use on the responses – this makes sure that the level of measurement is correct and that the data you get will be the correct type for the analysis you plan to do in order to test your hypotheses and answer research questions.

Many poorly trained researchers are so over-keen to collect their data that they ignore these steps and end up having done lots of work collecting data that they cannot analyse to answer their research questions. Warning! Do not let this happen to you. Use a process trail.

> The process trail is important for another reason. When you start writing your thesis, you must justify your reasons for the questions or statements you included in your questionnaire. If you already have a process trail, the writing of this rationale will be relatively easy.

Pretesting Your Items and Pilot Testing Your Questionnaire

You have made up a lot of items that you think will give you answers to your research problem. But, will they? One way to find out is to get critical reactions from a small group of people who are familiar with the variables you are studying – they do not even have to be randomly selected. This is the pre-testing aspect of the formation of your questionnaire.[1] Critical evaluations of items can catch unforeseen problems that can be solved before you design and print out your final formatted questionnaire.

In the initial testing of your questionnaire, ask a small group of people to answer each item as if they were really responding to your questionnaire and discuss each item with them while they are responding to the question or statement (a focus group discussion). Once they have answered the questionnaire, they can tell you what items they found ambiguous and what may need to be eliminated. They may even suggest other ways of asking the question. In short, you can iron out a lot of problems when you do a pretest run.

The Pilot Test

When you think you have created a questionnaire with responses to items that will answer your research questions, you are ready to do the all important pilot test.

1.   Administer the questionnaire to a number of respondents, (between 20 - 30) who are representative of those with whom the questionnaire will be used. You can also ask the people in your pilot project to write, in their own words, what they think each item means or you can discuss the items with them. If there are still ambiguities, revise and retest the items until the members of the pilot group understand each item.

---

1. Do not get "pretesting your items" mixed up with pretests and post-tests. Pretesting means that you are trying out your materials or questionnaires to make sure that items are unambiguous and that participants can understand what to do.

2.   After you have compiled a questionnaire with a minimum of ambiguous items, and administered it to your pilot group, you should compute each individual's total score by adding his or her item scores. If you are using a different type of scoring scheme (for example, by indicators), then consult your code book, and try out your scoring and types of analysis to make sure that you won't get any nasty surprises when you have a large number of questionnaires to analyse.

3.   Score responses to the various items in such a way that a response indicative of the most favourable attitude is given the highest score.

4.   For a uni-dimensional scale (that is, all items measure a single construct), use Cronbach's alpha[2] to analyse the responses to determine which items discriminate most clearly between the high scorers and the low scorers on the total scale. Items that do not show a substantial correlation with the total score, or those that do not elicit different responses from those who score high and those who score low on the total test can be eliminated. This elimination ensures that the questionnaire is "internally consistent" – this simply means that every item on the scale is related to the same general construct.

5.   Select the items that have the highest discriminatory coefficients, that is, use all of the scale items with values between 8.0 and 8.9.

Above all, do not get worried about computing and analysing scores. Once you have entered all the data into Excel or the SPSS data file, you just tell the computer what to do. How to tell the computer what to do is explained in Part 5.

If your research only involves a questionnaire, then go to:

Chapter 12 to learn how to enter your data into Excel, save your data files and then how to get into the SPSS programme, then to

Chapter 15 to learn how to increase the reliability and validity of your questions.

BUT FIRST

Carefully read "Part 4: Almost There" to make sure that you know all about the ethics of carrying out your research.

---

2. How to analyse your items (and why) with Cronbach's alpha is explained fully in Chapter 14.

A Final Check List

First decide on a time frame. Then check off each item as you have completed it.

DATE	DONE?	"THINGS" THAT MUST BE DONE
		Define research problem
		Formulate hypotheses
		Check with expert about definitions of constructs
		Define constructs
		Operationally define the major variables so they can be measured
		Develop outline of questionnaire
		Define population who will answer the questionnaire
		Write cover letter(s)
		Develop and construct items / select standardised instrument
		Decide how to analyse responses (construct a scoring system)
		Pre-testing run
		Revise items, etc., if necessary
		Pilot test
		Revise items, etc., if necessary
		Analyse individual items or group of items and throw out items to ensure that test is internally consistent
		Finalise sample and ensure they can be randomly selected
		Train assistants/interviewers, if necessary
		Administer questionnaire
		Analyse responses
		Synthesise results with previous findings

We have stated that you should be ready to write your proposal at this stage, BUT, there are still a few important points to consider and you should take time to think about them before you settle down to write the final draft of your proposal. These important considerations are (i) the reliability and validity of your research, (ii) ethical considerations and (iii) the cover letter(s). They have been placed in this section, Almost There!, so that you can read them carefully before beginning the research process and, of course, for a final review when you are writing your research thesis.

(i) Reliability and Validity: Although we have mentioned both of these terms throughout the text, we felt that they merited their own special section. *Reliability* refers to the consistency of the measurements used in your experiments, tests and questionnaires. It means that you should have measuring instruments that can be trusted. When we talk about *validity*, we are referring to information based on evidence and sound reasoning. The inferences that we make from our research findings must be supported by the evidence from the collection and analyses of data and should be appropriate, meaningful and useful.

(ii) Ethics: Our dictionary defines ethics as "...standards of conduct and moral judgement." When you apply this to the research process, ethics refer to questions about what is "right" and what is "wrong" while carrying out your research and when reporting your results. There are four main ethical considerations: protection of participants from harm, ensuring confidentiality of data, the use of deception, and informed consent.

(iii) The Cover Letter(s): We have found out that students often forget about the cover letter (or letters) until they are ready to begin their research. As you will read, the way the cover letter is written and formatted is a very important aspect of the research process. It is the introduction of your own research to the people whom you would like to be the participants. A good cover letter sets the stage for your research and goes a long way in ensuring that your research will take place when and where you need it to be.

This section finishes with a 'generic' format (a basic recipe) for writing your research proposal. It is generic because different faculties and/or organisations may require a slightly different format or word count. As we have stated so often, you must check with your own faculty or organisation to determine specific requirements and where the different information should be placed. The format presented in this text, however, has listed the essentials needed for most proposals.

10
Reliability, Validity, Ethics and Cover Letter

Reliability = Consistency

Reliability

Reliability of research refers to the consistency of the methods, conditions and results of whatever research is being carried out. It also is related to the extent to which the research can be replicated by independent researchers. To ensure *internal reliability* of research, you must take great care that you do not vary the methods you use or change conditions – particularly when you have different groups of people, when you are administering some form of measuring scale to many different groups or when your research requires research assistants. Additionally, you must take great care in how you analyse and interpret the data. You just can't fiddle with data because you are not getting the results you expected! This leads us to *external reliability* of research which means that other researchers would achieve similar results if they attempted to replicate your study under similar conditions.

Reliability of a test or measurement refers to the *consistency* of the measurement and the consistency of the test – how reliable or consistent is the test – and how reliable or consistent are the results. If, for example, you have created a test to measure a specific ability (such as academic ability or intelligence) or a specific characteristic (such as personality type, locus of control or motivation to do something), then an individual who scores high on one measure should also score high on a similar type of measure. Of course, that person will not get exactly the same scores every time he or she writes a similar test, but that person's set of scores should be highly related to each other as long as the tests or measurements were reliable and consistent.

Think About This ...

Notice that when we talk about measurement error of a test, we are not talking about differences in scores of groups of people taking the same test because their scores will certainly vary! Otherwise, why give the test?

We are talking about the scores of one person taking a number of tests that measure the same ability, characteristic, skill or perception. Scores or rankings from reliable tests or measurements should be similarly ranked for that person.

The Classical Test Theory and Measurement Error

Although a person's score or ranking on a number of tests or measurements should be similar, it is rare that the scores will be identical. This difference in test scores is what is known as the measurement error. According to the Classical Test Theory, an individual's performance on a test reflects both the individual's true score – that is, the actual amount of the characteristic, ability or skill that the test measured and the person actually possesses – and a measurement error that is randomly distributed. This means that measurement errors are not constant – you cannot pinpoint any one particular error and no one test taker makes exactly the same mistake as another test taker. Note that according to the Classical Test Theory, if scores have large errors, then the reliability is considered low; if few errors, then the reliability is considered high.

> Measurement error is defined as "...the difference between the individual's true scores on a test and the scores that he or she actually obtains over a variety of conditions."[1]

Factors That Might Cause Measurement Errors

1.   The items in a test are only a sample of the total domain of possible items that might be used to represent the trait, personality, aptitude or other construct being measured. Measurement error can occur if different items on the test are not equivalent in how they sample the construct.

2.   Test administrators may introduce measurement error by failing to administer the test consistently. Testing conditions, such as noisy or exceedingly warm rooms, inadequate lighting, different times of day, may cause individuals to perform atypically on a test.

3.   Test scorers may create measurement errors by not following consistent scoring procedures.

4.   The feelings or physical condition of the individual taking the test may vary (for example, being sick on the test day) and cause atypical scores. When you are working with young children, the researcher has to pay particular attention to the time of day. Children are fresher and more willing to do their best in the mornings but perhaps not late in the afternoon when they have been working hard at school all day.

Three of the major empirical methods used to estimate reliability of tests are:

1.   **Test-retest Method:** An individual takes the same test on two different occasions and the coefficient of stability is calculated between the two sets of scores. There may be problems using this method because the person might remember the questions and responses from the first test and the correlations might be artificially high. On the other hand, if the tests are too far apart, then the person might have changed his or her opinions, etc., and the correlations might be artificially low.

---

1. Gall, Gall, & Borg, 2003, p. 196

2.   **Alternate-Form Reliability:** An individual takes one form of the test and then a parallel form of the same test and the scores are measured by a coefficient of equivalence. The parallel forms of a test can consist of two separate but very similar questions or statements, by using alternate questions of each form or by using the first part of a test as one form and the second part of the same test as the alternate form. This is difficult to do because (1) it is very time consuming and expensive to make up two forms of the same test and (2) you can never be exactly sure that the two forms are identical.

3.   **Split-Half Reliability:** A test is split into two comparable halves and administered to the same individual. This can be done in a number of different ways: placing all the even numbered questions in one test and the odd numbered questions in the second test and/or using a random numbers table to decide which questions go into which half. The major problem with using a split-half test is that the correlation coefficient gives you an estimate of the reliability between responses to the two sets of tests but not of the full test. If you considered using this method to determine the reliability of all of the full test items, the Spearman-Brown formula should be used.

If you are using standardised tests for your own research, be sure to check on their reliability. Because of the time and expense involved developing reliability measurement of a test, this might not have been done.

If a group of people are observing behaviours, you have to make sure that all observers note the same things and then check that the scores are similar (a high correlation of at least 0.90 among scorers is required).

It is important to describe the reliability of the measurement you used in your discussion of instrumentation in the Methods section.

Internal consistency of test scores refers to the estimation of the reliability of individual items of a test. To do this, you would need to give one administration of the test and then analyse the scores from that test using Cronbach's alpha when the scores are not dichotomous or by one of the Kruder-Richardson formulas if the items are scored dichotomously (e.g., yes/no; correct/incorrect; always/never). Again, you do not have to work this out for yourself as the SPSS programme (Chapter 15) will give you results and let you know the reliability.

Do not forget that reliability also refers to the consistency or trustworthiness of the measuring instrument. For example, you would throw a watch out or get it fixed if it ran too fast or too slow because you certainly could not depend on it to give you a reliable measurement every time you looked at it. The same thing holds true with any measuring instruments used during the research process. If the measuring instrument is not reliable, then you can be sure that the results will not be reliable.

Validity

Validity of a test was once defined simply as whether a test really measured what it was supposed to measure.[2] The definition of validity has been changed, however and in 1999, the Standards for Educational and Psychological Testing defined validity as the "...degree to which evidence and theory support the interpretation of test scores entailed by proposed use of tests" (p. 9). This is an important point to consider because, when you think about it, anyone can make up a test and score it but it is much more difficult and requires much more thinking to make sure that the test is appropriate, meaningful and useful *based on the information that the test score gives.*

> Validity now refers to how a test score is interpreted and what the scores mean and not the instrument itself.

There are three different ways to gather information about validity. You should be specifically concerned about the first two, *content-related validity* and *construct-related evidence* as these are very important when you are constructing questionnaires. The third, *criterion-related validity* is of great importance when you are using measurements that are to be compared with other valid measurements (the criterion).

Content-related validity uses evidence from the actual content of the test and refers to the relationship between the test questions and the construct it is supposed to measure.

Questions to ask:
- ❑ Is the content appropriate for the person who will be taking this test?
- ❑ Do the questions cover the content that the test is supposed to measure?
- ❑ How much of the content do the questions measure?
- ❑ Is the test format appropriate? (Does it follow the GAMTEAP Principles?)

You can make sure that your test has an acceptable content-validity by asking someone who is competent in the field of your particular topic to look at the questionnaire items or experimental conditions and judge whether they are appropriate and cover the domain adequately.

> Content-related validity is an important concept in selecting tests involving the effect of instructional methods.

Construct-related evidence: This is a difficult aspect of test construction and involves (i) precise definition(s) of the construct(s) being measured; (ii) hypotheses about what the actual scores mean (e.g., do high scores on a motivation to read test really mean that the person is highly motivated to read?) and (iii) the testing of these hypotheses.

---

2. In simplistic terms, if you want to find out how well a student can read, then giving a mathematic test certainly would not be a valid measure of reading ability.

Questions to ask:

❑ Have the constructs been precisely defined so that test items or questions represent what the researcher is investigating?

❑ If you received one set of scores on a test, would you be able to state that high scores mean one thing and low scores mean another?

❑ Can you verify that these scores accurately reflect the personality, ability, skill, etc., of the person taking that test or responding to that questionnaire?

❑ Can you verify that these scores do actually reflect the construct you are measuring?

Criterion-related validity refers to the relationship between scores from your test and scores from another valid external test or other measurement (the criteria). For example, if you are looking at some educational attainment based on a researcher-made measurement, then the scores from your test can be compared with scores from the one of the national achievement tests (e.g., GSAT) which would be considered the criterion.

Questions to ask:

❑ Do the test scores correlate positively with scores on other measures that are supposed to measure a similar construct?

❑ Do the test scores correlate negatively with scores on other measures that are presumed to measure a different construct?

❑ Do the test scores indicate how accurately test scores can predict criterion scores obtained at a later point in time?

Remember assessments can be reliable but not be valid!

Ethics in Carrying Out Research

In Jamaica, there seems to have been only limited attention paid to ethical considerations while carrying out research. This is particularly true of the research carried out by students who wish to complete their Master's degree – generally, they just go ahead and present their questionnaires to students or other adults without first obtaining informed consent. This, however, should change as the newly formed Jamaican Psychological Association is in the process of drawing up ethical guidelines for practitioners and researchers in Jamaica.

There are four major principals that must be observed when conducting research:

1. **Protection From Harm:** The most important ethical principal is that all research must be conducted so that the participants who are taking part in your research are not harmed in any way. Harm covers physical, psychological or legal considerations. Fortunately, much of our research does not set out to deliberately physically harm individuals but there might be problems if the effects of some new exercise programme are being investigated and the health of the participants had not previously been investigated.

Additionally, if the investigation involves controversial topics such as HIV, drug usage, or homosexuality, then the participants might be harmed physically or psychologically if knowledge of their attitudes or attributes is given out to the 'wrong' people. Psychological harm will most likely ensue if tests and measures are interpreted wrongly as, for example, when a person has been wrongly labelled as having low intelligence and is subsequently placed in an inappropriate educational setting.

2. **Ensuring Privacy and Confidentiality:** Researchers must guard the privacy and confidentiality of each participant in their studies. Researchers must ensure that no unauthorised persons will have access to their data *and* the participants must be told in advance who will have access to the information collected. This is of prime importance, particularly if some controversial topic, such as HIV, prostitution, homosexuality or drug use, has been selected. In some cases, the amount of money earned per year and even the age of the respondents should be treated as confidential. In these events, you have to ensure that your data is kept carefully guarded so that your participants cannot be identified. Protection of the participants must be of prime concern.

Sometimes, the research design is one in which multiple scores are required and this means keeping track of each participant by name (using a linkage system). One method of maintaining confidentiality has been discussed in the section on questionnaire items when it was suggested that a specific code be assigned to each participant. In most cases, the linkages have to be preserved only until all the data have been entered and verified and then the names of the participants can be removed so that not even the researcher knows the identity of the participants. The best way to do this, if you have to have linkages, is to write the name or the code number on the top right-hand corner of the questionnaire or test and then simply cut it off whenever you feel happy that the data has been entered correctly.

One of the main problems in conducting research in a small community is that others might want to know "what you found." As a researcher, when you write your thesis, you must discuss your findings but not in such a way that any one individual can be identified.

When you are writing your final thesis,
NEVER, NEVER
mention any participant or organisation by name or write your findings so that the participants or organisations can be identified.

3. **Fair Selection of the Participants:** The participants must be selected fairly so that every participant has an equal chance of being selected. For example, it would not be fair to ask a teacher to select students for your project because these students might be selected on the basis of some reward system. The teacher might choose the best and brightest students to take part and then you would certainly have biased results! The fairest method is to first identify your population sample and then randomly select participants according to a method decided in advance (e.g., by using a table of random numbers).

4. **The Need for Informed Consent:** All participants must be informed about what will occur in the study, what kind of information will be required from them and how the research will be used. They need to know that they have the right to withdraw from the study for any reason and at any time. If the participants are adults, they must give their consent to take part in your study.

    Children are different as they cannot give consent (only adults can do this). In this case, parents or the primary care-givers must give informed consent on behalf of the child and the appropriate school personnel must give permission for any research to be carried out in schools. Informed consent is crucial if you plan to change something, such as teaching a subject using a different method or if you plan to give them something to eat (such as sweets).

    Note that when you are investigating behaviours of children, many ethics committees require the researcher to ask parents or other primary care-takers to sign a consent form. These aspects are required by the ethics committees in some countries, irrespective of the needs of the respondents or the writer of the questionnaire. Although the rules set down by ethics committees may change, they generally are applied indiscriminately. This means that you have no choice but to do what you are told or your institution will not allow or accept your research or your publisher will reject your manuscript.

    In many societies, it is also considered unethical to ask questions that cannot be justified on a principle of utilitarianism, that is, questions that waste the respondents' time and effort. This means that you must realise that every question you put on your questionnaire must have a pre-planned purpose.

    Although everyone must be informed of the right to withdraw, remember that children often do not know how to say they want to stop. It is the researcher's moral responsibility to watch out for signs of discomfort or uneasiness in the child and suggest stopping.

The Use of Deception

In some cases, research designs require that the participants be deceived. In this case, the information to be gained from the research must be weighed with the amount of harm that might be caused. Placing children in a success or failure condition is such an example. For the research on learned helplessness, the ethics committee decided that knowledge of behaviours following exposure to a short failure experience would outweigh possible psychological harm. The researcher, however, had to explain in great detail how she was going to remove the "stigma" of failure before the proposal was accepted and this had to be built into her research design.

A major reason for deception is that if your participants know what you are trying to investigate, they may behave differently and you would not get valid results. For example, if a researcher wanted to investigate differential feedback from teachers according to gender and the teachers knew what the researcher was looking for, then it is quite likely that teachers would be very careful NOT to give different feedback to boys and girls.

In all cases where deception is required, the researcher should agree to tell the participants about the purpose of the research after data has been collected. In cases where participants have been deliberately deceived about test scores (in order to get their reaction to the scores, for example), at the end of the research, the researcher must show the participant the true scores and explain why the deception had been carried out – this is called *debriefing*.

The Cover Letter

The cover letter is usually a neglected aspect of the research design. Researchers become so involved in thinking about their questionnaire or research project that it sometimes comes as a shock to realise that a cover letter MUST be written. An important GAMTEAP Principle is that it is the cover letter that introduces the research to participants, persuades the participants that your research is important and motivates the participants to want to take part in your research or to want to respond to your questionnaire.

Realise that in some instances, you may need to write more than one cover letter for your research, to the head of a company or the principal of a school requesting permission to carry out your research in their territory, to the people who you wish to take part in your study and maybe, to the parents or primary care-givers of children asking for consent. The contents of each letter should be carefully thought out.

> A **GAMTEAP** Principle
> The main objective of writing a cover letter is to get a high return rate.

Although the contents of a cover letter were briefly discussed in the GAMTEAP section (p. 98) as an essential part of any questionnaire, each part of the cover letter is discussed in greater depth.

1. First, the cover letter should be brief. It should be no longer than one typewritten page and should look as if you have taken some time in composing it. This is an important GAMTEAP Principle: If you don't care how you introduce your research to others, the others won't care if they respond or not.

2. Secondly, the letter should be addressed directly to the individual. For example, if you want to carry out your research in a particular school, the letter should be addressed to the principal by name and not "Dear Principal." The idea here is that if you couldn't be bothered to find out the name of the principal, why should the principal trouble him or herself to help you? If, however, you are informing a large number of people about your research involving responding to a questionnaire, then it would be permissible to write "Dear Participant" or "Dear Student."

3. In the very first paragraph, explain the purpose of your research and why the person was chosen to take part in it. It should also give an overview of what the participant will be required to do.

4. The importance of the research should be specified. This should motivate the participant to want to be a part of your research.

5. Next, the ethical issues of confidentiality and the right to be able to withdraw from the task should be clearly stated. In this section, the researcher should also explain how he/she plans to safeguard the data being collected (e.g., using a code that only the researcher will have, using no names at all, having a name on the top right-hand corner that will be destroyed). If necessary, you can state that confidentiality is an important ethical responsibility of the researcher and required by your university.

6. Give an approximate length of time that this research will take. For example, if you are asking permission for students to answer a questionnaire, state that it is expected that the full time needed will be only $1/2$ hour.

7. End up by thanking the reader for his/her time and co-operation.

8. Sign the letter personally. Try not to make the cover letter look like a form letter.

Extras to Give Your Research Project Some Validity

♦ If the research is part of a university requirement, then it is a good idea to state that this research has been accepted by the review committee.

♦ Have the introductory cover letter written on the university letterhead or on the letter head of a company or association. For student researchers, the use of the university letterhead is logical as the research proposal has been approved by the review board and is being carried on under university sponsorship. Ask your supervisor (the person who is in charge of your research) to sign the letter. It is interesting to note that people tend to respond to an authority to which they have some knowledge and it is likely that when your letter looks official, it will probably receive a better response.

If you are asking permission from the head of an organisation, such as a school, hospital or workplace, then the cover letter serves as an introduction to the person in charge. This letter must be clear and concise and follow the general format. Additionally, it should state when you would like to be able to carry out your research and ask if this time is convenient. Follow up the initial letter and set exact days and times when you will be allowed to carry out your research.

You might have to write a second letter to others who will be involved in your research (e.g., the teachers in the classroom, nurses in a hospital, workers in a factory, parents of young children) using the same basic format. If you are carrying out some form of experimental condition, a letter of consent must be sent to all parents or primary care-givers, asking for consent for their child to take part in the research.

Figure 10.1 is an example of a cover letter and consent form used in the learned helplessness research. It was sent to all parents of the children taking part in the learned helplessness research.

Date

Dear Mr. And Mrs. **Name of each parent/care-giver filled in here**

    I am investigating how children learn under different conditions. The study consists of two sections. In the first section, your child will be asked about events regarding about how he or she feels about events that can occur in everyday living and also given a short test assessing mental maturity. In the second section, your child will be given a learning task and then given another short task. In this section, should a child not be able to do the task correctly, he or she will be told why and allowed to do the task correctly before being returned to the classroom.

    Each child will be accompanied by a trained research assistant and is expected to be out of the classroom for only about 20 minutes each session. The principal of the school is aware of the research and has given permission for this research to be carried out. In addition, the Review Board and Ethics Committee of the University of XXX has approved of this research. There will be a large number of children taking part in this study and all scores will be kept confidential. The results of this investigation will be reported so that no one child will be able to be identified.

    It is believed that the results of this research will be beneficial to the educational system in Jamaica in that it might help explain why some children fail to learn even though they have to ability to do so. Additionally, it is felt that the knowledge gained from this study will help foreign educators understand how immigrant children learn under different situations.

    The participation of your child in this research is entirely voluntary and if you and you child wish to terminate the sessions for any reason, you are both free to do so. If you have any questions regarding the research, I will be at the school on **the date filled** in between the hours of 10:00 AM and 2:00 PM and will be able to answer any of your questions.

    If you agree to your child taking part in the research, would you please sign the enclosed consent form and give it to the principal.

Sincerely,

Signature _____

I agree that my child, **Name of Child** is allowed to participate in this research study investigating how children learn under different conditions. I understand I may withdraw my consent at any time and may stop my child from taking part in the study at any time.

Date _____

Signature of parent or guardian

The name of each parent was filled in by the researcher.

What the research is about and what the child will be required to do in the research.

The parent is assured that the child will not be harmed psychologically.

Awareness and acceptability of the research by the Ethics Committee, the Review Board of the university and by the principal of the school.

Assurance of confidentiality of results

Benefits of the research

Ability to withdraw and notice of consent form.

The signature was hand written

The consent form that each parent was asked to sign

Figure 10.1: A replica of the cover letter and the consent form sent to all parents of the children taking part in the research investigating learned helplessness behaviours in children.

11
Writing the Proposal

You have taken all the basic steps.......

1. decided on your research topic.
2. narrowed it down so it is do-able.
3. defined the constructs so that they are observable and measurable.
4. searched for information about your topic on the computer and in the. library so you are able to justify the need for your research.
5. decided on the appropriate research design.

Now...

You have to sell your idea for your research! Writing the research proposal provides the basis for the "powers that be" (an academic committee or a review board) to allow you to begin your research or for a funding group to provide the necessary funds for your research. The proposal is a blueprint of what you plan to do and it communicates your intentions to the review board. A good, well-thought out proposal shows that you have done your homework – that you have taken all the steps shown above. It also shows that your research or project is not just something to which you have given very little thought. You have to prove that the topic you have chosen will add to existing literature and make the readers think, "What a good idea!"

The proposal should be fairly short – each faculty or committee has its own number of pages or word count that are considered suitable for the proposal. It is always a good idea to find out how long the proposal should be before submitting it. Then it is an even better idea to keep within that limit! Above all, student researchers MUST listen to their academic advisors – forms of proposals differ and you MUST follow the guidelines.

Drawing your research design and using Word Maps will make the outline of your proposal clearer. When you know exactly what you want to do, this clarity comes across to your readers of your proposal. When you know in detail what you intend to do, you will find proposal writing is fairly simple.

When you worked on the "Building Your Research" exercises, you actually gathered most of the information required for your research proposal. You now have to round out what you have written.

A Suggested Format for the Research Proposal

The format that we suggest gives you a general idea of the essentials that should be included in each section. BUT, when you are writing your proposal, remember that this outline is not "written in stone!" Each faculty member, academic advisor or research committee has specific requirements that you should follow.

A research proposal has five major parts:
1. Purpose and Background
2. Review of Related Literature
3. Description and Procedure
4. Significance
5. References

1. Purpose and Background *or* Why Are You Doing This Research?

The purpose of your research should be written almost at the beginning of the proposal. No one likes to have to read through many pages before he or she finally discovers the topic. In fact, if people have to read a great many pages to discover what your research is about, it may only put them in a bad mood and you might have to fight to get your proposal accepted.

- Start with a few introductory sentences introducing the topic in general. If possible, integrate a reference or two of the related literature. This brief introduction provides the context for stating your specific research topic and should include your thesis statement – the first thing you wrote in Building Your Research I.

- Jump right into the "nitty-gritty," the specific purpose or reason for this particular research. This can come at the end of your first paragraph or the purpose can open the second paragraph.

For example, you can write:

The major purpose of this study is to identify ......
The major purpose of this study is to describe some of the reasons why........
The major objective of this study is to determine whether.......
The major purpose of this study is to investigate ....
The research questions are to address............
This study will attempt to identify.......

> If you have many hypotheses, you can always state:
> A second purpose of this study is to .... *or* Additionally, this study will investigate (determine, analyse) .... *or* The three objectives of this study are to ....

Try to make your purposes or the objectives of the study in the form of hypotheses. Each hypothesis (or, if you must, question but **not** both!) should be accompanied by a rationale to explain why you are investigating this particular topic or what you expect to find. You could state something to the effect of: "The major objective of this study is to determine whether......" (*your problem statement*). Then: "Based on previous research, it is expected that ...." (*your hypothesis*) or "Although research on this topic appears to be limited in the Caribbean, it is expected that findings will be similar (or different) to those found by researchers in the USA (last name, DATE)"[1] or "Findings from other studies (e.g., last name, DATE; last name, DATE) have shown that .... and it is expected that data obtained from this research will be ...... (*your hypothesis.*)

---

1. The name and date of an article taken from your literature review.

In Figure 11.1, you can see an example of an introduction to a proposal. In the column at the right are some comments that point out specific aspects of the writing.

	Comments
Children are identified as demonstrating learned helplessness behaviours by their general tendency to give up or by showing decrements in performance following experiences with failure, even though they have the intellectual ability to make appropriate responses (Fincham, Hokoda, & Sanders, 1989; Licht & Dweck, 1984). The focus of many studies investigating learned helplessness behaviours in children is to examine causal attributions of failure made prior to experimental manipulations of success or failure and behaviours observed on tasks following the experimental manipulations (Butkowski & Willows, 1980; Craske, 1988).	A general introduction to the topic that sets the scene: children and learned helplessness. Note the references to work that has already been done in this field.
The major purpose of this study will be to investigate the extent to which experimental manipulations of success or failure influence a variety of behaviours on subsequent tasks. A second concern will be to investigate the interaction of the experimental conditions with subject variables, that is, school type, grade level, achievement ranking, and gender. Based on previous research (Diener & Dweck, 1980; Fowler & Peterson, 1981)[2], it is expected that children placed in the failure condition will exhibit a greater degree of behaviours associated with learned helplessness than those placed in the success condition. (The researcher then continued with more hypotheses and rationale)	The "nitty-gritty". Jump right in with the purpose of your study. Note that the alternate hypothesis is used because previous research had indicated that this would most likely be true.

Figure 11.1: An example of the beginning of a proposal.

Operational Definitions of Key Terms

When you operationalise the key terms, you are identifying the actions or operations necessary to measure or identify the terms used in *your own research*. Remember that key terms are those that describe the constructs and/or variables of your study and should be limited to your study. The terms should not be so broad (such as "teacher," "motivation," "attribution" or "interest") so that they could be applied to just about anything.

Remember (in Chapter 2 of this text) how you had to operationalise and narrow down your variables so that you could do a computer search? The same principle applies here. Motivation should be narrowed to "motivation of grade one students to learn to read" and interest to "interest in computer studies in science as displayed by the following behaviours." In the learned helplessness research, one of the key terms was: learned helplessness behaviours in children and was operationalised by specifically mentioning the specific behaviours that could be observed and measured (e.g., perserverence at a task). Notice that it was not learned helplessness in general.

---

2. This is an example of "LAST NAME, DATE," as required in the APA format.

2. The Review of Related Literature

As required by your department, committee or faculty advisor, the literature review can either consist of a second chapter or it can be integrated into the introduction using a subheading – whatever is required. When you write this section, you have to be selective and choose the research that is most critical and most pertinent to your research topic.

First, discuss in greater detail the research mentioned in your introduction. Then, bring in and integrate other research that is *relevant to your topic*. This is where an outline is most useful as it keeps you focussed on "what should go where." If at all possible, try to identify gaps in existing studies as this provides extra arguments why you should be allowed to carry out your research.

Sometimes, students get carried away by the amount of material they have already collected and the literature review turns out to be almost a complete manuscript. Cover the main topics in brief but, above all, be selective and remember the word count or a page limit set by the governing body. You should try to end with a brief summary or recap of your major points. Never leave your readers "dangling!"

An abbreviated version of the continuation of the proposal is shown in Figure 11.2.

The majority of the previous research investigating learned helplessness behaviours in children relied heavily on attributional methodologies as the basis of research (Deener & Deck, 1978; Licht et al., 1985). Thus, the focus has been on attributional styles, rather on experimental procedures. Consequently, a number of issues have been raised regarding the theoretical and operational model of learned helplessness behaviours in children (see Fincham & Cain, 1985; Peterson, 1985). These issues include (1) the definition of learned helplessness, (2) the extent to which causal attributions to failure mediate learned helplessness behaviours, (3) the ontogenesis of learned helplessness behaviours, and (4) the consequence of prior exposure to noncontingent events.

The researcher then continued with a summary of important points of each of the three issues that she wanted to address.

Comments

This is a form of advance organiser for the discussion that follows. It allows the reader to follow a logical train of thought in the review of literature.

Figure 11.2: Continuation of Figure 11.1

This section is important because it shows the review board that you have given your research topic some serious thinking and not just pulled your topic "out of a hat!"
In the proposal, the review of related literature is not as complete as it will be for your final thesis paper – but it will serve as the foundation so KEEP IT to build on!
It is time consuming and tedious but will save time when you are writing your final thesis.

3. The Purpose and Description of What You Are Planning To Do

You now have to propose a design for your study and describe in depth how you will carry out your data collection. To do this, you have to describe (a) the research design, (b) the population (your sample), (c) instrumentation, (d) details of the procedures to be used, and (e) data analysis. If you have completed the "Word Map" for your research, you have all the basic material you need.

(a) The research design

1. State what type of research you are planning to do: descriptive, correlational, experimental, non-experimental or a mixture.
2. State why you think that this is appropriate for your data and hypotheses.

(b) Population or Sample

1. Describe in detail who your participants will be and how and why you will select them (try for random sampling!
2. Explain why your sample is considered representative of a larger population – this is your rationale for choosing these particular participants.
3. If you are planning to divide groups (e.g., according to gender, school type, SES, age, and so on), state the rationale for the division. This rationale could already have been stated clearly in the introduction, but now you show why the division is necessary for your data collection and hypotheses.
4. This is where you must also state the procedures you will take regarding informed consent – knowledge of ethical considerations is a very important aspect of good research.
5. State what cover letters will have to be written.
6. You should also mention any confounding variables and what you plan to do about them – a form of limitations of the study.

(c) Instrumentation (Questionnaires, etc.)

1. If you are using an experimental or treatment condition, state exactly what the experimental or treatment condition is and why you will be using it.
2. If you are using a questionnaire, you must describe how you arrived at the questions or items (e.g., focus group discussions, interviews with professionals in this field, based on previous research). The construct under investigation should have been mentioned in your literature review. This increases the validity of your questionnaire.

> Do not be ambiguous and just state "questionnaires will be used." Describe at least some of the items in the questionnaire in as much depth as possible.

3. State how you will be interpreting the questionnaires or tests. If you plan to use a questionnaire or any other test, state what the scores might signify, for example, "The Motivation to Learn French Questionnaire" will have a total of

10 points. Scores of 7+ will signify an above average motivation while scores 4 and less will signify low motivation."

4. If you are using a researcher-made questionnaire, state how it will be pilot tested.

> Instrumentation is important because you have discussed the variables to be measured in the introduction and literature review and you now have to state how you will be measuring them.

(d) Details of the Procedures to be Used

Describe how you plan to gain access to your sample, how you will be collecting your data, cover letters, consent forms and how you plan to protect the participants in your study (i.e., ethics, confidentiality), etc. If you are planning to pilot test your questionnaire, this is where it must be mentioned.

(e) Data Analyses

Use the decision chart to help you decide what type of analysis will be most appropriate for your research design. You might want to state that you first plan to analyse your data to determine if it fulfills the assumptions for using parametric statistical methods and, depending on the results, what specific statistical analyses would be most appropriate.

Statistical analyses are used to test each hypothesis and it is important to understand why you are using a particular test.

1. Remember that you can use more than one type of analysis. You can use Pearson *r*, *t*-tests and ANOVA all in one piece of research.
2. If you have divided your sample, show how you plan to analyse the data according to group divisions (e.g., scores by gender and/or SES).
3. The description of the data analysis is tentative and does not have to be in depth – just enough to let the review board realise that you do know what you will be doing.
4. In this section, it is also advisable to state the limitations of your study (e.g., small group size, only one gender used in the sample). This shows the reader that you have seriously thought about your research and understand its possible failings.

Leedy & Ormrod (2001) point out that some researchers employ such vague and generalised language when discussing how the data will be analysed that "...their statements are worthless from a practical research planning and design standpoint" (p. 133). They advise researchers to give some serious thought to this section even though it may be tedious and time consuming.

4. Significance of the Research

Finally, you have to prove to the Review Board (the "powers-that-be") that your research is worthwhile and why you should be allowed to carry it out. In other words, you have to justify your research. It is important that you also refer to the literature that you have reviewed and show what has been accomplished and how you will be adding to it or you have uncovered some 'gaps' in the research and this is where you can show how your research will be filling some of these gaps.

In Jamaica, you also might be able to state that while much research has been carried out in other countries (e.g., Canada: Last name, DATE; USA: Last name, Date; Trinidad: Last name, DATE; Africa: Last name, DATE), it is hoped that your research "...can contribute to the extension of knowledge in the area....so that gaps in existing knowledge may be filled" (Wiersma, 1995, p. 409). For example, you could state that your findings may have implications for policy formations, curriculum changes, improvement of learning, development of methodological tools, allows for comparisons between contexts, and so on. Remember all the reasons for carrying out research that were given in Chapter One. USE THEM!

5. References

Appendix D shows the different types of reference styles accepted by the departments of UWI. Check with your own department, advisor or publisher and find out which format is required. *Then use that format throughout the proposal.*

The most commonly used standard manual for educational research (especially for citing sources in the body of your research proposal and for the reference section at the end of the proposal) is the *Publication Manual of the American Psychological Association*, 5th ed. (Gall, Gall & Borg, 2003, p. 52). It is your responsibility, however, to check the appropriate manual in either the "Doc Centre" or the library and make sure that your references are the ones required for your field of study so that they can be correctly written.

DO NOT GET SLOPPY here! Dot every *i* and cross every *t*! Put in the correct punctuation and specifically check to see how electronic or on-line references are written. In referring to the use of references and the reference section, Gall, Gall and Borg (2003) stated: "...it reflects poorly on your scholarship to make errors in style, especially in your citations" (p. 52).

Finally, Leedy and Ormrod (2001) spelled out the importance of taking time and effort when writing your proposal. They wrote:

> *A proposal for any research merits words that are carefully chosen, a style that is clear and concise, an attention to the most minute procedural detail, and for each procedure, a rationale that is logically and clearly stated. (p. 139)*

References

Fraenkel, J. R., & Wallen, N. E. (2000). *How to design and evaluate research in education* (6th ed.). Boston: Mcgraw Hill.

Gall, M. D., Gall, J. P., & Borg, W. R. (2003). *Educational research: An introduction* (7th ed.). Boston: Allyn and Bacon.

Leedy, P. D., & Ormrod, J. E. (2001). *Practical research.* Upper Saddle River, NJ: Prentice-Hall.

Wiersma, W. (1995). *Research methods in education: An introduction* (6th ed.). Boston: Allyn and Bacon.

> Did you notice how references and citations have been interspersed throughout this section on writing the proposal? This was done on purpose to give you an idea of how to use citations and references. The small reference section, using the APA format, was included to show what it should look like.

Statistical Analysis

Once you have finally arrived at this section, all the preparatory work needed to analyse your data should have been completed. You know how many variables you have, which ones are qualitative and which ones are quantitative. If you are looking for differences between measures, you should now know which variables are independent and which ones are dependent. If you are investigating relationships, as in the case of correlation or regression research, you know which variables are "X" and which are "Y." You should also know what type of measurement (nominal? ordinal? interval? ratio? frequencies?) you used when collecting your data and whether you will be using parametric or non-parametric statistical tests. Now, you have to find out what to do with all this data and discover whether you can reject (or fail to reject) your hypothesis.

Although the word "statistics" usually sends shivers up and down most people's spines, the statistical programmes nowadays make analyses of data an exciting prospect rather than a chore to be dreaded.

This is actually a very exciting part of your research.

12
Data Entering

Entering Your Raw Data

If you want to find out the meaning of all the measurements you have collected – in other words, interpret your findings – the data must first be organised into a pattern so that you can provide accurate statistical summaries. Begin by entering your raw data into Excel[1] – a programme found in Microsoft Office that is designed to create databases from worksheets. We have recommended the Excel programme because it is included with most computer programmes and, hence, is available to most researchers. Additionally, it is relatively easy to type in data using this programme and it is also relatively easy to import the Excel files into other statistical packages.

Another reason for placing your data into Excel is that the SPSS (Statistical Package for the Social Sciences) programme will automatically pick up your variable names from the top row of your Excel file and you do not have to do a lot of extra work creating these names. Once you have your data correctly entered in the Excel file, the worksheet (this is similar to a spreadsheet) can be saved to a floppy disk and used as the data base for other statistical software packages (such as SPSS).

Entering your data (also called "creating an data matrix") means putting all the precious measures (the raw data) you have collected into a format that a statistical programme can read and do all the things that you will tell it to do. **Before** you start entering data into the Excel programme, you should sit down and make up a list of your variables and assign a code to each category of the nominal variables. Earlier we mentioned "coding" and have shown you some examples of how to code, such as: males = 1, females = 2; private schools = 1, government schools = 2.

> These numbers do not mean anything, it is just a way of transforming nominal (categorical/organismic/demographic) data into numbers so that they can be used more easily in statistic programmes.

Making a list and coding your variables should be fairly easy if you have already drawn a word map of your research. You know how many variables you have, which ones are nominal, or which ones are independent and which ones are dependent variables. You have even noted what confounding variables might appear. You also know if you are doing research investigating relationships, you just use variable names (not dependent and independent variables). An example of a variable list can look similar to that shown in Figure 12.1. You just keep adding the names of your variables and whatever categories you need to sort out your data for analyses.

---

1. We are assuming that you already know how to open the Excel programme, what the different keystrokes mean, and how to enter data. If you don't know much about computers in general, we suggest you purchase Computers in the Classroom available at M.P.U. Excel for Dummies shows how to use the Excel programmes and can be purchased at most computer or book stores.

At the same time as you write the names of the variables, you should also write their category codes in a code book. This code book is very important because if you should ever lose it, you would not have a clue what information you are looking at. We have seen researchers make abbreviations of titles for their data and then not remember what the abbreviations stood for when it was time to write their theses.

Gender (abbreviated to gen): males = 1, females = 2

Grade (abbreviated to gr): Grade 5 = 1, Grade 7 = 2

School type (abbreviated to sct): Government = 1, Private = 2

Socio-economic Status (abbreviated to SES): Low SES = 1, Low Middle SES = 2, Middle SES = 3, Middle High SES = 4, High SES = 5

Figure 12.1: An example of a list of variables with their respective codes created before entering your data. Notice that the abbreviations used for each variable are also written down.

For example, you want to design a questionnaire investigating some particular behaviour (e.g., a questionnaire about bullying in schools or a scale involving career motivation) and you have four indicators for each construct you want to investigate. When you are entering the data for each of the four distinct (but hopefully) related concepts, make sure that the abbreviation for each indicator is clearly different from the other and keep a record of what each abbreviation means. If you do not give each indicator an identifying label, but call the first indicator Var 1, the second Var 2, and so on, after three months, you would have to really think what "Var 1" means. And does Var 2 mean the measures entered for the second concept or is it the second variable for the first construct?

Remember to make all your variable names fairly short and use some abbreviation that makes sense. This is because when you enter your data into the SPSS programme, SPSS will only accept variable names up to 8 characters long.

Back to entering data into Excel....The list of variables is entered as text and should be written across the top row of the worksheet (starting in cell A1). They are the abbreviated variable names and you enter all the data that pertain to each name in columns *underneath* each name. Figure 12.2 shows an example of where the names should be placed and we have placed some hypothetical data entries underneath each variable name.

	A	B	C	D	E	F	G	H
1	St. ID	Gender	Grade	School	SES	Test A	Test B	TotT
2	1	1	1	1	2	60	70	130
3	2	2	1	2	4	75	83	158
4	3	1	2	1	3	75	85	160
5	4	2	2	2	5	69	79	148

Figure 12.2: An example of a worksheet in Excel.

You can read each data entry according to your code and where it is placed on the spread sheet. For example, using the code shown in Figure 12.1, the first data entry, reading across the rows, refers to a student (cell A2) with the numerical ID of 1, he is a boy (cell B2, code = 1) in Grade 5 (cell C2, code = 1) attending a government school (cell D2, code = 1) and from a middle-low SES family (cell E2, code = 2). His score on Test A was 60 (cell F2) and on Test B (cell G2) was 70. The next student with an ID of 2 (cell A3) was a girl (cell B3, code = 2), also in Grade 5 (cell C3, code = 1) attending a private school (cell D3, code = 2) and from a middle-high SES family (cell E3, code = 4). Her scores on Test A was 75 and on Test B, 83.

It is essential to keep a list of the codes you are using.

Right now, and maybe even for the next month, you might find it easy to remember the codes, but what happens at the end of six months when it is time to write your final thesis?

The reason why you write numbers and not words as shown in the case of nominal variables or dichotomous variables such as gender, is that the Excel programme reads the numbers and values you have entered and uses them for analyses. Any non-numbers and empty cells in the data entry are read as 0. This means that if you wanted to use the Excel programme to find out how scores from the boys differed from those of the girls and had written "boy" or "girl" instead of 1 or 2 under the gender label and then asked the programme to separate the scores according to gender, all entries under that label would be counted as 0 and you would not be able to get the information you needed. When you enter your data in the SPSS programme, it is also easier and quicker to work with numbers such as 1 and 2 rather than with labels such as boys and girls.

If you have missing values (suppose someone did not want to tell you how old they were, did not answer a question or you could not decipher the answer), then you would put -99 (or some other impossible figure such as 999) where the raw data should be. Note that you will have to assign different numbers for each reason the data is missing. If you are lucky enough to have someone else enter your data, make sure that you decide, *before entering the data*, what numbers are to be used for the missing values and that the person entering your data knows exactly what number to enter. The advantage of using specific numbers for missing data is that you will then be able to carry out a missing values analysis.

When you are entering data in any file, make frequent "saves." This is because something can go wrong and you may lose your entries. If you save your entries frequently, then you will not have to start all over from the beginning

Using the Formula Wizard in Excel

Look at Figure 12.3. In this figure, you can see the label "totT." This is the abbreviation for "Total Test Scores" and signifies that the scores from Test A and Test B have been added together. To get this number, Excel has provided a method of writing different formulae so that you can get different scores or values without having to calculate each one by hand. The formula is placed in the cell in which you need the answer and you do not see the formula, only the result of the function. For example, because we wanted the total scores of the two tests, when we came to Cell H2, we wrote =sum(F2:G2), and the value appeared in the correct cell. Note that before we added the two scores, we also created a new variable name "TotT."

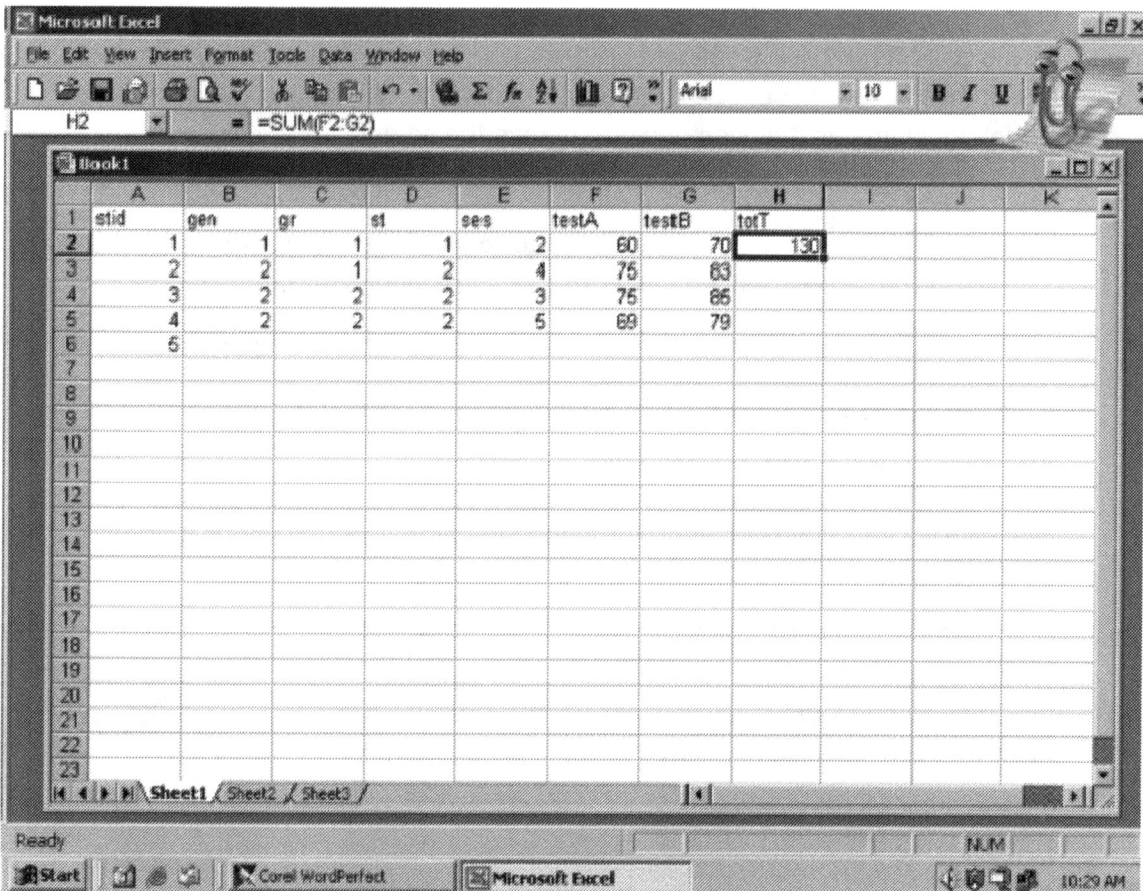

Figure 12.3: An example of using the formula wizard to create a new variable "Total Test Score."

Knowing how to use the different formulae is very helpful. Excel actually supplies you with a Function Wizard. Look at the menu bar in Figure 12.3 and find the *fx* that comes right after the Σ on the standard tool bar. When you click on *fx*, you will see a drop down menu of all the different formulae you can use.

An Example of using the Function Wizard in Excel

Suppose you wanted to find out the total scores of all the subjects in your study and you had 130 participants so that your data entries ended at row 131. At the bottom of the rows of scores and under the correct column (for example, F132 if you were using the F column and row 132), you would just click on the Formula Wizard and scroll down to SUM (found under the title Function Name). When you click on this, =SUM ( ) appears in the cell and on the formula bar.

Then you follow directions because you now have to fill in the space between the brackets ( ). In other words, you are telling the computer what to do. You should finish up with a formula that looked like =sum(F2:F131). This means that you have told the computer to add all the scores starting in cell F2 and ending in cell F131. The sum of the total scores will appear in cell F132. Notice that you do not start at F1 because you used Row 1 to put in the names or abbreviated labels of your variables.

In our example, you can see that we wrote =SUM (F2:G2) because we wanted to find the total scores from two columns (F and G) for each student. The correct sum appeared in H2. You do not have to write each formula out for each row. Simply place the cursor on the bottom right of the cell and drag your cursor down (or sideways) for as many rows or columns as you need. The programme automatically adjusts the number row and the alphabet column as it moves down or across the screen.

> If you have a chance to use Excel, try to play with the Wizard function as it can give you a lot of basic information.

Finally, **remember to save your Excel file**. When we were beginning to write this section, we made up some hypothetical data and created an Excel file called BMdemo.xls. We saved it in My Documents on the C: drive and we also made a backup copy on a floppy disk [A:BMdemo.xls]. Give your file a special name and remember that the name must be followed by .xls. This shows that it is an Excel file

> **Important**
> At all times, make a back up copy of your raw data file on another disk in case something happens and you lose all your data.

STEP 2 ▶ Checking Your Data

*D*ata checking means examining the data you have entered to make sure that you have entered all the numbers correctly. The expression "garbage in....garbage out" certainly applies here. If you enter some of the numbers incorrectly, then your results will be wrong. This is a very important task that many researchers forget to do. It is an extremely boring task and, unfortunately, many people just assume that the data has been entered correctly. Mistakes can be made, however, and these errors affect the validity and accuracy of your research. As an example, suppose, you were very tired when entering your data and you entered a test score of 37 instead of 73. Can you imagine what that number will do to your measures of central tendency?

We suggest three methods that can be used to check data, but bear in mind that there is just no easy way to ensure that your data has been entered correctly. The most boring way to make sure that your data entry is correct requires a print-out of the raw data and two people: one person reads out each number while the other checks whether the number read out is the same as the number on screen or on the printout. This is very time consuming but, at the end, you can be sure that no mistakes have been made.

Garbage In – Garbage Out (GI-GO)

Mistakes made when entering data can be costly and can give you some wrong results.

When you are checking scores, a second method is to put in a column after every fifth (or tenth score) for a total of the first five (or ten) scores. Then you tell the computer to find the total for the first five (or ten scores) and you then compare the computer's total with the total that you have computed by hand. A third method that you can use, particularly if your data is not too large, is to enter the same data in two different worksheets and tell the programme to compute the sum of the two sets of scores. You would then find the row totals, the column totals and the grand total for each data set. Then you compare the totals and if the totals correspond, then you KNOW that your data has probably been entered correctly. This is based on the assumption that you would not incorrectly enter the same measure twice.

Finally, a method for checking categorical data entries by frequencies can be done after you have entered your data into SPSS. This is explained later in this chapter.

STEP 3 Entering Your Data into SPSS from an Excel File

Although the Excel programme is useful for giving you basic information from your raw data, serious researchers need to perform higher levels of analyses to lend credence to their final thesis or journal article. In this case, we highly recommend that you use the SPSS.

There are two ways of placing your Excel file into the SPSS programme – a long way and a short cut. We start with the long way first:

1.   When you first open the SPSS programme, a dialog box appears that very politely asks: "What would you like to do?" You scroll down to **Open an existing data source**, click in the little box and then click **OK**.

2.   Now, another dialog box called **Open file** appears. It has a command that says **Look in** and then gives you some options. If you have saved your Excel file on a floppy disc, then you scroll down the list of where to look until you come to **Floppy [A:]**. Highlight this and click on **Open**.

3.   This click opens another dialog box showing all the files you have saved on the floppy disk A: In the grey area at the bottom of this window, you will see **File name** and just below this **:Files of type**. In this window, scroll down until you see **Excel [*.xls]** and click on this.

If you just click on Open and do not specify which file type it is, then all the files under Microsoft Word might be shown but not the Excel file. You might even see a blank window as shown in Figure 12.4. If you do not specify Excel file type, you might spend hours looking for your Excel file.

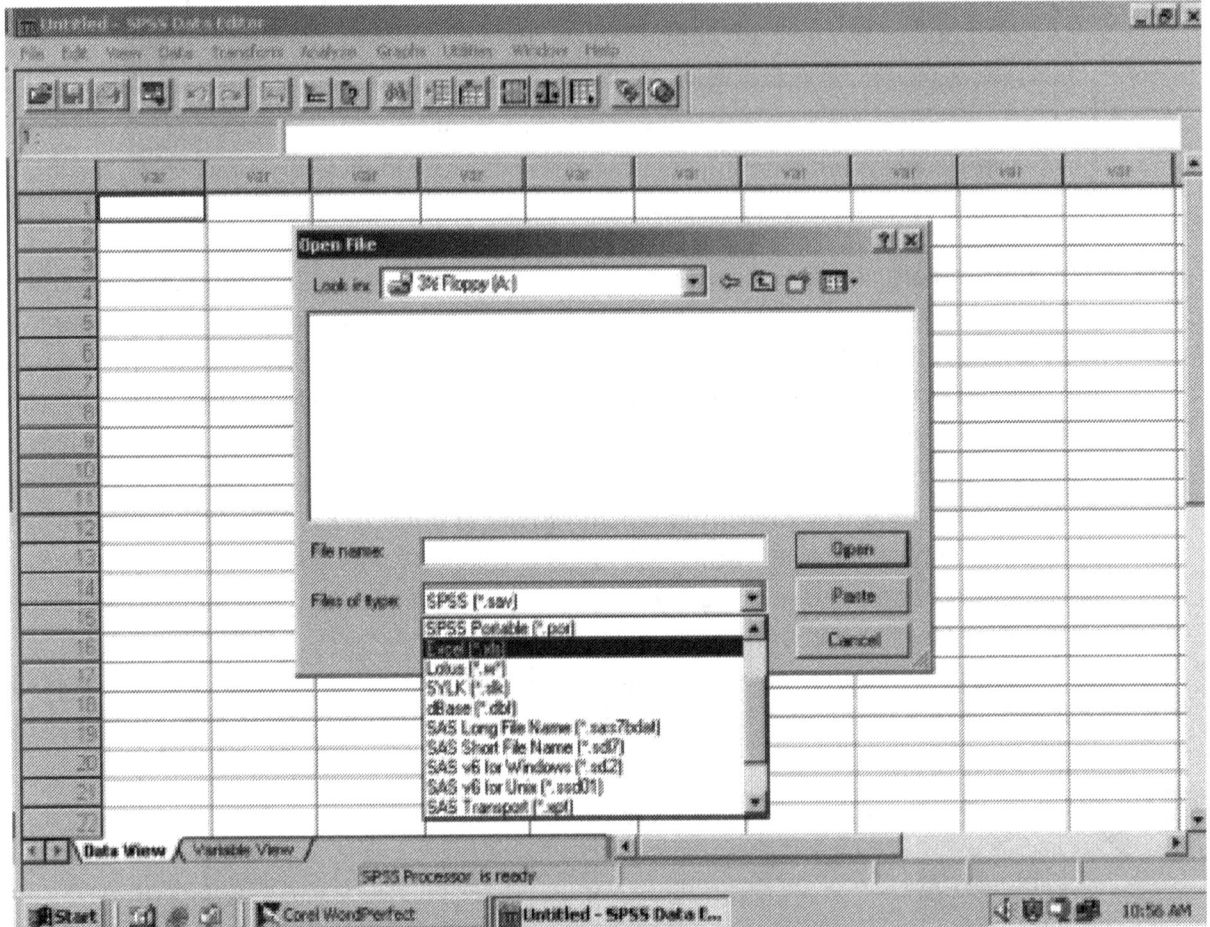

Figure 12.4: Locating the Excel file in the 'Files of Type" dialog box.

4. Scroll down in the top window until you see your Excel file and click on **Open**.
5. When you click Open, you will see another dialog box with an important question: **"Read variable names from first row of data?"** If you have already named your variables in Row A in the Excel file, you click in the little box and a ✔ appears.In this box, you will also see which worksheet you want. Usually, you leave it in the default because you want to enter the entire file. If, however, you only wanted to use the first ten variables and the data from the first twenty rows, you would look at the **"range."** The range states how many rows and columns from your Excel file you want to work on in the SPSS programme. For example, you would type in [A1:J20] and this would tell the computer to enter only the data that goes across from A to J (10 columns) and down 20 rows.
6. After you have done all this, highlight your file and click **Open**.
7. The SPSS opens your Excel file and places the value names on the top part of the file and all your raw data directly below each descriptive name.

The second way is a little shorter. When the polite dialog box appears, you just scroll to the bottom of the box and click on **Cancel** to close this box. Then:

1.   Look at the Data Editor window (the main menu) at the left top of your screen. Click on **File**. This is shown in Figure 12.5.

2.   Next click on **Open** and you will see a list headed by **Data**. Click on this and another list appears.

3.   This time, you click on **Open**. This opens another dialog box showing all the files you have saved on the floppy disk A: In the grey area at the bottom of this window, you will see File name and just below this **Files of type**. In this window, scroll down until you see **Excel [*.xls]** and click on this.

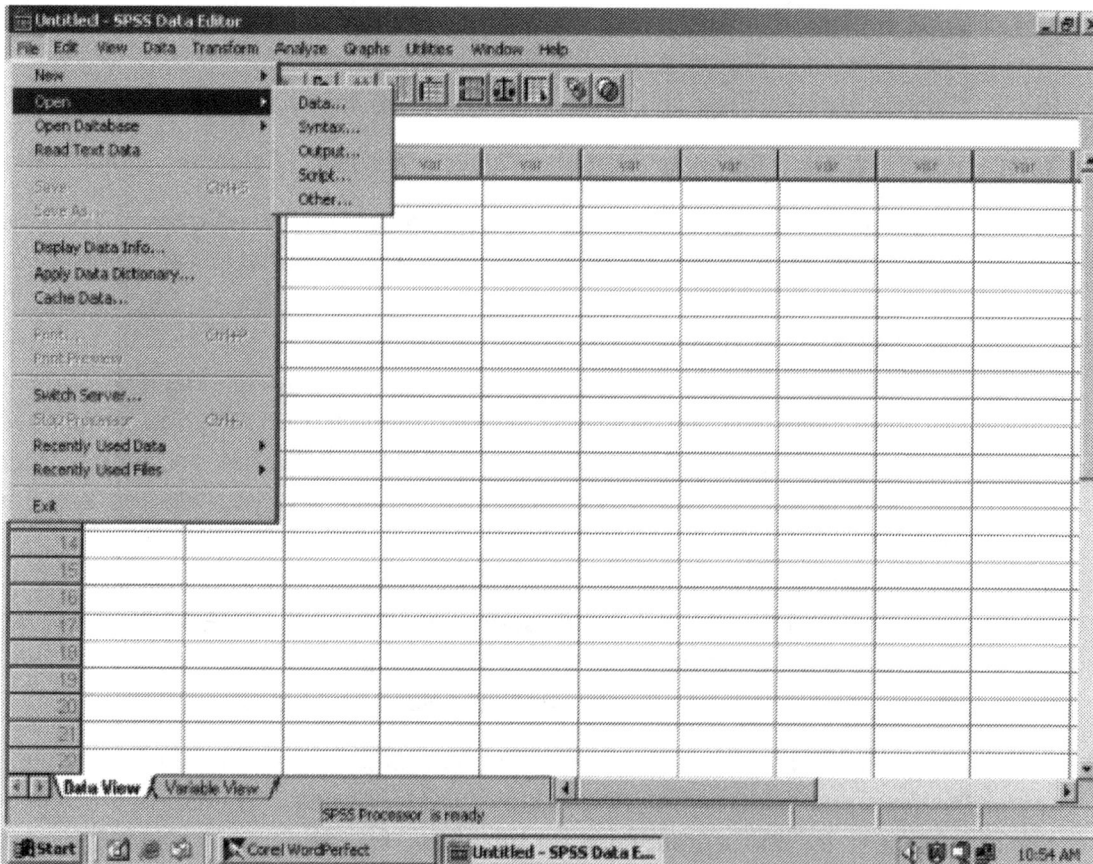

Figure 12.5: Opening the data file in the Open dialog box.

Remember, if you just click on the Open and do not specify which file type it is, then all the files under Microsoft Word might be shown but not the Excel file.

> **REMEMBER** to save your SPSS file on a floppy disk. You can give it some name that shows it is the raw data. For example, you can call it "My Raw Data Research." The SPSS programme will add the ending.

At the beginning, getting your data into the SPSS programme may seem bewildering. Remember: "Practice Makes Perfect!" Soon you will be opening your files like an old pro.

Coding Your Variables

When variables are nominal, their classifications or categories will have different values. You saw this when we divided our groups according to gender (one variable with two levels: male and female). When we define variables in the SPSS programme, we are actually assigning a value or code number to each level of the variable. This means that the next thing you must do is label each variable – in other words, enter the codes you are using and their labels. This is the SPSS equivalent of your personal code book and you use the codes you made up before you started entering the data (see Figure 12.1).

1.   Look at the bottom of the screen and you will see two tabs: **Data View** and **Variable View** (Shown in Figure 12.5).

2.   Click on **Variable View** and written along the top line, you will see:

Name   Type   Width   Decimals   Label   Values   Missing   Columns   Align   Measure

3.   Each variable is listed under the first column **Name**. Now go over to the column called **Values** and put your cursor on the row with the variable name you want (for example, gender). On that row, click on the three little dots ... (a grey area) and the **Value View** window appears.

      The first box in this window says **Value**, so, you type 1 in this box. The second box says **Value label** and you type in Male, then click on **Add**. You should see 1 = Male appear in the third box. Next you go back to **Value** box and type in 2, and in the **Value label**, you type in Female, click on **Add** and you will see 2 = Female added to the box.

4.   As you cannot have more than two values for gender, you will click on **OK**. But, if you were inserting the values for some variable such as SES with 5 levels, you just keep putting the number in the value box and the value label in its box and clicking on **ADD** after each entry until all values are coded.

This **Variable View** tab also allows you to add or remove the number of decimal places under **Decimals** and to define missing values (under **Missing**). To change the number of decimal places, for the appropriate variable (as for example, salaries), under the Decimals column, you will see two little arrows, one pointing up and the other pointing down. Each click on the up arrow increases (by one) the number of decimal places you need and, obviously, each click on the down arrow decreases the number of decimal places by one.

To add missing values, you do the same thing. Under the **Missing** column, click on the three little dots ... (a grey area). Of course, a window appears with a default saying "no missing values." You will click in a little box beside the next line that says: "**Discrete missing values**" and then type in -9 (or 999) for the variable that you think will have missing values. You have to repeat this step for each variable that might have missing values, but remember to use different numbers for each variable.

Labels for Your Variables

The next thing to do is make appropriate labels for your variables. This is an important step because when you want a printout of your data analysis, the computer will print out the full name of your variables instead of the SPSS abbreviated label of 8 characters or less.

1. Click on **Variable View** and you will see a list of your variables. The title across the page reads:

Name   Type   Width   Decimals   Label   Values   Missing   Columns   Align   Measure

2. This time, go to **Label** and the rest is easy. You just place your cursor in the appropriate cell and just type in the longer name of your variable. For example, instead of "Test A", you could type in "Reading Test Scores".

Although this may be time consuming, it is worth every minute that you will be spending learning to find your way around the SPSS programme. The good thing about this is that once you have all the basic data entered, you save it (on your floppy disk or on the hard drive) and you will never have to do this again. The next time you open the SPSS programme, all your raw data are there, properly labelled with correct values, just waiting for you to do something with it.

Opening Your SPSS File from Another Disk

Follow the same instructions showing you how to get your Excel data from a floppy disc into the SPSS programme. This time, when you open the SPSS programme, and after clicking cancel on the box that appears, click on **File** to open the drop down list. Scroll down until you see **Open ▶**, then click on **Data...** . This open the **Open File** dialog box. This time, instead of looking for an **.xls** file type, look for the file type **SPSS** or **.SAV**. Once you click on **SPSS** (or **.SAV**), all the files you have saved in SPSS format will be listed.

When you see the SPSS file you are working on, click on **Open** and your raw data file will appear on the screen.

Checking Your Categorical Data Using Frequency Counts

The easiest way to check categorical data (e.g., gender, marital status, etc.) that has already been entered in the SPSS programme is to look at the amount of times (the frequency) a value occurs. To do this in SPSS:

1. Look at the top of the screen and click on **Analyze**. When the dialog box appears, scroll down until you see **Descriptive Statistics ▶ Frequencies...** click on this.
2. In this window, you will see a list of your variables on the left. Click on the variable you want (e.g., gender), then click on the arrow and the variable will appear in the box on the right. Do this for all the variables you want to check on and then click **OK**.

The frequencies for each variable will appear in a Frequency Table. If you find that someone has entered a 3 for gender, this will show up in your frequency table and you can go back into your raw data and correct this immediately. If you have drawn a map of your research and know how many boys and how many girls are in each group, then the frequency count will let you check that the data is entered correctly. Notice that checking for frequencies is not recommended for large scores of test results unless you want to examine extreme scores.

To show you what a frequency table looks like, we used data taken from research that consisted of scores from 500 students and looked at the numbers of males and females in the total sample. When you enter your own data, your frequency table should look similar to that shown in Table 12.1. The first table shows the total number of records (N) and the second table shows you the number of males and females (n) and also gives you the percent of the number of students by gender in each category.

The minimum and maximum in the first table tells you that you have used only two numbers (1 and 2) that were the code for gender. If you had looked at the frequencies for SES, for example, with 5 levels, you would have seen Minimum 1 and Maximum 5. You will see a separate table for each variable you select.

Gender Statistics

N	Valid	500
	Missing	0
Minimum		1
Maximum		2

Gender

		Frequency	Percent	Valid Percent	Cumulative Percent
Valid	Males	280	56.0	56.0	56.0
	Females	220	44.0	44.0	100.0
	Total	500	100.0	100.0	

Table 12.1: *A Frequency Table Showing the Gender of 500 Students Participating in a Large Research Programme*

Finding Frequencies for Categorical Data Using Cross Tabs

When you are using data that is nominal and/or ordinal (ranked) scales, you can use Cross Tabs to find the frequencies. Using the SPSS programme:

1.   Look at the top of the screen and click on **Analyze**. When the dialog box appears, scroll down until you see **Descriptive Statistics ▸ Crosstabs...** click on this.
2.   You see the dialog window appear with your list of variables in the box on the left side. On the right, the first box you see is **Row(s)** and you choose the variable you want to use by highlighting one variable at a time and then clicking on the arrow to place them in the box at the right.
3.   Under this is another box **Column(s)**, you highlight each variable and move it into the appropriate boxes.

For this example, we entered "gender" in the Row box and then "school type" in the Column box. Next you see **Layer 1 of 1**, so we highlighted "grade" and moved it into that box. Note that the order we entered the variables is not written in stone, you can enter the variables in different orders if you want to. The way we entered the variables gave us a gender*school type*grade table. We could have also entered our variables as school type* grade*gender.

4.   Next, click on **Cells** to open the **Crosstabs: Cell Display** box.
5.   Under the **Counts** column, click on **Observed**.
6.   Under the **Percentages** column, click on **Row**, **Column**, and **Total**.
7.   Click on **Continue** and then click on **OK** and information similar to that reproduced in Table 12.2 should appear on the screen.

The results shown in Table 12.2 tell you the total number of participants (N = 500). In SPSS talk, this is known as the total number of records (N). It also tells you that your data has no missing cases. You can use this overall table to help check your data, for example, if you know that your research included 500 participants and the summary reported 495 with two pieces of missing data, then you just have to go back and check that the data was entered correctly.

CASES					
VALID		MISSING		TOTAL	
N	PERCENT	N	PERCENT	N	PERCENT
500	100.0%	0	100.0%	500	100.0%

GENDER*SCHOOL TYPE*GRADE CROSSTABULATION				
COUNT		SCHOOL TYPE		
GRADE		GOVERNMENT	PRIVATE	TOTAL
GRADE 1	GENDER MALE	60	70	130
	FEMALE	60	70	130
	TOTAL	120	140	260
GRADE 4	GENDER MALE	80	70	150
	FEMALE	50	40	90
	TOTAL	130	110	240

Table 12.2: *The Printout Showing Results of Using the Cross-tabulation Programme*

Table 12.3 gives you much more information. When we went into the Cells dialog box (Step 5), we actually asked the computer programme to show how many males and females were in each grade according to school type as well as the percentages of each group of participants (Step 6). By asking the computer to do this, it saved a lot of time and energy. This is so much easier than trying to count all 500 pieces of data yourself!

Think About This . . .
The computer programme does not make mistakes – people do!
If you are tired when you begin counting your pieces of data, you can miscount. Trust the computer, do not trust yourself!

For *categorical variables*, you should use **frequencies** because this will show you exactly how many "things" (participants, items, grade levels, etc.) are in a specific group. It is a waste of time to try to get means and standard deviations of dichotomous variables such as gender.

For *categorical* and *ranked variables*, use **Crosstabs**.

For *continuous variables*, use **Descriptive Statistical Frequencies...** (see the next chapter) because this will give you the means, standard deviation, median, etc., and other useful information.

Gender * School type * Grade Crosstabulation

Grade				Government	Private	Total
				School type		Total
Grade 1	Gender	Male	Count	60	70	130
			% within gender	46.2%	53.8%	100.0%
			% within school type	50.0%	50.0%	50.0%
			% of Total	23.1%	26.9%	50.0%
		Female	Count	60	70	130
			% within gender	46.2%	53.8%	100.0%
			% within school type	50.0%	50.0%	50.0%
			% of Total	23.1%	26.9%	50.0%
	Total		Count	120	140	260
			% within gender	46.2%	53.8%	100.0%
			% within school type	100.0%	100.0%	100.0%
			% of Total	46.2%	53.8%	100.0%
Grade 4	Gender	Male	Count	80	70	150
			% within gender	53.3%	46.7%	100.0%
			% within school type	61.5%	63.6%	62.5%
			% of Total	33.3%	29.2%	62.5%
		Female	Count	50	40	90
			% within gender	55.6%	44.4%	100.0%
			% within school type	38.5%	36.4%	37.5%
			% of Total	20.8%	16.7%	37.5%
	Total		Count	130	110	240
			% within gender	54.2%	45.8%	100.0%
			% within school type	100.0%	100.0%	100.0%
			% of Total	54.2%	45.8%	100.0%

Table 12.3: *A Summary of the Output from the Crosstabulation SPSS Programme*

The cross tabs programme is useful to know if you need to use the Chi-square test to explore the relationship between two categorical variables with two or more categories in each variable. The example we used to show you how to use Crosstabs had three categorical variables, each with two levels: gender (male and female), grade (grade 1 and grade 2) and school type (government and private).

Getting the SPSS Output into Your Written Report or Thesis

Finally, you should be able to import the SPSS output from the screen into your written report or thesis. Hopefully you have saved all the figures and tables that you have done on SPSS in their own files. When you write your research, you need to import these figures and tables into the correct places.

Remember that computer programmes allow you to have more than one window open at the same time and to import files from SPSS into a word programme, you must have both the SPSS file and whatever word programme you are using open at the same time.

1.   Minimise the word programme you are using (you do this by clicking on the "-" at the top right side of the screen) and open the SPSS file containing your saved files that you want to import.

2.   Click on the table or figure and a border will be placed around it.

3.   Look at the top of the page and click on **Edit** and then click on **Copy Objects**.
4.   Next maximise your word programme and move your cursor to the place that you want the figure or table to be placed.
5.   In the **File** menu for your word programme, click on **Edit** and then click on **Paste**.
6.   Click on **File** and **Save**.

> This is a very important thing to remember to do. After each **Paste** command, **SAVE** your word document.

You keep repeating these steps (minimise the word document, maximise the SPSS file, edit, copy, maximise the word document, paste and save) until you have imported all the figures and tables that you need for your thesis. **BUT, DON'T FORGET TO SAVE!**

So far, we have just used numbers to describe your variables in the "methods" section, but when you are describing your results in the results section, you will need to report some basic statistics, such as the means and standard deviations of scores. This is described in the next chapter.

You have done all the basic work. The hardest part was becoming familiar with the different statistical programmes. Now comes the fun part – learning how to make sense of your data collection.

13
Descriptive Statistics

The term "descriptive statistics" means exactly what it says. Statistics are numbers that describe the measures of the variables in your research. You have already learned to find the frequencies for categorical variables and how to describe continuous variables. To do this, we first look at measures of central tendency and then look at measures of variability.

If you have already studied statistics, ignore this next part.... it is simply an overview of the meanings of some of the terms that are commonly found when describing data.

Measures of Central Tendency

The *mean*, *mode* and the *median* are three statistics called the measures of central tendency. Each statistic is a single number that is at the middle of a (usually large) set of numbers. There are different ways of calculating these numbers: the mean is the average value of a set of numbers. When the numbers are arranged in increasing or decreasing order, the median is the middle value of that set of numbers and the mode is the value that occurs most often in that set.

In a normal curve, the positions of these measures of central tendency tend to be close together and form a symmetric distribution – the familiar bell-shaped curve. However, when there are more larger numbers (negative skew) or more smaller numbers (positive skew) than we would normally expect, then the three different calculations give different "middle" numbers.

Look at each figure in Figure 13.1 and notice the how positions of the mean, median and mode determine how the distribution looks in (a) a negative skew, (b) a normal distribution and (c) a positive skew.

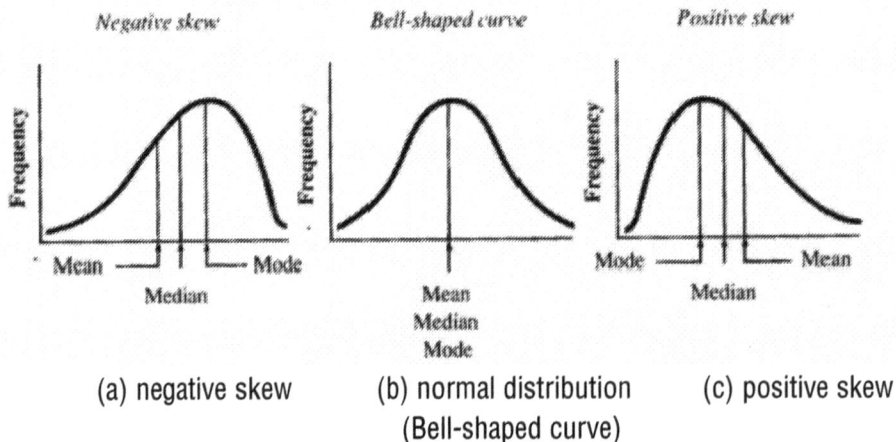

(a) negative skew   (b) normal distribution   (c) positive skew
(Bell-shaped curve)

Figure 13.1: How the positions of the mean, median and mode affect the distribution of a set of values.

Measures of Variability

Measures of variability include the range, interquartile range and deviations of scores of a distribution. These are numbers that give simple descriptions of the distribution (dispersion or spread) and refers to how spread out a group of scores is. It can also refer to how close the scores in a distribution are to the middle of a distribution.

- *Range:* is the difference between the lowest number and the highest number. It is obviously the easiest to determine but is also the most unreliable because it only uses two numbers – the lowest and the highest. If you have scores between 46 and 79, the range is 79 - 46 = 33.
- *Interquartile range:* consists of all the scores in the middle 50% of a distribution. These are the scores that fall between the upper 25% and the bottom 25% of the distribution.
- *Deviation:* is defined as the distance of measurements away from the mean and shows how a single score differs (deviates) from the average of many scores. For example, if one person received a score of 70 on a test and the mean score for all persons taking the test was 50, the deviation would be 20 (70-50 = +20). If the test score was 85, the deviation would be -15. A deviation score, however, only shows how the score of one person deviates from the mean of all scores.
- *Variance* is the sum of the squared deviations of n measurements from their mean divided by (n - 1). (Remember that the square of a negative number is positive.) It reflects the difference in dispersion but it is not often used because it gives a squared unit of measurement.
- *Standard deviation (SD):* is defined as the positive square root of the variance and shows the spread or scatter of *all the deviations* about the mean scores from a sample population. This is the most commonly used indicator of degree of variability and is considered the most reliable of the measures of variability. The SD is used in determining reliability of the differences between the means, coefficients of correlation, regression equations, etc.

  The standard deviation gives us a measure of dispersion relative to the mean and is sensitive to each score in the distribution. For example, if one score is moved closer to the mean, then the standard deviation will be smaller.

A rule of thumb for the most efficient use of each measure

Use the mean when you want the greatest reliability, for determining measures of variability.

Use the median when distributions are badly skewed, including when extreme measurements are at one side of the distribution.

Use the mode when you want to find out which is the most common case, otherwise use the mean.

Use the range when you need information concerning extreme scores.

Use standard deviations when you require the greatest dependability of values and when interpretation is related to the normal curve.

Why Do You Need Descriptive Statistics?

To start off, in the method section of your written thesis, you will need to describe the participants. As an example using the data given in the Crosstabulation output shown in Table 12.3, you might state: "The participants were 240 first- and fourth-grade Jamaican-born students attending private and government schools in a large urban area of Jamaica, West Indies. One hundred and thirty students attended government schools and 110 attended private schools. There were 140 boys and 110 girls taking part in this study." Then if you felt the need, you could draw a table showing exactly how many boys and girls were in each grade and which school type each student attended.

Suppose, however, you gave a questionnaire to a large number of students and wanted to sort the students into different categories for reporting in your methods section. You need to find out how many males and how many females answered your questionnaire, how many males were in Grade 1 and how many in Grade 4, how many females in each grade and what type of school each attended. Then rather than sit down and try to figure this all out, you would make the SPSS programme do the work for you. You would use **Frequencies** (for continuous data) or **Crosstabs** (for nominal and/or ordinal data as in the example given above) to give you all this information.

Descriptives Using Continuous Variables

So far, we have just used numbers to describe the variables in the "methods" section, but when you are describing your results in the results section, you will need more than the description of "how many" was in what group. You now need to use descriptive statistics to describe and make sense of the continuous variables – the raw measures – so you can report some basic statistics such as the means and standard deviations of scores. For this example, we have used the data given in the CD labelled Descriptives13.sav.[1] Take the time to enter this in your SPSS programme and follow along.

To do this using the SPSS programme:

1.   Open your SPSS file containing the data from **Descriptives13.sav** and place your cursor on **Analyze**, scroll down until you see **Descriptive Statistics ▶**. Move your cursor over until you highlight **Descriptives** and click on it.
2.   In the box that appears, place your cursor on each continuous variable that you need and then click on the arrow to move it into the **Variables Box** on the right. You can use as many variables as you need. In our example, we used scores from Test A and Test B.
3.   Next click on **Options** and the **Descriptive: Options** dialog box appears. Then click on **mean, standard deviation, range, maximum** and **minimum.** You could also click on what other statistics you need as, for example, skewness and kurtosis.
4.   Click on **Continue** then click on **OK.**

---

1. This is the data is also found in Appendix A: "Descriptives Data."

Descriptives Output

In the first box, titled "statistics," you see the overall N (total number) of the subjects (or items, questions, etc.) according to the variables selected. Scroll down the screen and you will see **Descriptives Statistics** Table. Each table gives you the count of how many cases there are in that particular variable. The output of "Descriptives" should look similar to that shown in Table 13.1. As we also entered skewness and kurtosis, the table was expanded and included the two extra columns shown in Table 13.2.

Table 13.1: *A Descriptives Table Showing the Total Number (N) of Cases for Each Value Label, the Minimum, Maximum and Standard Deviation*

Descriptive Statistics

	N	Range	Minimum	Maximum	Mean	Std.
	Statistic	Statistic	Statistic	Statistic	Statistic	Statistic
TestA	50	72	55	127	93.30	19.306
TestB	50	62	36	98	78.60	16.059
Valid N (listwise)	50					

Table 13.2: *A Descriptives Table Showing the Total Number (N) of Cases for Each Value Label, and the Skewness and Kurtosis*

Descriptive Statistics

	N	Skewedness		Kurtosis	
	Statistic	Statistic	Std. Error	Statistic	Std. Error
TestA	50	-.184	.337	-1.175	.662
TestB	50	-.924	.337	.200	.662
Valid N (listwise	50				

Looking at Table 13.1, you can see that we have data for 50 participants, the scores ranged from 55 to 127 on Test A with a mean of 93.306 and a standard deviation of 19.306 and from 36 to 98 on Test B with a mean of 78.60 and a standard deviation of 16.059. The Skewness values shown in Table 13.2 gives an indication of the symmetry of the distribution. If the number is positive, the scores are clustered to the left of the low values and, if negative, the numbers are clustered to the right of the low values. In this table, the numbers for both tests are negative indicating a cluster of scores at the low end (left side) of the graph.

The Kurtosis value shows how the scores peak. The negative value of Test A scores shows that the values of our set of scores are relatively flat and may have scores in the extremes. When you learn how to draw histograms (in Chapter 14) you can see whether this is true or not.

You will use these statistics when you are reporting on the outcome of your experiment or responses to your questionnaire in the results section. Remember that these are all descriptive statistics of a sample and need to be used with tests of significance to interpret if differences in the sample might apply to the population that the sample represents. For example, when you look at the mean of the test scores in Table 13.1, the mean scores from Test A appear to be higher than the mean scores from Test B. They certainly look higher but you can't be sure that these scores are significantly different from each other or that you did not obtain these scores by chance until you use a *t*-test (described in Chapter 16).

Do Your Scores Come From a Normal Distribution?

When you need to determine whether the distribution of scores is normal in order to use the more powerful parametric tests, you can use the Kolmogorov-Smirnov Test (we just call it the K-S test) – a nonparametric test that compares the measures you obtained for a variable with a specified distribution, in our particular case, for a normal distribution.

> When you use the K-S test, remember, you are actually testing the hypothesis: "The data from the scores did **not** from a normal distribution." This means that any number under the sig. column that is greater than 0.05 (i.e., a non-significant result) indicates normality of the distribution.

After you open your SPSS file:

1. Click on **Analyze**. Scroll down until you see **Nonparametric Tests ▶** and you will see a list of tests. Click on **1-Sample K-S**.
2. The dialog box appears and you click the variables that are the measures or scores. In our case, we wanted to find out if the test scores came from a normal distribution, so we put the two variable labels (Test A and Test B) by highlighting each one in turn and clicking on the arrow so that they go into the box at the right.
3. Go to the grey area at the bottom of the box and click on **Normal** under **Test Distribution**. Click on **OK**.

The next thing you see is a summary of the K-S results similar to the one shown in Table 13.3 Look at the last line that reads "Asympt Sig (2-tailed)" that gives the significance of the K-S *Z*. In this case, it is 0.332 for Test A and 0.08 for Test B. As both or these are higher than 0.05, you would read these results with relief because you really want scores from a normal distribution so you can use parametric tests!)

> Do not make the mistake of thinking that the note "a. Test distribution is normal" that appears under every K-S output tells you that your data set comes from a normal distribution. Make sure you look at the numbers on the same line as Asympt Sig. (2-tailed) .

Table 13.3: *An Example of the SPSS Printout of the Results of the K-S 1-Sample Test*

One-Sample Kolmogorov-Smirnov Test

		TestA	TestB
N		50	50
Normal Parameters[a,b]	Mean	93.30	78.60
	Std. Deviation	19.306	16.059
Most Extreme Differences	Absolute	.134	.180
	Positive	.106	.114
	Negative	-.134	-.180
Kolmogorov-Smirnov Z		.947	1.270
Asymp. Sig. (2-tailed)		.332	.080

[a.] Test distribution is Normal.

[b.] Calculated from data.

Anything over 0.05 is acceptable but the higher the Z score, the better. This means that when you see the final results, you can report (in the results section of your thesis), something similar to: "To determine whether the test scores came from a normal distribution, they were analysed using the Kolmogorov-Smirnov Test (K-S). Results showed that the K-S Z =0.95 (significance = 0.33) for Test A scores and 1.27 (significance = 0.08) for Test B scores. The hypothesis assuming that the distribution of the scores was not normal was rejected." You see, in Part 2, we promised that this would be easy!

Choosing a Level of Significance

When we used the K-S test to check for normalcy of the data distribution, we stated that a significance of any number higher than 0.05 means that you can reject your hypothesis. The 0.05 stands for level of significance and at the beginning of your study you should choose one level of significance to use throughout the entire study. In educational studies, $p < 0.05$ is usually chosen. The p stands for probability of error and $p = 0.05$ can be interpreted as: "There are 5 chances in 100 that the scores were due to chance fluctuation or other errors." Obviously, the smaller the p, the stronger are the results. For example, $p = 0.001$ would mean 1 chance in 1000 and $p = 0.0001$ would mean 1 chance in 10,000 that these scores were obtained by chance.

Note that significance levels (whether you use z, r, t or F statistics) tell us the percentage probability that the data we analysed were due to chance fluctuations as per the null hypothesis. (Remember that the null hypothesis states that there will be no difference?) When we see that $r = 0.809$ and that $p < 0.001$, or that $t = 2.477$ and $p = 0.05$ or that $F = 7.20$ and $p < 0.003$, this means that we can reject the null hypothesis of no difference (and breathe a sigh of relief!)

To choose the best significance level we use the principle of *minimising the disutility of error*. This means: "*Make the choice so as to reduce the cost of being wrong.*" Even if you find a result that is statistically significant, the variables being studied depend on the phenomenon under investigation. Sometimes you can be wrong by mistakenly getting a significant result due to a fluke of sampling. In this case, making this mistake would involve a high cost. For example, when people might get hurt or someone might lose a lot of money, then you should choose $p < 0.01$, or smaller, to reduce these chance results. Where a mistaken result is extremely costly, as in the case of testing drugs that could kill people, then a much more stringent level of significance should be used: $p < 0.001$ or less. It is sad to see, from comparing the significance levels used in education with those used in other areas, that mistakes made in educational research are considered less costly than the same level of mistakes in other areas.

14
Parametric Tests

(i) Bivariate Correlations

Correlation refers to the concordance or agreement of pairs of values from two variables. The minimum requirements are that (i) you have two variables, usually continuous such as age, test or questionnaire scores or when one of the variables is continuous and the other is dichotomous (having only two values) and (ii) the data should be normally distributed. Although correlation research designs were described in Part Two, correlations are one of the most basic and common forms of descriptive analysis that you will use. In the educational field, many students fulfill their research requirement by focussing on relationships between variables and using correlations as the major data analyses. In fact, many theses and projects consist only of correlational studies – students measure variables, with no experimental manipulation, and then interpret the relationship between them. This means that you will need to understand exactly what simple correlations are and what they do.[1]

Look at Table 14.1 showing the headings (or labels) S, V1 and V2. Under the column headed S are the subjects' identification numbers – these are called "cases" in SPSS talk. Note that this data is found on the CD labelled "Correlate13.sav" and in Appendix B1.

Table 14.1: *An Example of a Matrix With S (Subject Number), Scores from V1 and V2 and the Scatterplot of V1 and V2*

S	V1	V2
1	65	97
2	41	73
3	13	18
4	8	32
5	2	6
6	56	57
7	41	82
8	91	94
9	87	98
10	57	72
11	24	14
12	60	40
13	26	58
14	25	39
15	86	86
16	83	71
17	46	13
18	64	78
19	8	5

Correlation of V1 with V2   r(V1,V2)= 0.811

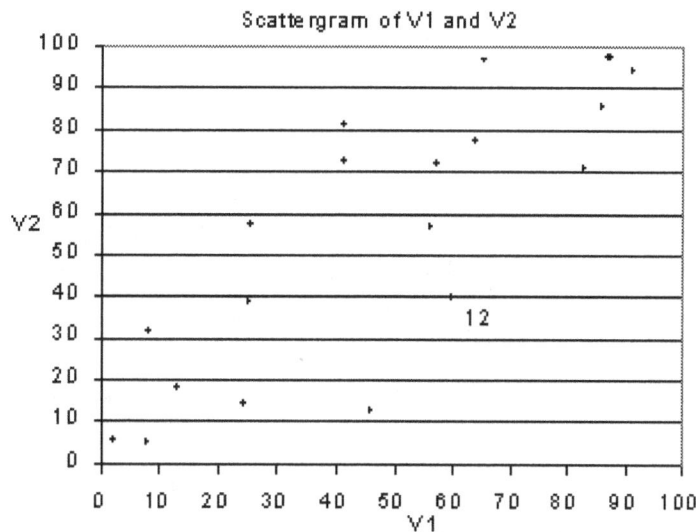

Scattergram of V1 and V2

---

1. If you need to, review *Correlational Designs* in Chapter 5

The first row holds the identification for the first subject S=1. V1 and V2 have their own columns and the pairs of number scores for each subject are entered below each column. Under V1, in Row 1, is the score that Subject 1 obtained on the first test and under V2, Row 1 the score obtained on the second test, and all the way down until Row 19 for Subject 19. The two selected variables, V1 and V2, are treated as a list of pairs of numbers. Correlation simply relates the numbers in one variable to the numbers in the other variable – pair by pair. When you do a correlation analysis, you are asking, "Are high numbers in one variable, that is the first number of each pair, associated with high numbers in the other variable, that is the second number in each pair?" If they are, this is called a **positive correlation**.

Note that we have just called these variables "V1" and "V2" but they can be almost any measure you have taken for each subject. For example, V1 could be scores on a mathematic test and V2 could be scores on an English test or V1 might be pretest scores and V2 post-test scores. *Whatever variables you are using, do not forget to give them their proper labels!*

> Whenever you see the word *correlation* ask yourself, "What are the two variables that have been measured for each case?" Then, check that the two measures are correct and that each case has two measures.

Exercise 14.1
Import the data called "Correlate13.sav" from the CD into your SPSS programme or type in the data from Appendix B1 so that you can follow along as we explain the concept of correlations. This will improve your skills and give you confidence in your new data analysis abilities.

Drawing Scatterplots[2] with SPSS

Before, we look at correlations in depth, it is a good idea to be able to produce scatterplots. Scatterplots allow you to visualise the relationship between two variables.[3] Scatterplots provide a picture so that you can see at a glance whether some form of relationship exists between the two sets of numbers. In a scatterplot, the variables are plotted on a graph – one of the variables is plotted on the abscissa (the horizontal line or X axis) and the other variable is plotted on the ordinate (the vertical line or Y axis). To put it another way, a scatterplot is a graph of paired X and Y values.

The SPSS programme makes drawing a scatterplot very easy and when you have imported your Excel data matrix into SPSS, you can use the SPSS programme to produce a scatterplot to "cut-n-paste" into your report.[4] Figure 14.1 shows the data imported into SPSS.

---

2. We prefer the word "scattergram" but SPSS refers to this as a "scatterplot" so this is the term we are using.
3. Although we loosely say "relationship," the numbers alone only show us a numerical association.
4. *See Getting the SPSS Output into your Thesis,* pp. 150-151.

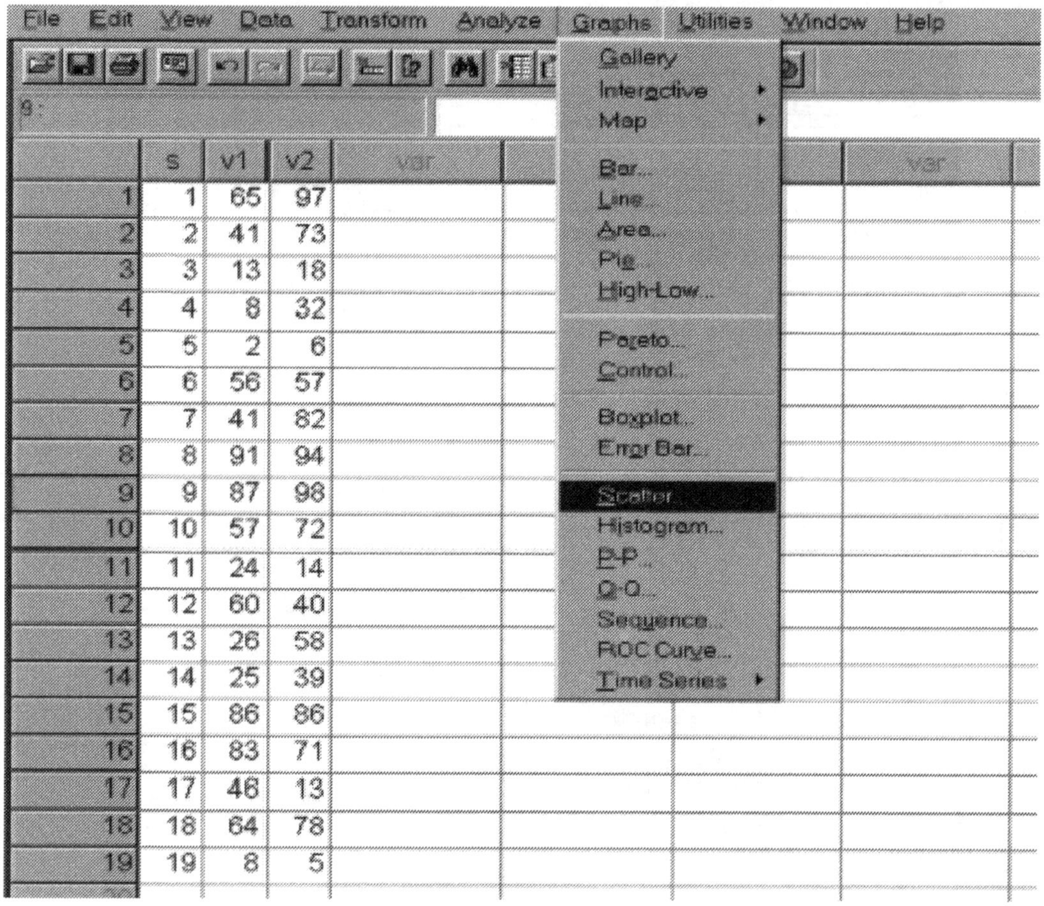

Figure 14.1: An example showing data from Table 14.1 imported into SPSS as well as the sequence 'Graphs - Scatter' needed to get the scatter pop-up box.

To create a scatterplot using the SPSS programme:

1. Open your file in SPSS and click on **Graphs** so that the Graph dialog box appears (as shown in Figure 14.1).
2. Click on **Scatter...** and the Scatterplot pop-up box will be the next thing you see. In this box, first click on **Simple** then click on **Define**.
3. This brings up the **Variable Choice** dialog box. Highlight **V1** by first clicking on it and then on the arrow pointing to the **X-axis** box as shown in Figure 14.2.
4. Next highlight **V2** by clicking on it, then on the arrow beside the **Y-axis box**. As you can see in Figure 14.2, we have already put V2 into the Y-axis box.
5. Click on **OK** and SPSS will produce a scatterplot similar to the one shown in Figure 14.3.

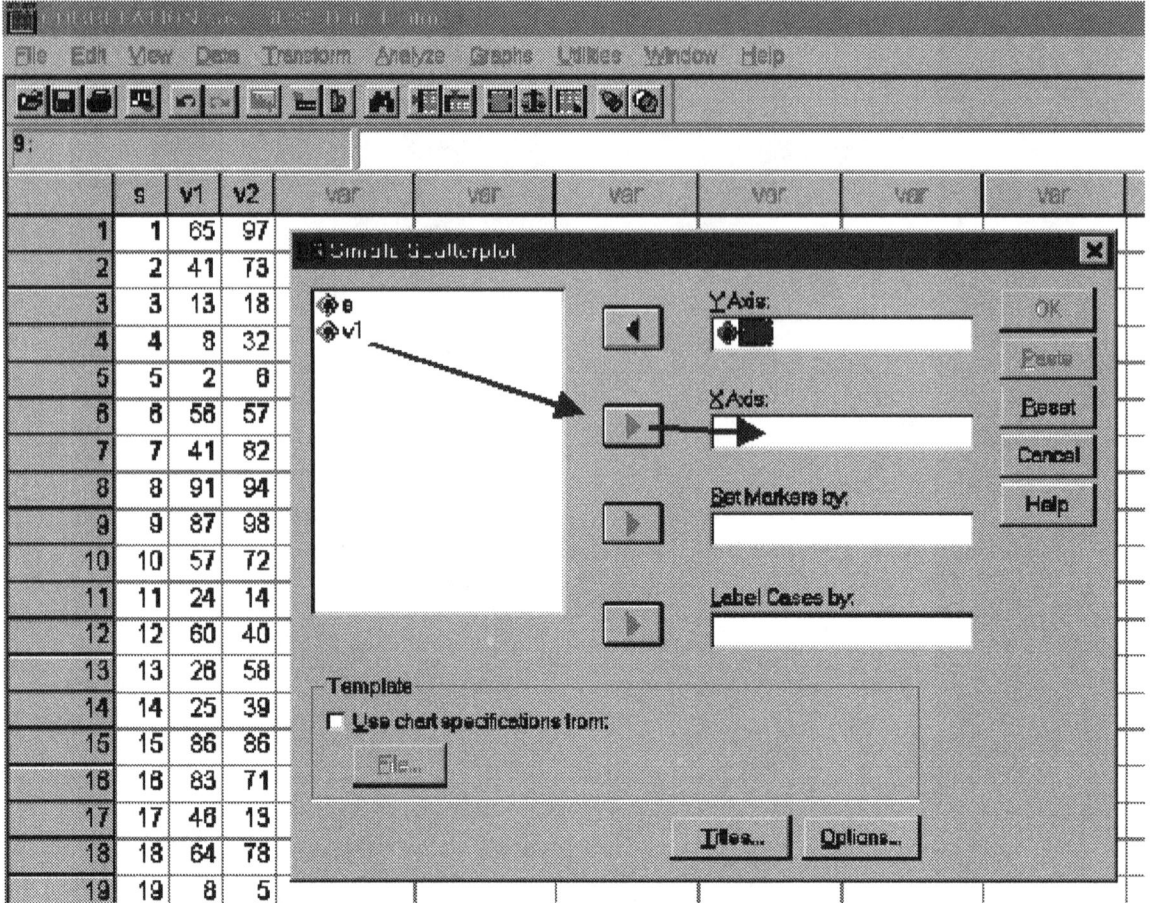

Figure 14.2: Placing the variables into the Y-axis and X-axis boxes.

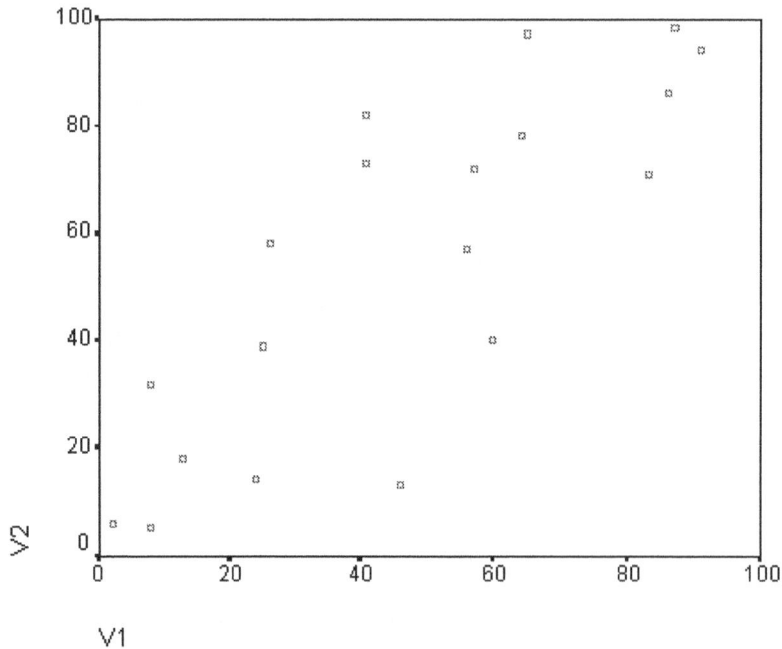

Figure 14.3: How a scatterplot using data from Figure 14.1 should look.

You can ask SPSS to label each square with the number of the subject it represents (as long as the data consist of less than about 50 numbers or the numbers will 'run' into each other). When you are entering your own data, this is also a good method to check that it has been entered correctly.

To label each square:

1.   Double-click anywhere on your scatterplot and a new chart editing window, **Chart - SPSS Chart Editor** will open.
2.   Click on **Chart** and then on **Options**. This will open the **Scatterplot Options** dialog box shown in Figure 14.4. Note that it pops up over the scatterplot on the screen.
3.   Set **Case Labels** to **On**, then click **OK**. Note that the Case Labels have the same meaning as our subject numbers, that is, the first case is the first subject. This command places the number of each subject directly over the little square on the scatterplot as shown in Figure 14.5.
4.   To return to your SPSS output, close the Scatterplot Options window by clicking on the **X** at the top right of the window.

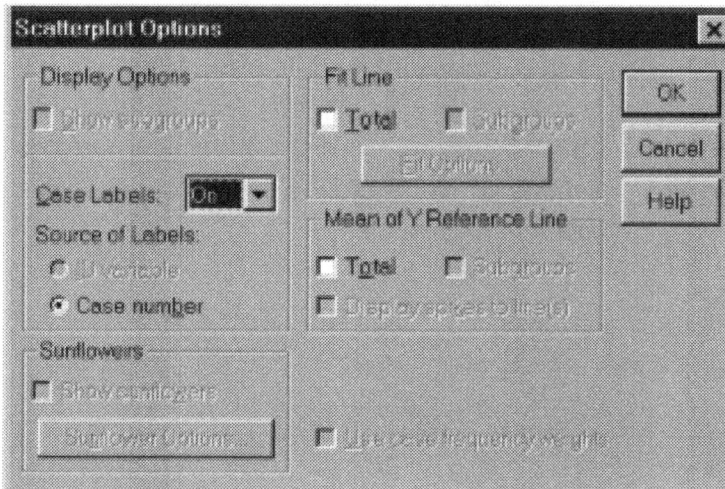

Figure 14.4: The Scatterplot Options box.

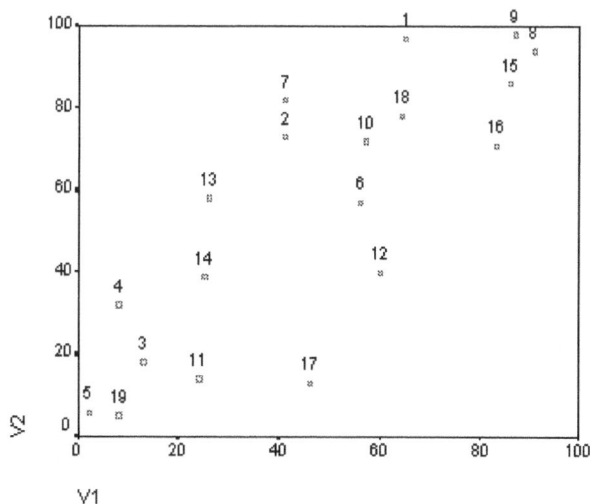

Figure 14.5: The result of using the Scatterplot Options box. Each square representing a pair of scores now has the number of the participant above it.

Remember that each square on the scatterplot represents two scores for one subject. The position of the subject's square is given by his or her V1 and V2 values. For example, in Table 14.5, you can see that Subject 12 has turned up in the right place, at V1=60 and V2=40. The little square for Subject 12 is placed where the imaginary line up from V1=60 crosses with the imaginary line across from V2=40.

Exercise 14.2

In Table14.1, look for subjects 3, 5, 8, 9, 15 and 19 and see if you can find and label their dots on the scatterplot shown in Figure 14.3.

As you work through your research, you should always check for errors. One way of doing this is to keep checking the consistency of your work – that things are progressing as expected.

Estimating the Correlation from a Scatterplot

A scatterplot gives you the overall picture of the relationship between two values. Remember that each dot on the scatterplot represents one subject and the position of the subject's dot is given by his or her V1 and V2 values. An easy way to estimate a correlation from the scatterplot, is to draw a "fish" over the scatterplot and see if it includes most of the dots (see Figure 14.6).

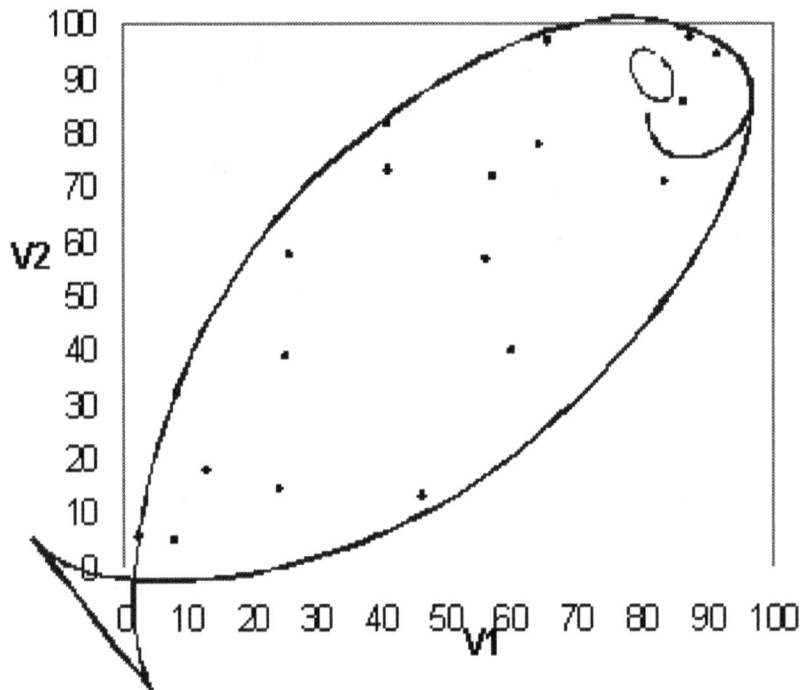

Figure 14.6: An outline of a fish has been drawn to include all of the V1 and V2 values from Table 14.1

If the dots in the scatterplot are clumped, bent or scattered around with little or no pattern as shown in Figure 14.7 in such a way that it is impossible to draw a 'normal' fish, then one of your variables is not sufficiently normal and you should not use the normal linear correlation. In particular, look out for one or two dots that do not follow a pattern. They may be outliers (discussed later) or measurement errors that may affect your results. Compare the positions of the dots in the three scatterplots shown in Figure 14.7 with that shown in Figure 14.6.

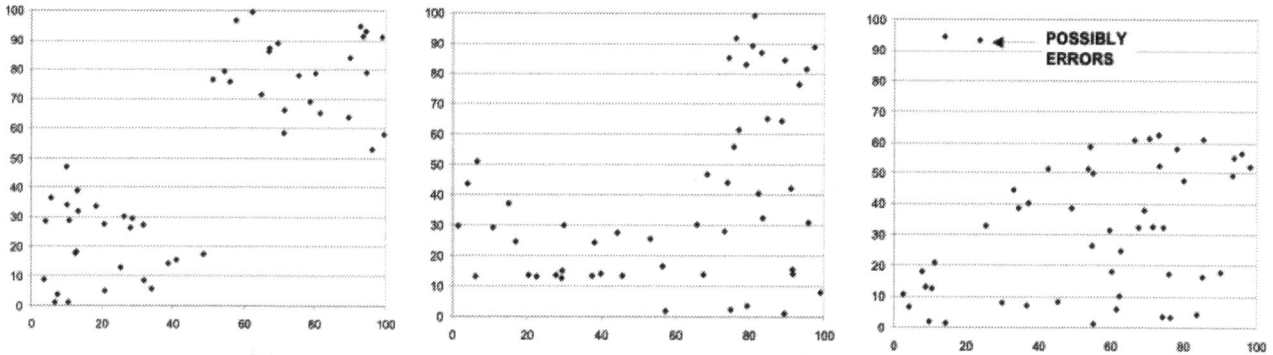

Figure 14.7: Examples of pairs of variables that are not linearly distributed.

The size of a correlation ranges between +1.00 and -1.00. If the fish is facing the top-right corner, the correlation is positive. This means that high measures from one variable tend to be related to high measures on the other variable. For example, by just looking at the numbers in Table 14.1, we can see the majority of the subjects who scored high on V1 also scored high on V2. At the same time, we can see that subjects who scored low on V1 also scored low on V2. This means that high scores go with high scores and low scores go with low scores (a positive correlation).

Examine the shape of each fish shown in Figure 14.8 and look at the shape of the fish around the dots on the scatterplot. It is the *fatness* of the fish that allows you to estimate the size of the correlation. When the fish is a thin line – almost like a 1, the correlation is nearly 1. When the fish is round and fat, and looks like a zero, the correlation is nearly zero. Examine the shape of each fish in Figure 14.7. The correlation for fish (a) is relatively high ($r = 0.811$), the very thin fish (b) is very high, nearly 1 ($r = 0.975$) and for the fat fish (c), the correlation is very low, nearly zero ($r = 0.012$).

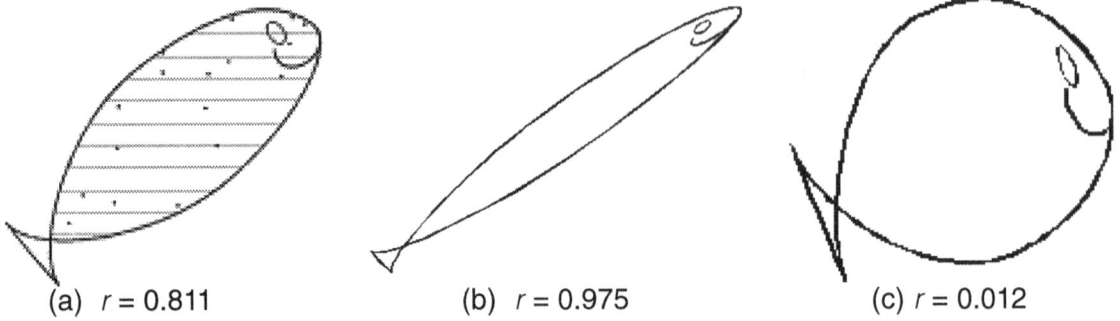

(a) *r* = 0.811   (b) *r* = 0.975   (c) *r* = 0.012

Figure 14.8: You can estimate the size of the correlation from the shape of the fish.

When the fish are facing the other way – to the top-left instead of the top-right, the correlations have the same size but are negative. A negative correlation means that high scores on one variable tend to be associated with low scores on the second variable. This is the inverse of positive correlations: high scores go with low scores and low scores go with high scores. In Figure 14.9, you can see the correlations for (a), r = -0.811, for (b), r = -0.975 and for (c) r = -0.012. These are the negative numbers of those shown in Figure 14.7.

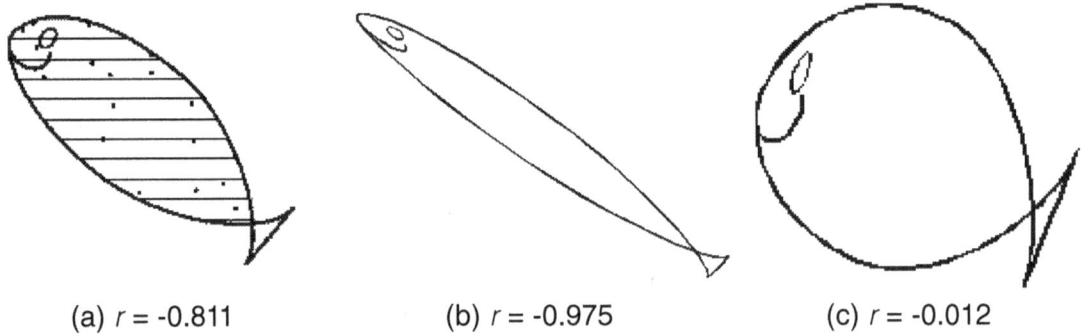

(a) *r* = -0.811   (b) *r* = -0.975   (c) *r* = -0.012

Figure 14.9: An example of the look of the size of negative correlations.

Test Yourself 7
We have changed the numbers for subjects 3, 5, 8, 9, 15 and 19 and renamed it "Non linear13.sav" (Appendix B2). Create a new scatterplot so you can see where the new values are repositioned. Is there any correlation between these pairs of numbers?

Answers can be found at the end of the text.

In Test Yourself 7, we changed the scores for S3, S5, S8, S9, S15 and S19. This made a difference in the measures for V1 and V2 and also changed the placement of the dots. If you were able to draw a fish around the dots in this scatterplot, the new fish would be much rounder and fatter and would probably represent a correlation close to zero as shown in Table 14.2.

S	V1	V2
1	65	97
2	41	73
3	75	18
4	8	32
5	51	6
6	56	57
7	41	82
8	27	94
9	87	46
10	57	72
11	24	14
12	60	40
13	26	58
14	25	39
15	86	28
16	83	71
17	46	13
18	64	78
19	66	15

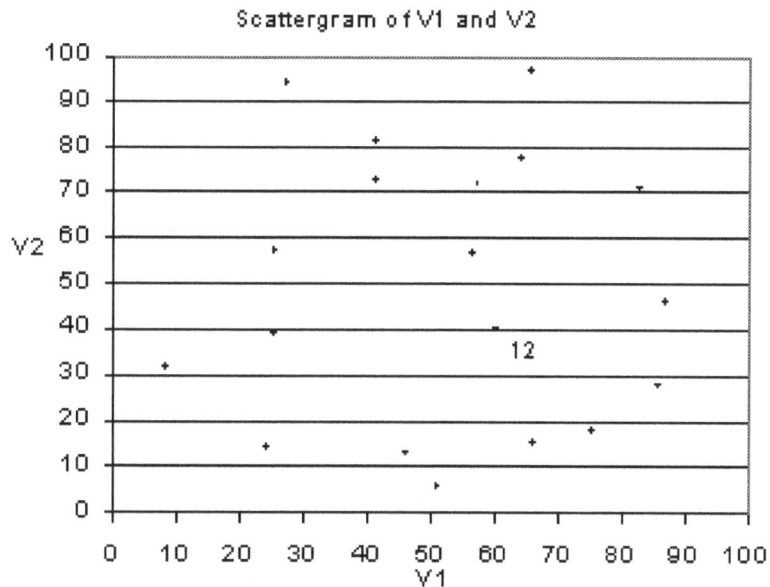

Table 14.2: *Data Matrix with Changed Scores and Scatterplot Showing Zero Correlation*

You can also tell by looking at the scatterplot whether your two variables are normally distributed and correlated. If the variables are normally distributed and correlated, the scatterplot should look like a relatively slim fish. In other words, the data should be linear and not curved and there should be more dots in the middle than at the ends.

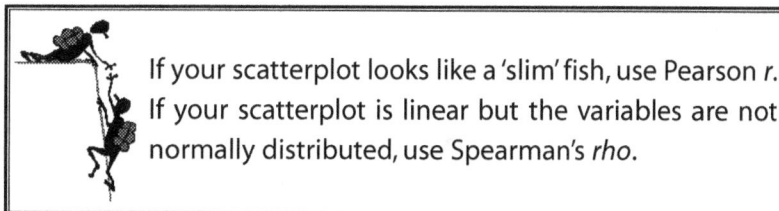

If your scatterplot looks like a 'slim' fish, use Pearson *r*.
If your scatterplot is linear but the variables are not normally distributed, use Spearman's *rho*.

Drawing Pie-Charts, Bar-Graphs and Histograms

You may wish to draw a *pie-chart* to show relative proportions of each category to each other and to the whole, a *bar graph* to display the frequency of a continuous variable at each level of a categorical variable, or a *histogram* to see how your continuous variables are distributed.

> • You use bar graphs or pie-charts when you have categorical variables with different levels or groupings, such as salary level, age grouping, years of experience, gender, makes of cars, types of schools, etc. For bar graphs, this method displays the *names of the categories* along the X-axis and the frequencies on the Y-axis.
>
> • You generally use histograms when you want to display the distribution of a continuous variable, such as scores from tests or questionnaires. This method places the *numbers* along the X-axis and the frequencies of the scores on the Y-axis.

Drawing Pie-charts

Pie-charts are useful when you want to show relative proportions. Generally, you use a pie-chart only when you have only a few categories because they can become difficult to read when there are more than about 5 or 6 categories.

Using the data from Descriptives13.sav, we first explain how to draw a pie-chart for the gender variable. Open your SPSS file and:

1. Click on **Graphs**, scroll down until you see **Pie...** and click on it to open the **Pie Charts** dialog box (see Figure 14.10).
2. In the **Pie Charts** box, click in the box beside **Summaries for groups of cases** dialog box.
3. Click **Define**. This brings up the **Define Pie: Summaries for Groups of Cases** dialog box.

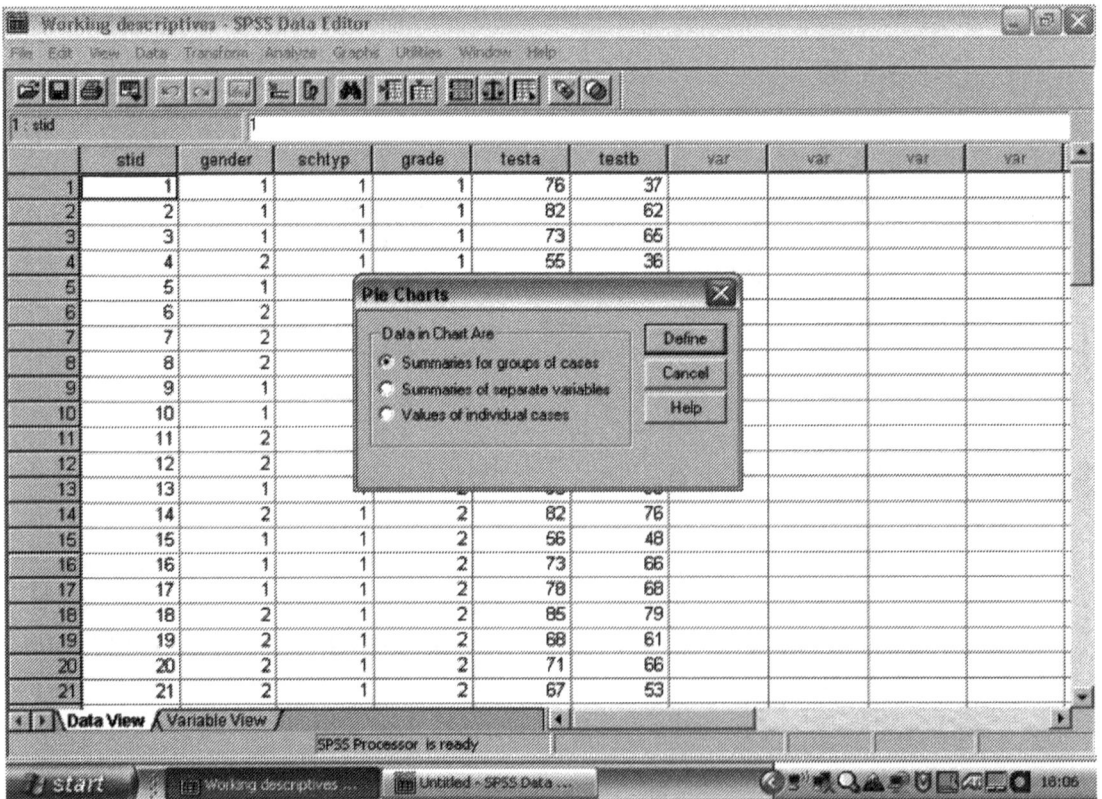

Figure 14.10

4. In the Define Pie dialog box, (i) under the heading **Slices Represent' chose** the option **N of cases**. (ii) In the space under **Define Slices by**, move whatever variable you wish to use into the space. In our example, we used *gender*.
5. Click **OK**. This brings up a pie-chart with no labels.

To place labels, numbers, percentages on your pie-chart:
6. Right double-click anywhere on the chart to open **Chart 1: SPSS Chart Editor**.
7. In the Chart Editor's menu, click on **Chart** and
8. Click on **Options** to open the **Pie Options** dialog box (as shown in Figure 14.11).

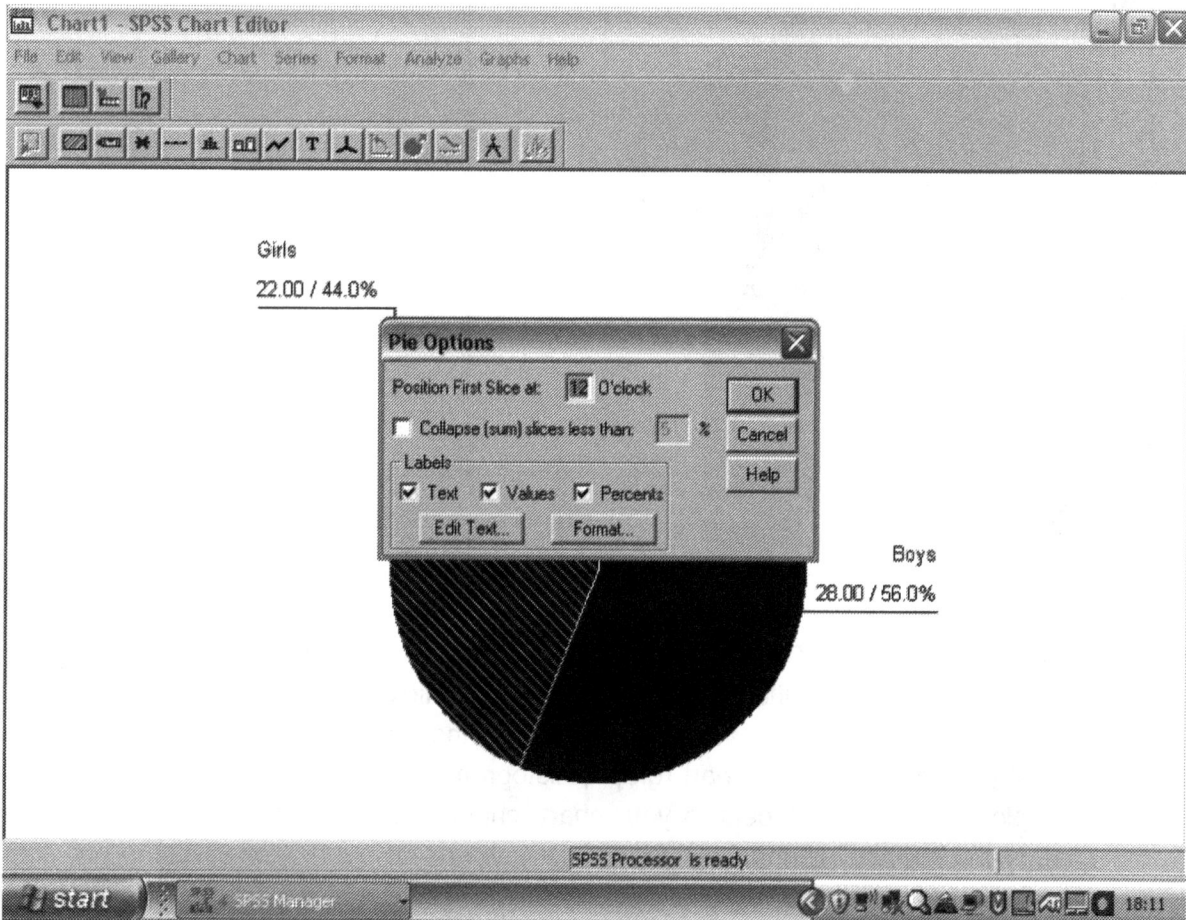

Figure 14.11

9. In this box, (i) choose a specific time where you want the first slice to go in **Position First Slices at ? O'clock**. (We chose 12 o'clock.)
10. Under **labels**, click beside **Text, Values, Percents**.
11. Click **Format** and change the decimal places box to **0**. We only chose this option because we didn't need any decimal places for gender.
12. Click **Continue**.
13. Close both the Format box and the Chart 1: SPSS Chart Editor box by clicking on the red **X** at the top right of the screen in both boxes.

This procedure produces a standard coloured and labelled pie-chart that should be similar to that shown in Figure 14.12. Although this may have seemed like a lot of steps to produce a pie-chart, the outcome is well worth it!

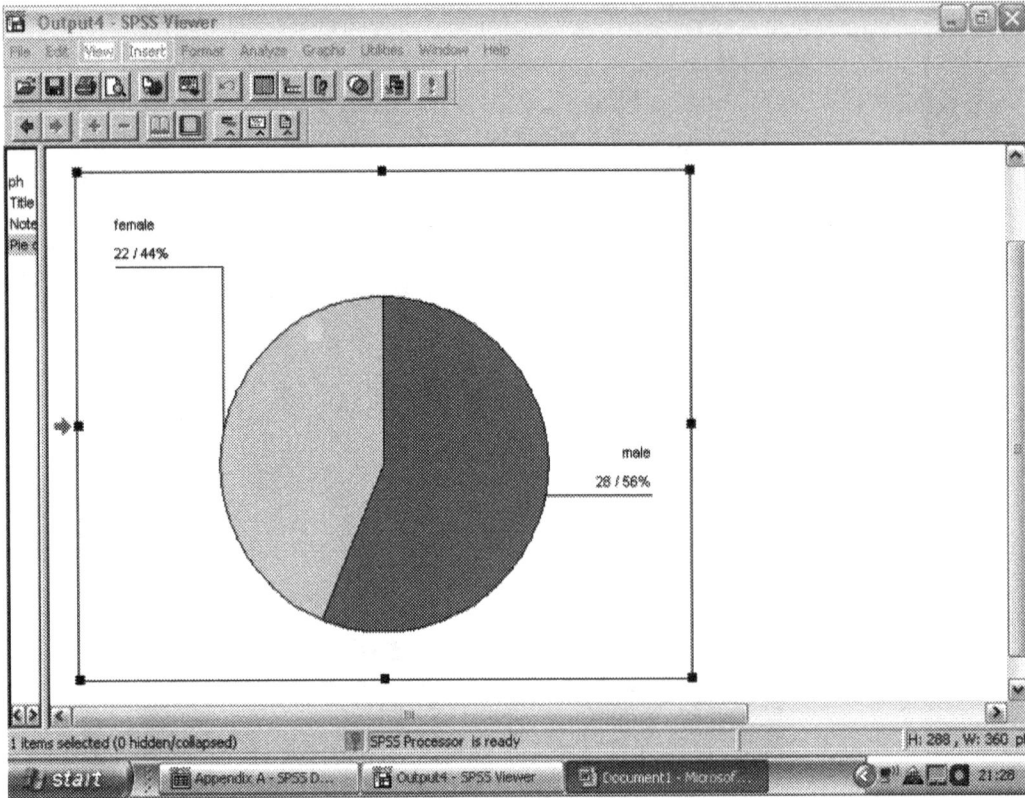

Figure 14.12

A Note About the SPSS Chart Editor

To open the **Chart Editor**, you just double right click any where in box (it does not matter what graph or chart you are using). You then see a complete menu of all the 'things' you can do to your chart (graph, histogram) to enhance your presentation. For example, you can add labels to your chart, change font type and size, add legends, change the colours, change the fill and fill patterns. It even allows you to get some descriptive statistics.

Go into the Chart Editor and experiment! It takes very little time and is a lot of fun. Above all, this extra information adds to your finished paper.

Drawing Bar Graphs

To draw a bar graph, you need two variables – one categorical and one continuous. (Note that you can also use more than one continuous variable.) The major use of a bar-graph is when you want to show the number of cases in different categories (for example, the number of students in five parishes of Jamaica who sat the GSAT in 2006) or it can show the scores on some continuous variable according to the different categories (scores on the GSAT according to five parishes).

Although it is rather pointless to draw a bar-graph for only two categories, we are using the same data from Appendix A and the same variable, "gender" so you can see how similar the two processes are.

1. Click on **Graphs,** scroll down until you see **Bar...** and click on it to open the **Bar Charts** dialogue box shown in Figure 14.13.

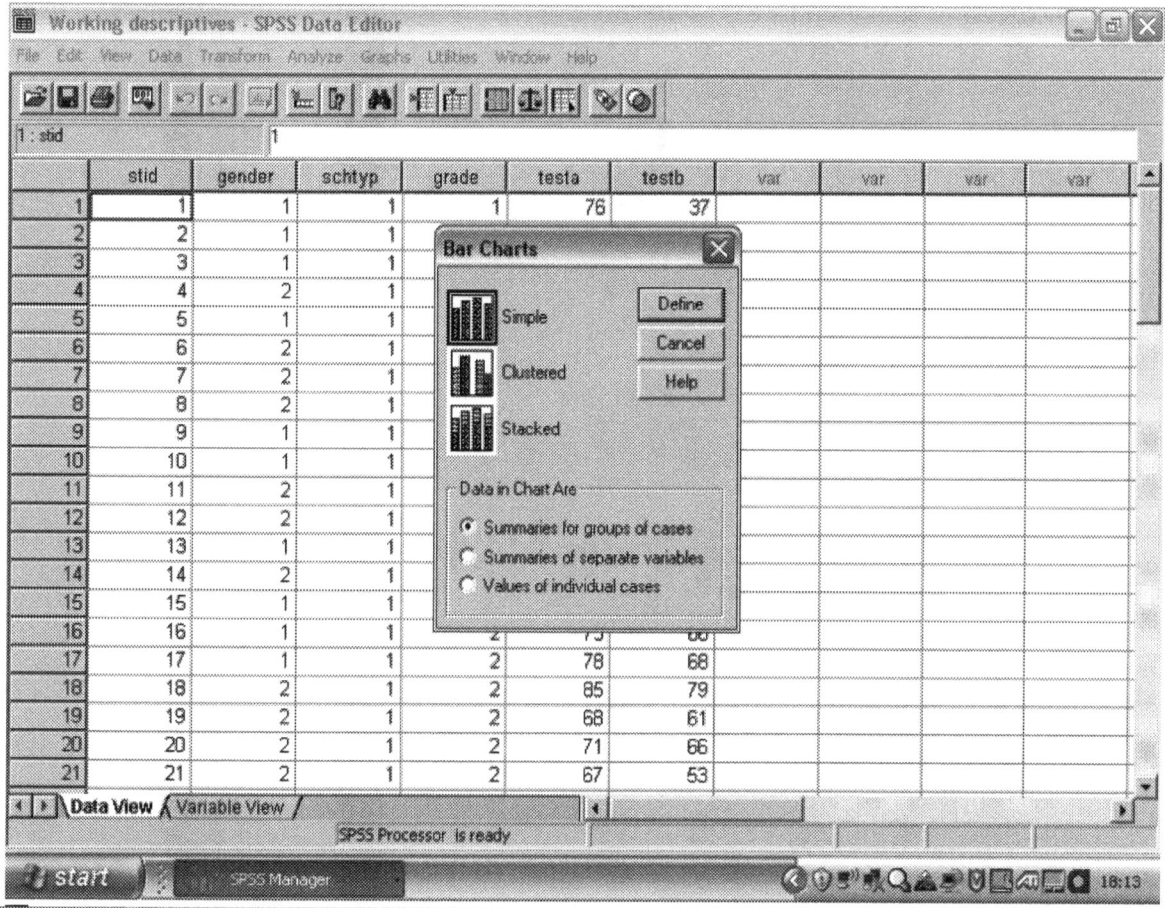

Figure 14.13

2. In the **Bar Charts** dialog box, click on the example of a bar graph marked **Simple**. Under **Data in Chart Are**, click on **Summaries for groups of cases**.
3. Click on **Define** to open the **Define Sample Bar: Summaries for Groups of Cases** (Figure 14.14)
4. In the **Define Simple Bar** dialog box, (i) under the heading **Bars Represent** chose the option **N of cases**. (ii) In the space under **Category Axis**, move whatever variable you wish to use into the space. In our example, we used *gender.*
5. Click **OK**. This brings up the bar-chart with no labels. To add the labels, double right click anywhere on the bar chart to open the **Chart editor** dialog box and follow Step 6 (described in drawing a Pie-chart) to change colours, put different labels on, or clicking on the scale to start at 0 as we have done for Figure 14.15.

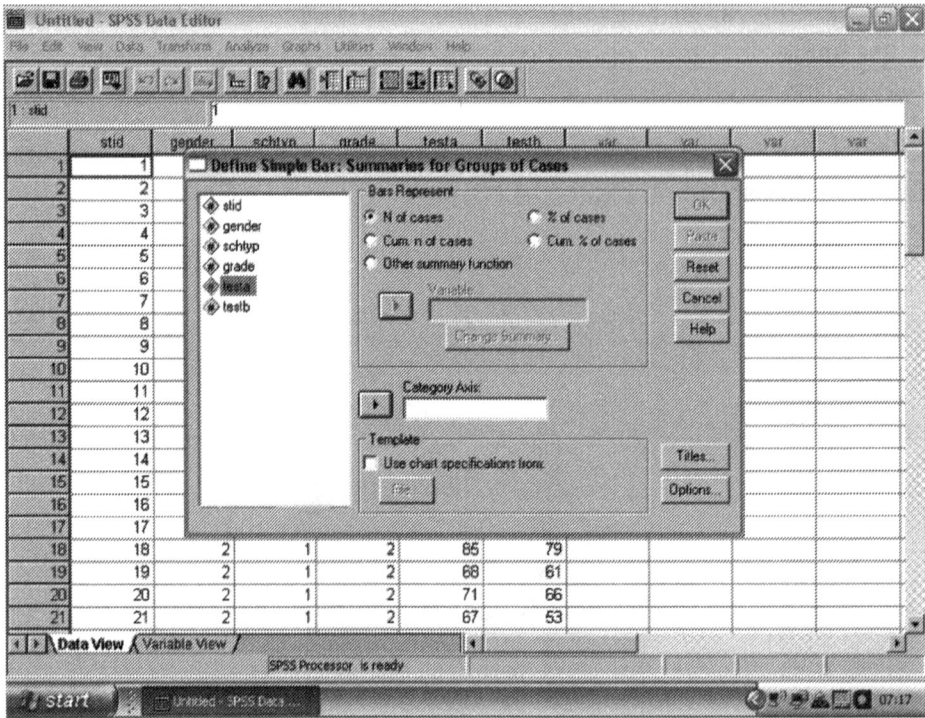

Figure 14.14

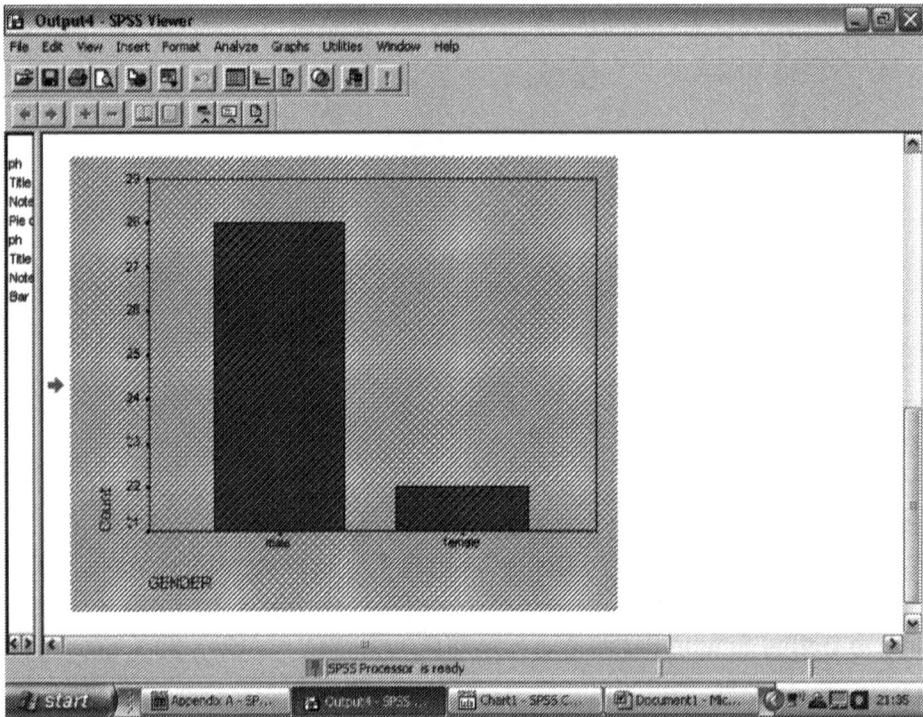

Figure 14.15: A completed bar graph showing the number of males and females for the categorical variable 'gender.'

Note that we chose the option 'Simple" but you can choose any of the other two options, Clustered or Stacked. Play around with these options to see which one best visually describes your data. Go into the SPSS Chart Editor and experiment with the output.

Drawing Histograms

There are many options for drawing histograms: (i) the **Graphs** options, under the **Descriptives menu** (ii) the **Frequencies** option, and (iii) the **Explore** option.

Drawing a Histogram Using the Graph Option

The Graph options is useful for displaying a single continuous variable. By now, you should be adept at using the Graph options. Using the same data from Descriptives13.sav, we are using scores from Test A because this data consist of many values (scores) in a continuous variable. Also, it seems pointless to draw a histogram of gender as it only has two values and the data is dichotomous, not continuous.

1. Click on **Graphs**, scroll down until you see **Histograms...** and click on it to open the **Histogram** dialogue box
2. In the Histogram dialog box, click on **Test A** and move it into the **Variable** box.
3. If you want to superimpose the normal curve, click in the box beside **Display Normal Curve**.
4. Click **OK**. This brings up the histogram showing the mean score, the standard deviation and total number of students. This is shown in Figure 14.16. Remember this is a histogram of the scores for all the students and has not been separated according to gender, school type or grade. As before, go into the **SPSS Chart Editor** to add labels, change font size and so on....whatever you think will be necessary to add to your histogram.

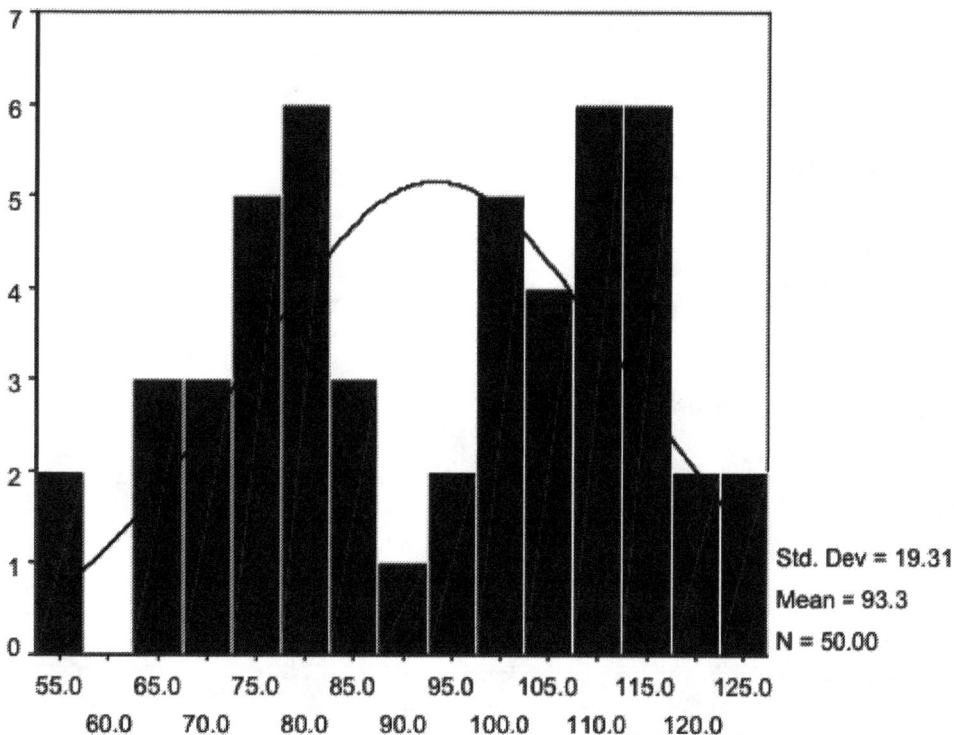

Std. Dev = 19.31
Mean = 93.3
N = 50.00

TestA

Figure 14.16

Think About This

In Figure 14.16, a normal curve with the same mean and standard deviation as the variable has been superimposed over the histogram so you can compare where the two graphs do or do not match up. Looking at this figure can suggest insights about our data that might lead to further knowledge.

For example, it is interesting to see that the histogram does not look Normal because it goes down in the middle and looks as if it is made up of two Normal distributions – one with a low mean and one with a high mean. You might hypothesise that there were two groups of students who took this test and one group of students scored higher than the other.

Drawing a Histogram Using the Frequencies Option

The frequencies option is similar to that of the Graph option in that it also requires one continuous variable. It is useful because you can create many histograms at one time. We used the scores from Test A and from Test B from Descriptives13.sav in this example.

1. Click on **Analyse**, scroll down until you see **Descriptive Statistics** and click on it to open the Frequencies dialog box (see Figure 14.17).

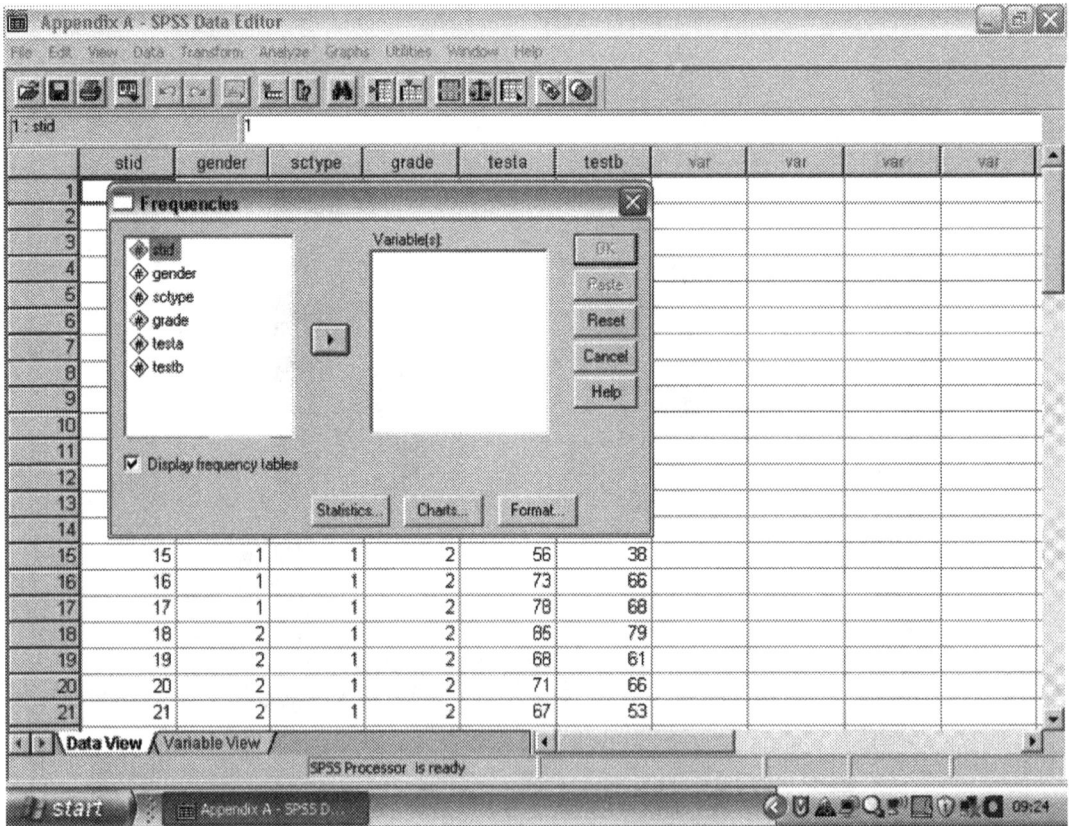

Figure 14.17

2. In the Frequencies dialog box, click on Test A and Test B and move them into the **Variable(s)** box. You need to click on the **Display frequency tables** because although this generates an unnecessary output (it gives the frequency of every single score in your data!), if you turn it off, you get a warning message.

Think About This . . .

Note that although we have only entered two variables, you can enter as many variables as you wish into the Variable(s) box. It is very easy to generate charts, graphs and histograms using the SPSS programmes. BUT, be warned, you must write about EVERY one of them that you put into your paper, project or thesis.

3. Click on **Charts** to open the **Frequencies: Charts** dialog box, then click on **Histograms**. If you want to superimpose the normal curve, click in the box beside **With normal curve**.
4. Click on **Continue** to return you to the main Frequencies box.
5. Click on **OK**.

This brings up two histograms shown in Figure 14.18 (a) and (b) showing the mean score, the standard deviation and total number of students for Test A (a) and Test B (b). Remember these are histograms of the two sets of scores for all the students. The scores have not been separated according to gender, school type or grade.

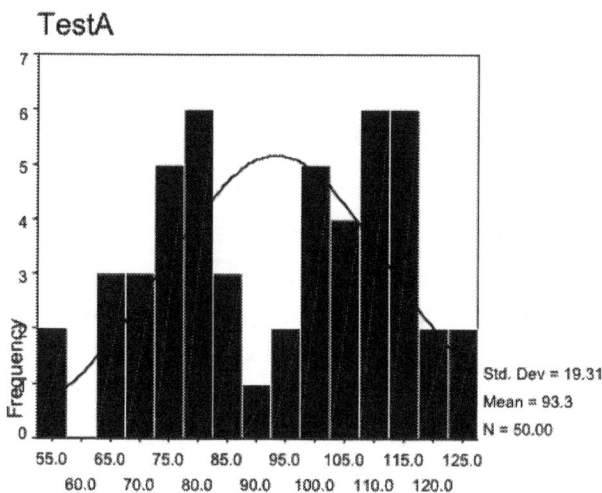

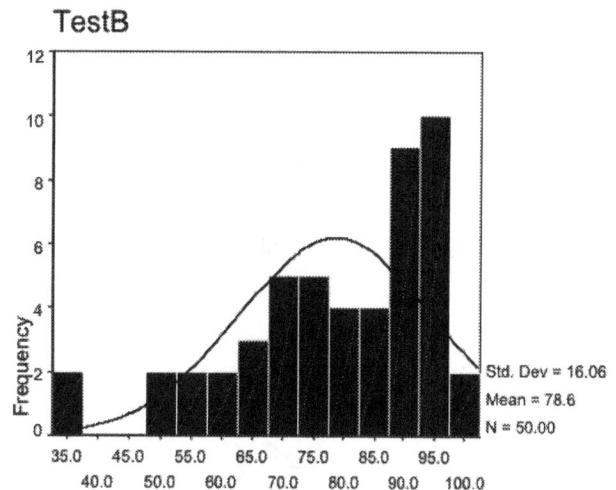

(a)   (b)

Figure 14.18: Histograms of the scores for Test A (a) and Test B (b). The mean scores, standard deviations and total number of students are shown for each test.

As before, go into the SPSS Chart Editor to add labels, change font size and so on....whatever you think will be necessary to add to your histogram.

Drawing a Histogram Using the Explore Option

The Explore option in the SPSS programme gives you a lot of information that has already been covered, but you might wish to use this option when you are ready to start putting your data into order.

To use this programme:
Using data from Descriptives13.sav...
1. Open your file in SPSS and on the menu at the top, click on **Analyze**. Scroll down until you see **Descriptive Statistics ▶**. Move your cursor over until you highlight **Explore...** and click on it so that the Explore dialog box appears.
2. Highlight the variable you want to investigate. Click on the ▶ to move it into the **Dependent List** box at the right. You can use as many variables as you wish.

In this example, we placed the data from Test A in the dependent variable box and 'school type' in the factor list box. (This means that we are telling the SPSS programme to produce a histogram that separates the scores of Test A by school type.) However, if you want to sort your data by other grouping variables (such as gender, age group, grade, etc.), you would highlight each of these variables and put each one into the Factor List box.

3. Under **Display**, make sure that the box beside **Both** is checked.
4. Click on **Plots...** to open the **Explore: Plots** pop-up box.
5. In this box, look for the list under **Descriptives** and click on **Histogram**.
6. Click on **Normality plots with tests**.
7. Click on **Continue** to return to the first box.

If you know you have missing cases (data), then you would click on **Options** and in the **Missing Values** box, you would click on **Exclude cases pairwise**. Then click on **Continue**.

8. Click on **OK**.

You will next see a screen chock full of information. The output should be similar to that shown in Tables 14.3 and 14.4. Table 14.3 shows you how many cases were processed and that there were no missing data. Table 14.4 is labelled "Descriptives" and gives you information about the variables. In this example, because we used data from 'Test A' and school type as the factor, you can see the measures of central tendencies: mean, median, standard deviation, minimum, maximum, range, skewness and kurtosis according to each type of school.

The Explore option box also gives much more information such as the 5% Trimmed Mean. The 5% Trimmed Mean shows that the SPSS programme has removed the top and bottom 5% of the scores and computed a new mean score. If this number and the mean score for your raw data are very different, it means that you must go back and investigate your raw data because there could be some extreme scores that might affect the mean.

Table 14.3: *Output from the Explore Option Showing the "Case Processing Summary" for Test A*

Case Processing Summary

		Cases					
		Valid		Missing		Total	
	School Type	N	Percent	N	Percent	N	Percent
TestA	Government	25	100.0%	0	.0%	25	100.0%
	Private	25	100.0%	0	.0%	25	100.0%

Table 14.4: *The Output from the Explore Option Showing Descriptive Data for Test A*

Descriptives

	School Type			Statistic	Std. Error
TestA	Government	Mean		76.52	2.136
		95% Confidence Interval for Mean	Lower Bound	72.11	
			Upper Bound	80.93	
		5% Trimmed Mean		76.39	
		Median		77.00	
		Variance		114.010	
		Std. Deviation		10.678	
		Minimum		55	
		Maximum		102	
		Range		47	
		Interquartile Range		13.00	
		Skewness		.069	.464
		Kurtosis		.584	.902
	Private	Mean		110.08	1.553
		95% Confidence Interval for Mean	Lower Bound	106.87	
			Upper Bound	113.29	
		5% Trimmed Mean		109.94	
		Median		111.00	
		Variance		60.327	
		Std. Deviation		7.767	
		Minimum		96	
		Maximum		127	
		Range		31	
		Interquartile Range		11.00	
		Skewness		.079	.464
		Kurtosis		-.225	.902

In this programme, you can check for skewness and kurtosis and you can also check for normality using the Kolmogorov-Smirnov statistic. Results of the K-S test are shown in Table 14.5. Remember that you want a non-significant result (anything higher than 0.05) to show that your distribution of scores could have come from a normal population. For the scores from Test A, for both school types, the significance levels were over 0.05, so you could state that your scores could have come from a normal distribution and you can use parametric statistics to analyse your data.

Table 14.5: *Results of the K-S Test of Normality*

Tests of Normality

	School Type	Kolmogorov-Smirnov[a]			Shapiro-Wilk		
		Statistic	df	Sig.	Statistic	df	Sig.
TestA	Government	.094	25	.200*	.982	25	.918
	Private	.078	25	.200*	.984	25	.950

*. This is a lower bound of the true significance.

a. Lilliefors Significance Correction

Finally, Figures 14.19 (a) and (b) show histograms for each set of scores for pupils attending (a) government schools and (b) private schools. These are very poor examples of scores showing a normal curve but remember that this data was designed primarily to help you understand correlations and not for drawing histograms. We used the same data so that you would not have to enter new data if you were following our "how-to" use the options offered by SPSS.

Histogram

For SCHTYP= Government

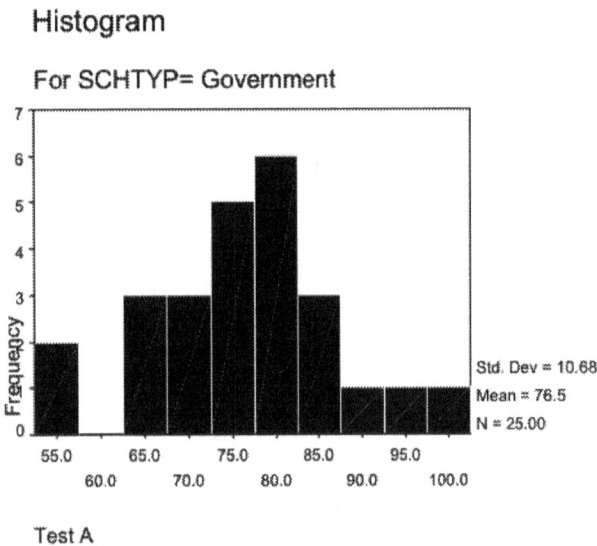

Std. Dev = 10.68
Mean = 76.5
N = 25.00

Test A

Histogram

For SCHTYP= Private

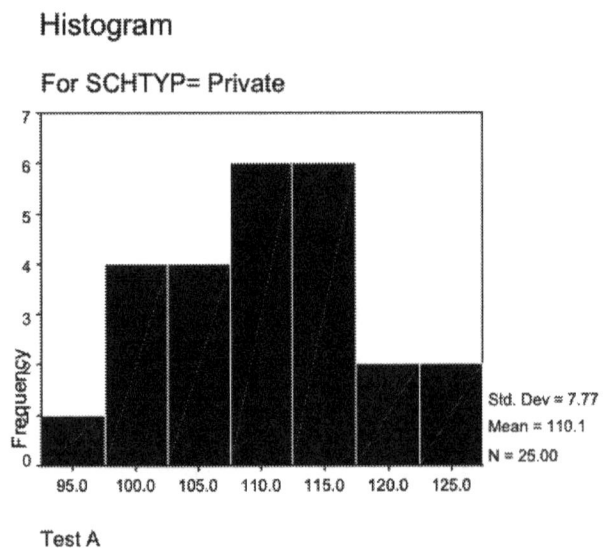

Std. Dev = 7.77
Mean = 110.1
N = 25.00

Test A

Figure 14.19 (a): A histogram showing the distribution of scores of Test A from students attending government schools.

Figure 14.19 (b): A histogram showing the distribution of scores of Test A from students attending private schools.

Now look at Figure 14.20, a QQ plot. This is also part of the information given when you use the Explore Histograms option. The QQ plot is used to check whether your sample could have come from a specific target population and is a useful tool for assessing normality. The Quartiles of the scores are on the horizontal axis and the expected normal scores are on the vertical axis.

Normal Q-Q Plot of TestA

For SCHTYP= Government

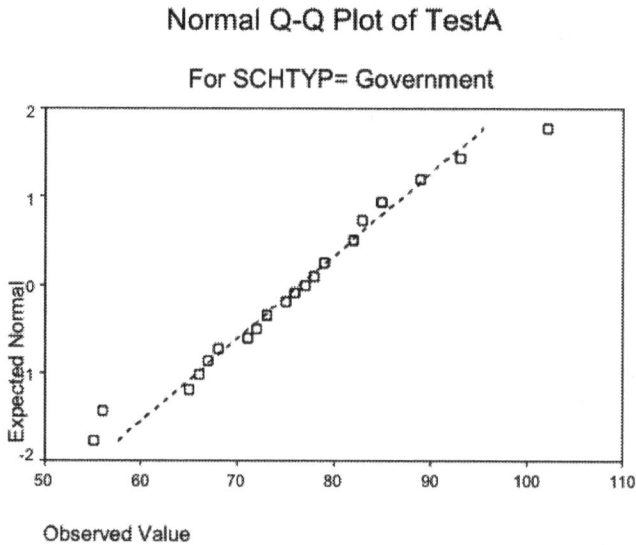

Figure 14.20: A QQ plot of the distribution of scores from Test A.

Rest assured that many of the variables used in social science research do not necessarily show the normal curve (as in our example). The scores may be skewed to the right or left or show a rectangular shape.

You should experiment with the many different options in the Descriptives options and find out how to do bar graphs and find outliers (scores that are very low or very high). Under the Graphs options, you can create line graphs, bar plots and scatterplots. These figures help in explaining your data and increase the credibility of your research.

Outliers

Outliers are scores or observations that are far above or below the majority of the other scores. You can easily recognise an outlier because it is the score that does not fall within most of the scores within a distribution or pattern. For example, you may have a distribution of scores between 15 and 30 and then find one score of 2 – this would be the outlier of that particular distribution. If you looked at a scatterplot of the scores, this one score would be all by itself. An example of outliers is shown in Figure 14.7.

One method is to look at the values given in the Descriptives table from the Explore Option box. Looking at this value will give you some idea whether your extreme score is influencing the mean to any great extent.

Another method to identify outliers is to use the Explore Option found in Descriptive statistics discussed above under Drawing Histograms.

To check for outliers:
1. Click on **Analyze** and scroll down to **Descriptive Statistics ▸** and click on **Explore**.
2. Place the continuous variable you are examining into the **Dependent List**.
3. Place the ID of the variable into the **Label Cases** box. This helps you identify the outlying cases.
4. Click on **Both** in the Display section.
5. Click on the **Statistics** box to open the **Explore: Statistics** box and click on **Outliers**.
6. Click on **Continue**.
7. Click on **Plots** and click on **Histogram**.
8. Click on **Continue** to return to the first menu.
9. Click on **OK**.

Look at the histogram in the output to determine whether any scores appear out of place. Then examine the boxplot to see if the SPSS programme was able to identify any outliers. These will show up as little circles either above or under the main boxplot (see also Figure 14.7 on page 165.) Each little circle has a number attached (the ID number). When you find an outlier, first check to see if the data was entered correctly. If this was correct and the score really is very much higher or lower than the rest of the distribution, then you need to decide what to do with it.

Calculating Correlations - Pearson r

You use Pearson *r* (also called the **Pearson Product Moment Correlation**) to determine whether variables are *associated or related with each other* (remember: high-high, low-low or high-low, low-high) – and not to find out whether the scores *are different from each other*. The Pearson *r* indicates the strength – it tells you how close the array of data points is to a straight line – and the plus or minus signs indicate the direction of the line.

The major requisites to be able to use the Pearson *r* are:
- the data consist of continuous variables (numerical scores) or when one of the variables is continuous and the other is dichotomous (such as gender: males/females).
- the data are normally distributed.

Using the SPSS Programme to Determine the Value of Pearson *r*

For this example, we used data from Correlate13.sav (Appendix B1):
1. Open your SPSS file and click on **Analyse**. Scroll down until you see **Correlate ▸** . Click on the ▸ to find the **Bivariate Correlations** dialog box. This is shown in Figure 14.21.
2. In this dialog box, all the variables are listed in the box on the left side. Highlight the first variable (in our example, V1), click on the ▸ to place it into the box at the right (called **Variables:**).
3. Repeat this step until you have placed all the variables you need into the Variable box. In our example, we only used V1 and V2 as shown in Figure 14.22.
4. At the left side of the Bivariate Correlations box can be seen **Correlation Coefficients**. This is a list of all the different types of correlation statistics that can be used. As we are using the Pearson *r*, click in the box beside **Pearson**.
5. Under **Test of Significance**, click on **Two-tailed**.
6. Click on the box beside **Flag significant correlations**. Click **OK**.

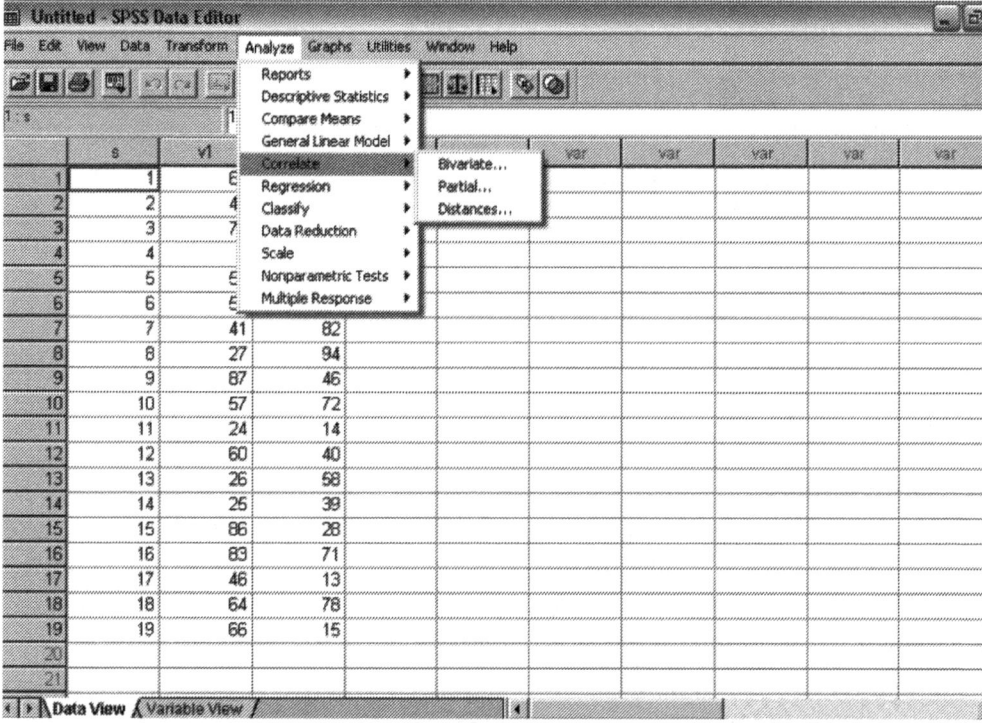
Figure 14.21

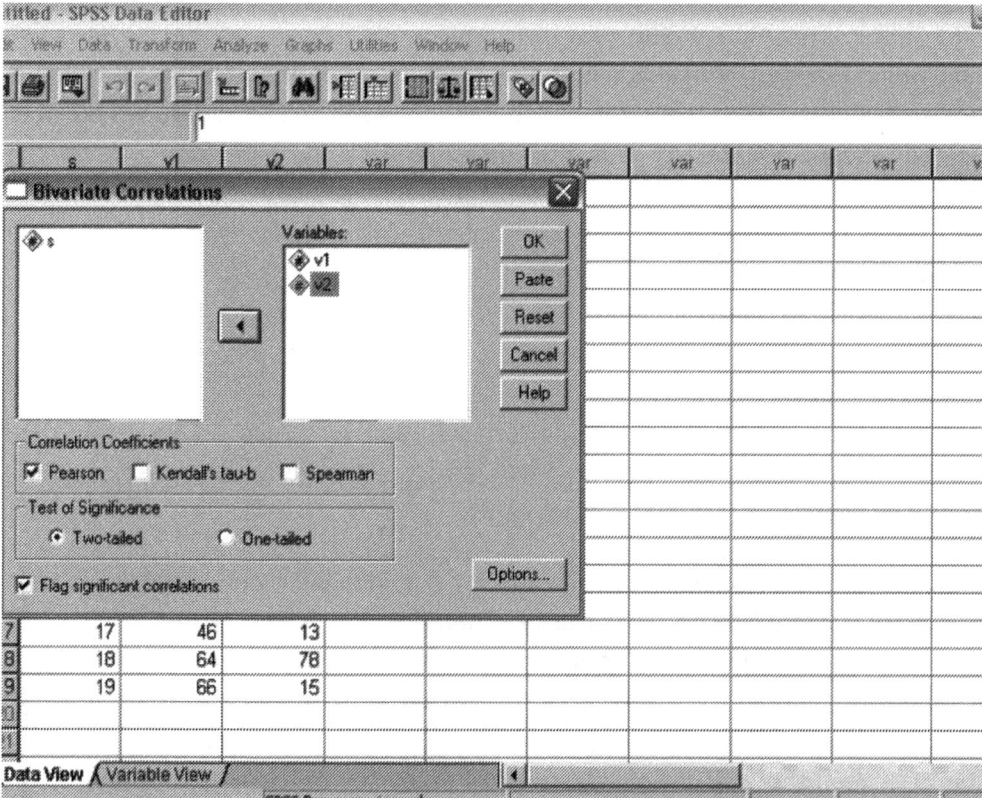
Figure 14.22

Steps 2 - 6 are shown in Figure 14.22. After you have clicked OK, the next thing that appears on your screen is the result of the computation – the SPSS output that should look similar to that shown in Table 14.6.

Correlations

		V1	V2
V1	Pearson Correlation	1	.809**
	Sig. (2-tailed)	.	.000
	N	19	19
V2	Pearson Correlation	.809**	1
	Sig. (2-tailed)	.000	.
	N	19	19

· Correlation is significant at the 0.01 level

Table 14.6: *An Example of a Correlation Table Showing the Magnitude and Direction of the Relationship between V1 and V2*

Interpreting the Correlation Table

Look at Table 14.6. There are three numbers that are important. We see that N =19 and by now, you should know that this means that there are 19 sets of scores (from 19 subjects). The N should be the first thing to check just to be sure that the computer has included all of your subjects and nothing else.

Next notice that r(V1, V2) = 0.809 has two stars (**). The two stars were produced because you choose **Flag significant correlations** in the Bivariate Correlations box (Step 6). Correlations can be flagged with 0, 1 or 2 stars and, just like hotels and restaurants, the more stars the better. Two stars mean that the significance, shown as 'Sig (2-tailed)' is less than 0.01 which is very good. Actually the significance is reported as .000, which is very, very good. When you write the significance value in your research, you would write it to two decimal places, $p < 0.01$ or $p < 0.05$ depending on the significance level you chose for your work.

Once you have discovered that your correlations are significant, you can state something to the effect:

> *The relationship between scores from Variable 1 and Variable 2 was investigated using the Pearson r statistic. There was a strong positive correlation between the two variables (r = 0.81, p < 0.01).*

Of course, because you have already performed other analyses on your raw data (such as the K-S test), you could also mention that preliminary analysis showed no violation of the assumption of normality and linearity.

NEVER, NEVER interpret the analysis by writing Variable 1 and Variable 2 (the way we just did). The variables must be identified by name.

If we had labelled V1 as 'hours' as in the amount of hours spent doing homework and V2 as 'scores' as in scores from a mathematics test, then we would have written:

"The association between the amount of hours spent studying for mathematics and the scores that students obtained on the mathematics test was significant." ($r = 0.81$, $p < 0.05$).

Then, we could continue:

"Results show that children who scored high on a mathematics test also tended to spend many hours in studying."

Calculating the Reliability Coefficient (r^2)

Remember that the Pearson *r* tells you only that there is a relationship between two variables. If your result is significant, the significance level merely tells you that it is unlikely that your measurements came from a population where there was NO correlation between variables. So a statistically significant result only means that there might be a non-zero correlation in the population. Significance does not tell you the size of the correlation or its importance.

One way to answer the 'importance' question is to calculate the coefficient of determination by simply squaring *r*. For example, if *r* = 0.809, then the effect size is = 0.809 x 0.809 = 0.654 or 65.4%. The coefficient of determination (r^2) gives the proportion or percentage of the variance shared by the two variables. In the example of the effect size being 65.4%, this means that 65.4% of the variance in one variable can be explained by the variance in other variable. Or, if you prefer, 34.6% of the variance is not explained by the correlation.

How important is this? It depends again on the cost caused by what is unexplained. You may need to know if the correlation is big enough to be important and this need to know depends on whether the cost of being wrong is important. For comparison, a test-retest correlation of 0.74 (55% variance accounted for) is usually considered an acceptable reliability – but no one is going to die from taking a low reliability test!

Correlations show association not causal relationship.
Correlations show that pairs of scores are related to each other.
Correlations do NOT show differences between scores.

Rules for Selecting Correlation Coefficients Statistics

- It is important to look at the scatterplot of your data to make sure that the relationship is linear before you try to compute any correlation analysis.
- Use Pearson r when the data are measured using continuous variables or when one variable is continuous and the other is dichotomous.
- Use Spearman's rho when the data are ranked.
- Use biserial correlation when one variable is, at least, interval and the other is dichotomous.[5]

Introduction to Partial Correlations

It has been repeatedly stated that a relationship between X and Y does not show that X "causes" Y or that Y "causes" X. You should also know that you can only report the correlation statistic as a numerical association between X and Y and not as a causal relationship. This section shows you how to explore possible causal relationships between variables in correlational or sectional research. You do this using *partial correlation.*

---

5. Not explained here. You have to use the **Data Editor** and the **Split File Option** to identify the groups in the **Compare Groups** box, you have to move the grouping variables into the box labelled **Groups based on**. Once you have identified the groups, you can then use the SPSS correlation programme.

Partial correlation is a very close relation to Pearson r statistic except that it allows you to add a third variable that you think might be influencing your results. It is a relatively simple technique that can give important information about how that third variable might be impacting on the correlation between the other two variables that you have examined. If you only used results from simple bivariate correlations, you might wrongly assume that one variable is a major influence on another and misguidedly go ahead and recommend more (or less) use of the variable you think is doing the "influencing."

An Example of Using Partial Correlations

You might be interested in finding out if assigning homework for mathematics is effective for improving children's mathematical attainment. To do this, you randomly select a group of children and obtain two measures for each child (i) how many hours of mathematics homework is done in a week (variable X) and (ii) the child's score on a standard mathematic test (variable Y). Using the data from Correlate13.sav we found that Pearson r between X and Y resulted in a correlation of $r = 0.8$. This is a large correlation with the coefficient of determination being $r^2_{xy} = 0.64$ (meaning that the amount of time spent in doing mathematic homework accounted for 64% of the mathematic test result). As the homework is done before the test, you decide that you could logically assume that more time spent in doing math homework is causing higher attainment, so you recommend giving more homework.

Simple? Too simple! (If only life were this simple.) This is one of those cases where you should not assume that X causes Y because it is highly likely that no major increase in attainment would result if more homework were given to these children. Think of some of the reasons why. In other words, think of some of those confounding variables that might influence scores on the mathematics test.

Have you noticed that children who have educationally supportive parents are usually the ones who do the most homework and are also the same ones who do better on tests? Perhaps the major influencing variable is not the doing of homework but it might be parental support. If you give more homework, it is very likely that the children without parental support will not do it and it is also likely that the children with parental support are already doing as much homework as they can. So giving more homework is unlikely to produce the result you expected from the correlation.

If you added a third variable called "amount of parental support" (variable Z) for each child, then you could partial out its effect using partial correlation analysis. You might find that the partial correlation of X and Y (controlling for Z) is only $r_{xy.z} = 0.08$. This is very small, much smaller than the simple zero-order bivariate correlation $r_{xy} = 0.8$. It is almost certain to be not significant, as the coefficient of determination is now $r^2_{xy.z} = 0.0064$ which is much less than 1%. It appears that giving more homework may not have the effect you expected. The partial correlation result showed that it was the amount of parental support that was improving the mathematics test results. In the above example, the third variable can be referred to as a *masking variable* or sometimes a *suppressor* or *lurking* variable.

Test Yourself 8

Read the following examples and recommendations. Then see if you can determine a plausible masking variable that gives a misleading causal interpretation to the resulting correlations. Some of these examples are counter intuitive and are just given to see if you can think of a possible masking variable that should have been measured so that a partial correlation could have been calculated. If you cannot think of a likely masking variable, then read the answers that produced the correlation as this might help you.

Example 1 : Tall children are better at geography. Why?

Research: One hundred children were chosen at random and asked to complete a standardised geography test (variable X). The height of each child was measured (variable Y). The correlation $r_{xy}=0.876$ was highly significant. The research concluded that taller children were better at geography.

Recommendation: Promote equity by giving extra geography lessons to the disadvantaged shorter children.

Possible masking variable: z = ?

Example 2 : More firemen attending a fire cause more damage. Why?

Research: One hundred fires in cities in the USA were chosen at random. The number of firemen attending each fire (X) and the cost of the damage (Y) were tabulated. The large correlation $r_{xy}=0.892$ was highly significant. The researcher concluded that when more firemen attended a fire then the more damage they caused.

Recommendation: To keep cost of damage as low as possible, send as few firemen as possible to attend fires.

Possible masking variable: z = ?

Example 3 : People who buy ice cream tend to be lightly dressed. Why?

Research: Over the period of six months, researchers observed, at random, 120 customers purchasing ice cream at each of 6 randomly chosen ice-cream retailers. Each customer was asked how much he or she had just spent on ice-cream (X) and an assessment was made on a 100-point scale of the quantity of clothes he or she was wearing (Y). The correlation $r_{xy} = -0.742$ was highly significant. The researcher concluded that the fewer clothes people wear then the more ice-cream they buy.

Recommendation: Open ice-cream shops in nudist areas.

Possible masking variable: z = ?

Answers can be found at the end of the text.

How Partial Correlations Can Be Applied

Dobbelsteen, Levin and Oosterbeek (2002), investigated the correlations between class size and achievement. Previously, most research supported the conclusion that children can achieve higher standards in smaller classes and a recommendation was made to reduce class sizes in order to increase students' attainment. However, what the researchers found was that although there were often strong zero-order correlations both negative and positive between class size and attainment, there were other variables that influenced these correlations. For example, parental effects – caring parents tried to enroll their children where there were smaller classes. These parents also helped their children more so that their children had higher attainments. This resulted in children in smaller classes having higher attainments.

Contrary to this, schools often place children at risk in smaller classes for more intense instruction. In this case, smaller classes also correlate with lower attainment. The researchers found that when similar selection variables were partialled out, the correlations between class size and attainment came closer to zero.

> Generally, socioeconomic status (SES) is a strong lurking variable in many attainment studies. If you are conducting a study in which attainment is a dependent variable, you would be well advised to also measure SES as an independent variable so that you can control for it using partial correlation. (Or, you could also use ANCOVA or some other statistical method of "holding a variable constant.")

Calculating Partial Correlation Using SPSS

Using SPSS to calculate the partial correlation is very simple. You need three (or more) continuous variables (X, Y and Z): two of these variables are the ones you want to use to explore the relationship and the third is the variable you think is doing the influencing. When you have the partial correlation output, then all you have to do is to interpret the size and meaning of the result by comparing it with the corresponding zero-order correlation – the ordinary XY correlation.

In the following example showing you how to obtain partial correlations, we used data from a type of research that is fairly common in Education and Social Sciences. In order to test students' ability in a subject, they may be given two tests: a paper and pencil theory test and a hands-on practical test. What generally happens in lower ability classes is that the students do well on the practical and badly on the theory. This experience often leads to teachers, parents and the students themselves to say that paper and pencil tests do not show the "true" ability of the students and that hands-on authentic testing has more validity.

This is not always the case, but in the example we are using, it is true because the students in this class had low reading and writing ability which interfered with their ability to read and write examinations and most likely lead to lower scores on the written theory examinations. The teacher could have provided evidence for this because she had also given her students a test of reading and writing so that she could calculate the partial correlation to show this effect.

Experiment: In a cookery class, the cookery teacher assessed her class by giving her students both a practical and theory end-of-year examinations in cookery. She also gave them a test regarding their ability to read and write English. Figure 14.23 shows the SPSS data matrix of the results of the three tests entered into the SPSS programme for the first nine children. This data set is from file 'Covariate13.sav' on your CD (also in Appendix C).

Figure 14.23: An SPSS data matrix showing test results for first nineteen students on Cookery Theory (theory), Cookery Practical (pract) and English (reading and writing).

Once all the data has been entered, you use the SPSS Partial Correlations programme to calculate the zero-order correlations and the first-order partial correlation.

The number in this "order" terminology refers to how many variables are being partialled out (or controlled for – which means the same thing).

When we calculate the bivariate Pearson correlation, without any controls, it is called the zero-order correlation.

When we control for one variable, it is a first-order partial correlation.

When we control for two variables at the same time, it is called a second-order partial correlation.

SPSS has the option where you can control for whatever normally distributed variables you want to use.

To compute partial correlations using the SPSS programme...
1. From the menu at the top of the screen, click on **Analyze**. This opens the Analyze dialog box.
2. Scroll down until you see **Correlate**. Click on the arrow and then click on **Partial**.
3. This opens the **Partial Correlations** dialog box. Move the variables, 'Theory' and 'Pract' into the Variables box (on the left) by first clicking on the variables, then on the arrow.
4. Now move the suspected masking variable (in this case, 'English') into the **Controlling for** box to get a first-order partial correlation (shown in Figure14.24).

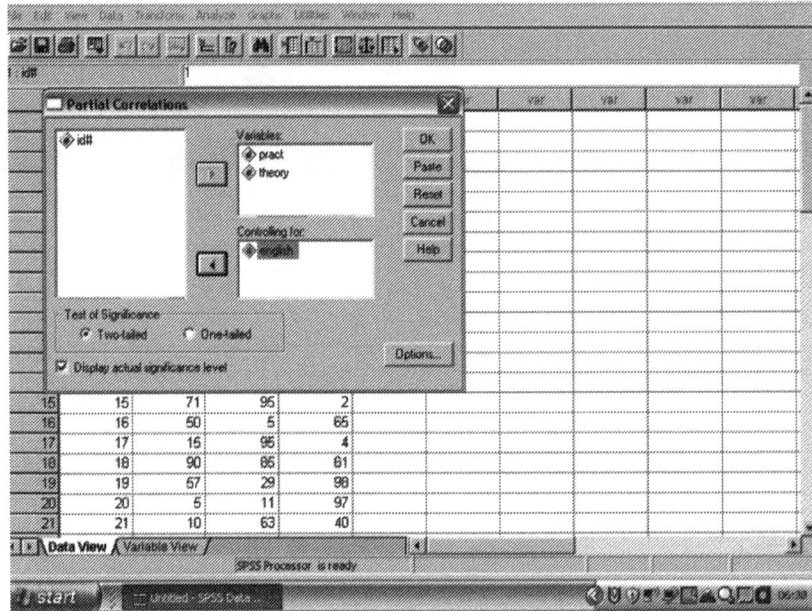

Figure 14.24: Partial Correlations dialog box showing the request for the correlation between theory and pract controlling for English.

Note that if you had more masking variables such as scores from a parental support questionnaire and/or level of motivation to learn cooking and entered them into the Controlling for box, you would also get an output for higher order partial correlations.

5. Under **Tests of Significance**, click in the circle beside **Two-tailed**.
6. Click in the square beside **Display actual significance level**.
7. Now click on the **Options**. This brings up the **Partial Correlations: Options** dialog box as shown in Figure 14.25.

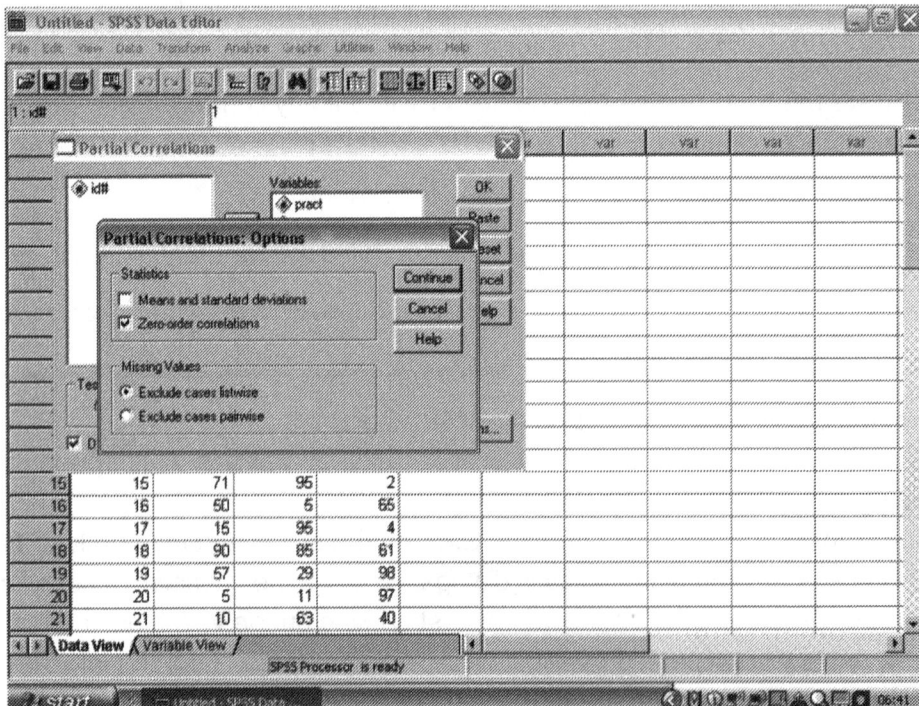

Figure 14.25: The Partial Correlations: Options dialog box.

8. Under **Statistics**, click in the box beside **Zero-order correlations**.
9. Under **Missing values**, click in the circle beside **Exclude cases pairwise**.
10. Click **Continue** to return to the **Partial Correlations** box and then click **OK**.

By requesting Zero-order correlations, you will be able to directly compare these with the partial correlation. By choosing Exclude cases pairwise, you will not lose too many cases if there were some missing values on the variables.

> Sometimes, when you have several variables with some scattered missing values among them and you do not use the "Exclude cases pairwise" option, SPSS can exclude so many cases that there would be too few left for the analysis or to calculate a suitable significance level. If this happens to you when using partial correlations (or, for that matter, any other SPSS programme), go back to the appropriate dialog box and check that you have chosen **Exclude cases pairwise** and not *Exclude cases listwise* and this may solve the problem.

Interpreting SPSS Output from the Partial Correlation Programme

The partial correlation output is interpreted by comparing the size of the original bivariate correlation coefficient with the resulting partial correlation coefficient. The SPSS output is very simple as shown in Table 14.7 (zero-order partials and partial correlations controlling for English).

From the correlation table shown in Table 14.7, you should be able to notice a very peculiar result. The correlation between scores from the Cookery Theory and Cookery Practical examinations is not significant at $r = -0.0084$ ($p = 0.95$). This would seem to mean, on the surface, that there is no relationship between achievement in Cookery Theory and achievement in Cookery Practice – a very strange result. Now, look at the correlation of English with Theory. It is positive and significant at $r = 0.39$; $p = 0.01$. This means that students who are good at reading and writing English scored well on the reading and writing test of Cookery Theory. On the other hand, the zero-order correlation between English and Cookery Practical was large and highly significant but negative, at $r = -0.7114$; $p<0.001$. This means that students who did well in the Practical did very poorly on the English test.

Taken together, these zero-order correlations suggest that the reason there is such a low correlation between Cooking Theory and Cooking Practice is not that the students who understand Cookery are not good at both Theory and Practice, but that many students who are good at the Practical have problems with reading and writing English. This is penalising them on the written Theory exam because it requires both reading and writing. We can test this by comparing the original Theory/Practical correlation of $r = -0.0084$ with the corresponding partial correlation that controls for differences in reading and writing by holding English constant.

From the output in Table 14.7, we see that the partial correlation of Theory with Practice (holding English constant) is $r = 0.41$ which is significant at $p = 0.018 < 0.05$.

Table 14.7: *SPSS Output Showing Zero Order Partials and Partial Correlations Controlling for English*

```
- - - P A R T I A L    C O R R E L A T I O N    C O E F F I C I E N T S
- - -

Zero Order Partials

                PRACT         THEORY        ENGLISH

PRACT           1.0000        -.0084        -.7114
                (     0)      (    38)      (    38)
                P=            P= .959       P= .000

THEORY          -.0084        1.0000        .3899
                (    38)      (     0)      (    38)
                P= .959       P=            P= .013

ENGLISH         -.7114        .3899         1.0000
                (    38)      (    38)      (     0)
                P= .000       P= .013       P=

(Coefficient / (D.F.) / 2-tailed Significance)

" . " is printed if a coefficient cannot be computed
```

```
- - - P A R T I A L    C O R R E L A T I O N    C O E F F I C I E N T S
- - -

Controlling for    ENGLISH

                PRACT         THEORY

PRACT           1.0000        .4157
                (     0)      (    37)
                P=            P= .008

THEORY          .4157         1.0000
                (    37)      (     0)
                P= .008       P=

(Coefficient / (D.F.) / 2-tailed Significance)

" . " is printed if a coefficient cannot be computed
```

This partial Theory/Practical correlation is much bigger than the original bivariate correlation between Cooking Theory and Cooking Practice ($r = 0.41$ is much larger than -0.0084) and tends to confirm that students who were proficient in reading and writing English were able to easily write their Cookery Theory examination whilst students who had difficulties reading and writing English were being unfairly penalised on the Theory exam. You could then report your results something similar to the following:

Partial correlation was used to explore the relationship between the students' scores in Practical Cooking (Pract) and scores on the Theory of Cooking (Theory) while controlling for scores on a test requiring an ability to read and write standard English (English). Zero-order correlations showed that there was no relationship between the scores on the written Theory test of Cooking and the Practical test of Cooking (r = -0.0084, p > 0.05). There was, however, a positive and significant relationship between the scores on the English test and scores on the written Theory of Cooking test (r = 0.3899, p < 0.05) suggesting that students who achieved high scores on the reading and writing English examination also achieved high scores on the reading and writing test of Cookery Theory. On the other hand, the zero-order correlation between English and Cookery Practical was large and highly significant but negative, at r = -0.71, p< 0.05 indicating that students who achieved high scores on the Practical Cooking examination achieved low scores on the English test. These results suggest that an ability to read and write English has a strong effect on the written examination on the Theory of Cooking. This was confirmed by the significant partial correlation between the written Theory test of cooking and the Practical test of cooking (r = 0.41, p < 0.05) that controlled for students' ability to read and write in Standard English.

15
Increasing the Reliability and Efficiency of Your Questionnaire

When you pretest your questionnaire, you are trying to identify the 'best' questions.

By omitting the 'not-so-good' questions from the final version of your questionnaire, you save time and resources.

A questionnaire can be used to measure a person's perceptions, knowledge or understanding of one or more constructs, or the traits or characteristics of a person. For example, if a researcher wants to test the hypothesis that there might be a connection between 'fear of examinations' and 'locus of control,' then she would need to measure both of these constructs. She might design a questionnaire with as many as 60 questions – twenty of these questions might ask about a student's fear of examinations (one construct) and the other 40 might be intended to assess the student's locus of control (a second construct). When analysing the responses, the researcher would total the student's answers to the 'fear of examinations' questions (after remembering to code for any reverse-scored questions) and use this total as the index to measure the student's 'fear of examinations.'

Then, the researcher would add the student's responses for the 'locus of control' questions to create an index indicating the student's 'locus of control.' A score on any one of these constructs is usually found by adding up responses to each question that contributes to that specific construct. Each of these sets of questions investigating the two constructs is considered a "sub-scale."

For any sub-scale, some of the questions will be better indicators of the construct than others. Some of the not-so-good questions might actually be tapping into some other construct and not contributing to what we think we are measuring at all. These questions reduce the reliability of our index and waste our time and resources. Remember, a 60-item questionnaire violates GAMTEAP Principles! This is why it is always best to pretest a questionnaire on a small sample (about 20 or more) so that the very best questions to use can be identified and the others discarded in the final version of the questionnaire.

Cronbach's Alpha

To identify the 'not-so-good' questions, use a statistic called Cronbach's alpha (C-alpha for short). C-alpha is based on the average correlation between questions so it is a reliability statistic measuring how consistently your questions in one sub-scale measure the same construct. This is useful because if all the questions are measuring the same construct then they will be highly correlated with each other and their average correlation will be high. A not-so-good question will not be measuring the same construct as the others and so will not be so highly correlated with them. Excluding this question will raise the overall average and the C-alpha will increase.

$$\alpha = \frac{N \cdot \bar{r}}{1 + (N-1) \cdot \bar{r}}$$

C-alpha uses the formula where N is the number of questions and r is the average correlation among the questions. You may notice from this formula that as the Number of questions increases so does the reliability, even if the average correlation stays the same. This is important to note because our method shows how to increase the reliability by actually reducing the Number of questions and, at the same time, increasing the efficiency of the questionnaire. The method is simply to:

(i)   Calculate C-alpha and use it to identify the worst item.
(ii)   Take out this item, and
(iii)   Precalculate C-alpha without the item to see if C-alpha increases.

If C-alpha does increase then you have done two useful things. You have reduced the number of questions by one and so made your questionnaire more efficient (a GAMTEAP Principle). You have also increased the reliability of your questionnaire. Do (i), (ii) and (iii) again, and again and again, until you can no longer increase C-alpha by dropping out questions from your questionnaire.

> Using C-alpha to identify the 'worst' items only works for unidimensional scales (sub-scales). A unidimensional scale means that all the questions must be intended to measure the same construct. If you have more than one sub-scale (i.e., if you are measuring different constructs) in your questionnaire, then you can use this iterative technique on each one separately – *never on combined constructs in the scale.*

Using the SPSS Programme to Determine the Value of C-alpha

To illustrate how to do this with SPSS, we are using the data from a pretest of 12 questions administered to a sample of 158 subjects.[1] Figure 15.1 shows the SPSS data matrix for the first few subjects.

---

1. Although we would liked to have given you the complete data set for this exercise, it was just too large so you will have to calculate the C-alpha using your own data.

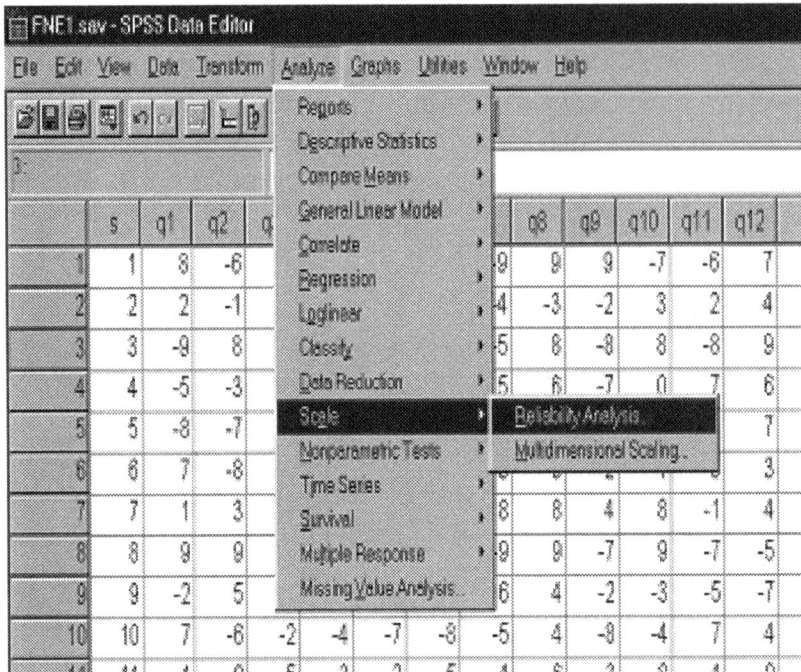

Figure 15.1: Sample data matrix for a 12-question draft questionnaire. S stands for "subject identification number" and q1 to q12 stands for the number of each item on the questionnaire.

To calculate C-alpha, open your SPSS file and:

1. Click on Analyze. Scroll down and click on **Scale ▶** .
2. Click on **Reliability Analysis...** (shown in Figure 15.1).
3. This brings up the **Reliability Analysis** dialog box shown in Figure 15.2.
4. Click and drag to highlight all the questions in your sub-scale. Then click on the arrow to place them into the space under **Items:**
5. Make sure that you select **Alpha** in the **Model:** box. This stands for C-alpha.

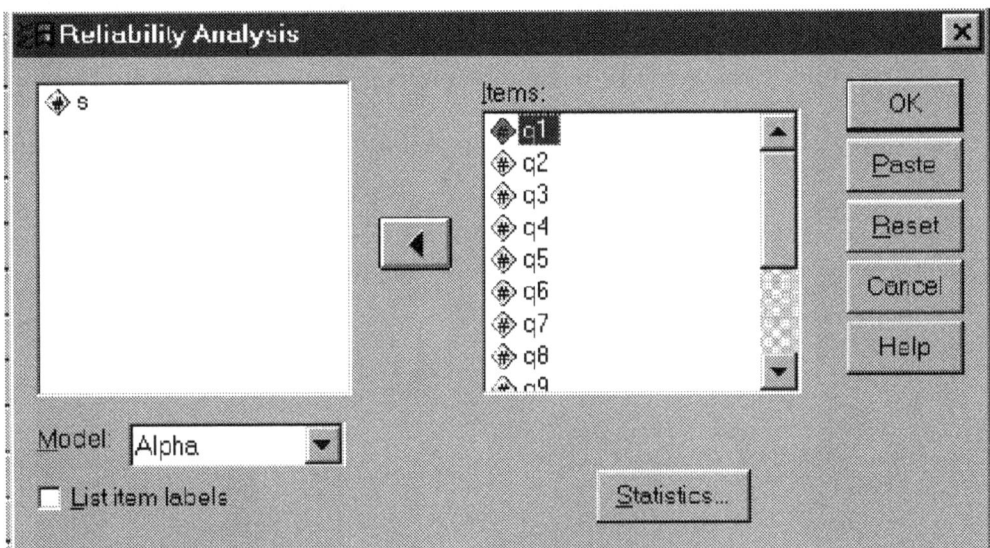

Figure 15.2: In the Statistics dialog box for Reliability Analysis, all questionnaire items have been placed into the Items: box and Alpha has been chosen for the Model.

6. Click on **Statistics ...** this brings up the **Reliability Analysis: Statistics** dialog box shown in **Figure 15.3.**

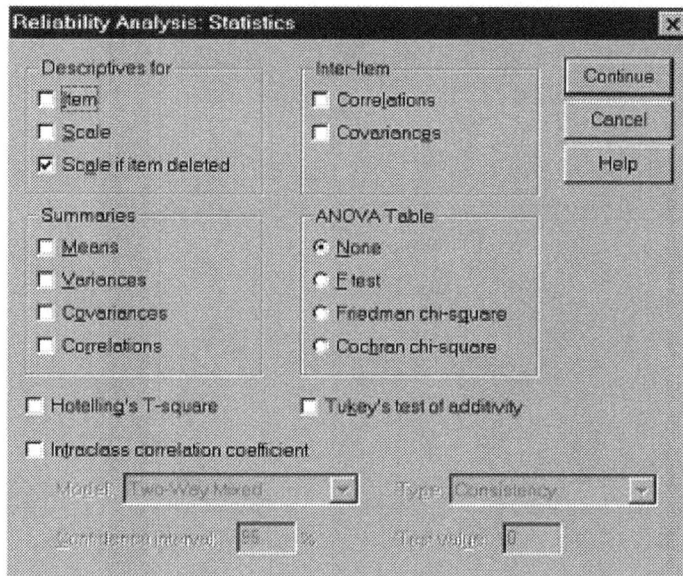

Figure 15.3: The Reliability Analysis:Statistics dialog box in the SPSS programme for reliability analysis.

7. Click in the box beside **Scale if item is deleted.**
8. Click **Continue** to return to the Reliability box and click **OK**.

The output from the SPSS programme should look similar to that shown in Table 15.1. Look at the last line of Table 15.1 and you can see that C-alpha of the pre-questionnaire items is only Alpha = 0.5701 but it should be at least 0.75 to be acceptable. Next, look under the column headed "Alpha if Item Deleted" (at the right) to identify the largest number. This is 0.6134, which corresponds to Question 1, so Q1 is the worst question. This means that if we deleted Q1 then the C-alpha of our scale would go up to 0.6134. This would be higher than if we deleted any of the other questions and would lead to an increase over the current C-alpha value of 0.5701. So, it is worth dropping this question and then recalculating the Reliability Analysis once Question 1 has been removed.

Finally, look under the column "Corrected Item-Total Correlation" and you will also see that Q1 shows the lowest correlation with the corrected total of the questions (-0.0646). This is a negative correlation indicating that it has been detracting from our sub-scale. This gives us further proof that we would be correct to remove it.

Table 15.1: *Typical Output from Entering 12 Questions in a Reliability Analysis for C-alpha.*

R E L I A B I L I T Y   A N A L Y S I S   -   S C A L E   (A L P H A)

Item-total Statistics

	Scale Mean if Item Deleted	Scale Variance if Item Deleted	Corrected Item-Total Correlation	Alpha if Item Deleted
Q1	8.1392	930.8467	-.0646	**.6134**
Q2	7.8544	764.5838	.3823	.5120
Q3	7.6266	926.3883	-.0420	.6046
Q4	9.7089	867.9402	.1253	.5714
Q5	9.2025	724.4810	.5511	.4723
Q6	9.2722	733.7535	.5071	.4822
Q7	8.0759	754.0579	.4355	.4999
Q8	7.6772	758.3983	.4394	.5003
Q9	7.3101	884.4319	.0626	.5860
Q10	8.1456	747.1952	.4315	.4990
Q11	8.0696	887.9633	.0788	.5796
Q12	6.2468	929.1043	-.0428	.6024

Reliability Coefficients

N of Cases =   158.0   N of Items = 12

Alpha =   .5701

Go back into the Reliability Analysis dialog box and remove Question 1 from the Items: box. You do this by clicking on Q1 to highlight it and then clicking on the arrow pointing to the box on the left. All the other settings remain the same so we don't have to change them.

After you have clicked OK, you will see a second table (Table 15.2) showing the new statistics with Q1 removed. Compare the C-alphas from the two tables and you can see that after removing Q 1, the C-alpha has increased to the number promised by results shown in Table 15.1, namely 0.6134.

Table 15.2: *Results of C-alpha When Q1 has Been Removed*

R E L I A B I L I T Y   A N A L Y S I S   -   S C A L E   (A L P H A)

Item-total Statistics

	Scale Mean if Item Deleted	Scale Variance if Item Deleted	Corrected Item-Total Correlation	Alpha if Item Deleted
Q2	7.1456	733.5774	.4357	.5523
Q3	6.9177	921.2225	-.0695	.6559
Q4	9.0000	848.2803	.1407	.6159
Q5	8.4937	711.9968	.5485	.5280
Q6	8.5633	705.8272	.5550	.5250
Q7	7.3671	722.6797	.4932	.5398
Q8	6.9684	731.0754	.4846	.5431
Q9	6.6013	881.8591	.0291	.6405
Q10	7.4367	724.4385	.4603	.5450
Q11	7.3608	881.5569	.0535	.6318
Q12	5.5380	926.8616	-.0801	.6550

Reliability Coefficients

N of Cases =   158.0   N of Items = 11

Alpha =   .6134

Notice that the new largest number in the column headed 'Alpha if Item Deleted' is now 0.6559 corresponding to Q3. This means that if we rerun the Reliability Analysis without Q3 then our C-alpha should go up to 0.6559. When we have correlated items contributing to an unidimensional scale, we can keep doing this iteration until we find that none of the numbers in the 'Alpha if Item Deleted' column promises a C-alpha larger than the one we last calculated. This is the time to stop dropping questions from the analysis, because if we continued then the C-alpha would start to go back down indicating that our questionnaire is becoming less reliable.

Table 15.3 shows consecutive iterations with these same data all in one table. You can see how, at each iteration, the worst question is identified and dropped from the analysis. Notice, however, that at iteration 7 the worst question is identified as Q10 and we are promised a C-alpha of 0.8129 if we drop Q10 from our questionnaire. BUT, at that stage we already have a bigger C-alpha of 0.8492 so we will lose reliability if we continue. Hence, with this data we would stop at iteration 7 with the questions we had been left with, viz. the six questions Q2, Q5, Q6, Q7, Q8 and Q10.

Table 15.3: *Consecutive Iterations With All the Data in One Table*

	Alpha if Item Deleted									
Iteration	1	2	3	4	5	6	7	8	9	10
Q1	**0.6134**									
Q2	0.5120	0.5523	0.6043	0.6622	0.7309	0.7775	0.8092	0.7848	**0.7646**	
Q3	0.6046	**0.6559**								
Q4	0.5714	0.6169	0.6583	0.7114	0.7742	**0.8294**				
Q5	0.4723	0.5280	0.5750	0.6382	0.7087	0.7643	0.7924	0.7680	0.7400	0.6441
Q6	0.4822	0.5250	0.5664	0.6360	0.7045	0.7541	0.7895	0.7640	0.7372	0.6820
Q7	0.4999	0.5398	0.5820	0.6422	0.7108	0.7640	0.7978	0.7657	0.7522	**0.7248**
Q8	0.5003	0.5431	0.5864	0.6500	0.7147	0.7702	0.8097	**0.7988**		
Q9	0.5860	0.6406	0.7021	**0.7616**						
Q10	0.4990	0.5460	0.5924	0.6532	0.7191	0.7742	**0.8129**			
Q11	0.5796	0.6318	0.6808	0.7373	**0.8033**					
Q12	0.6024	0.6550	**0.7068**							
C-alpha	0.5701	0.6134	0.6559	0.7068	0.7616	0.8033	0.8294	0.8129	0.7988	0.7646
Maximum	**0.6134**	**0.6559**	**0.7068**	**0.7616**	**0.8033**	**0.8294**	**0.8129**	**0.7988**	**0.7646**	**0.7248**
difference	0.0433	0.0425	0.0509	0.0548	0.0417	0.0261	-0.0165	-0.0141	-0.0342	-0.0398

This example illustrates how unacceptable items of a questionnaire may be deleted using C-alpha. In our example, we increased the initial value of C-alpha = 0.5701 by identifying, one-by-one, the most unreliable items in the sub-scale and then deleting them, again one-by-one, to get a very acceptable maximum reliability of C-alpha = 0.8294. Note that the new questionnaire now has half the number of questions but it can be considered more reliable!

You must take care when using this technique because the concept of unidimensionality is all 'in the mind.' It is just the degree of approximation you make that allows you to ignore the differences between things and consider them to be countable the same. Every time a question is dropped you will lose the information that it offered. Hence, look at the content of the question and the actual increase in reliability you will get if you drop it. Then make the choice of what you need more – the increase in reliability or the extra information the question offered.

> It is usually better to be approximately right than precisely wrong!

Data Reduction - Exploratory Factor Analysis

After your participants have answered your questionnaire, you can find out which factors[2] were important, which were inter correlated, and which items in your questionnaire were most important. Although there are several types of factor analyses, they are all used to look at long lists of variables in order to find which variables from similar groups (or are 'clumped' together or belong together). As one example of using factor analyses, we may have a long list of questions on a questionnaire and we can use factor analysis to identify separate groups of questions in which each group of questions measures one particular aspect of the whole questionnaire. These groups of similar variables are called factors. Each factor (group of variables) will measure one particular aspect and we can identify what this aspect is simply by looking at what is common about the variables in that particular group.

For example, suppose we made up a Self-Esteem Questionnaire containing as many as 40 questions. If we used a factor analysis, we could identify perhaps three main groups of questions. When we look at the content of the questions in the first group we might realise that they are all about self-esteem at school, so we would call this factor something like "Academic Self-Esteem." The second group of questions might all be asking about relationships with friends, so we would call this factor something like "Peer Self-Esteem." The third group of questions might be asking about what the person looks like and so we could call this factor "Physical Self-Esteem."

There could also be some of the 40 questions left over that did not fit into any group and we could not find a fitting name for those. In addition, if these leftover questions were not very important when compared to the three factors, then we might not want to consider them any further and omit them from the questionnaire. You can understand from this example how the original 40 questions, which seemed to be asking about many aspects of Self-Esteem, have been grouped into only three named factors and the less important questions discarded. It is then possible to use the original 40 questions to work out just 3 scores (factor scores) for each respondent. Because of this conceptual reduction (that is reducing 40 items down to 3 factors), the method is sometimes known as a data reduction method.

---

2. Do not mix up factors within a questionnaire with factors as in factorial analysis. These particular factors are groups of similar variables that you identified as important in your questionnaire.

Varimax Factor Analysis

One of the most commonly used types of factor analyses, Varimax Factor Analysis, is explained in this section. The main advantage of this method is that the resulting factors are independent of each other. This means that they do not over-lap; because they are not related, each factor explains a completely different aspect of what is being measured.

When you are discussing your findings, you will need to be able to tell how important a factor is, which *factors* are more important, and also which *questions* within each factor are the most important. To decide on the importance of the factors, we look at how much of the variation within the data they can account for. A good set of factors will account for more than 50% of the variation between the responses to the questionnaire. However, if your respondents have not been answering the questions as systematically as you hoped (because they were not being conscientious or because the questions were on too many different topics), then there will be very little structure in the data for factor analysis to recognise – another case of GI-GO (garbage in – garbage out) and another reason to carefully plan and administer your questionnaire. If your factor analysis does result in recognisable factors, then you can tell which questions are the main ones in each group by their factor loading (correlation between the question and the factor).

The Varimax Factor Analysis method groups together those questions that are inter-correlated. This means that, as a rough guide, you will need at least 20 respondents for each pair of questions to get sufficient data for the computer programme to work on. For example, if you have 20 questions (that is 10 pairs) then you need at least 10 X 20 = 200 respondents who have answered **all** the questions. To allow for blanks and other missing data you should increase this to 225 for good measure.

Using Varimax Factor Rotation to Develop a Questionnaire

In order to develop questions for a questionnaire on what motivated people to choose teaching as a profession, 96 student teachers and 4 lecturers were individually interviewed and 30 other student teachers were interviewed in focus groups. Data from the 130 interviews were coalesced into 19 most prominent reasons and these formed the original set of questions that were then administered to 1,444 teacher trainees in Jamaica (Bastick, 2000). The example that follows used the Varimax Factor Analysis and led to the development of the final questionnaire called *The EIA Factor Model of Teacher Motivation* and is shown in Figure 15.4.

The data matrix was prepared in Excel and imported into SPSS for factor analysis in order to identify any important groups of questions that could better explain why teacher trainees choose to be teachers. Only 845 questionnaires had complete responses so only the analysis for these is illustrated. Figure 15.5 shows what the data file looked like in SPSS. It shows the responses of the first 8 respondents to all 19 questions, labeled Q1 to Q19.

Figure 15.4: The final version of the EIA Factor Model of Teacher Motivation

FACTOR 1		
Q11	0.701	Teaching is the profession with the most holidays
Q10	0.667	Fees for Teachers' College are affordable
Q7	0.648	I will have enough time to earn extra money
Q8	0.604	It allows me to be a manager
Q16	0.561	It offers job security
Q9	0.561	The salary will be adequate to meet my demands
Q4	0.508	Teachers enjoy good status in the society as a whole
FACTOR 2		
Q15	0.839	It is the profession I have always wanted
Q17	0.831	I wanted to
Q12	0.587	I see it as a life-long career
FACTOR 3		
Q19	0.770	I can make a worthwhile contribution to the social development of others
Q13	0.764	I can make a worthwhile contribution to the academic development of others
Q14	0.596	I love children

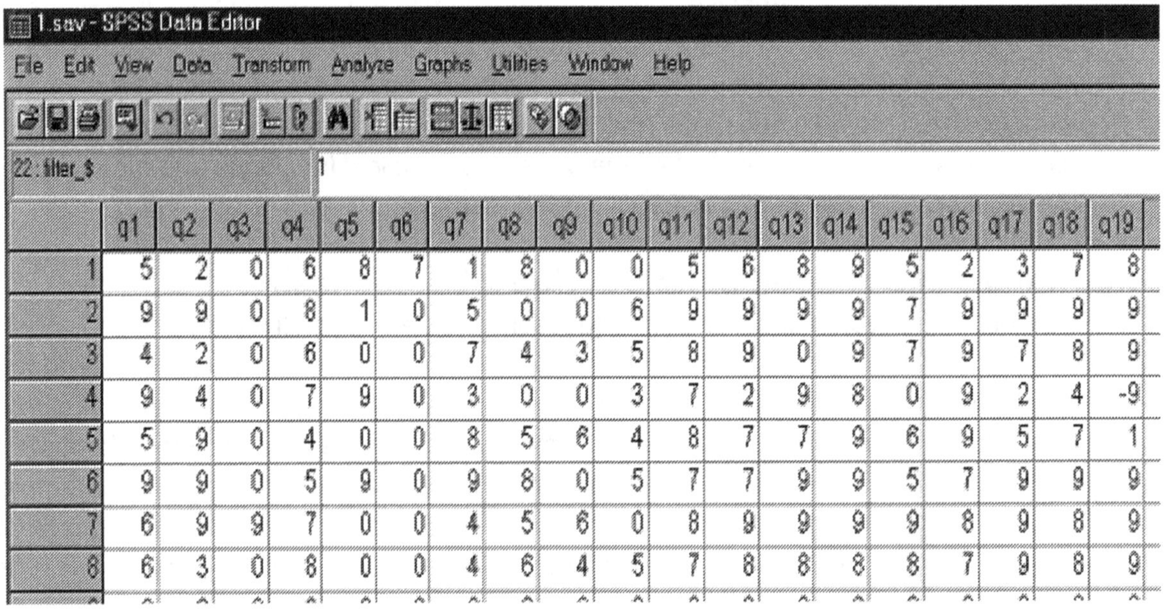

	q1	q2	q3	q4	q5	q6	q7	q8	q9	q10	q11	q12	q13	q14	q15	q16	q17	q18	q19
1	5	2	0	6	8	7	1	8	0	0	5	6	8	9	5	2	3	7	8
2	9	9	0	8	1	0	5	0	0	6	9	9	9	9	7	9	9	9	9
3	4	2	0	6	0	0	7	4	3	5	8	9	0	9	7	9	7	8	9
4	9	4	0	7	9	0	3	0	0	3	7	2	9	8	0	9	2	4	-9
5	5	9	0	4	0	0	8	5	6	4	8	7	7	9	6	9	5	7	1
6	9	9	0	5	9	0	9	8	0	5	7	7	9	9	5	7	9	9	9
7	6	9	9	7	0	0	4	5	6	0	8	9	9	9	9	8	9	8	9
8	6	3	0	8	0	0	4	6	4	5	7	8	8	8	8	7	9	8	9

Figure 15.5: An example of the SPSS data file for the first 8 respondents.

You do a factor analysis in two passes – the first time is to decide the best number of factors and the second time is to run the analysis with this chosen number of factors.

To compute the factor analysis

1. Open your SPSS file. Click on **Analyze** and scroll down until you see **Data Reduction – Factor.**
2. This brings up the **Factor Analysis** dialog box. You need to enter all the questions into the **Variables:** box on the left.
3. Click on **Extraction...** to open the **Factor Analysis: Extraction** dialog box shown in Figure 15.6.

4. In the **Extraction** dialog box, beside **Method:** make sure that **Principal components** is chosen. Under **Analyze**, click on the circle beside **Correlation matrix**. Under **Display**, click on both **Unrotated factor solution** and **Scree plot**. Under **Extract**, click in the circle beside **Eigenvalues over:** and then make sure that the box beside this is **1**.
5. Click **Continue** to return to the :**Factor Analysis** box
6. Click **Rotation...** to open the **Rotation** Dialog Box shown in Figure 15.7.
7. Under **Method,** click on the circle beside **Varimax** and make sure that all the other circles are blank.
8. Under **Display,** click on the square beside **Rotated solution.**You can leave **Maximum Iterations for Convergence:** as *set.*
9. Click **Continue** to return.

Figure 15.6

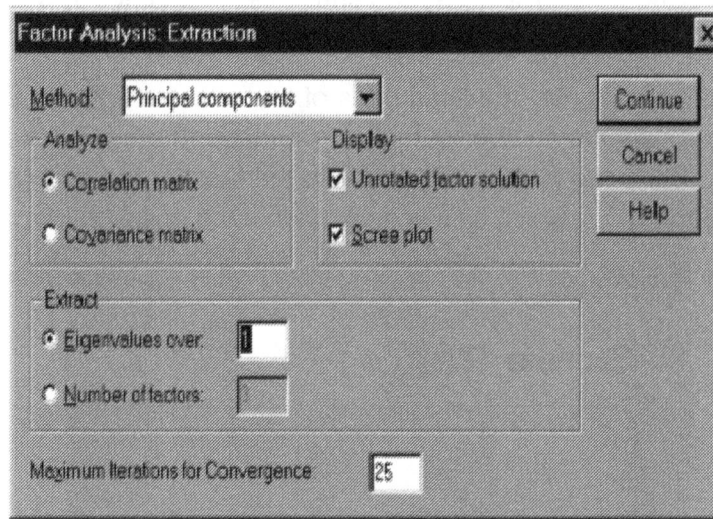

Figure 15.7

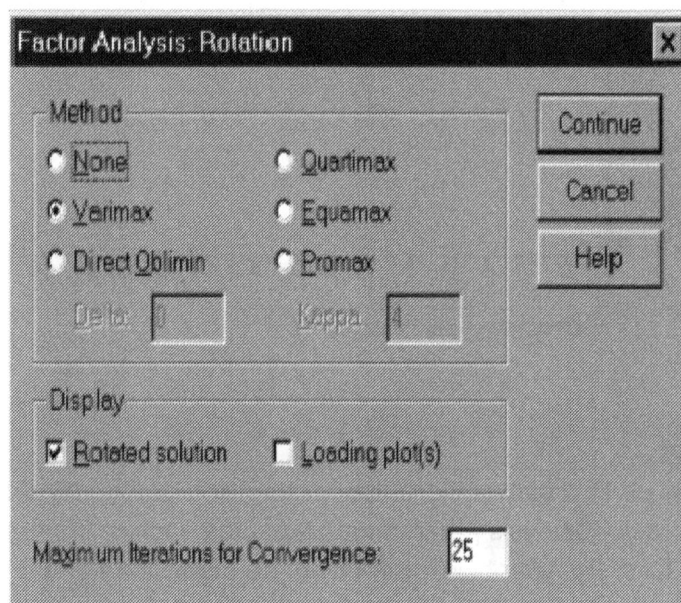

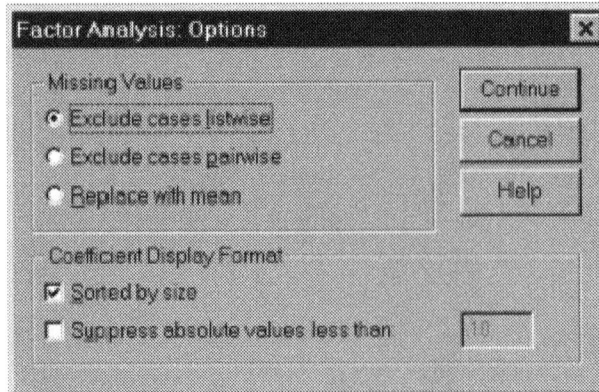

Figure 15.8

10. Click **Options…** to open the **Factor Analysis: Options** dialog box (Figure 15.8)
11. Under **Missing values**, click in the circle beside **Exclude cases listwise**.
12. Under **Coefficient Display Format**, click on **Sorted by Size**.
13. Click **Continue** to return to the main box and click **OK** to run the program.

In this first pass, the main parts of the output are (i) the Scree plot (see Figure 15.9) which shows the number of factors you need, (ii) the variance of the factors (see Table 15.4), which shows the importance of the factors and (iii) the rotated component matrix (see Table 15.5) which shows how much each question contributes to each factor.

Figure 15.9: A scree plot showing the point at which the shape of the curve changes direction.

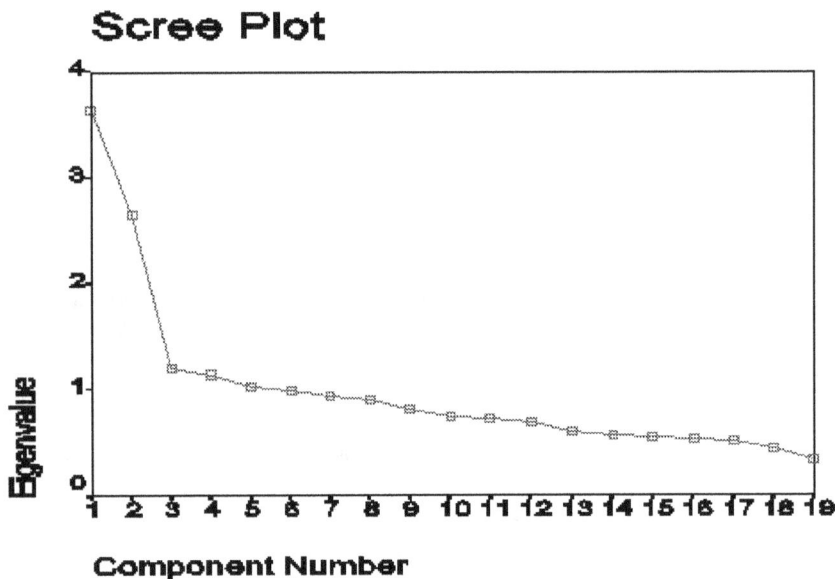

The Scree Plot

Figure 15.9 shows the output in the form of a scree plot. To obtain a scree plot, the SPSS factor analysis programme computes each of the eigenvalues and draws a plot of the results. For your own information: an eigenvalue of a factor denotes the total amount of variance explained by that factor. Each little box represents a factor (or component) and you can see that there are as many factors as there are questions (viz. 19). However, not all of these questions are important. The height of each little box (the Eigenvalue) shows the importance of each of the factors and the important factors come first, on the steep part of the diagram. As you can see, the line starts above the component number 1 at 3.68 goes sharply down to 2.64 above the component number 2, then to 1.19 above component number 3. The eigenvalues above the component numbers 4 -19 are all roughly similar – ranging from about 1.143 to about 0.332 above the component numbers.

In this example, three important factors have been identified and all the others are more or less no different from each other. The idea is to retain the most important factors (the ones above the "elbow" or bend) in the plot as they are the factors considered to contribute the most to an explanation of the variance found in the set of data.

Next, to see how important these factors are, look at part of the output labeled 'Total Variance Explained' (Table 15.4). This table corresponds to the Scree Plot. In the first column, "Total," you can see the actual numbers of the first three components. In the second column "% of Variance", the first three numbers are very different from each other (that is, there is a large difference between them), 19.084, 13.935 and 6.309. These correspond to the first three factors on the Scree Plot. This table confirms that we have three clear factors and that the three factors together account for 39.328% of the total variance among the 845 responses to the 19 questions.

> The numbers under component in the Total Variance Explained box are the numbers of the components **NOT** the question numbers!

Table 15.4: *Importance of the First Three Factors Shown by the SPSS Output of the Varimax Factor Analysis Programme.*

Total Variance Explained

Component	Initial Eigenvalues		
	Total	% of Variance	Cumulative %
1	3.626	19.084	19.084
2	2.648	13.935	33.019
3	1.199	6.309	39.328
4	1.143	6.016	45.344
5	1.036	5.453	50.798
6	.989	5.207	56.004
7	.936	4.926	60.930
8	.906	4.770	65.701
9	.808	4.255	69.956
10	.734	3.865	73.821
11	.725	3.816	77.637
12	.690	3.631	81.268
13	.609	3.205	84.473
14	.576	3.032	87.505
15	.551	2.900	90.405
16	.540	2.841	93.247
17	.510	2.684	95.930
18	.442	2.324	98.254
19	.332	1.746	100.000

Extraction Method: Principal Component Analysis.

Next, look at Table 15.5, the Rotated Component Matrix, to see which questions make up these three factor groups. This table shows all the factors that had eigenvalues greater than one, which is the SPSS default in the Extraction Dialog box. However we are only interested in the first three factors (or components). The numbers in the columns are called "factor loadings" and they show how important each question is to the factor for any column.

To choose the questions that are important for the first three factors go to Column 4. You use Column 4 because the scree plot showed us that component numbers 4 - 19 contributed little to the variance in our questionnaire. Look down the column and find the largest number, which is .830. This factor loading corresponds to Q2. Because we asked for 'Sort by size' in the Options dialog box, Q2 and all the questions below it are the ones that do not contribute much to the three factors. This means that Q2, Q1, Q6 and Q5 can be discarded in the second pass and go for three factors in the Extraction Dialog box. A finer analysis of the communalities and factor loadings for this data showed that Q3 and Q18 should also be dropped.

Table 15.5: *The Rotated Component Matrix Showing that Q2 Has the Largest Number in Component 4*

Rotated Component Matrix^a

	Component				
	1	2	3	4	5
Q11	.657	-7.3E-02	4.83E-02	7.98E-02	.229
Q10	.657	-2.0E-02	3.24E-02	-5.0E-02	6.79E-02
Q7	.634	7.83E-03	-.226	-3.5E-02	.189
Q8	.630	-8.7E-02	.210	5.71E-02	-.158
Q9	.604	.348	-.210	-2.0E-02	-.134
Q4	.522	.117	.147	.261	-.142
Q16	.490	.217	.302	5.07E-02	.339
Q15	-3.3E-02	.828	.163	.160	-4.8E-02
Q17	-4.5E-03	.798	.237	7.44E-02	-1.0E-02
Q12	.127	.586	.266	3.78E-03	-6.8E-02
Q19	-3.2E-02	.177	.747	9.55E-02	-1.4E-02
Q13	.124	.138	.634	.102	-.331
Q14	1.50E-02	.267	.539	8.38E-03	-7.4E-02
Q18	.223	.106	.524	4.92E-02	.442
Q3	.183	-.258	-.341	.115	.326
Q2	.148	-6.3E-02	4.94E-02	.830	-5.9E-02
Q1	-5.2E-02	.357	8.08E-02	.680	5.74E-03
Q6	.162	4.00E-02	-.177	-7.1E-02	.569
Q5	.172	.279	2.80E-02	4.20E-02	-.468

Extraction Method: Principal Component Analysis.
Rotation Method: Varimax with Kaiser Normalization.
a. Rotation converged in 7 iterations.

For the second pass, take out from the Variable Box the last six question in Table 15.5, namely Q2, Q1, Q6 and Q5, and also Q3 and Q18. In the Extraction box, we now ask for only three factors and rerun the analysis. The Rotated Component Matrix for the remaining 13 questions is shown in Table 15.6.

Table 15.6: *The SPSS Output Showing the Final Rotated Factor Matrix for 13 Questions.*

Rotated Component Matrix[a]

	Component		
	1	2	3
Q11	.701	-8.2E-02	1.66E-02
Q10	.667	-1.3E-02	-3.1E-02
Q7	.648	-6.3E-02	-.203
Q8	.604	-7.7E-02	.235
Q16	.561	.218	.184
Q9	.561	.394	-.194
Q4	.508	.187	.157
Q15	-3.2E-02	.839	.201
Q17	6.19E-03	.831	.185
Q12	.114	.587	.311
Q19	-1.4E-02	.182	.770
Q13	9.67E-02	.131	.764
Q14	2.17E-02	.230	.596

Extraction Method: Principal Component Analysis.
Rotation Method: Varimax with Kaiser Normalizatio

a. Rotation converged in 5 iterations.

To be able to interpret the information that can be found in Table 15.6, look at Figure 15.10. In this figure, we have removed some of the lines and added others to show you how to read the output. The next two paragraphs explain what all these numbers mean.

Rotated Component Matrix

		Component		
		1	2	3
	Q11	**0.701**	-0.082	0.017
	Q10	**0.667**	-0.013	-0.031
	Q7	**0.648**	-0.063	-0.203
	Q8	**0.604**	-0.077	0.235
Questions in Factor 1	Q16	**0.561**	0.218	0.184
	Q9	**0.561**	0.394	-0.194
	Q4	**0.508**	0.187	0.157
Questions in Factor 2	Q15	-0.032	**0.839**	0.201
	Q17	0.006	**0.831**	0.185
	Q12	0.114	**0.587**	0.311
Questions in Factor 3	Q19	-0.014	0.182	**0.770**
	Q13	0.097	0.131	**0.764**
	Q14	0.022	0.230	**0.596**

Largest # in column 2

Largest # in column 3

Figure 15.10: Rotated component matrix for 13 selected questions showing how to determine which questions define each factor.

To find the questions that define Factor 2, look down Column 2 for the largest factor loading. It is 0.839 and refers to Q15. This means that all of the questions above Q15 describe Factor 1. These are Q11, Q10, Q7, Q8, Q16, Q9 and Q4 in order of importance. The contribution of a question to a factor is given by its factor loading. You can see that the factor loadings have been sorted as we requested and that Q11 correlates 0.701 with Factor 1.

Next, look down Column 3 for the largest number to find the cut point for Factor 2. The largest number in Column 3 is 0.770 corresponding to Q19. Hence the questions above this cut point (that are not in the previous factor) will describe Factor 2. These questions are Q15, Q17 and Q12. The remaining three questions describe Factor 3.

The importance of these three factors is given by the variation that they explain as shown in the output 'Total Variance Explained' (Table 15.7). The first factor is very important at 24.24% compared to factor 2 at 18.144% and factor three at only 8.582%. However, together these three factors explain 50.966% of the variation in the responses to these 13 questions.

Table 15.7: *Output Showing the Total Variance Explained*

Total Variance Explained

Component	Initial Eigenvalues		
	Total	% of Variance	Cumulative %
1	3.151	24.240	24.240
2	2.359	18.144	42.384
3	1.116	8.582	50.966
4	.871	6.703	57.669
5	.810	6.229	63.898
6	.781	6.006	69.904
7	.722	5.556	75.460
8	.694	5.335	80.795
9	.587	4.516	85.311
10	.551	4.242	89.554
11	.543	4.180	93.734
12	.467	3.589	97.323
13	.348	2.677	100.000

Interpreting the Factors: What Is Each Factor Measuring?

This is a good model. But what are the meanings of the three factors? What are they measuring? To find out what each group of questions is measuring, you need to look at what each question in the factor is asking. Start with the most important questions to get a rough idea, and then refine your description by considering successively the less important questions in the group.

Look back at Figure 15.4 showing the final version of the EIA Factor Model of Teacher Motivation. As you read the most important question in each section you will begin to realise that Factor 1 is measuring Extrinsic Motivation, Factor 2 is measuring Intrinsic Motivation and Factor 3 is measuring Altruistic Motivation. Further, the relative importance of these factors in motivating teacher trainees to become teachers is given by the variation explained, viz. 24%, 18% and 8%. So we can see that teacher trainees are mainly extrinsically motivated. These 13 questions were renumbered and are given on the questionnaire shown in Figure 15.4. This is now called the EIA Factor Model of Teacher Motivation and it has been used to show that experienced teachers are much more intrinsically motivated than teacher trainees.

These three motivational measures for each respondent can be calculated and saved by the SPSS programme for further analyses. These are called Factor Scores and the three scores for each respondent will replace the original thirteen responses. To do this, simply select **Save as variables** in the Scores dialog box, and click **Continue** (see Figure 15.11).

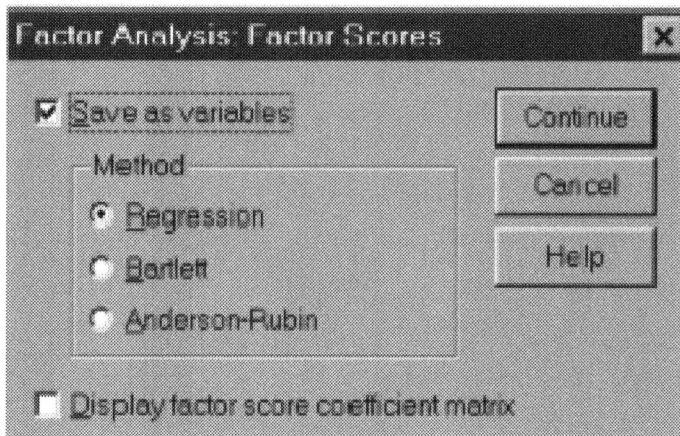

Figure 15.11: Saving factor scores as variables for each respondent.

In Figure 15.12, these new scores have been added to the end of your SPSS data under the headings of fac1_1, fac2_1 and fac3_1. These should be renamed with more meaningful names in the SPSS Variable View window. These variables can now be used for further analyses, as for example, to find if female teachers are more motivated than male teachers. Actually, our research discovered that they are more motivated and motivated differently. Similarly, we could test if older teacher trainees are more motivated than younger teachers or if primary school teachers are motivated differently than secondary school teachers. We can even use this questionnaire to compare the motivations of teachers in the classroom with those in administrative positions or to compare the motivations of teachers in different countries – all based on this EIA Factor Model of Teacher Motivation!

Figure 15.12: An example of the SPSS data matrix showing that the new variables have been added to the data collection.

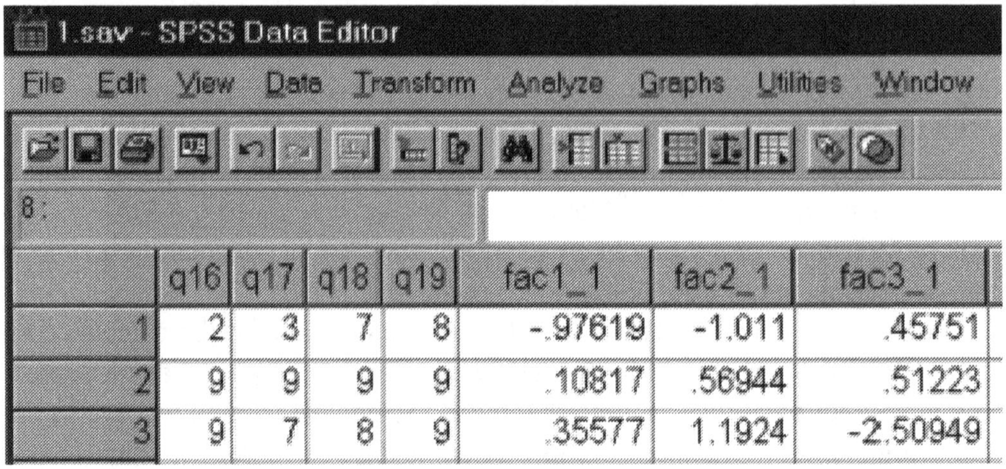
1.sav - SPSS Data Editor
File Edit View Data Transform Analyze Graphs Utilities Window
8 :
q16 q17 q18 q19 fac1_1 fac2_1 fac3_1
1 2 3 7 8 -.97619 -1.011 .45751
2 9 9 9 9 .10817 .56944 .51223
3 9 7 8 9 .35577 1.1924 -2.50949

16
Parametric Tests

(ii) The t-test
An Explanation of What the *t*-test Does

You use a *t*-test when you want to determine if the mean scores of *two sets of measures* differ significantly from each other. As an example of when to use a *t*-test, we might want to find out whether the average height of men is the same as the average height of women or whether the heights are significantly different from each other. In other words, we want to determine whether two sets of measurements differ. To find this out, we take a random sample of men and a random sample of women and measure their heights. We then calculate the average height of both our samples and compare these two averages by finding the difference between them.

Look at the shapes in Figure 16.1. Each curve represents the measurements found when measuring heights of males and females. The curve with the dotted line shows the sample of women with their average height marked in the middle by the dotted line. The curve with the single line shows the sample of men with their average height marked in the middle by a single line.

Figure 16.1: The dotted line in the middle of each curve represents the mean height for females and the straight line shows the mean height for males.

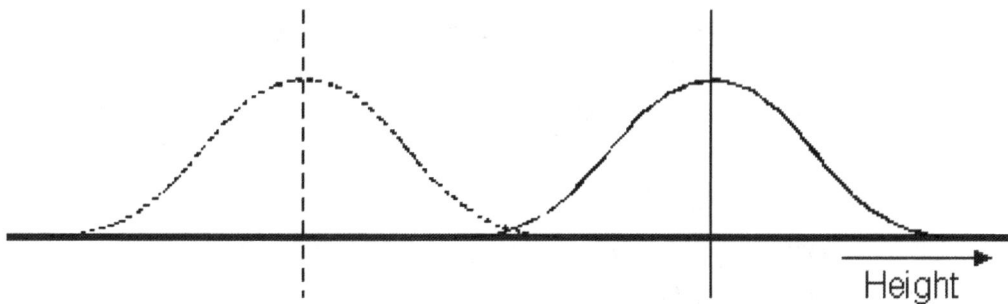

Figure 16.1 shows us that there was such a large difference between the means of the two samples that it is highly probable that the two samples came from two distributions – each with a different mean. This might have happened by chance, but if the samples were chosen at random, then it is highly improbable that such different samples could have come from distributions with the same means. In other words, our height measurements could not have come from a population in which men and women were, on average, of the same height. When there is a large difference between the sample means, this shows us that the measurements are unlikely to have come from populations with the same means.

When you used the *t*-test to determine whether the two measurements were significantly different from each other, the *t*-test would most likely give us something like a probability of less than 5% which is written in the standard form as $p < 0.05$.[1] We would report this difference as being significant at the 0.05 level. The null hypothesis was: "There was no difference between the mean height of men and the mean height of women in the population" and this would be rejected at the 5% level of significance.

Using SPSS for the *t*-test Statistic

In 'SPSS language,' related *t*-tests are referred to as *Paired-Samples t-tests* and unrelated *t*-tests are called *Independent Samples t-tests*. So, do not get confused if you see *t*-tests referred to as related or unrelated.

Use the *t*-test for paired samples if the data consists of two sets of scores measured on the *same* participant or thing, etc. (as in the data we have been using as an example for determining correlations). **One** person produced **two** sets of measurements.

Use the *t*-test for independent samples if the data consists of measures from *two different* sets of people, things, etc., (for example, the plants growing under blue or green lights or two different sets of people (a group of females and a group of males) writing the same test. **Two** different sets of people produced **one** measurement.)

t-tests for Related Measures (the Paired-Samples t-test)

To show you how to use the SPSS programme for *t*-tests we are using the same data that we used to show you how to calculate correlations (correlate13.sav). For this example, V1 represents scores from a reading test and V2 scores from a math test and we will use the null hypothesis stating that there will be no differences between the two scores. Because the same subjects wrote both sets of tests, we will use the Paired-Samples (related) *t*-test.

Open the SPSS programme:
1. Click on **Analyze**. Scroll down and click on **Compare Means ▶** .
2. Click on **Paired-Samples T Test**.
3. This opens the **Paired-Samples T Test** dialog window. In the space at the left where all the variables are displayed, click on V1 and on V2, then on the ▶ to move them both into the Paired Variable(s) side.
4. Click **OK**.

---

1. Remember that when you see $p < 0.05$, it means that there are only 5 chances in 100 that you got this result by chance. Alternatively, you can be 95% certain that you did *not* get this result by chance.

Once you click OK, the output of the *t*-test appears on the screen. The SPSS procedure gives you three pieces of information: Table 16.1(a) shows the means and standard deviations of the two sets of scores and the standard error of the means (which can be used for calculating confidence intervals). Note that these are descriptive statistics that should be reported in the results section. Table 16.1(b) gives the correlation between the paired samples. Note that if you compare this correlation to the correlation obtained for the Pearson *r* (*r* = 0.811) obtained in Table 14.1 (p. 159), you can see that they are similar. Finally you see the results of the *t*-test in Table 16.1(c), the *t*-test paired samples.

Table 16.1(a): *SPSS Output Showing the Means and Standard Deviation of Two Sets of Variables*

		Means	N	Std. Deviation	Std Error Mean
Pair 1	V1	46.47	19	28.96	6.636
	V2	54.37	19	32.449	7.444

Table 16.1(b): *SPSS Output Showing the Correlation between the Paired Samples*

	N	Correlation	Sig.
Pair 1 V1 & V2	19	0.809	0

Table 16.1(c): *SPSS Output Showing Results of the Paired-Samples Test (t-test)*

	Paired Differences							
				95% Confidence Interval of the Differences				
	Mean	Std. Deviation	Std Error Mean	Lower	Upper	t	df	Sig 2-tailed
Pair V1 - V2	-7.9	19.258	4.418	-17.18	1.39	-1.79	18	0.09

Interpreting the Results

To interpret these results, we have imagined that Variable 1 consisted of scores from a reading test and Variable 2 of scores from a math test. Both of these tests were written by the same set of students. Using these labels and the data from Table 16.1(b), you could state:

Data were analysed using a t-test for paired samples. Looking at results from the paired samples correlation (Table 16.1 (b)), you can see that the two sets of scores from the Reading test and the Mathematic test show a significant correlation (r = 0.809, p < .001). This means that students who obtained high scores on the reading Test also obtained high scores on the Mathematics Test.

You have to realise, however, that the mean scores from one test could be higher (or lower) than the mean scores from the other test. The question to now ask is: "Even though the scores are highly correlated, are the two means of the scores significantly different from each other?" The difference between the means of V1 and V2 is 7.89. Look at Table 16.1(c) (Paired Samples Test). The *t*-test results show that the difference of 7.89 between the two means is not significant ($t_{(1,18)}$ = -1.787, p = 0.091) and you would have to continue:

Contrary to previous findings showing that children who score high on reading tests do not score as high on mathematics tests (Name, date)[2], in this study, the students' mean scores of reading and mathematic tests did not differ from each other (t $_{(1,18)}$ = -1.787, p = 0.091).

This would then be followed by the appropriate tables, usually ones showing the means and standard deviations for the tests.

> This is an important aspect of your final thesis writing. You first state the important results of the analysis and state why it is important. Then, you insert the table (always after) and it must be appropriately numbered and titled.
>
> **Note** that you do not have to write about all of your findings, only what is pertinent to your research hypotheses.

Degrees of Freedom

Notice that we have introduced degrees of freedom in reporting the *t*-test when we stated that $t_{(1,18)}$ = -1.787. "Degrees of freedom" (*df*) is defined as: "The degrees of freedom for any statistic is the number of scores that are free to vary in calculating that statistic."[3] You do not need to use the Degrees of Freedom unless you want to look up the significance of the *t*-value in a Student's *t*-distribution table. You certainly do not have to do this when using SPSS because SPSS calculates the significance of the *t*-value for you so that you don't need to use the degrees of freedom.

The rule of thumb for determining the *df* for *t*-tests is to use N - 1. (The N equals the total number of participants and the 1 shows that only one value was fixed viz their mean.) Degrees of freedom were very important before computer programmes came into being because you used to have to look up the tables (usually found in the appendices at the back of every statistic text), then look for the "Critical Values of Student's *t* distribution," search until you saw the correct *df* and then determine whether the *t* was higher or lower than the critical value at a particular level of significance. Now, the computer printout gives you the exact critical values of *t* and the specified degrees of freedom. However, it is always a good idea to put in the degrees of freedom in brackets in subscript directly following the *t*.

---

2. You would put your reference here.

3. Pagano, (p. 279)

t-tests for Independent Samples

To show you how to find *t*-test results for independent samples, we are using the same data – but this time, we have included the gender of each student because we now want to find out if there is a significant difference between the mean scores on V1 and V2 for males and for females. We do this by coding 'male'=1 and 'female'=2 to label the two groups. This grouping variable is shown as 'Gender' in the data matrix in Figure 16.2. In this data matrix, the males are coded as "1" and the females as "2." Remember that these are only labels (nominal variables) and the codes do not imply that females are twice as good as males or that males come first whereas females come second.

Figure 16.2: A data matrix showing the variable "gender" has been included in the data collection (males = 1 and females = 2).

S	Gender	V1	V2
1	1	65	97
2	2	41	73
3	2	13	18
4	1	8	32
5	2	2	6
6	1	56	57
7	1	41	82
8	1	91	94
9	1	87	98
10	1	57	72
11	1	24	14
12	2	60	40
13	2	26	58
14	1	25	39
15	2	86	86
16	1	83	71
17	2	46	13
18	2	64	78
19	1	8	5

First, the difference between scores on the math test (Variable 1) achieved by males and females are compared. In other words, we are now comparing the means of *two different* groups who took the same test so the *t*-test for independent means must be used. If you add this 'Gender' variable to your SPSS data matrix, you can follow along with this example.

To use the independent samples *t*-test:
1. Click on **Analyze**. Scroll down and click on **Compare Means ▶**.
2. Click on **Independent-Samples T Test**. This is shown in Figure 16.3.

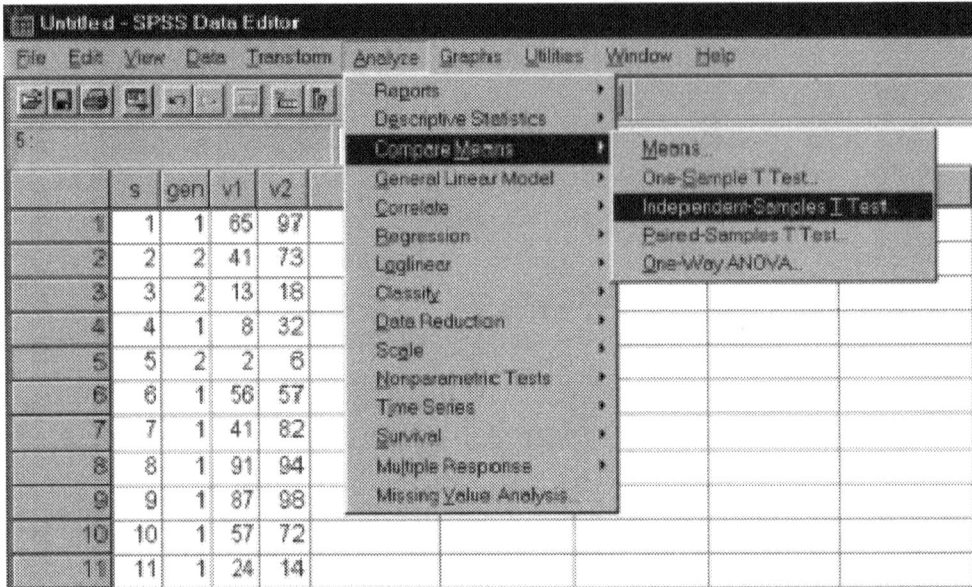

Figure 16.3: Choosing the Independent Samples T Test

3. This opens the **Independent-Samples T Test** dialog box shown in Figure 16.4. In the space at the left where the variables are displayed, click on V1 and on the ▶ to move it into the **Test Variable(s)** box.
4. Next click on **Gender** (in the space at the left) and move it into the **Grouping Variable: box.**
5. This opens the **Define groups...** box. Under Group1, enter "1" by typing in 1 in this space. Next, define the second group as "2" by typing in 2 as in Figure 16.4.
6. Click on **Continue** to close this box and return to the **Independent-samples** dialog window.
7. Click **OK**.

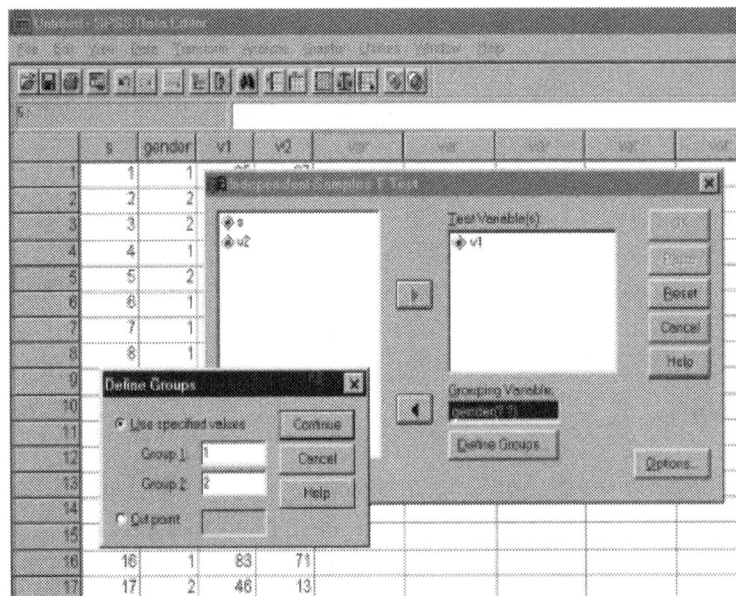

Figure 16.4: Defining the two groups for the "grouping variables" box when computing a *t*-test for independent samples.

The means and the standard deviations of the scores from each group are shown in Table 16.2. The mean scores for males (coded as "1") was 49.55[4] with a standard deviation of 30.59 and for females (coded as "2"), the mean score was 42.25 with a standard deviation of 27.92. The results of the t-test are shown in Table 16.3. Note that the means of the two sets of scores do not differ significantly from each other ($t = 0.532$, sig. = 0.60).

Table 16.2: *Means and Standard Deviations of Scores Obtained by Students*

Group Statistics

	Gender	N	Mean	Std. Deviation	Std. Error Mean
Math test	Males	11	49.55	30.589	9.223
	Females	8	42.25	27.922	9.872

Table 16.3: *SPSS Output Showing Results of the Independent Sample Test (t-test)*

Independent Samples Test

		Levene's Test for Equality of Variances		t-test for Equality of Means					95% Confidence Interval of the Difference	
		F	Sig.	t	df	Sig. (2-tailed)	Mean Difference	Std. Error Difference	Lower	Upper
Math test	Equal variances assumed	.341	.567	.532	17	.602	7.30	13.717	-21.644	36.235
	Equal variances not assumed			.540	16.013	.597	7.30	13.510	-21.342	35.933

Levene's Test for Equality of Variance

SPSS also gives us an extra feature, Levene's test for equality of variance (a method of testing for homogeneity of variance or HOV for short). This tests whether the two samples have the same variance. It simply divides one variance by the other. This ratio of variances is an F statistic and if the two variances are the same, then the top and bottom numbers of the fraction will be the same and the F value will be 1. It is unlikely to be exactly 1, and the significance of the F ratio tells you how likely the variances are to be equal. A $p < 0.05$ is usually taken to mean that the variances in the populations are likely to be equal so you can use the significance value of the t-test for equal variances. This is preferable because it gives an extra degree of freedom and hence a more powerful test. Look back at Table 16.3, you can see the $DF = 17$ for equal variances and 16.009 for unequal variances.

---

4. You only need to report results to two decimal places.

However, if the significance of the F is less than 0.05 you have to use the significance of the t-value based on unequal variances which makes a further assumption and so uses and extra degree of freedom resulting in lower significance of the t-statistic. Our result is $F = 0.341$ (and the significance $= 0.57$)[5], so we can conclude that the variances are equal and we need to report only the top numbers. If the results of Levene's test were significant, then we would report the numbers on the lower line.

Interpreting the Results

You could report the results as follows:

> Scores from the mathematics test were analysed using an Independent Samples t-test. Results showed that there was no significant difference in scores according to gender ($t_{(1,17)} = 0.539$, $p = 0.597$). The mean score of the boys $= 49.57$ and the girls $= 42.16$.

In some cases, however, you might prefer that the sets of scores differed from each other. For example, as shown in the non-significant results of the t-test for paired samples, we would be very disappointed to find out that there was no difference between the mean scores of a pretest and those of a post-test because that might imply that our intervention (or treatment) was not effective.

It is important to realise that the second measurement in each pair could be much higher than the first measurement. Although you would still find a significant correlation between the pairs of measures – in each pair, the large numbers that come first tend to go with the large numbers that come second, the second number could always be much higher than the first number. This would result in the mean of the second set of measures being much larger than the mean of the first set of measures and would produce a significant difference when the two sets of scores were analysed using a t-test.

Test Yourself 9

We used data from "Correlate13.sav" to show you how to compute the different t-tests. Now, it is your turn. Use the data from "Descriptive13.sav" to compute t-tests for:

(1)   the paired samples t-test. For (1) label Testa as "English" and Testb as "Math".
(2)   the independent samples t-test. For (2) use "Testa" as the dependent variable and "School Type" as the grouping variable (1 = government school; 2 = private school).

What results did you get? How would you report your results for each test?

Hint: Remember to go into variable view to use the label your variables option before you start.

Answers are found at the end of this text.

---

5. Remember that p should be more than 0.05 to consider the variances as equal.

An Example of Reporting Differences in Scores

In the example of reporting differences between two sets of scores, the research question concerned the "fairness" of culture fair tests. The null hypothesis tested was that culture fair scores did not differ regardless of the type of school the children attended. Table 16.4 shows the mean scores, standard deviations and results of the *t*-test. Notice that in this example, the two sets of information from the SPSS output have been combined because often it is not necessary to put all the details of the computer output into the thesis – just enough of the information necessary to answer your research question.

Table 16.4: *Mean Scores and Standard Deviations of CMMS Scores According to School Type*

School Type	Mean Scores	Std. Deviation	t	Sig. (2 tailed)
pri gov	110.71 92.31	12.05 11.29	1.96	0.03

N = 200
pri = private schools; gov = government schools

The results then could be written as follows:

> *To determine whether the means scores of the CMMS differed between students who attended government and private schools, the scores were analysed using an unrelated t-test. As can be seen in Table 16.4, the mean scores were significantly different from each other (t = 1.96, p = 0.03) with children who attended private schools obtaining higher scores ($\bar{X}$ score = 110.71) than their peers who attended government schools ($\bar{X}$ score = 92.31). Thus, it appears that results from this "culture fair" test show that children who attended government schools scored significantly lower than children who attended private schools. (See Appendix X for the t-test.)*

17
Parametric Tests

(iii) ANOVA

What Is the ANOVA?

ANOVA stands for the **AN**alysis **O**f **VA**riance and is a close relation to the *t*-tests that test for the difference between two means. Whilst the *t*-test uses the mean (the average score) as the basic statistic for analysing data, ANOVA uses the variance[1] of the measurements for testing the hypothesis (hence its name). The ANOVA programme produces a statistic called the *F* ratio which is actually the ratio of *between-groups* of estimated variance (the differences of scores **between** each group) and *within-groups* estimated variance (the differences of individual scores **within** each group). If the between-group variance is much larger than the *within-group* variance, the value of the *F* ratio will be high and imply that the results have not been obtained by chance.

> The ANOVA statistic is used to test whether there are any *differences between the variances of scores achieved by different* *groups*. The groups are the ***independent variables*** (with different levels of categories such as gender, religion, age, schools, grades; treatments or conditions such doses of medication, methods of teaching, working atmospheres – remember the list of groups is almost limitless!) The scores are always continuous variables.

The type of factorial analysis you use to test for differences of continuous variables depends mainly on the number of independent variables (factors) and the number of dependent variables that have been included in your research:

One-way ANOVA: use when you have one independent group variable (called a factor) with different levels and one continuous dependent variable

Two-way ANOVA: use when you have two independent grouping variables and one continuous dependent variable.

Three-way ANOVA: use when you have three independent grouping variable and one continuous dependent variable.

> In order to use any of the analyses of variance models, you need to make sure that your data collection has met the same assumptions required when doing *t*-tests: normal distribution, random sampling, and homogeneity of variance among variances of sets of scores for each group.

---

1. Remember that the variance is the square of the standard deviation and that variability has to do with how far the scores are spread out. Don't let all this information worry you! Remember that the SPSS programme does all the work for you. You just have to know why you are using this.

For your own information...

There are two more methods that can be used when carrying out factorial analyses: ANCOVA and MANOVA, but detailed descriptions of these are beyond the scope of this text. If you find that you need to carry out statistical analyses using either the ANCOVA or MANOVA, it is advised that you consult someone who is experienced in higher order statistical analyses.

ANCOVA: (Analysis of Co-Variance). This is very similar to the ANOVA except that it is used when you want to control for (or partial out) the effects of another continuous variable (the co-variate). As a simplified example, you may have decided to test an experimental hypothesis that one method of teaching reading was a better method to use than two other methods. (The dependent variable was reading scores; the independent variable was the methods were used.) The difference is that for this experiment, you also used three different groups of teachers for each method but you were not able to match each individual teacher on 'teaching experience' which most likely differed by teacher within each group. To control for the 'teaching experience' effect, you would use 'teaching experience' as the co-variate. Thus, you use the ANCOVA to remove the possibility that teaching experience might have accounted for differences in the reading scores.

MANCOVA: the Multivariate Analysis of Co-Variance is used when you want to test hypotheses for any crossed and/or nested research designs. It uses three types of variables: dependent variables that are continuous (Y); co-variate variables that are continuous (X) and factors that are categorical with more than 2 levels (e.g., A and B). The idea is that it specifies an analysis of co-variance model with Y as the dependent variable, X as the co-variate and A and B as factor variables with different levels.

The One-way ANOVA

The one-way ANOVA involves using one independent variable that has three or more different levels. Just to make things more difficult for you, different texts call the one-way ANOVA different names: the independent groups design, the single-factor experiment design, or the simple randomised group design. Don't let all these names confuse you – we just call it the one-way ANOVA and this is what we start off explaining.

In the SPSS programme, you should use:

(i)   **One-way repeated measures ANOVA:** *different measures* are obtained from *one group of people.* Data comes from three or more sets of measurements obtained from one group of people or things. For example, you might want to find out if there are any differences between the scores on a math test, an English test and a science test (the dependent variables) from a group of Grade Four students (the independent variable). In this example, we have three separate measurements (test scores) and one group of people (Grade Four students).

(ii) **One-way between-groups ANOVA:** *three different groups* of people provide *one set of measurements.* Data consists of three or more groups (as in age groups, salary groups, motivational levels, levels of SES, levels of Locus of Control, levels of achievement, and so on) and one set of measurements. For example, for the grouping variable (the independent variable), you could have three levels of motivation (high, medium and low) and for the measurement variable (the dependent variable), you could have scores on an achievement test. Then you would be able to find out if achievement scores differ according to different levels of motivation.

(iii)   A third way is to plan your research so that groups of people (things, etc.) receive different treatments or conditions (an experimental design). In other words, you randomly divide the participants (or things) into at least three different groups, measure them on something and look at the scores for each group. The results will show that the sample groups are different or similar (depending on the F value and level of alpha). This is just another way of saying *between-groups* because you still have different groups and one dependent variable.

Using the SPSS Programme for One-Way ANOVA With Contrasts

To show you how to compute and interpret a one-way ANOVA using the SPSS programme, we have used data from a hypothetical research:

An educational researcher wanted to investigate whether teachers who taught different subjects spent the same amount of time in marking students' homework assignments. She was an English teacher and had noticed that the math teachers seemed to spend less time marking homework than she did. She thought that this might be the case in all schools because math teachers mainly tick numerical answers as right or wrong while she had a lot of difficult handwriting to read and comments to make which is very time consuming. She wondered if this was generally true for both math and physics because these subjects seemed mainly numerical when compared to English and Social Sciences which seemed to require more reading and writing when marking homework. These groups of academic subjects (English/Social Sciences and Math/Physics) are "contrasts" that we shall later ask the SPSS programme to compute.

She asked secondary teachers, who were subject specialists (they only taught one subject) the following two questions:

Question 1:   What subject do you teach? (tick ✔ one)
Maths ( )   English ( )   Physics ( )   Social Science ( )   Other ( )

Question 2:   How many hours last week did you spend marking homework?____hours

This researcher had randomly selected the schools and also had randomly selected the teachers within each school so she could generalise her results to all the schools from which she had sampled. The first thing she did after collecting the questionnaire was to write a respondent's number in the top right-hand corner of the questionnaire for easy identification in case of errors while entering the data into Excel. The academic subjects were coded as follows: Maths = 1; English = 2; Physics = 3; Social Science = 4; Other = 5. This is an example of a between-groups one-way ANOVA because you have different groups as the independent variables (the subjects taught) and one dependent variable (amount of time marking homework).

Computing the One-Way ANOVA

By now, you should be an old hand when using the SPSS programme. When entering your data, remember to number code each group or each different condition that the participants are in, or in this example, the different academic subjects. Similar to entering data, such as gender, you use numbers for each group or condition and then use the value label so you know what these numbers mean. In the data we are using, we only have three columns: under the first column is an identification number given to each teacher[3], the second column is the code number of the subject being taught and the third column contains the number of hours each participant (teacher) reported that they spent marking homework.

At first, it will seem that there are a lot of steps just to get the ANOVA statistics. The thing to remember here is that we have combined finding the *F* ratio with finding a lot more information – measures of central tendency, descriptives, HOV and multiple comparisons. It is far easier to do everything at once than to keep going back and forth to the SPSS programme to find the extra information you might need for the same set of data.

1. Open your data in the SPSS programme, and scroll across the main menu until you see **Analyze**. This opens the drop down box.
2. Next click on **Compare Means ▶**, then click on **One-Way ANOVA...** this opens the One-Way ANOVA Dialog box as shown in Figure 17.1.

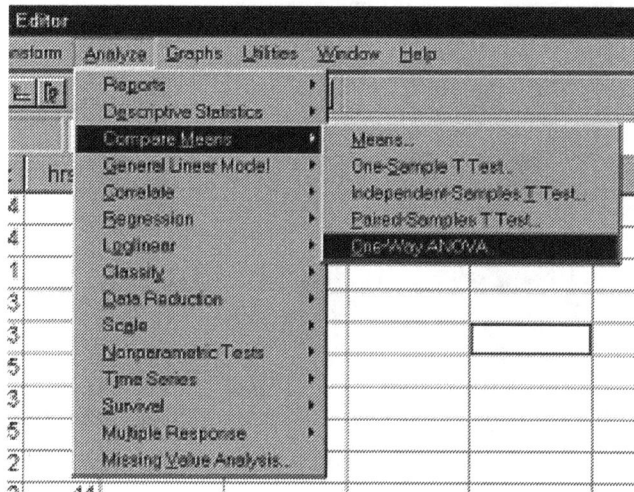

Figure 17.1: Going from *Analyze* to *Compare Means* to the *One-Way ANOVA* to open the dialog box.

3. In the left side of the One-Way ANOVA dialog box, you will see your list of variables. You scroll down this list until you see your dependent variable (now you should understand why it is so important to know what the dependent and independent variables are!) Highlight the DV, (which is number of hours) and click on the arrow to place it in the Dependent List.

3. This ID number is NOT to identify teachers but to use to check that the data has been entered correctly.

4. Go back to the list of variables and scroll down until you see the **independent variable (subject taught)**. Put this one in the **Factor**[4] box. This has been done in Figure 17.2.

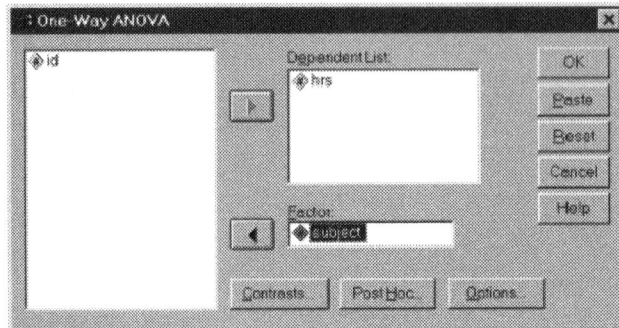

Figure 17.2: Placing the dependent variables and independent variables in the correct boxes.

5. Next click on **Options** to bring up the **One-Way ANOVA: Options** dialog box.
6. Click on the squares besides **Descriptive, Homogeneity-of-variance** and **Means Plot.** Underneath Missing values, click on **Exclude cases analysis by analysis** shown in Figure 17.3.

Note that in this example, we used the "Exclude cases analysis by analysis." However, if you are not sure about missing data, then it is generally better to choose pair-wise rather than case-wise because the pair-wise option leaves you with more respondents to analyse and, perhaps, more significant results.

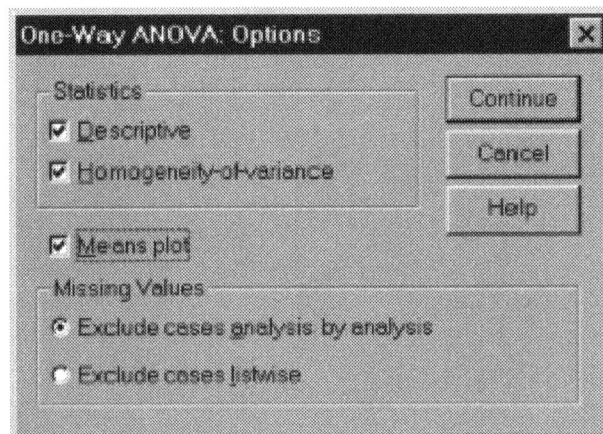

Figure 17.3: Using the Options dialog box to choose descriptive statistics, etc.

7. Click **Continue** and then when you get back to the :**One-Way ANOVA** dialog box, click on **Post Hoc...** to open the **One-Way ANOVA: Post Hoc Multiple Comparisons** dialog box. This is shown in Figure 17.4.
8. Click on both **Bonferroni** and **Tukey's b** so you can see a print-out of both results, then click on **Continue** to get back to the **One-Way ANOVA** dialog box. When you are doing your own data, you will decide which one you need. (More about this later on.)
9. Click on **Contrasts** and bring up the **One-Way ANOVA: Contrasts** box shown in Figure 17.5. This is the box that is used to request the special contrasts between groups.

---

4. Remember that a factor is a variable with more than one level. This research has five levels (five different subjects!)

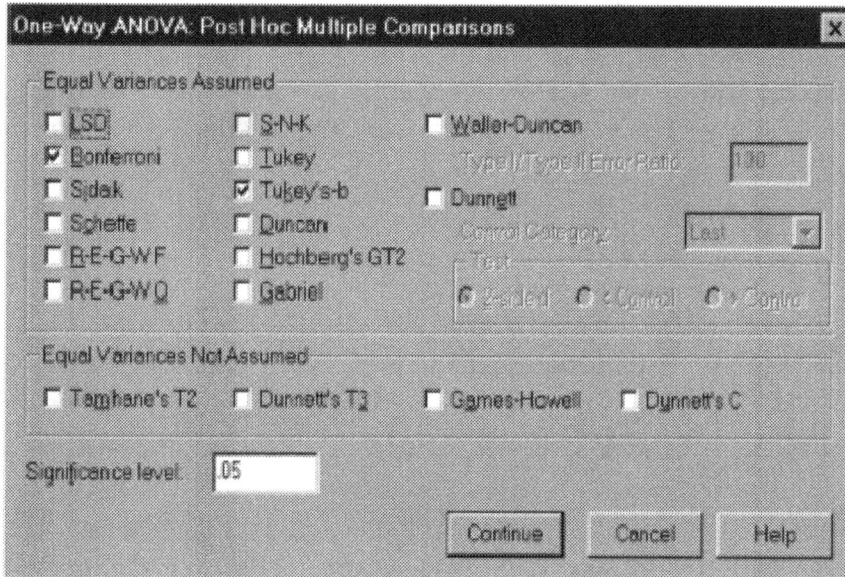

Figure 17.4: Choosing the required comparisons in the One-Way Post Hoc Multiple Comparisons Dialog box.

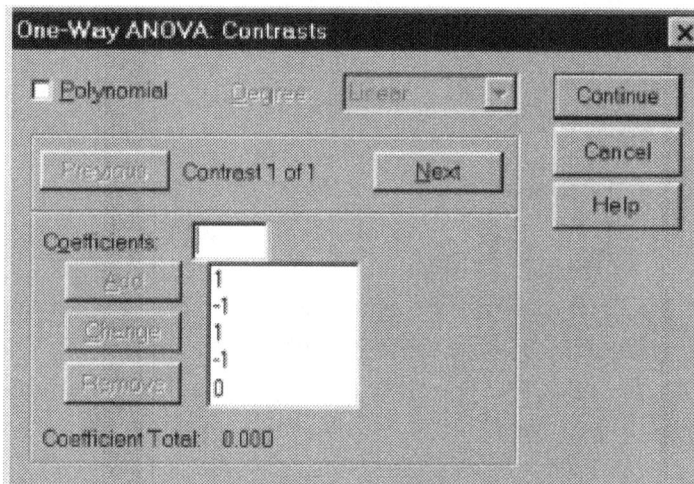

Figure 17.5: The One-Way ANOVA: Contrasts box showing how the coefficients have been added.

Remember that the researcher hypothesised that teachers who taught English and Social Sciences spent more time marking homework than teachers who taught Math and Physics. The Contrasts option allows her to see if this is true. She is using the Contrasts Option in order to compare (contrast) the amount of time marking two subjects (English and Social Sciences) with the other two subjects (Maths and Physics).

To make this concept more understandable, we have drawn out a contrast table (shown in Table 17.1) so you can see why the numbers were entered into the contrasts box. There are certain things to remember:

• The contrast coefficients must be entered in the same order as they were entered in the variable table. Look and see how the subjects were entered into the SPSS programme (Maths, English, Physics, Social Science and Other).

- Because the researcher wanted to contrast the hours spent marking English and Social Science homework (one group) with hours spent marking math and physics homework (the second group), she marked English and Social Science as -1 and Math and Physics as +1. She really wasn't interested in "Other" so she just put a 0 for this one.
- The sum of the contrast coefficients must add up to 0.

Table 17.1: *How to Specify Contrast Coefficients*

Maths	English	Physics	Social Science	Other
1	-1	1	-1	0

10. Enter these contrast coefficients into the box marked **Coefficients**. Type **1** first, then click on **ADD**, type **-1** next, **Add**, and keep doing this until all 5 numbers have been entered. *Make sure that the numbers are entered in the same order as they are in your variables list.* After all numbers have been entered, the dialog box should look similar to that shown in Figure 17.5. The **Coefficient Total:** shows that the sum of the coefficients = 0.
11. Click on **Continue** to return to the first box, then click on **OK**.

(WHEW!!!!)

You will get a lot of information after you have done all this work.

Examining the Results of the SPSS Output

First, in Step 6, we chose the **Descriptives** option in the One-Way ANOVA dialog box. This option presents a table similar to that shown in Table 17.2. The descriptive statistics are very useful for describing the numbers in your sample for the Methods Section of your thesis. It is also a general rule that you show the means and standard deviations when reporting your findings in the Results Section.

Under column N, you can see that the researcher actually collected a total of 64 questionnaires of which only 8 were from English teachers. This makes it an unbalanced design. The Mean column shows the average number of hours the teachers reported marking homework for each subject. The 95% Confidence Interval for Lower to Upper Bound means that, if the researcher did this survey 100 times, then for 95% of those times, the mean of each group would fall within these bounds. You generally do not need to reproduce the 95% level of confidence columns in your final written thesis unless it is needed as part of your method, e.g., as part of your hypotheses testing. The "Min" stands for the minimum number of hours and the "Max" stands for the maximum number of hours. The difference between the Min and the Max gives the range of the total number of hours the teachers spent marking their papers.

Table 17.2: *Descriptive Statistics Showing the Number of Teachers per Subject and the Mean and Standard Deviations of the Numbers of Hours Spent Marking Homework per Subject*

Descriptives

Hours

	N	Mean	Std. Deviation	Std. Error	95% Confidence Interval Lower Bound	95% Confidence Interval Upper Bound	Min	Max
Math	16	11.88	1.86	.46	10.89	12.86	9	15
English	8	15.50	1.77	.63	14.02	16.98	13	18
Physics	13	12.85	2.64	.73	11.25	14.44	8	16
Social Science	13	14.77	2.17	.60	13.46	16.08	11	18
Other	14	13.14	2.32	.62	11.81	14.48	10	17
Total	64	13.59	2.47	.31	12.77	14.01	51	89

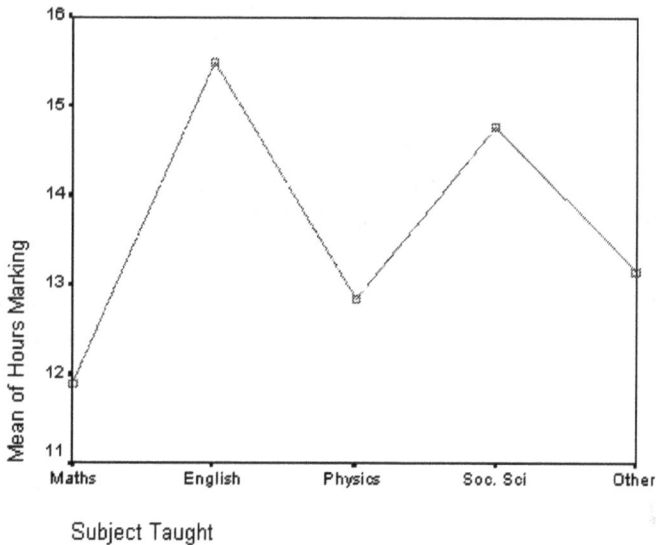

Figure 17.6: Group means output from the Means Plot option requested in Step 6.

Next, you will see the means plot because this is what we requested in Step 6. This should look similar to Figure 17.6. By just looking at this plot, you can see that the mean number of hours the teachers spent marking Maths and Physics is lower than those spent marking English and Social Sciences.

So far, we have seen that there are differences between the mean numbers of hours that teachers of different subjects spent marking homework, and the question now to ask is: "Are these differences significant?" The null hypothesis that the researcher is testing is: "There were no differences in the number of hours spent marking homework in maths, physics, English and social science." To find out whether this hypothesis should be rejected, you now look at the main ANOVA table shown in Table 17.3.

ANOVA

Hours Marking

	Sum of Squares	df	Mean Squares	F	Sig.
Between Groups	101.770	4	25.443	5.296	.000
Within Groups	283.464	1	4.804		
Total	385.234	59			

Table 17.3: *The Main ANOVA Table*

The first thing to look at is under the column headed "Sig." which is equal to 0.000. This shows that the difference is significant as it is less than 0.05 (our level of significance). For this analysis, you could write:

The data was analysed using an ANOVA to determine whether the mean hours spent marking homework differed according to subject taught. Results showed that there was a significant difference in the mean number of hours spent marking the different subjects ($F_{(4, 59)} = 5.29, p < 0.05$).

When you report the F value, you should reproduce the main parts of the ANOVA table as part of your thesis. If it is small like this one, it can go into the main text, but if it is long, then it can be placed into an Appendix. Note that you do not have to report the actual significance level but you could write ($F_{(4, 59)} = 5.29, p < 0.05$) if you have chosen 0.05 as your level of significance. The $_{(4, 59)}$ written after the F shows the degrees of freedom and is useful to someone with a great deal of knowledge who wants to check your analysis. It is always a good idea to include this information when reporting your results.

The Effect Size (η^2)

An important point to note is that many journals now require the *effect size* to be reported. This is because the differences can become "significantly significant" just through increasing the sample size and this can be misleading – particularly when comparing results from different research using different sample sizes. This statistic is used to indicate the relative magnitude between the means. The Effect Size statistic most commonly used to report ANOVA results is *eta squared* and is written η^2.

Unfortunately, the one-way ANOVA does not routinely offer this statistic, but it is very easy to compute it for yourself. The formula is:

$$\eta^2 = \frac{\text{between groups Sum of Squares}}{\text{within groups Sum of Squares}}$$

To get these numbers, just look at the main ANOVA table (Table 17.3) and look under the Sum of Squares. The effect size is calculated:

$$\eta^2 = \frac{101.770}{385.254} = 0.262$$

Probably one of the most cited references to interpret Effect Size is Cohen (1988). He stated that an effect size of 0.02 is small, from 0.06 is medium and from 0.14 is large. As 0.262 is a great deal larger than 0.14, this statistic means that the researcher has found a large effect size.

So far, we have found out that there are significant differences between the number of hours teachers of different subjects spent marking homework and the η^2 (effect size) shows that the effect size is large but neither the F or the η^2 tell you which set of mean scores differ from each other. Now you would add to your writing up of the analysis:

The data was analysed using an ANOVA to determine whether the mean hours spent marking homework differed according to subject taught. Results showed that there was a significant difference in the number of hours (F $_{(4,59)}$ = 5.29, p = 0.01) with an effect size (η^2= 0.262) indicating that the actual differences in the mean scores of each group was large.

Interpreting Multiple Comparisons

The *F* value just tells us that there is a difference in the measurements according to categories or levels of the independent variable – that the independent variable had a significant effect. Normally, analysis does not just stop at this point because you should also find out which category means differ from each other or whether two of them are similar and only one is different. The way to do this is by making *multiple comparisons* between pairs of group means. In the SPSS programme, in Step 7, we did just this when we went into the Post hoc Options box. The Bonferroni option produces an output shown in Table 17.4.

To interpret this table, look at each row of the table. The first two columns in the first row shows us that we are comparing the hours marking mathematic papers with the hours spent marking the other four subjects. The next column gives us the mean difference between the hours for marking maths and each subject, the next column shows the Standard Error and the next column (Sig.) is the important one! It tells us whether the Mean Difference is significant or not. This is the column you really want to read first. Run your eyes down this column and mark everything that is significant (in a red pencil – because this will focus your attention on what is important in your analyses).

Reading across the first row, you can now see that the amount of hours spent marking Maths was significantly different from the hours spent marking English, the mean difference is -3.63 and this is significant at 0.003. Still in the first row, you can see that the difference between Maths and Physics was -0.97 and this is not significant at all (1.000). Still reading across the first row, you can see that Maths was significantly different from both English and Social Science (sig. = .008) but not from Physics. In the second row, you can see that English was significantly different from Maths but not from Physics (sig. = .092) or Social Science (sig. = 1.000). In the fourth row, you can see that Social Sciences was significantly different from Maths (sig. = .008) but not from the other subjects.

Table 17.4: *Results of using the Bonferroni Option for Multiple Comparisons*

Dependent Variable: HRS (Hours Marking)

(I) SUBJECT Subject Taught	(J) SUBJECT Subject Taught	Mean Difference (I-J)	Std. Error	Sig.	95% Confidence Interval	
					Lower Bound	Upper Bound
1 Maths	2 English	-3.63	.95	.003	-6.39	-.86
	3 Physics	-.97	.82	1.000	-3.36	1.42
	4 Soc Sci	-2.89	.82	.008	-5.28	-.51
	5 Other	-1.27	.80	1.000	-3.61	1.07
2 English	1 Maths	-3.63	.95	.003	.86	6.39e
	3 Physics	2.65	.98	.092	-.22	5.53
	4 Soc Sci	.73	.98	1.000	-2.14	3.60
	5 Other	2.36	.97	.183	-.48	5.19
3 Physics	1 Maths	.97	.82	1.000	-1.42	3.36
	2 English	-2.65	.98	.092	-5.53	.22
	4 Soc Sci	-1.92	.96	.291	-4.43	.58
	5 Other	-.30	.84	1.000	-2.76	2.17
4 Soc Sci	1 Maths	2.89	.82	.008	.51	5.28
	2 English	-.73	.98	1.000	-3.60	2.14
	3 Physics	1.92	.86	.291	-.58	4.43
	5 Other	1.63	.84	.589	-.84	4.09
5 Other	1 Maths	1.27	.80	1.000	-1.07	3.61
	2 English	-2.36	.97	.183	-5.19	.48
	3 Physics	.30	.84	1.000	-2.17	2.76
	4 Soc Sci	-1.63	.84	.589	-4.09	.94

Actually, our researcher was really more interested in comparing similar groups of subjects and not in comparing single subjects as shown the Bonferroni test. This is why she also chose the *Tukey's b* in Step 8. The printout from this option should look similar to that shown in Table 17.5. An advantage of using the harmonic mean (Tukey's b) is that it compensates for differences in group size (remember that she had unequal measurements for each of the subjects and this made it an unbalanced design).

Table 17.5: *Multiple Comparisons Generated by the Tukey's-b Option in the One-Way ANOVA: Post Hoc Multiple Comparisons Dialog Box*

SUBJECT Subject Taught		N	Subject for Alpha = .05		
			1	2	3
Tukey B[a,t]	1 Maths	16	11.88		
	3 Physics	13	12.85	12.85	
	5 Other	14	13.14	13.14	
	4 Soc Sci	13		14.77	14.77
	2 English	8			15.50

Means for groups in homogeneous subsets are displayed
a. Uses harmonic mean Sample Size = 12.15
b. The group sizes are unequal. The harmonic mean of the group size is used. Type 1 error levels are not guaranteed.

Interpreting Table 17.5

First, draw a line through "Other" and reading the table will be much simpler. The alpha level was set at 0.05. Under "Subject for Alpha" column and 1, in terms of the amount of marking homework, Maths and Physics go together (11.88 and 12.85, respectively). Under the 3, English and Social Science go together (14.77 and 15.50, respectively). This is what the researcher expected when she first started her research.

Interpreting Contrasts

Finally, we come to the contrasts that we asked for in Steps 9 and 10 in the One-Way ANOVA programme. Contrasts are very sensitive to variations between groups and this is the main reason why we also ticked the "Homogeneity-of-variance" option in the One-Way ANOVA options box in Step 6. This gives the Levene Statistic shown in Table 17.6. It is included in One-Way ANOVA: Options box and it is always a good idea to include it. The Levene statistic is 0.552 – much greater than the required 0.05. This means that we can reject the hypothesis of "no HOV" and can assume that the groups have equal variances.

Table 17.6: *Levene Statistic from Homogeneity-of-Variance Option in the One-Way: ANOVA Options Dialog Box*

Levene's Test of Homogeneity-of-Variance

Dependent Variable: Hrs (Hours of marking)

Levene Statistic F	df1	df2	Sig.
0.765	4	59	0.55

Making sure that the groups have equal HOV is important when reading the results of the Contrast that we asked for in Steps 9 and 10. You will see two tables reported for contrasts. The first is shown in Table 17.7 (Confirmed Contrasts Coefficients) and shows that what we entered in Step 9 is correct. The results of the contrasts are shown in Table 17.8.

Table 17.7: *Confirmed Contrast Coefficients*

		Old Book	New Book	Average
GENDER	Male	25.3	25.8	25.6
	Female	19.6	19.2	19.4

Table 17.8: *Results of Contrasting Maths and Physics with English and Social Science*

Contrast Tests

Contrast		Value of Contrast	Std. Error	t	df	Sig. (2-tailed)
Hrs Hours marking	Assume equal variance	-5.55	1.28	-4.33	59	0.0001
	Does not assume equal	-5.55	1.23	-4.52	37.8	0

Because we can assume equal variances (from the results of the Levene's test of HOV shown in Table 17.6), we choose the top line of Table 17.8 showing that the researcher was correct. There is a significant difference in the time spent marking English and Social Science homework when compared with the amount of time marking Maths and Physics homework (t = -4.33, p = 0.001).

Once again we should report the effect size. This is a little more complicated formula and requires just a little more work: $\eta^2 = \dfrac{t^2}{t^2 + (n_1+n_2 - 2)}$

Explanation: t = - 4.33 (from first line of Table 17.8)
t^2 = (- 4.332 X -4.332) = 18.76

n_1 stands for the total number of teachers who marked Maths and Physics. There were 16 teachers marking Math and 13 teachers marking Physics for a total of 29. (This is found in the Descriptives Table 17.2).

n_2 stands for the total number of teachers marking English and Social Sciences (8 + 13 = 21).

Plugging in the numbers, the formula is $\eta^2 = \dfrac{18.766}{18.766 + (29 + 21 - 2)} = 0.279$

Looking back at how Cohen rated the effect size, this turns out to be very large.

The Final Version of the Results

After you have looked at all this information, your final report would read:

The data was analysed using a One-Way ANOVA to determine whether the mean hours spent marking homework differed according to subject taught. Table XX[5] shows the number of teachers per subject and the means and standard deviations of the amount of hours the teachers reported that they spent marking homework per subject. Results showed that there was a significant difference in the number of hours spent marking the different subjects ($F_{(4,59)}$ = 5.29, p = 0.01) (see Table XX). The size of the differences was large (η^2 = 0.262). Levene's test of HOV showed that there was equal variance between groups (equal variances is taken from the results of the Levene's test of HOV shown in Table 17.6). The contrast between the time taken for teachers to mark English and Social Science homework was significantly greater than the time taken to mark Math and Physics homework ($t_{1,59}$ = 4.333, p < 0.001). The size of the difference between the time taken to mark the word-based subjects (i.e., English and Social Science) and the number-based subjects (i.e., Math and Physics) was large η^2 = 0.28) indicating that the actual differences in the mean scores of each group was large.

---

5. This is taken from the Descriptives Table 17.6 and should be presented immediately following the written results. "XX" is just written to represent the number of your table and it should be written in Arabic numerals NOT Roman numerals.

Why Make Multiple Comparisons?

When you use an ANOVA, you are testing the null hypothesis that the differences among the scores of groups (conditions, treatments) are not significant. Based on the *F* value and the level of significance, you would either reject your hypothesis or fail to reject your hypothesis of no differences among the dependent variables. Once you reject the hypothesis, the story does not have to end there because now, you may want to find out which of the conditions are significant. This means that you can use *multiple comparisons*.

Rule of Thumb for Using Multiple Comparisons

When you open the Post Hoc dialog box, you can choose from a large list of comparisons tests. We recommend that you just use one of the following:

1. *For planned comparisons (a priori), use:*

Bonferroni to compare differences with minimum significant differences. The Bonferroni option gives us the significance of the group differences after controlling for Type 1 errors. It is considered very flexible in that it allows almost any number of contrasts to be made but at the same time, the number of comparisons should be relatively few in number and should be planned in advance.

2. *For unplanned comparisons (post hoc or a posteriori), use:*

Tukey (Honestly Significant Differences test) compares all possible pairs of means and maintains the Type 1 error rate at the same alpha level for all of the complete set of comparisons. Tukey's-b should be used when the groups are unequal in size (as in our example).

Newmann-Keuls test also compares all possible pairs but maintains the Type 1 error rate for each comparison. The Newmann-Keuls test is more powerful but has a somewhat higher error rate than Tukey's test.

- To avoid making many Type 1 errors, we recommend using Tukey's test.
- For both Tukey and Newmann-Keuls, use the "harmonic mean" when there are unequal numbers in each group.
- Both use the *Q* or studentised range statistic, so don't get alarmed if you see *Q* rather than *t*!

Things to Think About – Type 1 and Type 2 Errors

One question we often hear is "Why go to all this bother to find contrasts when we could do a lot of *t*-tests on the same data?" The answer to this question is that using a lot of *t*-tests on the same data might introduce Type 1 errors. When you use a *t*-test, you are only looking at the differences between two samples, but when you have many samples (as in the *F* statistic), the *t* statistic is no longer appropriate.

Making a Type 1 error means that you have rejected the null hypothesis but, in fact, the null hypothesis is true. The results of the analysis tell you that you should reject the hypothesis because the results may actually be due to chance. A Type 2 error is just the opposite. This time, you fail to reject the null hypothesis, but the null hypothesis is false.

In educational research, this might not be too serious, but just think of the consequences of making a Type 1 or a Type 2 error in the field of medicine or science! For example, a group of scientists might investigate a certain medicine to see if it is safe for public consumption. If they have rejected the null hypothesis of the medicine being safe, they might be throwing away something that could save countless lives (a Type 1 error). On the other hand, if they failed to reject the safety level of that medicine and declared it safe for public consumption, then they just might end up by making killing countless people (a Type 2 error).

You try to control against making Type 1 errors by correctly identifying the power of a test. You can do this by:

- Trying to design your research so that you can use parametric tests.
- Increasing your sample size. If you use small sample sizes (smaller than 20), then you may find a non-significant result due to insufficient power.
- Looking at the effect size. We did this in our One-Way ANOVA example and found a large effect.
- Setting the alpha level at an even more stringent level before you start to look for contrasts (e.g., $p = 0.03$ or $p = 0.01$, etc.) depending on how many groups you want to compare. The rule of thumb here is to divide your alpha level by the amount of comparisons you wish to make (e.g., if your alpha level is 0.05 and you wish to make 3 comparisons, then your new alpha level would be $0.05 \div 3 = 0.0166$ or 0.02).

Note that the number of paired comparisons increases more rapidly as more groups are used. Table 17.9 shows how rapidly the probability of making Type 1 errors increase as you consider more groups.

Table 17.9: *Increasing the Probability of Making Type 1 Errors as Number of Groups Increase*

Type 1 errors at $p = 0.05$

Groups	2	3	4	5	6	7	8	9	10	11	12
Comparisons	1	3	6	10	15	21	28	36	45	55	66
Probability of error	0	0.14	0.26	0.4	0.54	0.66	0.8	0.8	0.9	0.9	1

Now, back to why we use the ANOVA rather than a lot of *t*-tests. Think of throwing dice. If you throw only one die, the chance of a 6 coming up is only 1 in 6 throws. If, however, you threw a handful of dice, the chances are that in the one throw, you might get a lot more showing 6 and the 6 will appear more than once in 6 throws. When you do many *t*-tests on the same data, it is a bit like throwing a lot of dice at the same time. The chance of getting significant differences is much higher than the basic $p = 0.05$ that we chose as the level of significance.

The LSD option on the One-Way ANOVA: Post Hoc Multiple Comparisons box calculates the *t*-tests without making corrections for Type 1 errors.

DO NOT USE IT!

If we had used the LSD option with the five groups, then we could have had a massive 40% error.

The Two-Way and Three-way Analysis of Variance (GLM in SPSS talk)

When you start to analyse data and are using an ANOVA, an important question to ask is: "Should a one-way, a two-way or three-way ANOVA be used?" We have already explained when the one-way ANOVA should be used – when you have one independent variable with two or more groups and one continuous variable. This section explains when, why, and how to use the two-way and three-way ANOVAs – that is, when you have two or more group variables with two or more levels and one quantitative (independent) variable.

A simplistic definition of a factor is that it is an independent variable with two or more levels. When we showed you how to compute the F statistic for the one-way ANOVA, we used one independent variable with five levels and looked at the effect of the factor (or each level of the independent variable) on the dependent variable (the hours spent marking papers). In the two-way ANOVA, you need two independent grouping variables with two or more different levels so you can simultaneously investigate their individual effects (the main effects) and their joint effects (the interaction effect) on the dependent variable.

> The main reason for using the two-way and three-way ANOVAs is to test for possible interactions between the factors.

You can also use the two-way ANOVA if you have more than two dependent variables and you would then have two separate analyses: one for the first DV and one for the second DV. For example, a medical researcher wanted to find the effect of a specific drug on reaction time and eye-hand coordination. The two independent variables were drug treatment and gender. His two dependent variables were reaction time and eye-hand co-ordination. He randomly placed the participants in his study into four groups: people in Group 1 received a low dose of the drug, those in Group 2 a medium dose and those in Group 3 a high dose. The people in Group 4 were considered the control group and received a placebo. All participants were then tested on reaction time and eye-hand coordinating (the dependent variables). This is a 4 X 2 factorial design because there are four groups and two test scores. Because there are two test scores, the results can be analysed using 2 two-way ANOVAS. A 4 X 2 ANOVA can be processed first using the reaction time as the DV and then another 4 X 2 ANOVA can be processed using eye-hand co-ordination as the second DV.

> Here is where life gets a little difficult. There is no such thing as a two-way ANOVA on the SPSS programme. Instead, you have to use the **General Linear Model** (GLM). Remember that the two-way ANOVA programme is used to investigate differences between two dependent variables and the three-way ANOVA is used to investigate differences between three dependent variables.

The example that follows is an example of a three-way ANOVA.

Using the GLM SPSS Programme to Analyse Research Involving Three Factors.

Note that you go through the same steps to analyse data for both the two-way and three-way ANOVAs. We used the three-way ANOVA because we wanted to show you how to put in the extra factor.

Example of Research

We show you the steps involved in the GLM programme by using data from a 2 X 2 X 2 cross-sectional, factorial research design. The dependent variable consisted of scores from a culture fair test of mental maturity given to male and female students in Grades One and Four, attending private and government schools.[6] The three independent variables or factors were: gender (boys versus girls); by grade (Grade One versus Grade Four); by school type (private versus government. The researcher wanted to find out if culture fair tests were really "fair" for all children or whether test scores varied according to gender, grade level and/or type of school the children attended and whether there were any interactions between grade and school type, grade and gender or school type and gender. In other words, did the test scores from the culture fair test differ according to the levels of any of the three factors.

In Word Map 7 of the research design, you can see how the questions arose from the problem statement and how the hypotheses were a natural follow on. Note that the first three questions concern the main effects while the fourth question asked whether there were any interaction effects (look at hypotheses 4-7).

Table 17.10 shows you how the basic research design can be "drawn." We recommend that you always draw out your research design before you start deciding on how you will collect the data or designing questionnaires just to make sure that your research is do-able. In this table, we have filled in the numbers for each subgroup (n) with the big N = 50. This is a good way of determining about how many participants will be needed for your study. For example, if this was a "real" study, you would look at the number of females in Grade Four attending private school and you could see right away that you would need to find more participants for this subgroup. Frankly, if you wanted to generalise your results, you would need more participants for most of the other subgroups, as well.

Table 17.10: *A Drawing of a Research Design Showing the Levels of the Independent Variables and the Number of Participants in Each Subgroup*

Males				Females			
Government		Private		Government		Private	
Gr 1	Gr 4	Gr 1	Gr 4	Gr 1	Gr 4	Gr 1	Gr 4
n = 6	n = 8	n = 6	n = 5	n = 6	n = 7	n = 8	n = 4

N = 50

---

6. The actual sample was much larger (800 children) but we only used a small number in this example to make it easier for you to use the same data. If you want to follow along, use Descriptives13.sav or Appendix A for the numbers used in this example. If not, simply plug in your own numbers and your own variables.

```
┌─────────────────────────────────────────────────────────────────────┐
```

WORD MAP 7

Problem Statement: An investigation to determine whether scores from the CMMS, a culture fair test, differed according to school type, grade level or gender of children.

Questions to ask:
Q1: Did the scores differ according to the type of school the children are attending?
Q2: Was there be any differences in the scores according to gender?
Q3: Did the scores of children in Grade 1 differ from the children in Grade 4?
Q4: Did the children's scores from the CMMS vary according to how they were combined with gender, school type or grade level?

Hypotheses:
(1) H_0: Scores of the CMMS did not differ according to the type of school the children attend.
(2) H_0: Scores of the CMMS did not differ according to gender of the children.
(3) H_0: Scores of the CMMS did not differ according to grade level of the children.
(4) H_0: CMMS scores did not differ according to grade and school type.
(5) H_0: CMMS scores did not differ according to grade and gender.
(6) H_0: CMMS scores did not differ according to gender and school type.
(7) H_0: CMMS scores did not differ according to gender, school type and grade.

Operational definitions:
CMMS: A standardised culture fair test (CMMS) obtained from the Psychological Corporation. Age deviation scores were obtained from the raw scores
School type: government schools and private schools in an urban area of Jamaica
Grade level: Grade 1 and Grade 4

Independent Variables
Boys and girls attending Grades 1 and 4 in private and government schools

Dependent Variables
Age deviation scores obtained from the raw scores from the CMMS

Confounding Variables
Time of day. To try to control for this, all the children were tested in the mornings.

Analysis
ANOVA looking for main effects and interaction effects. By using the three-way ANOVA, all hypotheses can be tested at the same time.

Computing the Three-way ANOVA 2 X 2 X 2 Factorial Design

Place the data from the "Descriptives13.sav" into the SPSS programme and change the name of Test A to CMMS. The numbers under this column are what we are using as the continuous dependent variable.

1. Open your data, and click on **Analyze**. This opens the drop down dialog box.
2. Next click on **General Linear Model ▶ ...** and click on **Univariate**. This opens the Univariate dialog box.

3. On the left side of this box is the list of the variables. Highlight the **dependent variable (CMMS)** and click on the arrow to place it in the **Dependent Variable** box on the right.

4. Next, highlight each of the factors and place them in the **Fixed factor(s)** box at the right. In our example, we clicked on *gender, school type* and *grade* as these are the three factors (the independent variables) in our data collection.

5. Next click on the **Options** box to open the **Univariate: Options** dialog box. Under **Factor(s) and Factor Interactions**, click on whatever you think you will need. If you don't know what you will find, we advise you to click on all possible and logical interactions. In our example, we clicked on *gender, school type, grade (the factors)* and then on *gender*school type, gender*grade, school type*grade* and *gender*school type*grade* (the Factor Interactions). Then click on the ▶ to place them into the box at the right titled **Display Means for:**.

6. Under **Display**, click on **Descriptive Statistics, Estimates of effect size, Observed power** and **Homogeneity tests**.

7. Click **Continue** to return to the **Univariate** dialog box.

8. Click on **Plots** and when the dialog box opens, place one of the independent variables in the Horizontal box. We placed *School Type* in the Horizontal box.

> When entering data for plots, you usually place the independent variable that has the most levels in the horizontal box but, in this example, all of our IVs had only two levels. For example, if we had three grade levels, "Grades" would have been placed in the horizontal box.

9. Place the other independent variable (we placed Grade Level) in the box labelled **Separate Lines**.

10. *Do not forget to click on **Add**.* You should now see the two variables (school type and grade level) listed in the Plots section.

11. Click on **Model**, then click on **Full factorial**.

12. Click on **Continue** and click on **OK**.

The output from the SPSS programme gives you descriptive statistics and Levene's Test of Equality of Error Variance (asked for in Step 6) and the Tests of Between-Subjects Effects otherwise known as the three-way ANOVA).

Descriptive Statistics

The SPSS output is displayed in Table 17.11 and shows "who" is in what class, grade, and attending what type of school. It provides the mean scores, standard deviations and the number of students in each subgroup. This acts as a good way to check that you have entered your data correctly. For example, if you know that you had 25 students from each school type and saw 24 in one group but 26 in another, you should know right away that something was wrong.

> Use the basic data (e.g., subgroups and number in each subgroup) from the Descriptives table when you are describing your sample in the Methods section in Chapter 3.
> Use the mean scores and standard deviations from each subgroup from the Descriptives table when discussing your findings in the Results section in Chapter 4.

Table 17.11: *Results of Selecting Descriptive Statistics in the GLM Programme (Step 6)*

Descriptive Statistics

Dependent Variable: CMMS

Gender	School Type	Grade Level	Mean	Std. Deviation	N
Boys	Government	Grade 1	80.67	12.420	6
		Grade 4	75.25	11.196	8
		Total	77.57	11.600	14
	Private	Grade 1	107.67	4.457	6
		Grade 4	112.63	8.141	8
		Total	110.50	7.057	14
	Total	Grade 1	94.17	16.672	12
		Grade 4	93.94	21.493	16
		Total	94.04	19.232	28
Girls	Government	Grade 1	75.67	11.587	6
		Grade 4	74.60	8.325	5
		Total	75.18	9.755	11
	Private	Grade 1	105.14	7.669	7
		Grade 4	117.25	4.787	4
		Total	109.55	8.915	11
	Total	Grade 1	91.54	17.868	13
		Grade 4	93.56	23.421	9
		Total	92.36	19.810	22
Total	Government	Grade 1	78.17	11.746	12
		Grade 4	75.00	9.815	13
		Total	76.52	10.678	25
	Private	Grade 1	106.31	6.277	13
		Grade 4	114.17	7.322	12
		Total	110.08	7.767	25
	Total	Grade 1	92.80	16.995	25
		Grade 4	93.80	21.716	25
		Total	93.30	19.306	50

Levene's Test of Equality of Error Variance (from Step 6)

The results of the Levene's Test are shown in Table 17.12. This is one of the tests used to check that one of the basic assumptions – that of equality of means – are met before you start to interpret the two-way ANOVA statistics. You are trying to get a significance of any number greater than 0.05 so you can reject the hypothesis of inequality. If you can reject this hypothesis, then you can assume that the variance of the dependent variable across groups is equal. In our example, the significance is 0.621 and this means that we can look at the main effects and interactions secure in the knowledge that the assumption of homogeneity of variance has not been violated.

Levene's Test of Equality of Error Variances

Dependent Variable: CMMS

F	df1	df2	Sig.
.763	7	42	.621

Table 17.12: *Levene's Test of Equality of Error Variances*

Tests the null hypothesis that the error variance of the dependent variable is equal across groups.

a. Design:
Intercept+GENDER+SCHTYP+GRADE+GENDER * SCHTYP+GENDER * GRADE+SCHTYP * GRADE+GENDER * SCHTYP * GRADE

Reading an ANOVA Table

Before you look at the main three-way ANOVA table, realise that it contains a lot of numbers that look very frightening. You really do not have to worry because the good thing about all these numbers is that you mainly need to scan down the column headed by "Sig." and see which factors and interactions are equal to or less than 0.05. When you are using an ANOVA, significant probabilities are generally what most researchers look for. Remember that you are looking at this table to see if the scores were different according to the different factors.

Now, look at Table 17.13 and see how the results are organised. The first line shows the result of the overall analysis, $F = 24.59$ and $p = 0.0000$ so you know that the scores on the CMMS differed significantly from each other. Note that if the F had not been significant, it would have implied that all the students achieved similar scores and the researcher would have had to conclude that the culture fair test really was "fair."

Table 17.13: *An Example of a Three-Way ANOVA Table*

Dependent Variable: CMMS

Source	Type III Sum of Squares	df	Mean Square	F	Sig.	Partial Eta Squared	Noncent. Parameter	Observed Power[a]
Corrected Model	14680.318[b]	7	2097.188	24.589	.000	.804	172.122	1.000
Intercept	417619.306	1	417619.306	4896.460	.000	.991	4896.460	1.000
GENDER	9.379	1	9.379	.110	.742	.003	.110	.062
SCHTYP	13875.322	1	13875.322	162.684	.000	.795	162.684	1.000
GRADE	83.391	1	83.391	.978	.328	.023	.978	.162
GENDER * SCHTYP	44.741	1	44.741	.525	.473	.012	.525	.109
GENDER * GRADE	98.464	1	98.464	1.154	.289	.027	1.154	.183
SCHTYP * GRADE	412.960	1	412.960	4.842	.033	.103	4.842	.575
GENDER * SCHTYP * GRADE	5.833	1	5.833	.068	.795	.002	.068	.058
Error	3582.182	42	85.290					
Total	453507.000	50						
Corrected Total	18262.500	49						

a. Computed using alpha = .05

b. R Squared = .804 (Adjusted R Squared = .771)

Looking at Main Effects

Following the "Corrected Model" and "Intercept" are the results of individual factor analyses (each independent variable without the level considered) and these are called the **MAIN EFFECTS**. Analysis of the main effects means that all the scores from the CMMS were analysed according to each independent variable (and is 'sort of' equivalent to 3 *t*-tests). Of the three main effects, only "school type" was significant ($p = 0.0001$). From this, we can be certain that children attending one type of school achieved scores that were significantly different from children attending another type of school. We can also see that there was no gender difference between scores: boys and girls and obtained similar scores on the CMMS ($p = 0.74$). It also means that there were no main effects for grade level – scores achieved on the CMMS did not differ significantly among students in grades One and Four ($p = 0.328$). The only significant main effect was school type.

> Sometimes, at this stage, a researcher might just remove the two factors (gender and grade level) and analyse the results using only one factor as in a one-way ANOVA.
>
> The results from this example show why the GLM programme should be used – because now, we can see if there are any significant interactions.

The significant main effects showed that the scores differed according to the type of school the students attended ($F_{(1,49)} = 162.68$, $p < 0.05$). Because there were only two levels for each factor, it was easy to find out which group obtained the higher scores. All that was needed was to find the means and standard deviations for each factor – and you have done this using Descriptives on the SPSS programme (Step 6). Look at the Total (the last row) in Table 17.11. The total mean score for students attending government schools was 76.52 while the total mean score for students attending private schools was 106.31. The *F* statistic tells us that this difference was significant ($F_{(1,49)} = 24.59$, $p < 0.05$). We can now conclude that students in Grades One and Four attending private schools achieved higher scores on the Columbia Mental Maturity Scale than did their peers attending government schools. If you had more than two levels for each factor, you would carry out "contrasts" or multiple comparisons discussed in Chapter 16, *t*-test.

The Effect Size (η^2)

Under the column headed partial η^2 is the effect size for each factor. The type of school attended by the students was significant and the effect size is 0.795. Based on Cohen's criterion, this is indeed a large effect and shows that the actual difference between the mean scores is very large. Using the same criterion, the interaction effect of grade level by school type is significant and and this should be classified as a large effect size (0.103).

Think About This . . .
When writing the results, one school of thought states that you should never report main effects when you find significant interactions while another states that you can report significant main effects if they are *very* significant and contribute to more than 75% of the variance of the total scores.

The fact remains that you must always report the main effects *in terms of the interactions found.* Frankly, we feel that you can report significant main effects if you are also careful to state that these main effects are reported in terms of their interactions.

Looking at the Interaction Effects

The major benefit of using the GLM programme is that it gives interaction effects according to different levels of the other factor. After looking at the main effects, the next four lines show how each factor (independent variable) was paired with the next – these are the interactions. In our example, gender was paired with school type (gen*sctype), then with grade level (gen*grd). This continued until all three factors had been paired with each other and all three together – the final interaction was gender*school type*grade level.

The results of the GLM) show whether or not there were interaction effects. The interaction effect answers the question: "Did the dependent variable vary according to how it was combined with two or more independent variables?"

Using our example, we would ask: "Did the children's scores from the CMMS vary according to how they were combined with gender, school type and/or grade level?" By looking at the interaction effects (Table 17.13), we can see that the scores from the CMMS varied according to grade by school type ($F = 4.84$, $p = 0.03$) but nothing else.

What is an Interaction Effect????

One way to think of an interaction effect between two factors is that one factor works differently at the separate levels of another factor. For example, men may require a large dose of medicine, but, for the same effect, women might only need a smaller dose of the same medicine. Here, the effect of different levels of the drug dose (large or small) depends on the gender level (male or female). So, interaction means that effects at different levels of one factor are modified according to the levels of the other factor.

In other words, scores (the dependent variable) may change according to the different levels of the factors (the independent variables such as school type, grade or gender). If you plotted out the scores for an interaction effect, the lines would not be parallel. This can be contrasted with no interaction effect that happens when one independent variable has a uniform influence across all categories of the dependent variable, either increasing or decreasing it by the same amount. When there is no interaction, if you plotted the mean scores of the dependent variable at each level of the independent variables, the lines on the plot would be parallel.

This can be a difficult thing to understand and the best way is to look at the plot asked for in Step 10. Because the lines are not parallel, we can tell that there was an interaction effect and the result of the three-way ANOVA table shows that the differences were significant. In Figure 17.7 we have placed the Grade Levels (the IV) on the horizontal line and the CMMS scores (DV) according to School Type on the separated lines. The numbers on the side of the vertical lines represent the CMMS scores.

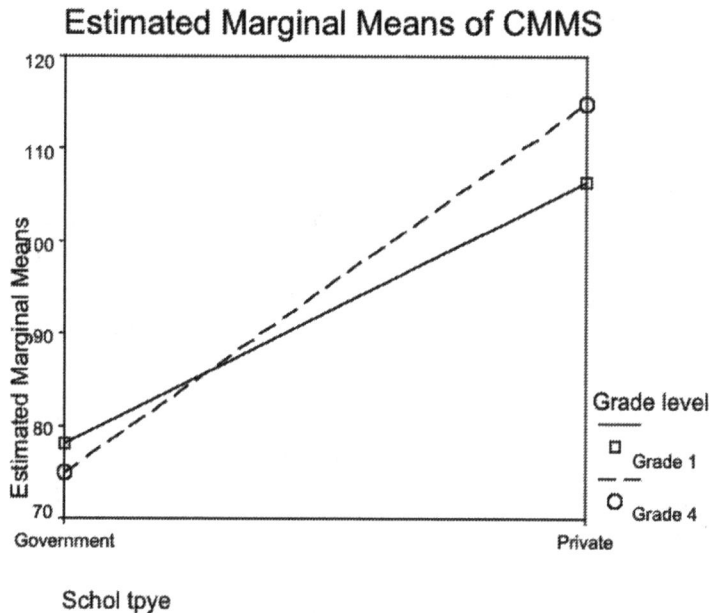

Figure 17.7: Results of selecting a plot placing the Grade Level on the horizontal line and School Type on the separated lines. This plot shows how the scores on the CMMS varied according to grade level and school type.

You can decide for yourself which plot you want to use. The researcher chose to put the plot pictured in Figure 17.7 into her final paper because the figure really showed how much higher the students attending private schools scored when compared to the students attending government schools. The plot also showed that the scores varied according to the grade level. In this plot, the Grade Four students attending private schools achieved higher scores on the CMMS than the Grade One students. It also looks as if the Grade Four students attending government schools achieved somewhat lower scores than the Grade One students but, according to the results of the ANOVA, they were not significantly lower. A picture is worth a thousand words and this picture was very powerful.[7]

If you want to work this out yourself, look at the Descriptives in Table 17.11. The mean scores for students attending government were 75.25 for the Grade One students and 75.00 for the Grade Four students. Then look at the scores for the students attending private schools: $\bar{x} = 106.31$ for students in Grade One and $\bar{x} = 114.08$ for students in Grade Four. You just have to draw the picture that best represents what you want to tell.

---

7. Matalon, B. (1999).

Interpreting the Results of the Three-Way ANOVA

Based on the results of the ANOVA output, you might write:

> *A three-way ANOVA was computed to investigate the impact of gender, grade level and school type on the scores from a culture fair test. The only significant main effect was school type (F $_{(1, 49)}$ = 19.57, p < 0.008) and the effect size (η^2 = 0.77) showed a large difference in the mean values of the scores. Students attending government schools scored significantly lower than their peers attending private schools (see Table XX for the mean scores and standard deviations for the students from each school type). There were no main effects for gender or grade level. The CMMS scores obtained by boys and girls in Grades One and Four did not differ significantly from each other.*
>
> *Although the ANOVA showed no significant main effects for grade level, there was a significant interaction effect between grade level and school type (F = 2.03, p < 0.05) with a large effect size (η^2 = 0.046). The mean scores of the Grade Four students attending private schools (mean score = 114.17, SD = 7.32) were higher than the mean scores of their counterparts in Grade One (mean score = 106.31, SD = 6.28) while the scores for students attending government schools were relatively similar in both grade levels (Grade One: mean score = 75.25, SD = 15.70; Grade Four: mean score = 75.00, SD = 9.81). This result shows that the mental maturity index had increased over years spent in school for students attending private schools but not for students attending government schools.*

Then, you would place Table 17.11 about here because the table always follows the verbal description.

More About Main Effects and Interactions

We are spending a lot of time on looking at and interpreting interactions because we have found that many researchers are either not aware of their implications or simply do not understand how to interpret them. When you use the two-way or the three-way ANOVA, you may find many different kinds of interactions. In our example using the three-way ANOVA, we saw significant grade level and school type interaction effects even though the main effect of grade level was not significant.

To further clarify the concept of main effects and interaction, we are using hypothetical data based on a research design involving the use of a new English book. The researchers wanted to investigate whether the use of it would lead to an increase in reading scores. The researchers formulated two null hypotheses (1) The use of a new book did not lead to an increase in reading scores of students in Grade 3, and (2) There was no gender difference in reading scores according to the type of book used. In this hypothetical research design, students in two Grade 3 classes were taught using the new book while in two other classes, the Grade 3 students were taught using the old book. In addition, the researchers wanted to find out if there was any gender difference: Was the book better for girls? or boys? or did it make any difference? This made the research a 2 X 2 factorial design (use of new book versus use of old book) by (males versus females).

Needless to state, before using the new book, all students were give a pretest to determine that their basic reading levels were similar. After the book had been used for more than six months, the researchers had to give all students a test to determine whether scores had increased. The post-test reading scores were the dependent variables.

The research design can be drawn out a number of ways. Table 17.14 shows two examples of drawing out the research design. In (a) the number beside each small n shows how many students were in each group. In (b), the groups were not given numbers but the numbers of students were placed in the appropriate box.

Table 17.14: *Two Ways to Draw a 2 x 2 Factorial Research Design*

		old book	new book
Gender	male	n1 = 10	n2 = 15
	female	n3 = 18	n4 = 12

(a)

old book		new book	
males	females	males	females
10	18	15	12

(b)

The factors were treatment groups (Group1 = old book, Group 2 = new book), and gender (males, females). The "scores from the reading test" was the dependent variable. If you were entering data, you would enter your data in the same manner as the previous example (e.g., student ID, treatment group, gender, reading scores).

Recognising and Interpreting Main Effects Only

In this example, you could have four possible outcomes in terms of the main effects: (1) no main effects, (2) main effect of gender (3) main effect of using the new book and (4) main effects of both gender and using the new book. Each of the following tables show different mean scores of the children according to gender and type of book.

To help you understand the concept of the different types of main effects and interactions, we used different data sets for each example. Each example has a table and a figure attached to it. Look at the numbers (the mean scores of the reading test) in the table first, then see how they have been drawn out in the graph. Realise that (a) the numbers used for the lines in the graph are taken from the table and (b) in the case where there is no interaction effects, the lines in the graph are relatively parallel.

1.   **No Main Effects:** Table 17.15 shows the mean scores that the children received according to gender and type of book used. When an ANOVA was calculated, the significance of F showed that regardless of which book was used or whether the children were boys or girls, scores were similar – there was no significant difference between reading scores regardless of which book was used or whether the children were boys or girls. Figure 17.8 shows a plot of the mean scores achieved by the children according to the type of book used.

Table 17.15: *Mean Scores of the Reading Test for Gender of Children and Type of Book Used*

		Old Book	New Book	Average
GENDER	Male	19.2	18.9	19.05
	Female	19.5	19.5	19.55
	Average	19.3	19.2	

Figure 17.8: A plot of the mean scores achieved by boys and girls according to the type of book used. This plot illustrates no main effects and no interactions as the lines are fairly close together and are relatively parallel.

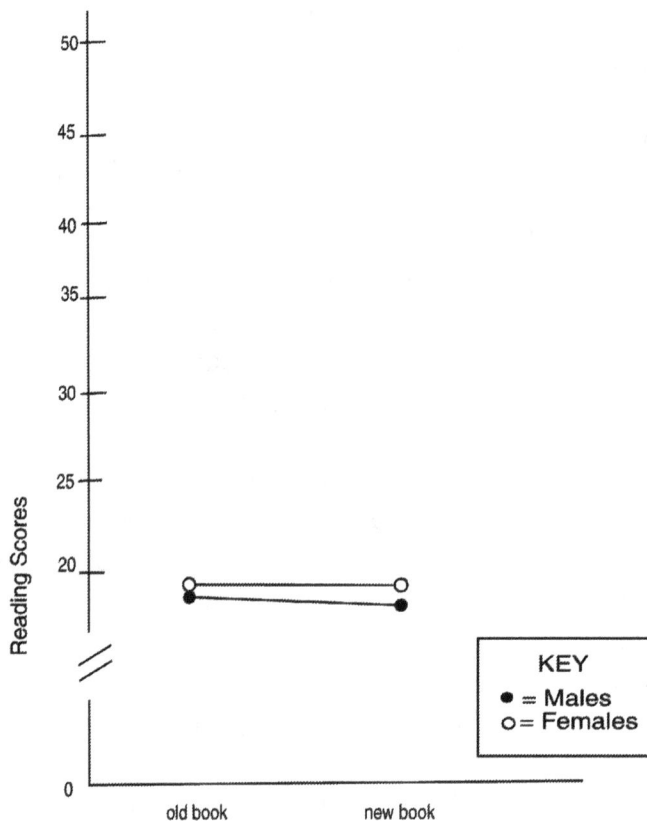

From the row averages in Table 17.11 you can see that there was no differences between the mean reading scores of the boys ($\bar{X}$ = 19.05) and girls ($\bar{X}$ = 19.55). When you look at the column averages, there is no difference in the average scores between the children who used the old book ($\bar{X}$ = 19.3) and those who used the new book ($\bar{X}$ = 19.2). When the researchers analysed their data using an ANOVA, they would have to conclude the new book had no effect on reading achievement.

Now look again at Figure 17.8 – this is a graphic illustration of how the scores did not differ significantly from each other. As you can see, the two sets of scores are very close to each other and the two lines are almost parallel. In other words, there are no main effects and no interactions. There is not much difference between the four sets of scores. All are clustered between 18.9 and 19.55.

When you draw a plot such as this, remember to always put in the key (e.g., males = ● and females = o so that the reader will understand which scores belong to which group of participants.

2. **Main effect of using the new book:** In this example, results of an ANOVA showed that the reading scores of all children taught using the new book increased significantly compared to the reading scores of children taught using the old book. The mean scores of the children according to gender and type of book are shown in Table 17.16 and the plot of the mean scores achieved by the children according to gender and type of book are shown in Figure 17.9.

Table 17.16: *The Mean Scores of the Reading Test According to Gender and Type of Book*

		Old Book	New Book	Average
GENDER	Male	19.2	25.3	22.5
	Female	19.6	26.2	22.9
	Average	19.4	25.7	

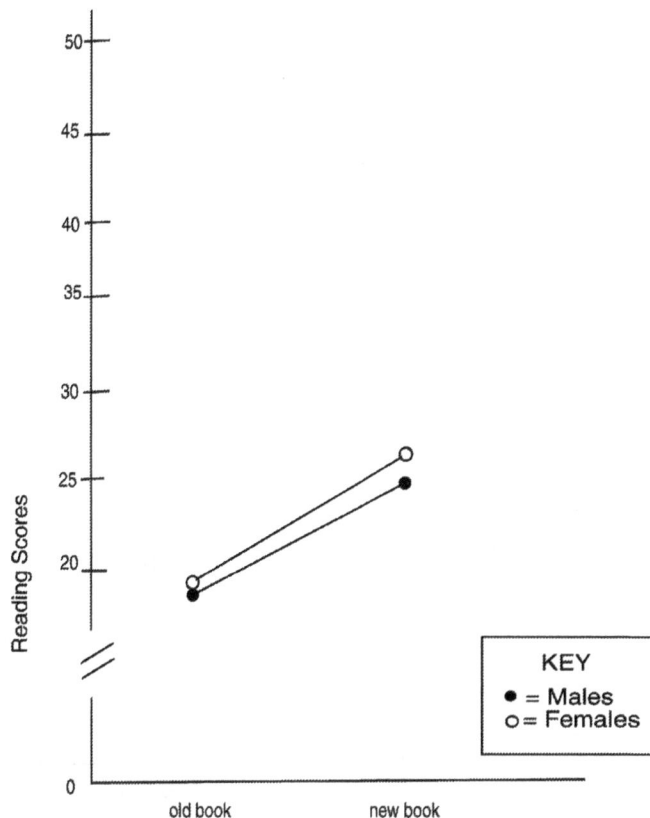

Figure 17.9: A plot of the mean scores achieved by boys and girls according to the type of book used. This plot illustrates a main effect of the type of book used but no interactions. The lines are still relatively parallel but show an increase in scores according to type of book used.

In Table 17.16, you can see that the scores differed according to the type of book used – the mean scores ranged between 19.2 and 19.6 for students taught using the old book but when students were taught using the new book, the mean scores were higher and ranged between 25.3 and 26.2. This is a graphic illustration of how the scores did differ from each other according to the type of book used. Note, however, that in Figure 17.9, the lines are still relatively parallel showing that there are no interactions.

3. **Main effect of gender only:** In Table 17.17, you can see that the reading scores changed only according to gender for all the children but not according to the type of book used. Results of an ANOVA showed that the reading scores of the boys were significantly higher than those of the girls regardless of what book was used. The scores are plotted in Figure 17.10.

Table 17.17: *Mean Scores of Students according to Gender and Type of Book.*

		Old Book	New Book	Average
GENDER	Male	25.3	25.8	25.6
	Female	19.6	19.2	19.4
	Average	22.45	22.5	

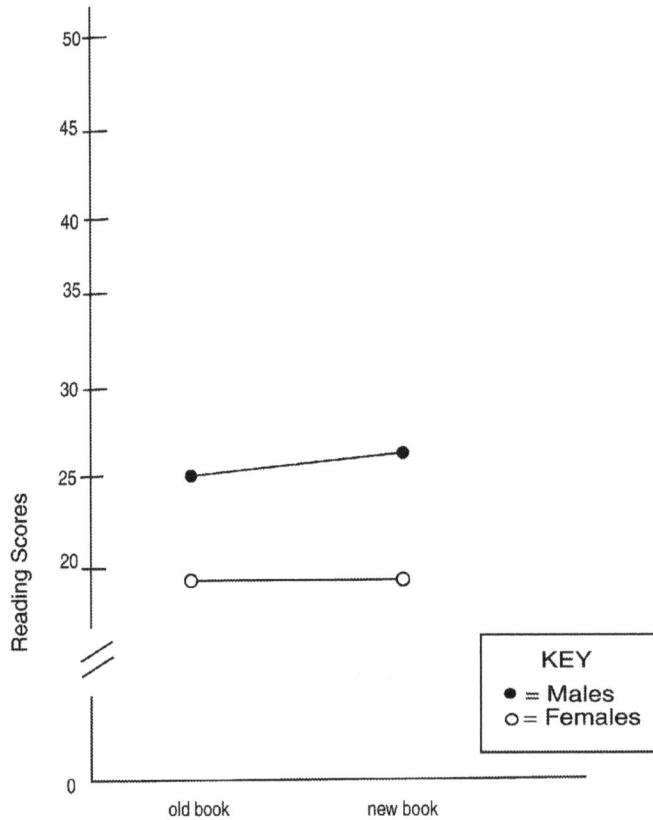

Figure 17.10: A plot of the mean scores achieved by boys and girls according to the type of book used. This plot illustrates that the scores differed according to gender but there is no interactions between gender and type of book. The lines are still relatively parallel and show a difference in scores only according to gender of the children.

4. **Mean Scores Showing Main Effects of both Gender and Use of the New Book:** In Table 17.18, you can see that the mean scores increased considerably when the new book was used (for the new book, $\bar{x} = 37.5$ which is much higher than $\bar{x} = 27.5$ for the old book) and there is also a difference in the reading scores by both boys and girls. Although the girls actually scored higher than the boys, both improved by roughly the same amount (about 10 points). Look at Figure 17.11, and you can see that the lines are still fairly parallel showing that use of the new book increased the mean scores of both boys and girls relatively equally.

Table 17.18: *Mean Reading Scores According to Gender and Type of Book Used*

		Old Book	New Book	Average
GENDER	Male	15.3	25.8	20.5
	Female	39.6	49.2	44.4
	Average	27.5	37.5	

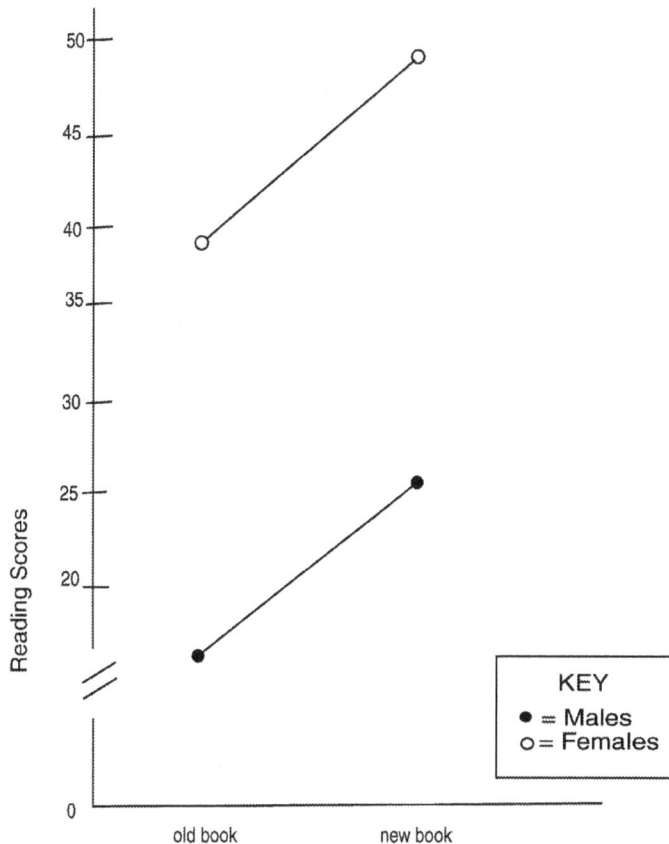

Figure 17.11: A plot of the mean scores achieved by boys and girls according to the type of book used. This plot illustrates the main effects of both type of book used and gender but no interactions as the lines are still relatively parallel to each other.

When one independent variable has a uniform influence across all categories of the other independent variables and either increases or decreases them all by the relatively same amounts, then there is no interaction effect.

Recognising and Interpreting Interaction Effects

The two factors were gender and use of book. When we look for interactions, we are trying to find out if mean scores of the dependent variable vary (increase or decrease) depending on both of the factors.

1. *No main effects BUT an interaction effect of book by gender:* If using the new book helped the boys but not the girls (or the other way around), we would get an interaction effect of gender*book.

This is one of the more interesting results because if you look at the column and row averages shown in Table 17.19, you would see similar averages. If you just looked at the main effects of results of a one-way ANOVA, you would have to conclude that the learning scores were similar regardless of gender of student or use of the new book. This, however, would be wrong! There is an overall gender and book effect but the average scores are working in opposite directions and they cancel each other out so that the actual effect of both gender and book is hidden when you only consider the overall row or column averages. (Note that this is exactly what happened with the scores of the CMMS in the example given using the three-way ANOVA)– the average scores of the Grades One and Four students cancelled each other out and you only were able to see the impact of Grade level and School type on the scores by looking at the interaction effect.

You would never discover the interesting interaction effect of gender by book unless you used the two-way ANOVA. In Figure 17.12, the mean scores obtained by boys and girls are plotted according to the type of book used. This plot shows that the type of book used had a great impact on the reading scores. If the new book was used to teach boys, then their scores increased but when it was used to teach girls, their scores decreased.

Table 17.19: *Average Scores of Children by Gender and Type of Book Showing No Main Effects But An Interaction Effect of Gender and Type of Book*

Gender	Book Used	Mean	N	Row Average
Males	New Book Old Book	40.08 20.12	30 30	30.14
Females	New Book Old Book	20.36 40.87	30 30	30.58
(Column Average) New Book Old Book		30.22 30.49	60 60	

Figure 17.12: A plot of the mean scores achieved by boys and girls according to the type of book

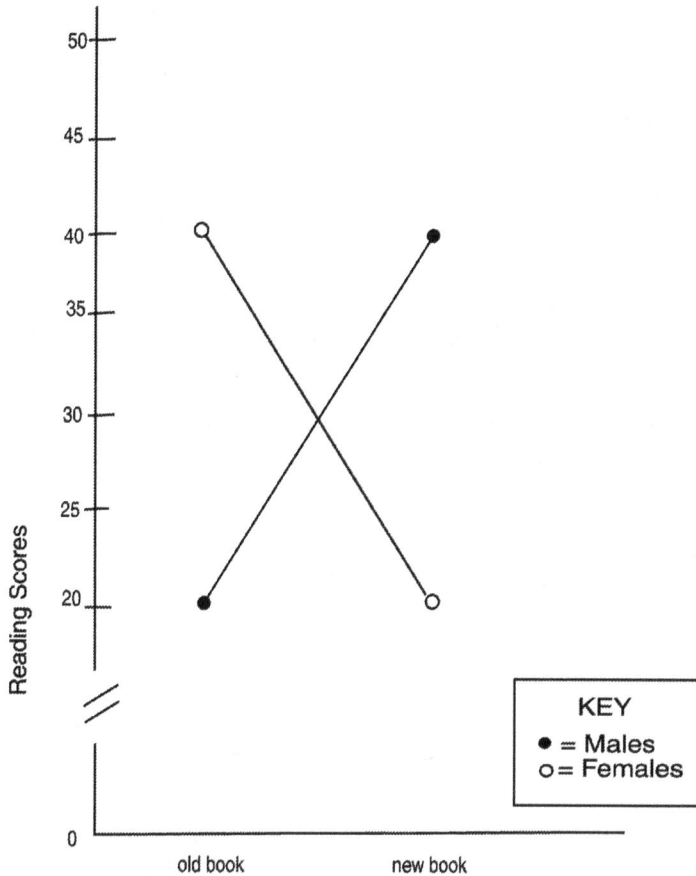

used. The lines are not parallel and show the interaction of book by gender.

To interpret this result, you would have to write something similar to the following:

> *Results of a two-way ANOVA using gender and use of book as the independent variables and the reading scores as the dependent variable showed no main effects for either gender (F = 0.765, p = 0.45) or use of book (F = 0.969, p = 0.86).[8] However, the interaction effects showed that scores of boys and girls differed significantly according to the book used for teaching (F= 5.936, p < 0.05). As can be seen in Table 17.19, when the boys were taught using the new book, their mean reading scores increased significantly. The boys taught using the old book obtained a mean score of 20.12 compared with the mean scores of boys using the new book (= 40.08). The mean scores for the girls also differed significantly, but $\bar{x}$ the opposite direction: girls taught using the new book obtained a mean score of 20.36 while the mean scores of the girls taught using the old book was 40.87. It appears that the new book is more efficient at increasing reading scores for boys than it is for their female peers.*

---

8. Although we have reported the *F* and *p* results, we have not put in the ANOVA tables. Just concentrate on understanding main effects and interactions.

> This is very important information and checking for this type of interaction effect is one of the main reasons for using the two-way ANOVA.
> The moral is: *Always check for possible interactions even if the main effects are not significant!*

2. *Main effect "gender" and an interaction effect of book by gender.* The data shown in Table 17.20 reveals that the students taught using the old book had similar reading scores (males $\bar{X}$ = 30.12 and females $\bar{X}$ = 30.87). The reading scores of students taught using the new book, however, differed according to the gender of the students. Looking at Table 17.20, you can see that following the use of the new book, the boys' mean scores decreased to $\bar{X}$ = 10.8 while the mean scores of the girls increased to $\bar{X}$ = 50.36.

Table 17.20: *Mean Scores of a Reading Test According to Gender and Type of Book Used*

Gender	Book Used	Mean	N	Gender Average
Males	New Book	10.08	30	20.14
	Old Book	30.12	30	
Females	New Book	50.36	30	40.58
	Old Book	30.87	30	
Book Average		30.22	60	
		30.49	60	

If you just looked at the book averages, you should see that there was no difference in the average reading learning improvement for those who used the book and those who did not (no main effect for the use of the book, x = 30.22 and x = 30.49). The row averages, however, show that the reading scores differed according to gender (a main effect for gender: x = 20.14 for boys and x = 40.58 for girls) and this shows up as an interaction effect. The use of the new book did not have the same effect on both boys and girls.

Figure 17.13 shows lines of different slopes, signalling an interaction. The use of the new book did change the reading scores but only in terms of the gender of the children using it. When boys were taught using the new book, their scores decreased and when girls were taught using the new book their scores increased. However, both boys and girls taught using the old book obtained similar scores.

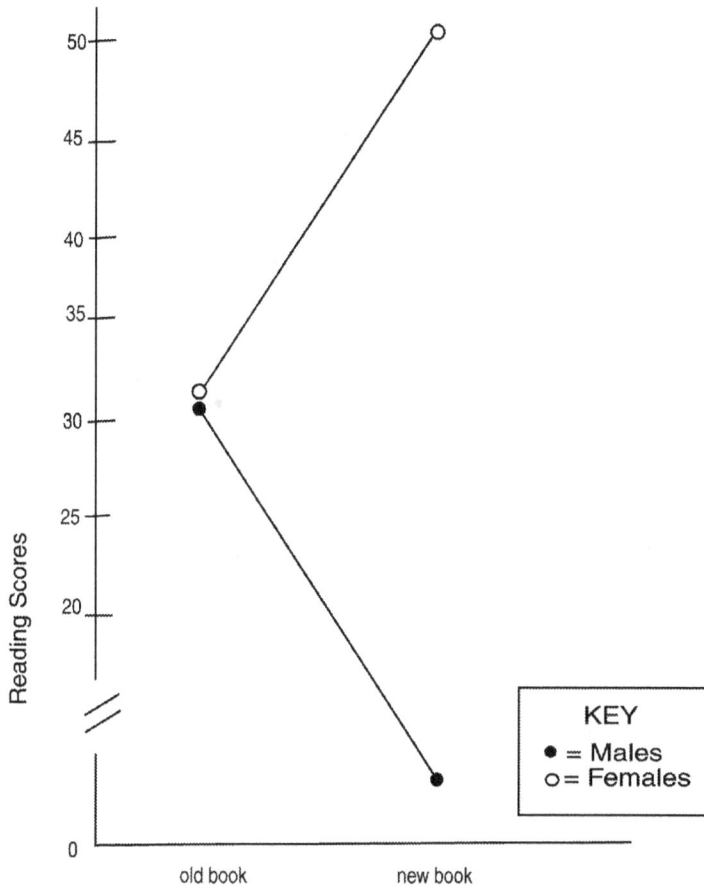

Figure 17.13: A plot of the mean scores achieved by boys and girls according to the type of book used. The interaction effect shows that reading scores of the males decreased after using the new book but that the reading scores of the females increased after using the new book. The lines are not parallel showing the interaction effect.

To report this interaction effect, you could state something to the effect:

> *Results of an ANOVA using type of book and gender as the independent variables and the reading scores as the dependent variable showed no main effects for type of book (F = 5.93, p < 0.45) used but a main effect for gender (F = 0.765, p < 0.05). However, the main effect of gender should be interpreted in terms of the interaction. The interaction effects showed that scores of boys and girls differed significantly according to the type of book used for teaching (F = 5.936, p <0.05). As can be seen in Table 17.20, both boys and girls obtained similar scores on their reading when taught using the old book, but when the students were taught using the new book, the mean scores of the boys decreased (x = 10.8) while the mean scores for the girls increased (x = 50.36). Results of a two-way ANOVA showed that these differences were significant (F = 5.03, p < 0.05) It appears that the new book is better to use with girls rather than with boys.*

3.   *Main effect "new book" **AND** an interaction effect of book by gender:* The reading scores of

the children taught using the new book increased significantly and you might want to conclude that using the new book is a good thing. But, is it? The interaction effect gives us a different story. Look at the scores of the boys and girls who used the new book. The reading scores of the boys stayed fairly stagnant – their scores did not increase at all, but the scores of the girls increased dramatically. This interaction effect is illustrated in Figure 17.14.

Table 17.21: *Mean Scores of a Reading Test According to Gender and Type of Book Used*

Book Used	Gender	Mean	N	Book Average
New Book	Males	30.08	30	40.22
Old Book	Females	50.36	30	
New Book	Males	30.12	30	25.50
Old Book	Females	20.87	30	
(Gender Average)			60	
Males		30.10	60	
Females		35.61		

Figure 17.14: The interaction effect illustrating that the reading scores of males did not increase

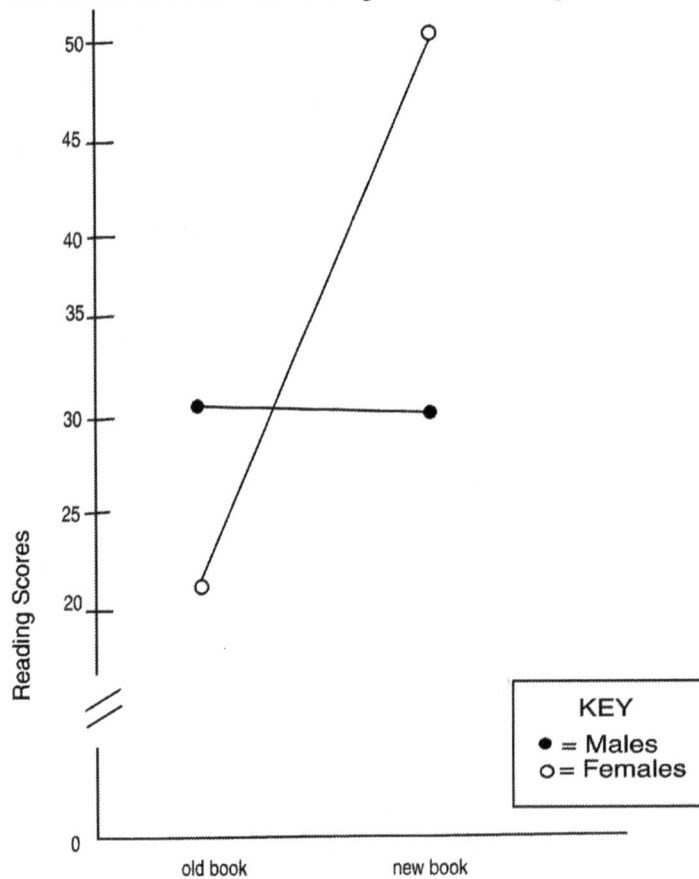

after using the new book but that the scores of the females increased.

To report this interaction effect, you could state something to the effect:

The results of an ANOVA using type of book and gender as the independent variable and the reading scores as the dependent variable showed no main effects for gender (F = 0.765, p = 0.45) but a main effect for the type of book used (F = 5.936, p < 0.05). However, the main effect of type of book used should be interpreted in terms of the interaction. The interaction effects showed that scores of boys and girls differed significantly according to the type of book used for teaching (F = 5.936, p < 0.03). As seen in Table 17.21, the boys obtained similar scores regardless of the type of book used (old book: $\bar{x}$ *= 30.12;new book:* $\bar{x}$ *= 30.08). When girls were taught using the new book, however, their scores increased significantly (old book: x = 20.87;* $\bar{x}$ *new book x = 50.36).* $\bar{x}$ *It appears that the type of book used did not have any impact on boys' reading scores but that using the* $\bar{x}$ *new book increased the* $\bar{x}$ *girls' scores significantly.*

4. *Interaction effects of both gender and use of the new book:* The reading scores changed according to both gender and the use of the new book. As you can see from looking at Table 17.22, the average reading scores differed according both to the book used and the gender of the students. The mean reading score from students who used the new book was 30.22 while the reading score from the students who were taught using the old book was only 20.49 – this is the main effect of the type of book used. At the same time, look at the scores according to gender: the boys achieved a mean reading score of 40.10 while the girls only achieved a reading score of 10.61. This is the main effect of gender. Obviously, reading scores were impacted by both the type of book used and the gender of the student. But, how?

   By looking at Figure 17.15, you can see that the reading scores of the girls stayed relatively the same. The new book did not seem to have any effect on their learning to read at all. The scores of the boys, however, increased.

Table 17.22: *Mean Scores of a Reading Test According to Gender and Type of Book Used*

Book Used	Gender	Mean	N	Book Average
New Book	Males	50.08	30	30.22
	Females	10.36	30	
Old Book	Males	30.12	30	20.49
	Females	10.87	30	
(Gender Average)	Males	40.10	60	
	Females	10.61	60	

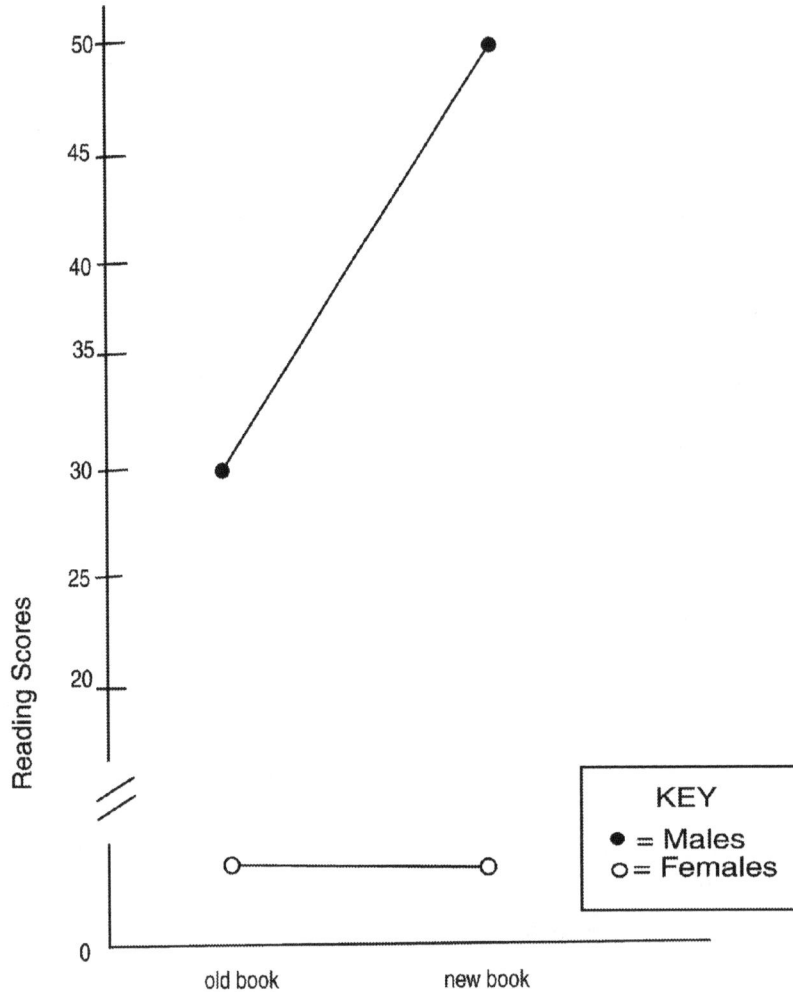

Figure 17.15: When the mean scores of the students were plotted on a graph according to gender and type of book used, you can see the interaction effect of both gender and book. This illustrates that the reading scores of females remained similar regardless of type of book used but that using the new book increased the scores of the males.

This is an example when you must interpret the main effects in terms of the interaction effect. You would have to state that the main effects of both gender and type of book used were significant (and put in the F and p values) but must be interpreted in terms of their interaction effects. Then you would write about how the scores differed only for boys when the new book was used but that the girls scores did not change regardless of the book being used to teach them.

There are many different combinations that could give interaction effects. What ever combination you get, it is hoped that these examples will help you interpret your results. The main thing to remember is that whenever you are doing a factorial research design, examine the interactions – even if there are no main effects!

18
Non-Parametric Tests

In Chapter 3, we asked the question: "*Parametric or non-parametric research designs?*" When you looked at the "Decision Chart," more reference was made to the differences between parametric and non-parametric statistical methods. In both these sections, we advised using parametric techniques whenever possible but there are certain cases in which non-parametric techniques are the correct statistical analyses to use. Non-parametric techniques can be very useful – particularly when you have data that is categorical or from a non-normal distribution. Of course, by now, you know that you must use non-parametric methods if your data is measured using nominal variables.

> To use non-parametric techniques to analyse your data, all the other assumptions are still required:
> (1) your sample population must be randomly selected and assigned, and
> (2) the observations must be independent.

Chi-Square Test for Independence

We begin this section with the chi-square test for independence because this is the one non-parametric test that has no parametric equivalent and it is a widely used non-parametric statistical technique. Chi is pronounced kye (rhymes with eye) and is the Greek letter for "ch." Chi-square is written as χ^2 so whenever you see this sign, you will know what it means.

The chi-square test must be used when you have categorical, dichotomous variables (not scores). Remember that a dichotomous variable can have only one possible level, such as gender – a person can be either a male or female, or "yes-no" answers – a person either answers "yes" or "no" or age groups – a person can only be in one age group such as "under 15," "16 to 20," "21 to 25," etc. Other examples of common nominal variables comprised as categories are parents (mother or father), demographics (urban or rural), and school (primary or secondary; new secondary or traditional, private or government). In all of these variables, a person can only be placed in one category. We often use these nominal or categorical variables in the demographics section at the beginning of a questionnaire.

> If you only consider this type of category variable, you will be very limited in the type of analysis you can do.

Example 1: Using the Chi-Square Test – a 2 X 2 Research Design

To determine frequencies, we simply count the number of people who fall into each category that we have decided to use. For example, we could count the number of males and females (gender) who use hard drugs (yes or no answers). This would make it a 2 X 2 research design – two levels of gender and two levels of answers. The data would then be placed in a table and might look something like that shown in Table 18.1.

Chi-square results are shown in a table called the *contingency table*. Each cell in the table represents one of the categories. The numbers in each cell are NOT scores – they are the numbers of people who fall into each category. The chi-square test compares the actual counts from the collected data with the numbers that you expect to get.[1]

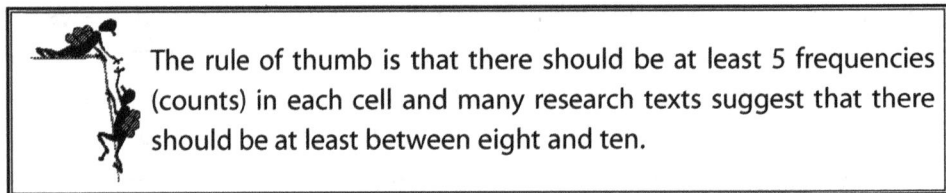

> The rule of thumb is that there should be at least 5 frequencies (counts) in each cell and many research texts suggest that there should be at least between eight and ten.

In our "hard drug use" example, we might have thought that half of all the males used drugs and half of all the females used drugs. This means that of the 50 males we asked, we would have expected that 25 were drug users and that 25 were not, and the same for females. The null hypothesis would read: "Half of the males and half of the females interviewed said they used hard drugs." However, the results of our questionnaire (see Table 18.1) showed different results. But, these results could have been due to sampling error rather than what was really happening in the population. This is where usefulness of the chi-square test is shown as it will tell us whether it is likely that we will get a difference this big even if we asked the same questions over and over again to many different people.

Table 18.1: *A Table Showing the Number of Males and Females who Used or Did Not Use Hard Drugs (N = 100).*

	Gender		
	Males	Females	Total
Use Hard Drugs	35 (70%)	20 (40%)	55 (55%)
Do Not Used Hard Drugs	15 (30%)	30 (60%)	45 (45%)
Total Gender	50	50	100

You first obtain the frequency counts by using the cross-tabs programme (see "Finding Frequencies for Categorical Data Using Cross Tabs" at the end of Chapter 12). Remember that finding the frequencies is an important part of the description of the sample and goes into Chapter 3: Methods of your final thesis. You use the frequency numbers or the percentages from the Crosstabulation frequency table when reporting your results in Chapter 4.

---

1. This is why it is also called the "goodness of fit test." It tests how good the fit is between your numbers and what was expected.

After you have used the Crosstabs programme, you can check that the totals are correct and you can also find the actual numbers and percentage of males and females who do and do not use hard drugs. Then you are ready to use the Chi-Square SPSS programme to find out if the differences between the obtained frequencies and the expected frequencies differ significantly from each other.

Calculating the Chi-square Using the SPSS Programme
1. Bring up your data in the SPSS files and click on **Analyze**.
2. When the dialog box appears, click on **Descriptive Statistics ▶ Crosstabs**.
3. This brings up the **Crosstabs: Statistics** dialog box.
4. Click on **Chi-square** in the top left hand box.
5. Click on **Continue** to open the **Crosstabs: Cell Display** dialog box.
6. In this box, click on **Observed** and **Expected**, then **Continue** to return to the **Crosstabs: Statistics** box. Click on **OK**.

> By clicking on Expected in the Crosstabs: cell Display box, you will see the expected cell counts calculated on the basis of the row and column totals in your sample. (Note, however, that you will rarely need these expected values for your report.) The output from the Chi-square test for this 2 X 2 research design will next appear on the screen and will look similar to Table 18.2.

Table 18.2: *Results of Computing the Chi-square Test*

	Value	df	Asymp. Sig. (2-sided)	Exact Sig. (2-sided)	Exact Sig. (1-sided)
Pearson Chi-Square	9.091[b]	1	.003		
Continuity Correction[a]	7.919	1	.005		
Liklihood Ratio	9.240	1	.002		
Fisher's Exact Test				0.005	0.002
Linear-by-Linear Association	9.000	1	.003		
N of Valid Cases	1000				

Notes:
a. Computed only for a 2 X 2 table
b. 0 cells (.0%) have expected count less than 5. The minimum expected count is 22.50.

In this example, the degrees of freedom = 1 (number of rows: 1 X the number of columns: 1) so it is usual to use the Continuity Correction (7.919) instead of the Pearson Chi-Square Value of 9.091. The Continuity Correction is significant at $p = 0.005$ and we will have to reject the null hypothesis stating that half of our population use hard drugs.

Look at Note b under Table 18.2. It states that no cells have an expected count of less than 5 and the minimum expected count is 22.50. If you find that some of the cells in your own data have an expected value of 0 and that less than 20% of the cells have expected values of more than 5, then you need to get a larger sample or combine cells to avoid these problems.

Interpreting the SPSS Output of the Chi-Square Computation

The statistic χ^2 reflects the size of the difference between the observed and expected frequencies. Obviously, the greater the difference, the more likely the results are to be significant so the χ^2 value should be equal to or less than the critical value of p = 0.05. You find this out by looking at the value under "Asymp. Sig. (2-sided)." In this example, the significant Continuity Correction χ^2 indicates that there are overall differences between the observed frequencies of the males and the females who take hard drugs. When you look at the crosstabulation table (Table 18.2) frequencies, you can state:

> *Based on the results of the chi-square test, the hypothesis that there is no association between gender and the use of hard drugs is rejected. More males (30 or 75% of the sample) took hard drugs than do females (20 or 40%) ($\chi^2 = 7.919$, p < 0.05).*

If you wanted to know the percentage of the sample as a whole who used hard drugs, you would look over at the Total row of the Crosstabulation results (Table 18.1) and state that 55% of the sample interviewed admitted taking hard drugs.

Example 2: Using the Chi-Square Test – a 2 X 3 Research Design

Here is an example of a question that uses frequency counts: 200 teachers were asked if they agreed or disagreed with a statement. We counted up the numbers of male and female teachers who either agreed, were neutral or disagreed with the statement.

Q1:   Please tick whether you are male ( ) or female ( )
Q2:   Please tick whether you agree ( ), disagree ( ) or are neutral ( )
with the statement

"Children are better behaved now than they used to be."

The responses were coded: Gender (male = 1 and female = 2), Agreement (Disagree = 1, Neutral = 2 and Agree = 3) making this a 2 X 3 research design. The null hypothesis was: "There was no association between gender and agreement with the statement." Using Crosstabs, we first found the frequency of each response according to the gender of the respondent (see Table 18.3). Look in Cell 1 and you can see that 20 males disagreed with the statement. These 20 male teachers were 21.1% of all males sampled and 10.0% of all the teachers in the sample.

Table 18.4 shows the results of the Chi-square test. In this example, the degree of freedom (*df*) = 2, so we must use the Pearson[2] Chi-Square value of 7.628 and the *p* value of 0.002. The results show that we must reject the null hypothesis of no association and we can write:

> *There was an association between gender and agreement with the statement: More males (58.8%) agreed with the statement than did females (41.2%) and more females (60%) disagreed with the statement than males (40%) ($\chi^2 = 7.63$, p < 0.05).[3]*

---

2. Although the mathematics for the chi-square test were worked out in 1850, it was Pearson who developed it as a goodness of fit test in 1900. So it bears his name and we use the Pearson chi-square value.

3. Look at cross tabulation Tables 18.3 and 18.4 for those figures.

Table 18.3: *Results of Crosstabulation (Three Levels of Agreement [Agremt] and Two Levels of Gender)*

Agreement*Gender Crosstabulation

				Gender		Total
				1 Male	2 Female	Total
Agremt	1 Disagree	Count		20	30	50
		% within Agremt		40.0%	60.0%	100.0%
		% within Gender		21.1%	28.6%	25.0%
		% of Total		10.0%	15.0%	25.0%
	2 Neutral	Count		25	40	65
		% within Agremt		38.5%	61.5%	100.0%
		% within Gender		26.3%	38.1%	32.5%
		% of Total		12.5%	20.0%	32.5%
	3 Agree	Count		50	35	85
		% within Agremt		58.8%	41.2%	100.0%
		% within Gender		52.6%	33.3%	42.5%
		% of Total		25.0%	17.5%	42.5%
Total		Count		95	105	200
		% within Agremt		47.5%	52.5%	100.0%
		% within Gender		100.0%	100.0%	100.0%
		% of Total		47.5%	52.5%	100.0%

Table 18.4: *Results of the Chi-Square Test of Agreement and Gender*

Chi-Square Tests

	Value	df	Asymp. Sig. (2-sided)
Pearson Chi-Square	7.628[a]	2	.022
Liklihood Ratio	7.667	2	.022
Linear-byLinear Association	5.538	1	.019
N of Valid Cases	200		

[a] 0 cells (.0%) have expected count less than 5. The minimum expected count is 23.75

Spearman's rho

Spearman's *rho* (also called Spearman's rank order correlation coefficient) is the non-parametric alternative to the parametric Pearson *r*. Similar to Pearson *r*, the *rho* is used to describe the direction and strength of the relationship between two variables. When you use Spearman's *rho*, however, at least one of the variables MUST be of ordinal scaling – both sets of scores, preferences, ratings, etc., have to be *ranked in terms of their relative order or size*.

> When you have two continuous variables with at least one using ordinal scaling, use Spearman's rank order correlation coefficient to calculate the strength of the relationship between them.

Computing Spearman's *rho* Using the SPSS Programme

For this example, we are using the same raw data we used to compute correlations for the Pearson *r* – "Correlate13.sav". This time instead of trying to determine whether two sets of scores are related, we now want to find out if the rank order of the students according to their pairs of scores are related. In other words, students who are ranked highly on one set of scores should also be ranked highly on the other set of scores. The same holds true for students who have low ranking on the first set of scores, they should also be of low ranking in the second set of scores.

This means that instead of using the actual scores, the students are ranked as being 1st, 2nd, 3rd, right down to 19th for each set of scores. The good thing about the SPSS programme is that you do not have to do the ranking by hand. As long as you have the scores, the programme will work out the rank order of each student for each set of scores for you.

1. Open your SPSS file and click on **Analyze**. Scroll down until you see **Correlate ▶**. Click on the ▶ to find the **Bivariate Correlations** dialog box.
2. Click on the two variables (**Var 1** and **Var 2**) and move them into the box marked **Variables**.
3. Click on **Spearman** in the **Correlation Coefficients** box.
4. Click **OK**.

The output of this programme should be similar to that shown in Table 18.5.

Table 18.5: *The Result of using the SPSS Programme to Compute Spearman Correlation Statistic*

Correlations

			V1	V2
Spearman's *rho*	V1	Correlation Coefficient	1.000	0.833**
		Sig. (2-tailed)	.	0.000
		N	19	19
	V2	Correlation Coefficient	0.833**	1.000
		Sig. (2-tailed)	0.000	.
		N	19	19

**Correlation is significant to the .01 level.

You read and interpret the Spearman correlation results the same way that you do for the Pearson correlations. The major difference is that you report by ranks and NOT by scores.

Notice that Pearson's correlations are usually larger and more significant than Spearman's for the same data. This is because the significance depends on how much information you have. The significance level of Spearman's *rho* will be less because we have lost information between the values when we replaced them by their rank orders.

Mann-Whitney U Test

The Mann-Whitney U test is the non-parametric equivalent of the *t*-test for independent samples. It requires one categorical variable with two groups (e.g., parents) and one continuous variable that is ordinal (e.g., some number as in scores showing the total interest that parents show in their children's academic work). It does not compare the mean scores of the two groups as does the *t*-test, but it compares the *median*[4] of the two groups.

Similar to the requirements of using the *t*-test for independent samples, the scores from the sample must be from two different groups and the analysis tells us if the difference between the two sets of scores determines whether chance alone accounted for the difference.

In our example, we used scores from a questionnaire to determine whether mothers or fathers showed the most interest in their child's academic work. A non-parametric analysis was used because we obtained data from parents whose children attended only one school and the sample was not randomly selected from a large number of schools. The null hypothesis was that there was no difference in the amount of interest shown by the parents: mothers and fathers showed similar interest in their children's work.

Actually, to make life easier for you, we used the same data from Descriptives13.sav, only this time, changed the variable name "schtype" to "parents" with father = 1 and mother = 2 and test a to "interest inventory".

Computing the Mann-Whitney U test Using the SPSS Programme

Open your SPSS file and click on **Analyze**. Scroll down until you see **Non-Parametric Tests**.

1. Click on **2 Independent Samples**.
2. Click on your continuous (dependent) variable (in our example, we clicked on *Interest Inventory*) and move it into the **Grouping Variable** box.
3. Click on the **Grouping Variable** (in our example, *Parents*) and move it into the **Grouping Variable** box.
4. Click on the **Define Groups...** button to open the **Two Independent Samples: Define Gr...** dialog box. Type in the value for each group. We typed in 1 for Group 1 (fathers) and 2 for Group 2 (mothers). Click on **Continue**.
5. Under **Test Type**, click on the **Mann-Whitney U** box.
6. As an option, you can click on **Options** to open the Options dialog box and click on **Descriptives**. Click on **Continue** to return to the first dialog box.
7. Click **OK**.

Because we clicked on **Descriptives**, the output shows the descriptive statistics (Table 18.6), the Mann-Whitney Test showing the ranks according to the groups (Table 18.7) and the Mann-Whitney U test statistics (Table 18.8). Each table is presented first, followed by a brief description of it.

---

4. Remember the median is the scale value below which 50% of the score fall.

Table 18.6: *The Output from the Descriptives Option (Step 7)*

Descriptive Statistics

	N	Mean	Std. Deviation	Minimum	Maximum
Interest shown	50	93.30	19.306	55	127
Parent	50	1.50	.505	1	2

This table tells us that we had 50 parents who responded. The mean scores of the Interest Inventory = 93.80 and the standard deviation = 18.60. In the Mann-Whitney U test, the scores on the continuous variables are automatically converted to ranks for each group and the rankings are evaluated to determine whether the two groups differ significantly.

Table 18.7: *The Output of the Mann-Whitney U Test Showing the Ranks of the Parents' Scores.*

Ranks

	Parent	N	Mean Rank	Sum of Ranks
Interest shown	Father	25	13.16	329.00
	Mother	25	37.84	946.00
	Total	50		

Right away, you can see that there was a difference between the two groups as the mean rank of the fathers = 13.6 and that of the mothers = 37.8. Whether or not the difference has occurred by chance is shown in Table 18.8, the test statistics for the Mann-Whitney U.

Test Statistics[a]

Table 18.8: *The Results of the Mann-Whitney U Test of Significance*

	Interest shown
Mann-Whitney U	4.000
Wilcoxon W	329.000
Z	-5.988
Asymp. Sig. (2-tailed)	.000

Interpreting the Mann-Whitney U Results

There are two values that tell you whether the differences have occurred by chance or whether you can reject your hypothesis. The first value is the Z (-5.989) and the second is Asymp. Sig. (2-tailed) = 0.000. This shows that the probability value (p) is far greater than 0.05 so you can reject the null hypothesis of no difference in the amount of interest shown by parents. Of the two groups, mothers showed a greater amount of interest in their children's academic work than did their fathers ($z = $ -5.989, $p < 0.05$). By looking at the Ranks (Table 18.7), you can report the differences in scores: Results of the Mann-Whitney U Test of Significance showed that mothers displayed a greater interest in their children's work than did fathers ($Z = $ -5.98, $p < 0.05$).On the Interest Inventory, fathers had a mean scores of 13.6 while mothers had a mean score of 37.8.

Wilcoxon Signed Rank Test

The Wilcoxon Signed rank test is also referred to as the *Wilcoxon matched pairs signed ranks test* and is the non-parametric equivalent of the repeated measures or matched-pairs *t*-test. The data required are two sets of scores from one group of people (scores from the same population sample that have been measured on two different occasions) that are ordinal in scaling. This type of design is most useful when you need to find out whether people's attitudes, perceptions or knowledge change following a specific treatment or condition. When you use this test, you are not only looking at the differences of scores from the sample population, you are also looking at the treatment effect. The following are some examples of how the Wilcoxon Signed rank test could be used:

1.   Give high school students a questionnaire about their knowledge of HIV, show them a film and then immediately test their knowledge about HIV following the film. Although we are looking at the effect of the film and not examining scores, the analysis will show us whether the scores differ significantly from each other.
2.   Give students a pretest investigating the amount of fear they have for completing a literature review in a research class, present them with an intervention designed give a post-test to see if their fear has been reduced. Again, we are looking at the effect of the intervention treatment and not at the scores from the questionnaire, but we report whether there is a difference between scores.
3.   Find out how parents feel about the value of education for their children, then hold a seminar about the different benefits that education provides for their children and give them a test to see if their attitude has changed following the seminar. Again, we will see if there is any change in scores but we are really trying to determine whether the seminar was effective in changing attitudes towards the value of education.

Computing the Wilcoxon Signed Rank Test Using the SPSS Programme

Suppose we wanted to use the second example, investigating the effect of an intervention teaching students how to conduct effective search for literature for the Literature Review Section of a thesis. We would use an intact class and give the students a questionnaire asking them how they feel about carrying out the literature review, whether they know how to use the library, how they feel about having to do this, and so on. Then, we would give the students a short course on how to conduct a literature search. After the course had been completed, we would then ask them to answer a second questionnaire that was similar or the same as the first. By finding out whether the scores on the second test differed significantly from the scores of the first test, we can also find out if the intervention was effective.

You would enter the data in the same way you enter data for the *t*-test: the first column would be student ID, the second column the results of the first test for fear of literature search (Fear I) and the third column the results of the second test (Fear II).

1. Open your SPSS file and click on **Analyze**. Scroll down until you see **Non-Parametric Tests**.
2. Click on **2 Related Samples** to open the **Two-Related Samples** dialog box.
3. Click on the **dependent variables** (in our case, we clicked on Fear I and Fear II) and move it into the **Test Pairs List** box.
4. Under **Test Type**, click on the **Wilcoxon** box.
5. If you want, you can click on **Options** to open the Options box, then click on **Descriptives**. Then click on **Continue** to return you to the **Two-Related samples** dialog box.
6. Click **OK**.

Table 18.9 shows the number of participants (N = 20) and shows how the ranks varied by responses. Table 18.10 is a summary of the computation of the Wilcoxon test.

Table 18.9: *Results of the Pretest/Post-test According to the Rankings of Responses*

Ranks

		N	Mean Rank	Sum of Ranks
Post-test- Pretest	Negative Ranks	19[a]	10.000	190.00
	Positive ranks	0[b]	.000	.00
	Ties	1[c]		
	Total	20		

a. Post-test <Pretest
b. Post-test >Pretest
c. Pretest = Post-test

Table 18.10: *Results of the Wilcoxon Signed Rank Test*

Test Statistics

	Post-test- pretest
Z	-3.854[a]
Asymp. Sig. (2-tailed)	.000

a. Based on Positive Ranks
b. Wilcoxon Signed Ranks Test

Interpreting the Wilcoxon Signed Rank Test

Look at the *z* score and the Asymp. Sig. (2-tailed) value. Once the Asymp. Sig. value is equal to or less than 0.05, you can conclude that the scores are significantly different from each other. In Table 18.10, the *z* score = -3.854 and the Asymp.Sig. value = 0.000 much less than 0.05. You can conclude that the two sets of scores are significantly different and that your intervention most likely made a difference.

Kruskal-Wallis Test

The Kruskal-Wallis test is similar in nature to the Mann-Whitney test but it allows you to compare more than two groups. In this respect, it is considered the non-parametric equivalent to the one-way ANOVA. Similar to the majority of the non-parametric tests, the scores are converted to ranks and the mean rank of each group is compared. As this is a "between-groups" design, the scores must come from different groups of people. Your data should consist of one categorical variable with three or more categories (e.g., age levels, types of schools, religions, SES, etc.) and one continuous variable (e.g., the total scores of a questionnaire).

Computing the Kruskal-Wallis Test Using the SPSS Programme

Suppose we were investigating motivation to succeed in high school across three different levels of SES. To do this we would give a "Motivation to Succeed" questionnaire to a group of high school students and then place them in different groups according to their SES (we would then code SES as 1 = High SES, 2 = Middle SES and 3 = Low SES). The null hypothesis was ;"There was no difference in motivation to succeed in school across different levels of SES.[5] The analysis has to be non-parametric because we just went into one large school and asked all the Grade 10 students to complete the questionnaire.

1. Open your SPSS file and click on **Analyze**. Scroll down until you see **Non-Parametric Tests**.
2. Click on **K Related Samples** to open the **Tests for Several Related Samples** dialog box.
3. Click on the **continuous (dependent) variable** (we would click on *Motive*) and move it into the **Test Variable List** box.
4. Click on the **categorical variable** (in our case *SES*) and move it into the **Grouping Variable** box.
5. Click on **Define Range...** button to open the **Two Independent Samples: Define Gr...** dialog box. Type in the first value of the categorical variable (e.g., 1) in the **Minimum** box. Type the largest value for your categorical variable (e.g., 3) in the **Maximum** box.
6. Click on **Continue**.
7. Under **Test Type**, click on the **Kruskal-Wallis H** box.
8. Click **OK**.

You will get two pieces of information. Table 18.11(a) shows the results of the rankings and Table 18.11(b) gives the test statistics.

Table 18.11 (b) gives the Chi-Square value, the degree of freedom and the Asymp. Sig. values. If the significance value is equal to or less than 0.05, then you can reject the null hypothesis of no difference in motivation. According to this result, we can reject the null hypothesis as Chi-Square = 7.439 and the significance level is 0.045 – which, when rounded, is equal to 0.05. We can conclude that the level of motivation differs across the three levels of SES.

---

5. This might make an interesting study using different school types. The question would be: "Does the amount of motivation to succeed in school vary according to SES?"

Table 18.11: *The Results of Using the Kruskal-Wallis Test Showing (a) Ranks and (b) the Test Statistics*

(a) **Ranks**

	Level of SES	N	Mean Rank
Total Motivation	High	256	203.19
	Middle	334	235.21
	Low	567	266.75
	Total	1057	

(b) **Test Statistics [a,b]**

	Total Motivation
Chi-Square	7.439
df	2
Asymp. Sig.	.045

[a] Kruskal Wallis Test
[b] Grouping Variables: SES

To find out where the scores differ, you look back at the mean ranks for groups given in Table 18.11(a). You can see that students from low SES families scored the highest on the motivation questionnaire with the students from high SES families scoring the lowest.

The Friedman Test

The final non-parametric test presented in this chapter is the Friedman Test which is the non-parametric equivalent of the one-way ANOVA for repeated measures. Similar to the repeated measures ANOVA, this test requires scores that come from the same set of individuals over three or more different times or under three or more different conditions. This means that your data consists of three or more scores from one person (Remember repeated measures?)

To show you how to analyse this type of research, let us refer to the data collected in the Fear of Doing a Literature Review example. Only this time, we want to find out if the students still feel better about doing the literature review six months after they were given the seminar. This means that we would now have three sets of data collection: the pretest (Fear I), the immediate post-test (Fear II) and the third questionnaire written six months later (Fear III). The same people have responded to each of these questionnaires so we can use the Friedman Test to investigate whether the students still felt they benefitted from the seminar.

Computing the Friedman Test Using the SPSS Programme

1. Open your SPSS file and click on **Analyze**. Scroll down until you see **Non-Parametric Tests**.
2. Click on **K Related Samples** to open the **Two-Related Samples** dialog box.
3. Click on the **dependent variables** (in our case, we clicked on Fear I, Fear II and Fear III) and move it into the **Test Pairs List** box.
4. Under **Test Type**, click on the **Friedman** option.
5. Click **OK**.

The output will be similar to that shown in Table 18.12(a) showing the rankings and (b) showing the test statistics.

Table 18.12: *The Output After Computing the Friedman Test in the SPSS Programme Showing the Ranks (a) and the Test Statistics (b)*

(a)   **Ranks**

	Mean Rank
Fear I	19.56
Fear II	16.03
Fear III	14.18

(b)   **Test Statistics** [a]

N	30
Chi-Square	35.375
df	2
Asymp.Sig	.003

[a] Friedman Test

Interpreting the Friedman Test

As you can see by looking at the Asymp. Sig. value in Table 18.12 (b), the value of 0.003 is much less than 0.05 so you can state that there are significant differences in the scores. By looking at the rankings in Table 18.12(a), you can see that the scores decreased over time. It appears that the seminar worked and that there was a decrease in the fear of writing a literature review by the students over a period of six months.

❖ Writing Your Thesis

> You can achieve clear communication, which is the primary objective of scientific reporting by presenting ideas in an orderly manner and by expressing yourself smoothly and precisely (APA Manual, 2002, p. 23)

This section is all (well, nearly all) about the conventions of writing a thesis. Regardless of the type of research you have carried out, there are some conventions that are required when writing a research thesis. These conventions include the layout of your thesis, the order in which you should present your information, how to use citations and how to write the reference section. The formal structure of a research thesis consists of the following sections: abstract, introduction, literature review, methods, results, and discussion. In keeping with our 'cookbook' theme, we first present the basic ingredients – an overview of what should be written and the chapter (or section of the chapter) in which each should appear.

The way the final thesis appears does *not* necessarily have to be the order in which each section can be written! For example, the abstract is placed at the beginning of the final thesis, but it is the *last* thing that should be written. This makes sense because an abstract is a very short synopsis of your entire research and it would be impossible to write the synopsis of something that hasn't yet been written. If you do not think that this is logical, read the section in Chapter 20 "*When to Write What.*"

Part Six does not provide "written-in-stone" information on the final format of a thesis because each faculty and journal has its own guidelines about the submission of the thesis or article. For example, the University of the West Indies publishes a small booklet, "*Thesis Guide: A Guide for the Preparation of Theses and Papers.*" On Page 1 of the guide, you will see "Candidates should consult their departments for specific Faculty requirements" and then very clearly warns students that: "A thesis which does not follow the approved format will not be accepted...".

Before you write the final draft of your thesis, we strongly advise that you listen to and carry out the advice given by your mentor. Also, journals usually have "Instructions to Authors" at the beginning of each issue and it is wise to look at (and follow) these instructions before submitting an article. Remember that the academic advisors or the journal editors have the "final say" as to how the final paper is presented and they are the ones who will accept or reject your research.

We use this symbol ✎ to draw your attention to our special hints and suggestions that you might want to incorporate into each section.

19
A Basic "Recipe" for Your Research Thesis

At last! You are now ready for the final leg of your long journey. The purpose of this chapter is to provide you with some guidelines as to "what goes where" in the final thesis. Remember that these are suggestions only. Listen to your supervisor and read the guidelines provided by your university, faculty or journal.

To start off… You must be knowledgeable of the conventions that make up a research thesis. The standard format of a completed research thesis or dissertation has seven major areas (or nine when you count the preliminaries and appendixes). Everything you learned about writing the proposal (review Chapter 11) holds true for the final thesis – except now you put your writing into chapters, you write mainly in the past tense (except for Chapter 4) and, of course, you write a lot more! If you have written a carefully thought-out proposal, much of what you have written can be elaborated and incorporated into your final paper.

In Order of Appearance: What Goes Where

1. The "Preliminaries" (including the Table of Contents)
2. Abstract
3. Chapter 1: Background and statement of the problem
4. Chapter 2: Review of relevant literature
5. Chapter 3: Methods
6. Chapter 4: Results
7. Chapter 5: Discussion
8. References
9. Appendixes

The "Preliminaries"

We have placed "Preliminaries" in quotation marks because it covers all the 'things' that are necessary to consider when you are ready to turn in your project or thesis. Generally, the "Preliminaries" consist of the title page, dedication (optional), acknowledgements (optional), Table of Contents, List of Tables and List of Figures. Although we have provided some basic guidelines, this is the area in which you must consult the guide published by a university or journal. The *Thesis Guide* published by the University of the West Indies (1998) tells you exactly how the title page should be formatted for the different faculties and how you should number the pages that are included in this section.

The Preliminaries are traditionally numbered using roman numerals placed at the centre bottom of each page. Although the title page is considered the first page, it is not numbered and the actual page numbering starts at page ii.

Check your guidelines for the order in which to place the preliminaries. For example, some faculties require the preliminaries placed in the following: Abstract, Dedication, Table of Contents, List of Tables, List of Figures, Acknowledgments; others require: Abstract, Dedication, Acknowledgments, Table of Contents, List of Tables, List of Figures.

FIND OUT FIRST!!!

The abstract is placed on page ii followed by the Table of Contents which starts on page iii (unless dedication and acknowledgments pages are included and then it starts on page iv or v). The main heading should be in capitols (TABLE OF CONTENTS) and centre justified. The title of each chapter and the headings and major sub-headings (optional) should match exactly what you wrote in the main body of the text – word for word. Leave double spaces between each chapter heading but the headings (or sub-headings) under each chapter may be single spaced.

References and Appendix should be included as part of the Table of Contents pages and the page numbers on which each start should be given. Each appendix (A, B, C, etc.) should have its own title. An example of how Table of Contents and how References and Appendix should be mentioned in the Table of Contents is shown in Figure 19.1.

TABLE OF CONTENTS	
Abstract	ii
Dedication	iii
Acknowledgments	iv
Chapter One: An Introduction to the Research	1
Background of the Problem	2
Purpose of the Study	4
Repeat this for the next four chapters, remembering to leave a double space between each chapter title.	
LIST OF TABLES	
Table 1: Exact Wording of Title of Table 1	XX
Table 2: Exact Wording of Title of Table 2	XX
LIST OF FIGURES	
Figure 1: Exact wording of title of Figure 1	XX
Figure 2: Exact wording of title of Figure 2	XX
(Note: Place the list of tables and figures on separate pages following the completed Table of Contents pages)	
REFERENCES	XX
APPENDICES	
Appendix A: A copy of the letter sent to the principals of the schools requesting permission to carry out the research	XX
Appendix B: A copy of the questionnaire given to the participants	XX

Figure 19.1. An example of the arrangement of the Table of Contents page. Remember to align the page numbers flush right.

The **LIST OF TABLES** and **LIST OF FIGURES** (if you have included figures in your text) should also be written in capitol letters and each requires a separate page following the Table of Contents page(s). The captions for each table and figure should be exactly the same as written in the text and, similar to the **TABLE OF CONTENTS**, the page numbers should be flush right.

> Be very careful to make sure that these pages look as if you have taken a lot of care to make sure that they are correctly done. If this section looks sloppy, the reader will assume that the rest of your paper is sloppy, too.
>
> Do NOT add decorations or extra graphics to these pages! You are supposed to be a serious researcher. 'Pretty' graphics subtract from the scientific look of the paper and no examiner or journal editor will take it seriously.

Formatting Tip

- All of the text (including the abstract) **MUST** be aligned left. Do **NOT** use full justification.
- The font size should be 12 points (preferably Times New Roman) and be the same throughout the text.
- Check for margin size: generally the left margin is 2 inches and the others are 1 inch.

Abstract

Note that although we have included the Abstract in the main body of the text, the abstract page should be placed immediately following the title page (and is numbered page ii). It precedes Acknowledgements, Table of Contents, List of Tables and List of Figures (i.e., the "Preliminaries").

Purpose:

- To represent the entire thesis so it can be used for bibliographic reference materials and give other readers a general idea of what your research is all about.
- The abstract must be easily understood without any reference to the major body of your thesis.

Content: Contains only a brief summary of your research in paragraph form. It should not be longer than one double-spaced typed page (120-250 words – many journals require only 80-100 words). Acronyms and abbreviations must be written in full when first mentioned.

Order: A good method of organising your abstract is to write one or two sentences summarising the following chapters: introduction, methods, results and discussion.

    (i)   Brief statement telling what research was done, that is, the objective(s) of the research or what is being investigated. (Information from Ch 1: The Introduction).

(ii)   Identification of source of data, such as the total number of participants where your research took place, etc. (Information from Chapter 3: Methods)

(iii)   Identification of variables such as materials used, treatment given. (Information from Chapter 3: Methods)

(iv)   Summary of results without going into too much detail. (Information from Chapter 4: Results)

(v)   Summary of your conclusions (not an evaluation.) (Information from Chapter 5: Discussion)

Key Words: This is just a short list of about three to five of the major terms used in your research. (It can be similar to the key words you used for a computer search.) The key words must be directly related to your research and should not be so broad, such as "perception," "motivation," etc. that they could refer to a myriad of other things.

An example of an abstract written for a journal article is shown in Figure 19.2. Although it is only 88 words long, it is concise and informs a reader about the research that was carried out.

(For a university thesis, leave 3 spaces from the top of the page)

Are Culture-Fair Tests Really Fair?

(For a university thesis, leave 3 more spaces and remember to double space the text)

The mental abilities of 800 students in Grades One and Four, living in a large urban city in Jamaica, West Indies, were assessed by means of the Columbia Mental Maturity Scale, a culture-fair test. Results showed that children from families of low socioeconomic status (SES) scored significantly lower than children from families of high-middle and upper socioeconomic status. These findings are discussed in terms of conditions associated with low SES, the inadequacy of early childhood education facilities and the "unfairness" of culture-fair tests.

Key Words: Columbia Mental Maturity Scale; culture fair tests; SES

Figure 19.2: An example of an abstract written for a journal article.

The abstract is written when your research has been completed. If you are preparing a paper for publication, follow the guidelines of the journal to which you are submitting.

The Main Body of the Text

Under the general title of each chapter, you will first see "Purpose." This is the summary of each section. Next, read what should go into each chapter, write your chapter and when you think you have finished writing a section, look at the "Check List." Think of this list as the basic ingredients needed for the chapter and check off each section that you have completed. In this way, we are trying to help you understand what should go where when you begin to write your thesis.

Good Writing Tip
Remember that ALL chapters have an introduction and a conclusion. Also remember that your first draft will not be your last! Be prepared to write, edit, amend and write some more.

Chapter I: Introduction (Nature of the Study)

If you have written a good proposal, a lot of the introduction to your proposal can be incorporated into Chapter One of your thesis as both are fairly similar. You just need to elaborate and bring information up-to-date for your thesis. BUT, remember to use the PAST TENSE because this is work that you have completed.

Purpose:

- To communicate the exact purpose of the study, that is, to identify the research problem. It serves as a general introduction to your research.
- To give a concise history and background of your topic – the rationale for your research and reasons why this research is important.
- To build a case for the importance of the problem or questions under investigation.

Contents: (A 'recipe' for Chapter 1)
1. **Short introductory comments:** 1 - 2 paragraphs giving a little background or some general information about your topic.

   Your opening sentence and the first paragraph should set the 'mood' for the reader. There are two things that you must do within the first two or three paragraphs: (i) whet the reader's appetite for the topic and (ii) tell the reader why he or she is reading the paper. We have seen too many papers in which the researcher has been carried away with the introduction and has written page after page before introducing the topic of research. As external examiners, every so often we just have to flip through the first eight or nine pages (and, in one occasion, seventeen pages) to find out exactly why we are reading this paper.

   Begin with a general introduction of or background to the topic you have investigated. If the beginning is not interesting, the reader (if an examiner) will know that this is a paper that must be read but will not read the rest of the thesis with much enthusiasm. The journal editor may just put it aside for a rejection slip. One researcher started his paper with: "The concept of intelligence testing has created controversy since the late nineteenth century when Sir Francis Galton assumed that intelligence was a single inherited trait." This showed the reader that the researcher had 'done his homework' by mentioning Galton and led the reader to want to continue reading it.

> **STOP**   Warning... We have seen some research theses starting right off with "The purpose of this research is..." This is not a good idea! Think of an interesting and thought-provoking first sentence to introduce your research.

---

2. **A general and brief statement of the goal of your research.** Give the reader the "big picture." State the problem or question being investigated, that is, the overall purpose of what is being done. Tell the reader directly what the research is all about – your thesis or problem statement.

At this time, try to avoid very technical details as you will present them later in the text. You could state, for example: "The major purpose of the present research was to determine whether ....." or "The present research investigated the extent to which ...."or "The purpose of this study was to investigate ...." or "The present research was designed to determine whether ....."

Although the statement of what the research is about should be brief and fairly general, it must not be too general. For example, do not state: The research was designed to investigate the effect of some variables on the learning potential of school children. Instead, state: The major purpose of this research was to investigate the possibility of using a culture fair test to determine whether it could be used to assess the learning potential of Jamaican elementary school children.

Remember that you are still writing in a general way.

3.   **Your rationale for doing the study.** Explain why this study is being carried out. Give a brief overview or highlights of some of the relevant research that has been carried out on your topic. (You will enlarge this later in your literature review). Briefly explain what others have found. By discussing what has or has not been done by other researchers, you provide a strong argument for and provide the rationale for carrying out your own particular research.

4.   **Although you have already given a general idea (the 'big picture') of what the study is about, you must now be specific.**

This follows on from your rationale stated in Section 3. This section should include (1) all related hypotheses (or the specific questions being investigated) and (2) the rationale or justification for including them in your research design. For example: This research was designed specifically to address... (to examine...) (to investigate...) (to discover whether...) Then continue with the related hypotheses. Give some idea of what you expect to find – your assumptions – and the reasons for your expectations. But, do not base your rationale or assumptions solely on your own opinion. This is why you did a thorough literature search and mentioned some of this in the preceding paragraphs.

If you are only using questions (not advised!), this is the section they must be discussed in full – why you have asked them, what you expected to find and why you expected these results.

An Example of Introducing Your Research Hypotheses

The present research was designed to determine whether a culture-fair test could be used to assess the learning potential of the majority of Jamaican children. Based on the definition of a culture fair test, it was hypothesised that differences among the scores indicated differences in cognitive functioning only and there were no differences between scores for any of the independent variables, that is, SES, gender and grade level. This hypothesis was based on research by Diener and Dweck (1989) showing that .....

As you discuss your hypotheses, you introduce all necessary technical terms. Try to give the definition of special terms when you first introduce the construct or concept. Remember that your definitions define exactly what you are investigating and measuring. A major difference between the proposal and the thesis concerns the placement of the definitions of key terms – some supervisors require that all definitions be placed at the end of the first chapter. We recommend that when you first introduce a term that is fundamental to your research, you also define it and give the rational for its use. This means that the reader does not have to wait until the end of the chapter to find out the exact meaning of a specific term or concept.

5.   **A brief overview of how your research is being carried out** (the research design) and the importance of your research (the implications for carrying out this research).

6.   **Finish with a brief summary to conclude the chapter.** Do not leave the writer thinking he or she will turn the page to go on reading more of Chapter One.

This section should include why this study or research was important and how it relates to the current situation in Jamaica (or any other country). Remember that we stated in the section about writing the proposal that research in the Caribbean appears to be limited so you can discuss this (e.g., point out what is lacking) and explain that your particular research will contribute to the information research base or help in decision making or guide other professionals, and so on. This also sets the stage for your discussions and recommendations in Chapter 5.

Most of this chapter has already been written as part of your proposal. You must remember, however, that your proposal was written when you were just beginning your research and did not know very much, so expect to expand on what had previously been written. You also have to remember that your proposal was written in the future tense. If you are using parts of your proposal, remember to use the appropriate tense (see the section, Using the Appropriate Tense, in the next chapter). **Finally, do not forget to summarise!**

Good Writing Tip

What you write in one section should become the 'lead in' for the next. All this contributes to the readability of your thesis and makes it more acceptable to internal and external examiners or journal editors who will accept or reject your research paper.

A Checklist for Chapter 1

6-10 pages		
	Introduction: (interesting and exciting) 1 -2 paragraphs	
	Introduction to research problem; e.g., "The major purpose of the present research was to…". Give the 'big picture.' 1 -2 paragraphs	
	Rationale for investigating this topic: reasons why, overview of research showing what has been done or what has not been done in Jamaica. 3+ paragraphs	
	This ties in to formation of questions or hypotheses All must be stated specifically Variables should be defined here as part of text (not in list format!) Assumptions of what you expect to find (based on previous research) or rationale why each question was asked or hypothesis generated	
	Brief overview of how research is being carried out	
	Statement of importance of research. Conclusion to Chapter one	

Chapter 2: A Review of Related Literature

Purpose:

- To provide the background as well as limit and identify the context (reasons) for the research hypotheses.
- To inform readers that you are aware of what research has already been done in this field.
- To identify gaps in the research and show that your research is worth while.
- To demonstrate how your research fits into previous research.
- To provide validation for your research design and methodology used.
- To provide background for interpreting results.

Content:

1. **Start off with a brief introduction to direct your reader**. For example, you could begin by stating that in this chapter, the literature was organised according to history of the construct being investigated or according to topics posed in your research questions or according to the different hypotheses.

2. **You can organise this chapter in a number of different ways:** according to (i) the chronology of the construct – from oldest to latest, (ii) by topic, (iii) by specific areas within your research topic, etc. The choice is yours. This is where the note cards come in useful...you just shuffle them around and put them in the order that you want to write this chapter.

3. **Finally, remember to briefly summarise your literature review.** You can do this by briefly summarising the major findings under each topic area or presenting some conclusions of what you found while doing your literature research.

   - You now expand on the research you mentioned briefly in Chapter 1.
   - The studies reviewed must be relevant and limited to the current research. You should not just summarise other research, you should critique it and evaluate it!
   - Use only the details relevant to the present research, for example, the major findings as they relate to what you are doing. This way, you are making a case for your own research by showing what research has already been carried out, the findings of previous research, criticisms of what has been done, and any gaps that need filling. You can state that the research area reviewed is limited as this implies the need for doing your own research and gives ideas for further research.
   - Above all, try to have some form of outline when writing this section or you will find that you have left some important information out or repeated the same information in another section.

Good Writing Tip

In this chapter, you will be liberally sprinkling a lot of citations and references throughout. Be sure to read the section on Citations, Quotations, and Paraphrases and References in Chapter 20.

In the Caribbean, very often the information available on a particular topic is very limited or is buried away somewhere and you simply cannot find anything that has been done, so you, as the researcher can state this. However, **never** state that no research has been done on your topic. This is a very sweeping statement and you will probably be proved wrong. Relevant references from other countries should be documented as these can be used later in your discussion as comparisons and can prove very useful.

Nag, Nag, Nag!

When starting your review of literature, make your bibliographical note cards as complete as possible. Be sure to write down the author's name, name of book, text, journal, etc. and page number, also the date published, city and name of publishers. If a journal, write down the name of the journal, volume number and page numbers of the article. We know that we have already stated this in Part One – but keeping detailed bibliographic notes is important and many naive researchers just do not bother doing this. This will not only save you a lot of time when you have to write the references but it will also help you put your topics in order when you begin writing this chapter.

> This chapter is a review of what others have written.
> Your own views and opinions do not count in this section!

A Check List for Chapter Two

20-30 pages	Introduction of how you are presenting your literature review. 1 -2 paragraphs	
	Format can vary: Chronological review (from early to most recent) By topic relating to your research Example: Topic I, Topic II, Topic III, etc. End each topic with a brief summary or evaluation of the research reviewed	
	Evaluate important findings as it pertains to your topic Point out main points and identify any gaps Try to give both sides of the research	
	Conclusion; a brief summary of main points Remember to point out any gaps in existing research (as in Chapter One, also for Chapter Five)	

Chapter 3: Methods

Purpose:

- To tell the reader exactly how the study was conducted and/or how the hypotheses were tested.
- To permit the reader to evaluate the appropriateness of the procedures employed, and of the study itself.
- To enable other researchers to replicate the study.

Content: **Usually divided into three sections: Participants and Participant Selection, Materials/Apparatus, Procedures.** However, similar to all other chapters, this chapter should also start with a brief introduction – a recap of the hypotheses to be tested or the questions to be answered and a brief overview of how you have accomplished this.

1.   **Brief introduction:** Restate hypotheses or questions – a form of "executive summary." You can state something to the effect of: "This research was designed to investigate the effect of...... To this end, three hypotheses were formulated: (Write the hypotheses here. In order to test these hypotheses, students were first presented with a questionnaire asking about .....(an abbreviated summary of what you did).

2.   **Participants and their Selection:** Detailed description about the population sample used in your study including: the population from which they were selected, how they were selected, if they were randomly selected and how they were randomly selected, give the total population from which they were selected, how many were selected and some summary statistics. Give the rationale for selecting this particular population.

   You should, for example, state how many males and how many females, age group, grade, school type, work experience, salary, etc. You can also place a table here if you like. This table could be similar to tables produced by the SPSS Frequencies Option (Table 12.1, p. 148), the Crosstabs Option (Table 12.2, p. 149) or the Explore Option (Table 14.3, p. 177).

   On no account, must the participants be able to identify themselves or any reader be able to identify the participants. This would violate the ethical considerations of any research.

   A Poor Example: participants consisted of students attending Grade Four in the three largest government schools located in downtown Kingston, Jamaica.

   A Better Example using general terms: Participants consisted of Grade Four students attending government schools in an urban area of Jamaica.

   When necessary, this section can also include details of other research assistants, how many, why used as research assistants, how they were trained, and how you arrived at inter-rater or inter-observer reliability.

3.   **Instrumentation, Apparatus or Materials:** Describe the materials or apparatus used and how they were used in the present study. You must include the fine details of

measures used and rationale for using them. Although some writers place the details of questionnaires, materials used, etc. in the first section, many others (including the authors of this text!) prefer to read about the materials used in the research in this section. Questionnaires and other materials used must be reproduced in an appendix. In this case, you would state: *A copy of the final questionnaire can be found in Appendix X.*

- Descriptions of all measures included in the research, evidence of validity and relationship of measure to research questions or hypotheses (based on previous research or manuals provided by the writer of the measure being used).
- If measurements are novel, explain the rationale for using them, nature of items and its validity and reliability (this is generally based on previous research or results of pilot studies).
- Scoring procedures should be described in detail. For example, "Scores for the questionnaire could range from 0 to 10; scores between 0 - 3 indicated a low level of learned helplessness behaviours and scores higher than 8 denoted high levels of learned helplessness behaviours."

The description of the measures used and the rationale for using them should refer mainly to the information already mentioned in the literature review in Chapter 2. If the instrumentation is novel (i.e., author created), then reference must be made about how or why certain indicators, questions, etc. were used. As the author of this research, you did not pull the procedures or questions out of the air and should reference them to give validity to the methods used. For example, you could state: "The questionnaire investigating causal attributions for negative events (CANE) was an amalgam of items from the Intellectual Achievement Responsibility Scale (Crandall, Katkovsky, & Crandall, 1965), the Stanford Preschool Internal-External Inventory (Mischel et al., 1974) and the Primary Internal-External Scale (Nowicki & Duke, 1974)."

Think About This...

In Chapter 9, "The Nitty-Gritty of Preplanning Your Questionnaire," we advised you to keep a "process trail" or notes of how you organised and formulated your questionnaire. This process trail will prove very useful at this stage of your writing.

As a researcher, you do not have to keep reinventing the wheel! If you have found a suitable questionnaire, do not be afraid to use it (but, remember, give credit). However, you should also state the reliability published by the authors of the questionnaire or test. In some situations, questions may have to be adapted to the current situation. In this case, (i) show how the questions have been changed and (ii) give valid reasons why. Example: "*An adaptive behaviour scale was developed by the researcher because many of the items on the commercial scales that are used locally were considered culturally biased.*"[1] Then, the researcher described each question that could be considered biased, why it was biased and how it had been adapted and why.

---

1. Malcolm, L. M. (2000, p. 248).

If you are using a questionnaire that has been used by others, it is always a good idea to pretest the items using a small group similar to those who will be responding to the questionnaire. This is done to ensure that the questions will be understood by your target group. Remember to discuss the pre-test outcome in this section.

When pilot testing for the materials or questionnaire was carried out, then this must be discussed before the procedure actually used in the research is discussed and the C-Alpha must be mentioned. This shows how the materials were derived and adds validity to your research.

3.   **Procedure:** Everything that happened in the study should be described sufficiently in order to permit replication and to allow the reader to understand what was done. This includes:

    a.   Details of the cover letters that were sent out. The actual letters should be reproduced in the appendix. You can state: Letters were first sent to the principals of the schools requesting permission to carry out the present research (a copy of the letter can be found in Appendix E) and letters were sent to the teachers in the schools informing them of the research (see Appendix F for a copy of this letter).

    b.   Participants' consent to take part in study. If you used parental consent forms, this should also be mentioned and a copy of the consent form placed in the appendix.

    c.   If applicable, describe how participants were assigned to groups. For example: randomly selected, intact groups, etc.

    d.   Instruction given to groups – these can be paraphrased, summarised or included in full in an appendix.

Finally, explain in detail how the actual research was carried out. Did you, as the researcher, actually hand out the questionnaires to your participants? Read the questions to the participants? Carry out the treatment procedures? How long did this research take? Where, when and on what were participants measured?

A Check List for Chapter Three

5-7 pages	Introduction: purpose of research Restate hypotheses or questions 1 -2 paragraphs	
	Participants and their selection: how and why selected If applicable: how randomization process was carried out	
	Materials used Discussion of how and why you arrived at using these materials (based on literature review from Chapter Two and from other professionals, etc.)	
	Discussion of pretesting and results of pilot testing (C-alpha) if applicable	
	Discussion of how materials were scored and what these scores mean	
	Procedure in full detail: How research was carried out Cover letters, consent forms, etc (to be included in appendix)	

Chapter 4: Results

As in all other chapters, begin with a brief introduction of how you are presenting your findings. You can start by stating (again!) the purpose of your research and your research questions or hypotheses. Results can be organised around the study's hypotheses, questions or objectives. For example, the first hypothesis or question can be stated in the same form presented in the introduction and all findings related to this hypothesis or question can be reported. Then, go on to the next hypothesis.

Similar to all of the other sections, make an outline of what you are going to write. If you plan to report your data according to the hypotheses, then make sure that you know which data is for what hypothesis. If you are going to report your results according to chronological order, then put your results in that order.

Purpose:
- To clearly and succinctly allow the reader to understand exactly what was found on analyses of your data.
- To show that you have enough data to support your conclusions, discussion and recommendations in Chapter 5.
- Statistical analyses are carried out to shed some light on the research and must be explained.

Good Writing Tip

This chapter is intended to report, explain and interpret your findings and not to draw conclusions or inferences. Save this for Chapter 5.

Content: **Brief description of procedures for processing and analysing the data.** This includes: general organisation of the data, missing data, computer programmes used to process the data, transformation of scores, and any other relevant information.

Although some writers prefer to combine the results and discussion sections, we feel that each section should be separate because the discussion section is a very important aspect of your thesis and demonstrates your ability to synthesise your analyses of the results with previous research and with your hypotheses.

Report the statistical significance first followed by the practical significance (interpretation) of the results. Remember to interpret your findings as they relate to your hypothesis. Saying that Variable 1 is highly correlated to Variable 2 does not mean anything. Look at the difference when you read the following statements. The second statement plainly tells the reader the results of your analysis (the statistical significance) and tells the reader what the statistics mean (the practical significance).

Poor: *As shown in Table 1, Variable 1 was highly correlated with Variable 2, (r = 0.96).*

Better: *As shown in Table 1, correlations between the amount of hours studied and test grades were significant (r = 0.96). Based on this result, it can be concluded that association between the amount of hours spent studying and test grades is strongly positively correlated – students who studied longer hours tended to obtain higher test grades.*

Remember that not all data have to be reported. If findings are statistically significant and they tie in with what you are trying to prove, then report them. If findings are not statistically significant and previous research has shown that they should be, then report this. However, if you are not planning to comment on some findings in the discussion, you can simply state something to the effect: A complete analysis of variance table can be found in Appendix X.

Report the probability level for each statistical test as well as the statistic itself. For example: F, R or t, its attendant degrees of freedom (in parenthesis in subscript), the criterion value (written as $p =$, $<$ or $>$), also an indicator of strength, as in R^2. Remember that the effect size (η^2) should be included.

Figures and Tables

- Tables present quantitative data; figures contain all other types of illustration or information. The title for a table is placed at the top of the table and the title for a figure is placed immediately below the figure. (See Tables and Figures in Chapter 20).
- All tables and figures must be introduced in the text first. They should be clearly labelled and placed directly after the text introducing them.
- There must be a reference to the table or figure in the text although each table and figure must be self-explanatory without any reference to the text.
- Tables must have keys showing what the abbreviations mean. Fortunately, SPSS printouts provide labels for the variables so you do not have to figure out what is which!

An Example of Reference to a Table in the Text:

The data in Table 19.4 shows the mean scores and standard deviations by school type, gender and grade. ANOVA results showed that there were no statistical differences between average scores from boys or girls ($F = 1.95$, $p = .21$) or between students in Grades One or Four ($F = 1.58$, $p = .17$). It appears that school type alone is the major factor determining differences in scores ($F = 116.23$, $p < .001$). The complete ANOVA table can be found in Appendix X.

Table 19.4: *Mean Scores and Standard Deviations (SD) Achieved by Students on the Columbia Mental Maturity Scale by School Type, Gender and Grade*

FACTOR/LEVEL	MEAN SCORE	SD
Schools *		
Private	112.25	13.83
Government	93.22	11.35
CMMS Scores X Gender		
Males	101.56	16.14
Females	103.89	15.46
CMMS Scores X Grades		
Grade 1	101.34	14.47
Grade 4	103.96	17.07

Note: n = 400, * p = .001)

Do not believe that you can just look at your computer printout and write this section. As you look at each result, keep notes (and remember the red pencil technique) on what you are finding – particularly the 'interesting things.' These notes serve two purposes: to aid you in writing this section and to prompt you while you are writing your discussion.

Remember to end with a brief overview of your findings. Do not let the reader "hang in the air" wondering what is coming next!

Think About This....

Realise that while looking at results can be the most exciting aspect of your research, writing the results section is probably the most boring aspect of your entire thesis paper. You just report one result after another and it is difficult to be 'creative' in this section. Grit your teeth and write. Save your creativity and enthusiasm for the Discussion Section.

A Check List for Chapter Four

5-10 pages	Introduction: How you are presenting your research findings (A form of executive summary) Restate hypotheses or questions 1 -2 paragraphs	
	Present results according to hypotheses OR by topic	
	Lots of tables and figures in this section. In text, introduce table or figure first (by name! e.g., "Table 1 shows the results of a t-test....") Then present table or figure.	
	Conclusion: finish with a summary (the big picture) of your findings	

Chapter 5: Summary, Discussion and Recommendations

*B*efore you start to write this chapter, ask yourself the following questions:

1. What are the major hypotheses? Or, What questions did I ask?
2. Are results noteworthy and if so, why?
3. Are results consistent with results of previous research? If not, why not?
4. What other explanations can you offer to explain your results?
5. Do results suggest new theories?
6. Do results merit further investigation? What kind?

Answers to these questions are of interest to other readers and give meaning to your research.

Purpose:
- To explain by identifying and interpreting the important statistical results so that readers can understand the purpose of the present research.
- To draw conclusions and suggest implications about what you have found.
- To suggest how this particular research could have been improved (i.e., the limitations) so others can benefit from your experience.
- To compare your results with existing research so you can make recommendations for future research.

Content:

1. The summary
- A brief overview of the purpose of the study.
- A brief discussion of how these purposes were met.

Examples of beginning the summary
- The major concern of this study (research) was to (contribute / investigate / describe .....
- The present study investigated / described / examined ....
- The present study was designed to investigate / describe / examine .....
- In this study, the following areas were investigated / examined ......

This is followed by a brief description of what you did find.
- The results showed that....
- Another interesting result was that .....

> This is the fun part! You can now come up with identifying your important findings and stating why you think they are important. Unlike the literature review where you reported what others have written, this is the time to think and write about the implications of your own research. You interpret what the results mean and how they can be applied. You can ask questions and provide implications for the results of your research.

In the following sections, speculations, implications and recommendations can be presented – as long as they tie in with the research you have just finished carrying out. Do not suddenly bring in new material at this point! Make sure that your speculations, implications and recommendations are based on what has been written in the introduction, the literature review sections and your own research findings.

2. Discussion
Suggestions for the discussion section:
- Explain why the results occurred, which results were expected or were a surprise and why.
  You can discuss your findings by hypotheses or by topic.
- Tie the discussion into your literature review and your hypotheses or questions. Did other researchers find similar results? If so, you can compare results. Did you find different results? If so, give some possible reasons why. For each,

explain or give some plausible reasons why (e.g., cultural differences? societal reasons?)

- Discuss the materials used. Were they the same or different from previous research? Did this make a difference?
- Are your results typical and can they be generalised to other situations or populations? If not, why?

3. **Limitations of the study.** In this section of this chapter, you should discuss any problems you had with the procedures, data collection or whatever. You can also note how your research could have been improved or enlarged. You can state: "There are some limitations of this study (research) that should be noted. First,..... " or " One limitation of the study (research) was ...... As such, findings may be considered ......"

- Include sample size, reliability of measurements, generalisability of findings, and so on.
- This is where you point out how your study could have been improved. Many students do not think that their study had any flaws at all but research by Hall, Ward & Conner (1988) showed that 31% of the 54 studies they reviewed had specific shortcomings because the limitations of the study were not stated. As Stojmenovic (2005) clearly stated, it is preferable for you to point out the flaws in your study rather than "leave such pleasure to examiners and referees" (n.p., para 5).
- Use the limitations of your study to point out the need for future research in the next section.
- Sometimes, naive researchers write that the major limitation of their study was "lack of time" and/or "lack of money." Understand that these limitations are researcher limitations and not research limitations!

4. **Recommendations and Suggestions for Future Research:**

- This section is all about implications of the findings for practical purposes – show how it added to the knowledge base or provided information for policy makers and how your research could lead to further research in this field. Recall all the reasons why research is carried out (Chapter 1of this text) and build on this.
- In the recommendation section, many students mistakenly make all sorts of sweeping 'recommendations' that are just their own personal beliefs or wish lists and have not been evidenced by the research. Do not make mistakes like this! For example, if you have found that children from single-parent families are not doing as well as children from nuclear families and your research did not include any measures of their daily diets, then you can not suddenly recommend that these students be given free lunches, no matter how nice this sounds!
- Remember that research should be designed to raise questions and these questions should be asked now. Because you have carried out your own research and examined its limitations, you are in a good position to suggest what more can be done to shed greater light on or increase the knowledge base of your topic.

- Base implications for further research on your limitations and all the questions you thought of when writing your thesis. Usually, in Jamaica or other Caribbean countries, your research is just the 'tip of the iceberg' and so it is necessary for much more research to be carried out to prove what you found was valid. Explain why it is important to do more research similar to the you just carried out.

    You can state: "Further research should focus on....." and discuss why. Remember, however, all suggestions or follow-up research should be related to your findings and to the implications from your findings – not from something you think might be interesting to do!

6. The Conclusion

- Your conclusion is important in that it 'wraps up' everything that you have done. It should demonstrate that you have fulfilled the aim of your research.
- You can state: " Results of this study provided support for...." as it was found that ... (give another brief overview of your findings)" or, " Results of this study were surprising in that it was found that ... (give another brief overview of your 'surprising' findings). This is in direct opposition to findings of research carried out in other countries. " "It was hypothesised that .... Thus, it follows that ...." or "A good beginning was made towards building a strong research-based library that can be used when making decisions for...."
- Remember to draw conclusions only from the discussions of your research.
- When you are writing the conclusion, try to avoid such words as, "in conclusion," "to summarise" or "finally."
- Also, while you should never finish with a new idea, it is considered acceptable to end with a rhetorical question that restates an issue raised in your discussion.
- You should try to end your thesis with something worthwhile so that the reader is left feeling that your research was definitely worth reading and will add to the knowledge base.
- The conclusion must have a satisfactory, 'final sounding' ending so that readers will know the Chapter 5 (and your thesis) has ended.
- Remember to finish with a brief summary to give closure to your thesis. Do not let the reader turn the page and then suddenly realise that the thesis had finished – that this was it!

Heavens forbid! Never, never make any grandiose statements about your research proving conclusively that something has taken place. Somebody will prove you wrong!

All you have accomplished is to gather evidence that allowed you to either support or fail to support your hypotheses.

Checklist for Chapter 5

10-20 pages	Introduction: a brief overview of the purpose of the study. Include thesis statement and hypotheses or questions 1 -2 paragraphs	
	Brief discussion of whether this purpose was met. 1 -2 paragraphs	
	NOT BRIEF (main body of Chapter Five) Discussion of your major findings Give possible explanations for your results Discuss whether same or different from previous research (from Chapter Two) Discuss possible reasons why your results were similar or different Tie your results to literature review from chapters One and Two Analyse, synthesise and evaluate!!!	
	Limitations of the study Include sample size, lack of generalization, etc., any other problems you encountered while carrying out your research. (Not researcher limitations)	
	Recommendations and implications for future research: Base this on your limitations (e.g., suggest several recommendations how your own research could be improved.) Show how your research can be carried out on different populations, in other areas, etc. Explain why it is important for more of this type of research to be carried out (e.g., "Future research should focus on...." and explain why!	
	Summary of your findings and importance of your research. "This study provides strong support for...." "a good beginning was made towards building a strong research-based library that can be used when making decisions for..."	
	Conclusion to Chapter Five: provide a satisfactory ending so that readers know your thesis is completed.	

References

Whoever you cited in your thesis **MUST** be referenced in the reference list. Many of the corrections that our students have to make in order for a final acceptance of their theses are due to the fact that references have been omitted. We advise you to review the importance of writing correct references in Chapter 20 as it is **VERY** important that your reference list be written and formatted correctly.

Appendices

Each appendix should be on a separate page and the page numbers should be a continuation of the Arabic numerals. Appendices are titled as Appendix A, Appendix B and so on and the content of each appendix should appear in the order in which they were introduced in the main text. For example, if your research involved the use of a questionnaire and you mentioned cover letters before you discussed your questionnaire, then you might have: Appendix A: Cover Letter to the Principals; Appendix B: Cover Letter to the Participants; Appendix C: A Copy of the Questionnaire.

Material presented in this section can consist of replicas of the cover letters, questionnaires used, instructions given to the participants, extra tables, etc.

Include everything that was novel to your research. By this, you should gather that everything included in the appendix is not really essential to your study but is of great interest to your readers. This is particularly true when it comes to writing theses – examiners of theses look at these very closely to determine whether you really did what you thought you were doing.

20
When to Write What

Some supervisors worry that their students may not be able to take the 'cognitive load' of a research project or that their students will not be able to finish in the required time. Even though the research has hardly begun, they suggest that their students start writing draft chapters. The advantage is that the student feels secure and a sense of accomplishment in seeing parts of the work being completed. It can be compared to going on a journey, seeing the road pass beneath you, and knowing that you are covering the distance between you and your destination. It makes you feel that you are getting somewhere.

Many students do not realise that the order in which you write your research thesis or article is not necessarily the same order in which you actually carry out the research. A disadvantage in writing chapter-by-chapter is that the first chapter is written when the student knows little about the subject but that chapter determines the rest of the work.[1] This is particularly true if the advisor does not insist on on-going revisions! It can also mean that the finished project will be limited by how little the student knew before starting the research. Over the years, we have found that our students can still feel a sense of accomplishment when they start writing if they do "bits and pieces" of their thesis at different times. We suggest writing the first few drafts of the thesis in the following order:

The Literature Review: This is often the first section that is written, but this section should be considered as an ongoing process. You can use your results to find published research relevant to your findings and, if you find it necessary, you can either add or remove information when you find it does (or does not) pertain to your research. Then when you write your introduction, your literature review will be related not only to your findings, but also to your hypotheses, methods and results.

Methods Section: You start writing parts of this as soon as you start making up your questionnaire or experimental treatments. You have your reasons for using certain items or materials and these reasons form your rationale for using your materials. Keep notes (a process trail) on how you selected your participants, how you decided on the different items for your questionnaire, who you consulted, and how you collected your data. At the beginning, this looks like a journal of what you are doing, but then you start to follow the "recipe" for writing this section and tighten up each part for your final draft.

At the same time that you are working on the literature review and the methods section, you start thinking how you are going to introduce your work in Chapter One – the all-important introduction to your research. Think of at least three interesting introductory sentences – ones that will grab your reader's interest. Remember that an opening sentence sets the tone for your paper.

---

1. It is fine to start writing chapters in order but be prepared to expand some topics and cut others!

Results Section: This section is written after you have collected your data and analysed it. (Actually, you should write sections of the results section while you analyse your data!) Remember to keep notes on what findings are important and why you think they are important. We recommend placing a big red star beside important findings as this will jog your memory for writing about it in the discussion.

Discussion: This section is based on your findings and the findings from previous research as noted in the literature review.

Abstract: The last to be written.

As you can see, you will be working on three things almost simultaneously. You are designing your questionnaire (or your treatment conditions) which will be reported in the methods section and this is based mainly on the literature review. Your introduction is also based on your literature review and includes what you have done and the rationale of why your research is important. Your discussion (written after you have analysed your results) also is a combination of your analyses and the literature review.

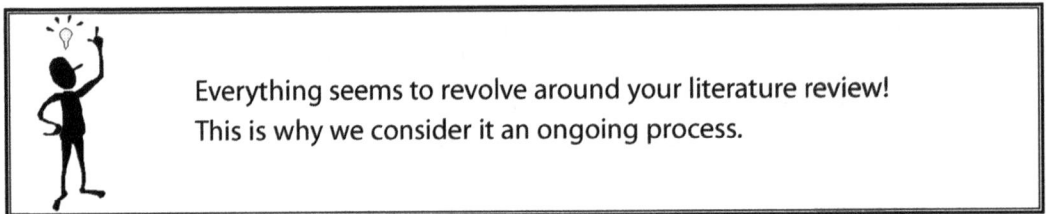

> Everything seems to revolve around your literature review!
> This is why we consider it an ongoing process.

Higher quality integrated research can be achieved by planning ahead and putting these integrated plans into order. At the beginning, it may seem that nothing concrete is being accomplished, but you will soon see that all these "bits" are gradually coming together. Unlike the method of 'chapter-by-chapter' writing, you don't just see the road passing beneath you. You now have a good idea of what is important and so can now plan the best route.

Suggestions for Effective Research Writing

Making an Outline

Before you start writing any section, it is wise to make an initial 'skeleton' outline – a working outline – of what you want to write. The idea of making outlines for each section of a research paper is not widely practised here but most texts about research writing advise starting with an outline. We are no different! The concept of writing an outline applies to all sections of the thesis – not only your literature review. An outline brings related material together under general headings and keeps your thoughts in order. It also prevents you from going around in writing-circles! Outlines tell you what has to be written and approximately where it fits in to your thesis paper. You use your outline to classify the segments of your research into clear divisions.

One way of making sense of all the notes you have made when doing the literature review (preferably on the note cards suggested in Part One) is to sort them into categories. Then you start thinking of how each category leads to the next. For example, for the literature review, notes for the learned helplessness research were placed into several different orders. The first order started with a chronological order of research that had taken place, followed by theoretical papers. This proved too confusing, so the cards were sorted again. After a few tries, the final topic outline was something similar to that shown in Figure 20.1.

Although Figure 20.1 shows only the major headings, you can still see how the finished section would flow from one topic to the next. The finished product was one that led the reader from the creation of the term, learned helplessness, to the current investigations being carried out, with the major emphasis on research involving children. Obviously, much more information was collected than was finally used and the author was able to pick and choose the articles that were pertinent to the study.

Following the introduction in which the topic "learned helplessness" was introduced and the construct was defined. The outline of the rest of the literature review follows:

I   Early and Pertinent Current Research
    A.   Seligman and his dogs
    B.   Adult research: early to current
    C.   Child research: early to current

II   The Measurement of Learned Helplessness Behaviours of Children
    A.   How LH is defined in terms of child research
    B.   Response-initiation
    C.   Perseverance at task
    D.   Perception of control
    E.   Locus of Control Scales

III Issues Emerging from Learned Helpless Research with Children
    A.   Ambiguous Definitions (- procedure? effect? or both?)
    B.   Dependence on attributional methodologies
    C.   Dependence on academic failure

Figure 20.1:   An example of an outline used to write the literature review on learned helplessness behaviours in children.

Remember your thesis statement and confine your writing to what is pertinent to your research. This can be difficult because, by now, you have collected a large amount of material and you would like to show off your scholarship. Probably, when you started your research by reviewing the literature, you felt like most other student researchers who thought that they would find it difficult to write such a long paper and that they would have to 'pad it out' to make up the number of words required. You will find, however, that when your project becomes part of you, your problem will be keeping within the limits set by your institution. It is actually much harder (and personally very painful) to 'cut-down' a finished thesis than it is to write it in the first place. This is an important reason for doing a lot of planning and making outlines at the start rather than rushing into final chapter-by-chapter drafts.

You have to make sure that there is a solid chain of theory and logic from thesis statement and literature review through the analyses and down to your discussion. You also need to ensure that (i) there are no 'slippages' of meanings between what your thesis refers to and what you actually measured (the operational definitions), (ii) that the analyses are appropriate to the measures, and (iii) the results are interpreted and discussed appropriately in relation to what has been done.

Pseudo-Academic Language

When you look at finished studies, research questions are sometimes written in 'fancy' language so that the study appears extremely academic. For example, research investigating how children feel about school becomes "Affective Response Tendencies in School Aged Children." This is what we mean when we titled this section "Pseudo-Academic Language."

Long abstract words can be used to hide the fact that the thesis is not worth very much. It is unfortunate but true, that 'fancy' language impresses some people more than hard earned simplicity – particularly if they don't intend to fully read the work. You also have to remember that your thesis will be read by at least three other people who already have received their doctorates or that your paper to be published in a journal will be peer-reviewed. All the pseudo-academic language in the world will not impress these readers. What will impress them is the quality of your research.

When you are in the planning stage, you should use plain, clear language with which you can work and feel comfortable. The language you use, however, must be in keeping with the discipline of your field of research and you should become comfortable with the terminology. For example, if you are using a Likert-type scale to measure your data, you must say so and your readers will understand. If you start off scribbling your thoughts in technical terminology that you really don't know (but you think you should use), then you may never clarify your ideas and your writing will reflect this.

When you actually begin serious writing, you should imagine that you are explaining each section of your research to your supervisor who keeps stopping you and saying "What exactly do you mean by that?" It can be very difficult to present a complex issue in simple words but at least, it will make sense to you and your readers.

> Say only what needs to be said. The author who is frugal with words not only writes a more readable manuscript but also increases the chances that the manuscript will be accepted for publication (APA Manual, 2002, p. 26).

Using the Appropriate Tense

When you wrote your proposal, you wrote in the future tense because it was what you hoped you would be allowed to do in the future. When you start writing your thesis, you must be consistent in your use of the verb tense. A simple 'rule of thumb' is to write mainly in the past tense for Chapter 1 and Chapter 2. In Chapter 1, for example, the introduction to your research can begin: The present study investig**ated**..... and in Chapter 2 for the literature review: Professor Smith (1999) stat**ed** that..... or Brown (2000) point**ed** out that .... or researchers **have shown** that.... as long as it is a description of past events.

When you describe the results and conclusions from your own research in Chapter 4, you use the present tense, e.g., Results of a *t*-test **indicate** that ..... BUT, in the discussion section of Chapter 5, use the past tense: The results of this experiment **were similar** in nature to...... perhaps because the participants **were**....... Another factor that **may have affected** the outcome **was** ....

If possible, try to use the active voice. Considered the following: *Brown (1999) obtained similar results* (active) to *Similar results were obtained by Brown, (1999)* (passive).

Citations, Quotations and Paraphrases

A citation means that you are referring to the work of another author who must be given credit.[2] You use citations as either a direct quotation that someone else has written or as a paraphrase of someone's theory or research. Every time you use a quotation or paraphrase something that someone else has written, you must give credit to that person or persons.

1.   **To paraphrase:** you report the findings of previous research or theories presented by an author: *In recent research, Bastick (2000) found that ...* and then you discuss the major findings of that research **in your own words**. You may also paraphrase a theoretical position taken by different authors as for example: *Some psychologists, such as Smith (1998) and Brown (1999) wrote that...* then discuss what they wrote **in your own words**. You can continue: *On the other hand, others (e.g., Green, 2001; Jones, 1999) held an opposite point of view when they stated that ....* You now state their position **in your own words**.

   In your own words has been stressed because when you paraphrase, you make statements without using quotation marks. Although you will be giving credit to the different authors, what you have written is how you have interpreted a specific passage written by someone else. To make sure that you have not misinterpreted them or that you are not guilty of plagiarism, refer to the notes you made when conducting your literature review.

> Plagiarism is a deadly sin! It is thought of in the same vein as cheating on an examination.
> Be very careful that you have not copied anyone's work and tried to pass it off as your own.

---

2. Make sure you keep a bibliography card for each reference you use because all citations **must** be included in the "reference" section.

2.   **To use a direct quotation:** If you are using a direct quote, you should introduce the speaker (the author), the date and, if possible, some identifying phrase. You end the quote with the page number (in brackets) from which the quotation is found. All direct quotations must be enclosed by quotation marks (" ") and must be followed by a specific page number. The period follows the page number. The following is an example of how to write a quotation correctly: *Vygotsky (1988), a well known social psychologist, stated "To understand a child's egocentric utterance, one should know beforehand the subject of the child's speech..." (p. 247).*

If the direct quote starts with a capital letter, then so must your quote. If you are quoting something from the middle of a sentence, then you must insert "... (3 dots or periods) after the first quotation mark to show that you are not quoting the full sentence. As shown in the example above, the quotation ended before the end of the sentence and this was shown by the same ..."

Note that the full stop (the period) punctuation mark comes **after** the author's name, date and page number and following the brackets. The period ties the sentence and the reference together. For example: *Some researchers believed that effective early childhood education is the cornerstone on which future learning is built (Brown, 2001; Green, 2002; Smith, 2000).* This sentence could also be written as: *Some researchers (e.g., Brown, 2001; Green, 2002; Smith, 2000) believed that effective early childhood education is the cornerstone on which future learning is built.*

Good Writing Tips

- In your text, when you are citing a list of two or more authors as reference, remember to put the last names of the authors in alphabetical order, as shown above. Do NOT place them according to date of publication.
- If the quotation is less than 40 words, it can be included as part of the paragraph. The page number is placed at the end of the quote in ( ) and *the full stop come after the brackets.*
- If the quotation is longer than 40 words, it should be given its own space indented 10 spaces from the inside margin. There are no " " marks around a long quote. Additionally, it is no longer required to keep the double spacing when you have a long quote and it can be written using single spacing. End the quote with a full stop and the page number in brackets follows the full stop.
- Make sure that the quote or the paraphrase is properly introduced. Never just plonk a quotation down somewhere in your paper because it looks nice and shows off your scholarship. It must fit into your thesis and you have only used it because you think that you cannot say it as well as the original!
- Be careful not to pepper your thesis paper with too many quotations. Even though you cannot be accused of plagiarism by ensuring that you have given due credit to the authors, your paper should reflect your own thoughts once you have synthesised the notes you made while doing your literature review. Rosnow and Rosnow, (1995) authors of "Writing Papers in Psychology" have termed the use of too many quotations as "Lazy Writing." They said that "Quoting a simple sentence that can easily be paraphrased signals lazy writing" (p. 57).

We endorse these views. When you use too many quotes or too many paraphrases, it is a sure sign that you have not bothered to think about what you have read. Your job is to evaluate, analyse and synthesise what you have read – not just to compile it. When you are writing this chapter, you must also vary how you report the literature.

We have seen far too many research papers that consisted of a series of paragraphs beginning with a researcher's name at the beginning of the paragraph and then the rest of the paragraph consists of nothing more than an outline of the research. This is boring to read and shows the reader that the writer did not attempt to understand, interpret, analyse or synthesize the importance of the research being reviewed. Furthermore, using only the summary of someone's research does not show how it fits into your own research topic. Think about what is important in your own research and then analyse how the findings of each of these reviewed studies are connected with what you are investigating. Then, integrate these different studies into comprehensive paragraphs – not choppy, boring-to-read ones!

Finally, we have noted that some writers overuse "according to..." One of the authors remembers reading a paper and being absolutely amazed by the number of "according to..." (13 on two pages)! The other overused word is "therefore." Think of other ways to introduce authors or to join thoughts!

Good Writing Tips

Note that when you cite an author first, the name must be followed by the date. If you refer to the same author in the same paragraph, you do not need to use the date again. BUT, you must give the date if you mention the same author in a different paragraph.

When you mention two authors of the same article in the text, you join the names together with 'and' as for example, Bastick and Matalon (2006) stated that students should ….. But, when you enclose the two names in a parenthesis following a quote, you use the ampersand (&) to join the two names (Bastick & Matalon, 2006).

References

In Appendix D, you will find an overview of the different research styles that are accepted in each faculty. NOTE: This was published by UWI in 1998 and has not yet been updated, so it is a good idea to check with your own faculty to determine exactly what is required. Then you must check Internet sites or the Doc centre and look at research style manuals.

The manuals show you, among other things, what goes into different types of references – references to chapters in edited books, in journal and newspaper articles, ways to reference different electronic media, etc. When you see how you must write the different types of references, you must make sure that you have collected that specific information when you take your notes.

You can buy books on standard styles and if you are going to be a serious researcher you should buy one for continued reference. However, for a one-time piece of research, you can save your money by typing 'APA style sheet' or 'MLA style sheet' into a search engine such as htpp://www.goggle.com or htpp://metacrawler.com and you will be guided to hundreds of sites with free overviews of the standard styles. The university library and the "Doc centre" also have current issues of APA and other manuals needed to write correct citations and references.[4]

Important

Make sure that you use current references and Internet sites!

Tables and Figures

Even though we stated that writing the results section can be boring, finding out what your data means is very exciting. One of the best ways to present your results is through the use of tables and figures. A table is a systematic arrangement of numbers usually arranged in columns while a figure is everything else (a picture, diagram, map, etc.).

Using the APA style, each table is consecutively numbered in Arabic numerals starting at Table 1 (not Table 1.1) regardless of where it appears in the text. The same holds true with figures – they also start with Figure 1 and are numbered consecutively throughout the text. In other words, don't try to number the tables (or figures either) according to the chapter or use Roman numerals.

The caption for a table has the first letter of each main word in upper-case letters. The caption for a figure begins with an upper-case letter, the remaining words are written in lower case the sentence ends with a full stop.

Captions for tables are placed above the table while captions for figures are placed below the figure. These captions should be self-explanatory and the reader should not have to keep going back to the text to find out what is meant by Fac or TotT. Remember to explain any abbreviations (but not for some statistical term such as SD, N and $\bar{X}$) and identify your units of measurement.

The function of a table or a figure is to supplement the text. Many writers do not realise that the major findings must be discussed in the text *before* they are presented in the text as tables or figures. They seem to assume that the table explains everything and it does not need to be mentioned. The table just appears out of nowhere! They also do not seem to realise that the table must be mentioned in the text by its number.

A good rule to remember when using tables and figures:
Try to write your table as if it does not need to be explained and try to write your text as if you are not using a table!

Remember that statistical tables are *summaries* of your data. You do not have to explain every result but only the major findings. You can write something to the effect: "Results of the ANOVA showed significant main effects for experimental conditions ($F_{(1, 160)}$ = 358.99, $p < .01$), type of school ($F_{(1, 160)}$ = 82.07, $p < 0.01$). There were no

---

4. In fact the library at the Mona campus provides students with seminars on how to use the different types of references and how to carry out computer searches.

significant main effects for gender ($F_{(1, 160)} = 0.31$, $p = .58$). Table 1 shows the mean scores and standard deviations for the main effects. The full ANOVA table can be found in Appendix X."

Finally – and this is what most students do NOT do – **Write your thesis in a draft format first.** You cannot expect to write a thesis and turn in the first draft as the finished article. Go through each chapter – section by section – and make sure that you have taken special care to look for typographic errors, misplaced punctuation marks and all the other things we have warned you about. Read the thesis aloud to yourself and see "how" it reads. If it sounds choppy to you, then it will read choppy to others.

HAPPY WRITING!

A Final Check List

		Date	
Topic Have you	had your topic approved by the Review Board and/or accepted by a supervisor?		
	consulted with your supervisor to make sure your research is do-able?		
Literature review Have you	become familiar with your library?		
	found information from recent articles?		
	made many appropriate notes and references?		
	completed your set of bibliography cards with author's name, date of publication, etc.?		
	ensured that you have avoided plagiarism?		
Writing Have you	selected an appropriate title?		
	developed an outline for writing each chapter?		
	used the correct tense for each chapter?		
	correctly written all the citations and quotations?		
	used the correct spelling? punctuation? grammar?		
	written an introduction and a conclusion for each chapter?		
The Final Draft Have you	used the correct format for the "preliminaries"?		
	used the correct sized margins, capitalisation, headings, placed the page numbers correctly?		
	introduced the tables and figures in the main body of the text? correctly labelled each?		
	numbered the tables and figures appropriately and placed the captions for each in the appropriate place		
	put in the limitations of the research?		
	made several suggestions for future research?		
References Have you	made sure that you have a reference for every work cited in your thesis?		
	used the correct format required by your faculty?		
Finally Have you	dotted every i and crossed every t?		

Test Yourself Answers

Test Yourself 1 (p. 19)

This is exactly what we mean when we stated that you should be very specific in who you are going to measure! Not all males are men and not all females are women so the research question and the null hypothesis are not logically equivalent. For example, we could test a random sample of 10 year-old males and females and we would find that the girls were taller than the boys at that age, whereas adult men are on average taller than adult women.

The research community has often accepted a 'proven' result only to find out later that it is not generally true because of assumptions that seemed to match the research question to the hypothesis. For example, you might find out that something scientists believed was generally true is not so in Jamaica or the Caribbean because they made assumptions that are not true here. This is where your unique personal experience can lead you to original research.

Test Yourself 2 (p. 20)

1.   You can phrase the 'no difference' statement in different ways:
     There was no difference in mean perseverance scores shown by children given solvable or unsolvable tasks.

OR   *Children who were given solvable tasks displayed the same amount of perseverance as children who were given unsolvable tasks.*

OR   *There was no difference between the amount of perseverance shown by children who were given solvable tasks and the amount of perseverance shown by children who were given unsolvable tasks.*

2. H_0: The amount of interest in schooling and academic performance taken by parents of Grade 10 high school students had no affect on their children's overall academic achievement.

     H_1: Grade 10 students whose parents took an interest in their school and academic achievement exhibited higher academic achievement than Grade 10 students whose parents took no interest.

3. H_0: Over a six months training session, math scores of Grade 3 students did not differ according to whether they were taught using a computer-assisted programme or by a lecture method.

     H_1: Over a six months training session, math scores of Grade 3 students taught using a computer-assisted programme were higher than scores of than Grade 3 students taught using a lecture method.

Test Yourself 3 (p. 23)

1. Ratio
2. Nominal
3. Ordinal
4. Ratio
5. Interval

Test Yourself 4 (p. 28)

Question A is perception and Question B is prevalence. If John and Mary both answered 5 to Question B then you would know that they had both a read a book the same number of times last week. You can add and average the responses to Question B to get the total and average number of times your subjects read a book last week. However, you must realise that the answers to Question A do not tell you how often people read books. For example, although John and Mary both read the same number of times, This might seem 'very often' to John but 'not often' to Mary. You cannot add or average the responses to Question A find out how often people read books.

Prevalence variables are of two types, Frequence and Degree. Question B above only asks for the Frequency 'how many'. It does not ask 'how long' which is the degree (force or strength) with which each event happened. If Question B has asked "How many hours did you spend reading books last week?" then Mary could have answered 8 for Question B and John only 2 and you would be right in assuming that 8 means more reading than 2. If John read for 3 hours each time but Mary only read for 5 minutes each time. John's total reading would have been 2 x 3 hours = 6 hours but Mary's was only 8 x 5 mins = 40 minutes. So it is more meaningful to use both degree and frequency variables than it is to use perception variables.

Test Yourself 5 (p. 31)

Answers will vary according to how you have defined each construct.

The first five constructs marked with * are "invented" constructs. They are non-observable entities and this means that we have to infer the behaviours that are associated with them from the behaviour or reports of the participants in the research. In other words, researchers have to look at behaviours associated with a particular construct to measure that construct.

Other constructs may be relatively easy to measure. For example, intelligence can be measured by a score on a standardised intelligence test and socioeconomic status (SES) by the relative ranking of occupation, income, education, etc., locus of control can be measured by a number scored on various standardised tests and so on.

Whatever you are measuring, remember to answer the question "what?" For example, if you are investigating motivation, answer "Motivation to do what?" for level of training, answer "Level of training in what?"

Test Yourself 6 (p. 67)

Problem 1:

The research would be quasi-experimental because the researcher is using an intact group of workers in one company. This is also a repeated measures design because the output of the workers will be measured first on the number of garments they would produce if paid for each piece and second on the number of garments they would produce if they were paid by the week. Each condition would last for two months and at the end of the two months, the data would be collected and analysed.

Note that this research could also be carried out by randomly selecting workers to be placed in either Condition A (paid by the piece) or Condition B (paid by the week) . This design, however, might have too many confounding variables – for example, there might be too many slow workers placed in one group or the level of motivation may differ with each person. In this case, you would have to determine a baseline of production for each worker first!

Word Map for Problem 1

Problem Statement: A study to investigate whether production of garments will increase if workers are paid by the piece or by the week.

H_0: The number of garments produced by the workers is similar regardless of how they are paid.

Operational Definitions

      Participants: All the workers at one factory

      Garment production: the number of garments produced per week

Condition A: Workers are paid at the end of each week according to how many garments they produced (i.e., by the piece)

Condition B: Workers are paid at the end of each week regardless of how many garments they produced.

Independent Variables	*Dependent Variable*
Condition A and Condition B	The total number of garments produced under each of the two conditions

Possible Confounding Variables

Level of motivation– for example, if workers are highly motivated to earn more money, they might produce more garments under Condition A

Analyses: *t*-test to determine which condition lead to an increased production of garments.

Problem 2:

This is an experimental research design using independent groups because the researcher has access to a large population and can randomly select participants for the research. After randomly selecting participants, he can then randomly assign each participant to one of four groups: low level dosage, medium level dosage, high-level dosage and placebo (a "pretend" drug – no drug at all). Following administration of the drug, he can then measure the reaction time of each participant of a computer-simulated driving test.

Word Map for Problem 2

Problem Statement: A study to investigate whether different levels of a drug will have any effect on reaction time while participants were given a computer-simulated driving test.

H_0: The drug, regardless of the strength given, had no effect on the reaction time of people who are driving cars.

Operational Definitions

Drug: Brand X of a drug supplied by a large drug manufacturing company

Dosage: Low-level: 2mm pill; medium-level: 4.5mm pill; high-level: 8mm pill.

Reaction time while driving: Use of a computer simulation driving teat that gives reaction time in half seconds. This needs to be measured prior to taking the drug (a pretest) and 10 minutes after taking the drug (a post-test).

Independent Variables	*Dependent Variables*
Group 1: People given a low-level dosage	Scores on pretest reaction time
Group 2: People given a medium-level dosage	Scores on post-test reaction time
Group 3: People given a high-level dosage	
Group 4: People given the placebo (no drug)	

Confounding Variables: Knowledge of computer games, individual differences of eye-hand coordination. Random selection should keep these differences to a minimum and these differences should be randomly distributed across the groups. However, both knowledge and eye-hand coordination could be measured and then, based on pretest scores, subjects could be placed into one of the four groups. In this case, the research design would be a matched-pairs design.

Analyses:

(1)   a *t*-test to determine whether the two sets of scores differ significantly. This would only tell you whether the drug increased or decreased reaction time.

(2)   Comparisons of the four levels of drugs to show which level of drug had the most effect on reaction time.

^Note: It is assumed that all participants have been medically examined and found healthy and that there would be no possible way that the drug could cause any form of physical harm to them.

Test Yourself 7 (p. 166)

The answer is that there is no relationship between the two variables. Look at Table 14.2 (page 167) to check whether your graph corresponded to ours.

Test Yourself 8 (p. 185)

This was a "fun" exercise as the masking variables are very obvious!

Example 1: The possible masking variable is: age of the children.

Reason: As a rule, taller children are older than shorter children – just compare the height of an eight-year old with that of a twelve year-old!. It stands to reason that the taller children will be at a higher grade level and have learned more about geography than the shorter and younger students.

Example 2: The possible masking variable is: the type of fires that require many firemen.

Reason: When a fire is large, it generally requires many firemen working together to contain it or extinguish it. Obviously, if a fire is large, it will require a lot of water causing water damage. (Additionally, firemen often have to take some extreme measures to get close to where the flames are (e.g., cutting through a roof) which also causes damage.

Example 3: The possible masking variable is: the time of year when the study was conducted.

Reason: In the summer time, when it is very warm outside, more people tend to dress lightly.

Test Yourself 9 (p. 215)

Part 1 (Paired-samples *t*-test)

For the paired-samples *t*-test, you used the two sets of test scores to see if there was any difference between Testa (renamed Reading Scores) and Testb (renamed Math Scores) achieved by all 50 students. Using the method to compute the *t*-test given in Chapter 16, your results should be similar to the following:

(a) Table 1 shows the simple statistics giving the mean score and standard deviations for each set. In the table it can be seen that the mean score for the Reading test was 93.3 (SD = 19.30) and for the Math test, the mean score was 78.60 (SD = 16.06).

Table 1

Paired Samples Statistics

		Mean	N	Std. Deviation	Std. Error Mean
Pair 1	English	93.30	50	19.306	2.730
	math	78.60	50	16.059	2.271

(b) Table 2 shows the correlations between the two sets of scores. The results show that there was a significant positive correlation between the two sets of scores ($r = .89$, $p < 0.05$) signifying that children who obtained high scores on the Reading Test also obtained high scores on the Math test.

Table 2: Results of the Paired-Samples Correlation for the Reading Test and Math Test Scores

Paired Samples Correlations

		N	Correlation	Sig.
Pair 1	English & math	50	.897	.000

(c)   Table 3 shows the results of the *t*-test for paired samples. The results show that the scores differ from each other ($t_{(1, 49)}$ = 13.78, $p < 0.05$).

Table 3: Results of the t-test Showing a Significant Difference Between the Two Scores

Paired Samples Test

		Paired Differences							
		Mean	Std. Deviation	Std. Error Mean	95% Confidence Interval of the Difference		t	df	Sig. (2-tailed)
					Lower	Upper			
Pair 1	English – math	14.70	8.631	1.221	12.25	17.15	12.043	49	.000

Now that you have established that the two scores differ from each other, refer to Table 1 and look at the mean scores to find out which score is higher. In this case, the mean score was 92.60 for the Reading test and 78.00 for the Math test. This means that we can conclude that children scored higher on the reading test than they did on the math test. You could write these results in something similar to the following:

> *A paired samples t-test was conducted to determine whether Reading test scores differed from Math test scores. Results showed that the scores differed significantly from each other ($t_{(1, 49)}$ = 12.04, p < 0.05). (see Table 3). Scores on the Reading test were higher than scores on the Math test with the mean score for the Reading test being 93.30 and for the Math test 78.60. It appears that in this study, the students were better readers than mathematicians.*

Part 2 (Independent-samples *t*-test)

For the independent-samples *t*-test, you used the scores from Testa (renamed I-Q test) to see if there was any difference between the scores of the students according to the type of school (Private and Government) they attended.

(a)   Table 1 shows the number of students attending each school and gives the mean scores and standard deviations obtained by the students according to each school type. The mean score for students attending government schools was 76.52 (SD = 10.69 and for those attending private schools, the mean score was 110.08 (SD = 7.77).

Table 1

Group Statistics

	School type	N	Mean	Std. Deviation	Std. Error Mean
CMMS	Government	25	76.52	10.678	2.136
	Private	25	110.08	7.767	1.553

(b)   Table 2 shows the results of the t-test for independent-samples. The results show that the scores differ from each other according to school type ($t_{(1, 48)}$ = -12.71, p < 0.05).

Table 2

Independent Samples Test

		Levene's Test for Equality of Variances		t-test for Equality of Means					95% Confidence Interval of the Difference	
		F	Sig.	t	df	Sig. (2-tailed)	Mean Difference	Std. Error Difference	Lower	Upper
CMMS	Equal variances assumed	1.418	.240	-12.709	48	.000	-33.56	2.641	-38.870	-28.250
	Equal variances not assumed			-12.709	43.843	.000	-33.56	2.641	-38.883	-28.237

Now that you have established that the scores of the IQ test differed according to the type of school the children attended, refer to Table 1 and look at the mean scores to find out which score was higher. In this case, the mean score was 76.52 for the students attending government schools and 110.08 for the students attending private schools. This means that we can conclude that children who attended private schools achieved higher scores on an IQ test than did children attending government schools.

You could write these results in something similar to the following:

An independent samples t-test was conducted to determine whether IQ scores differed according to the type of school the students attended. Results showed that the scores differed significantly from each other (t $_{(-2,48)}$ = -12.71, p < 0.05). (see Table 2). IQ Scores achieved by children attending private schools were higher than IQ scores achieved by children attending government schools with the mean score for children attending private schools equal to 107.92 and for children attending government schools the mean of the IQ test was 78.46. It appears that in this study, the students attending private schools achieve higher scores on IQ tests than do children attending government schools.

Note: this data was used to show you how to use the GLM (three-way ANOVA) in Chapter 17. A word map was drawn on page 234 and the results were interpreted on page 241. As IQ scores are largely based on learning experiences, the researcher asked the question: "What are we doing to our children attending government schools?"

Appendix A

Detail of Descriptives.13 data file

Id	Gend	SchT	Gr	Testa	Testb	Id	Gen	SchT	Gr	Testa	Testb
1	1	1	1	76	37	26	1	2	1	102	87
2	1	1	1	82	62	27	2	2	1	98	79
3	1	1	1	73	65	28	2	2	1	103	85
4	2	1	1	55	36	29	1	2	1	106	89
5	1	1	1	66	71	30	1	2	1	105	89
6	2	1	1	82	79	31	2	2	1	96	87
7	2	1	1	72	69	32	2	2	1	102	88
8	2	1	1	79	73	33	1	2	1	113	92
9	1	1	1	85	55	34	1	2	1	107	91
10	1	1	1	102	89	35	2	2	1	110	93
11	2	1	1	89	75	36	2	2	1	109	94
12	2	1	1	77	68	37	2	2	1	118	97
13	1	1	2	93	95	38	1	2	1	113	93
14	2	1	2	82	76	39	1	2	2	98	80
15	1	1	2	56	48	40	1	2	2	114	95
16	1	1	2	73	66	41	2	2	2	123	98
17	1	1	2	78	68	42	2	2	2	119	93
18	2	1	2	85	79	43	1	2	2	108	89
18	2	1	2	68	61	44	2	2	2	112	91
20	2	1	2	71	66	45	1	2	2	111	90
21	1	1	2	67	53	46	1	2	2	115	94
22	1	1	2	75	68	47	1	2	2	116	93
23	1	1	2	79	76	48	2	2	2	115	95
24	1	1	2	65	52	49	1	2	2	127	98
25	1	1	2	83	76	50	1	2	2	112	87

An example of possible codes and labels you can use for the data analyses
Gend = Gender: 1 = Males; 2 = Females
SchT = School Type: 1 = Government; 2 = Private
Gr = Grade Level: 1 = Grade 1; 2 = Grade 2

Remember to properly label your variables when you enter the data into SPSS.

Appendix B

Details of data for Correlate.13 (Appendix B1) and NonLinear .13 (Appendix B2)

Appendix B1: Correlate.13

Appendix B2: NonLinear

S	V1	V2		S	V1	V2
1	65	97		1	65	97
2	41	73		2	41	73
3	13	18		3	75	18
4	8	32		4	8	32
5	2	6		5	51	6
6	56	57		6	56	57
7	41	82		7	41	82
8	91	94		8	27	94
9	87	98		9	87	46
10	57	72		10	57	72
11	24	14		11	24	14
12	60	40		12	60	40
13	26	58		13	26	58
14	25	39		14	25	39
15	86	86		15	86	28
16	83	71		16	83	71
17	46	13		17	46	13
18	64	78		18	64	78
19	8	5		19	66	15

Appendix C

Detail of data for Covariate13

Id#	Theory	Pract	English		Id#	Theory	Pract	English
1	14	20	76		21	10	63	40
2	61	88	2		22	70	17	78
3	60	8	77		23	54	93	4
4	78	81	84		24	98	20	90
5	8	27	59		25	48	91	20
6	96	81	30		26	3	94	3
7	33	23	40		27	98	3	99
8	75	2	81		28	61	47	80
9	92	54	50		29	25	7	72
10	10	79	13		30	85	65	85
11	88	18	87		31	8	37	3
12	45	68	60		32	30	47	31
13	10	4	83		33	80	12	70
14	33	76	3		34	85	13	89
15	71	95	2		35	93	65	58
16	50	5	65		36	87	87	2
17	15	95	4		37	94	95	67
18	90	85	61		38	88	7	98
19	57	29	96		39	5	59	10
20	5	11	97		40	15	64	7

Key: Pract = Practical work

Appendix D
Recommended Style Manuals for Theses and Research Papers for Faculties at UWI
Adapted from: *The University of the West Indies Thesis Guide,* December, 1998. Appendix X (p. 28).

Faculty of Agriculture & Natural Science, Pure & Applied Science, Science & Technology

Agriculture	*Chicago Manual of Style,* University of Chicago Press (latest edition).
Biology	*Scientific Style and Format: The CBE Manual for Authors, Editors and Publishers (6th ed.).* Cambridge: Cambridge University Press, 1994.
Chemistry	*Handbook for Authors of Papers in American Chemical Society Publications.* Washington, DC: American Chemical Society, 1998.
Mathematics	*A Manual for Authors of Mathematical Papers (8th ed.)* Providence, RI: American Mathematics Society, 1984.
Natural Sciences	*Chicago Manual of Style,* University of Chicago Press (latest edition.) *The ACS Style Guide: A manual for authors and editors.* Janet S. Dodd, Editor. Washington: American Chemical Society, 1986 *AIP Style Manual for Physicists.* New York: American Institute of Physics (latest edition).

Faculty of Arts & Education; Humanities; Humanities & Education
Arts
(Undergraduate students)

MLA Handbook for Writers of Research Papers (latest edition). New York: Modern Language Association. (1998).

Chicago Manual of Style (latest edition) Chicago: University of Chicago Press.

(Graduate students)

A Manual for Writers of Term papers, Theses and Dissertations (6th ed.). Kate L. Turabin. Chicago: University of Chicago (1996) (Based on the Chicago Manual of Style).

Education
(Educational Psychology)
Psychology

Publication Manual of the American Psychological Association (APA) (latest edition). Washington, DC: American Psychological Society. (2001).

Humanities
(Undergraduate students)

MLA Handbook for Writers of Research Papers (latest edition). New York: Modern Language Association of America, 1998.

Humanities
(Graduate students)

MLA Style Manual and Guide to Scholarly Publishing (latest edition). New York: Modern Language Association of America, 1998.

MHRA Style Book (2ⁿᵈ ed.) London: Modern Humanities Research Association, 1978. (for the UK)

Faculty of Engineering

Chicago Manual of Style (latest edition). Chicago: University of Chicago Press, 1993.

ASTM Style Manual. Philadelphia: Committee on Publication, American Society for Testing and Materials, 1973.

Faculty of Medical Sciences

Publication Manual of the American Psychological Association (APA) (latest edition). Washington, DC: American Psychological Society. 1994.

International Committee of Medical Journal Editors.

Uniform requirements for Biomedical Journals (rev.). British Medical Journal, 302, 338-341. 1991.

The Oxford Dictionary for Scientific Writers. Oxford: Oxford University Press. (latest edition)

Nursing

Writing for Nursing Publications. Thorofare, NJ: Slack, 1981.

Publication Manual of the American Psychological Association (APA) (latest edition). Washington, DC: American Psychological Society.

Faculty of Social Sciences

Chicago Manual of Style (latest edition). Chicago: University of Chicago Press, 1993.

Political Science

Political Science Student Writer's Manual. Englewood Cliffs, NJ: Prentice Hall, 1995.

Faculty of Law

Chicago Manual of Style (latest edition). Chicago: University of Chicago Press, 1993

The Bluebook: A Uniform System of Citation. Cambridge, MS: Harvard Law Review Association, 1996.

As of printing this text, the latest edition of:
APA is the 5ᵗʰ edition
Chicago is the 15ᵗʰ edition
MLA is the 14ᵗʰ edition

References

American Psychological Association. (2001). *Publication manual of the American Psychological Association* (5th ed.). Washington, DC: Author.

Bastick, T. (2003). *Is validity more reliable than reliability is valid? Education Theory and Practice* (2nd ed.). Kingston, Jamaica: Department of Educational Studies, University of the West Indies, Mona Campus.

Bastick, T. (2000). Why teachers trainees choose the teaching profession. *International Review of Education*, (3/4), 343-349.

Bryman, A., & Crammer, D. (2005). *Qualitative data analysis with SPSS release 10 for Windows: A guide for social scientists.* East Sussex, GB: Routledge.

Chmura, H., Thieman, S., & Denenburg, V. (1987). *How many subjects? Statistical power analysis in research.* London, GB: Saga Publications.

Cohen, J. (1988). *Statistical power analysis for the behavioral sciences.* Hillsdale, NJ: Erlbaum.

Cook, L., & Bastick, T. (2003). Improving Teaching Quality: An examination of two locus of control instruments for monitoring internality training. *Journal of Education and Development in the Caribbean, 7* (1&2), 43-57.

Denscombe, M. (2003). *The good research guide* (2nd ed.). Maidenhead, GB: Open University Press.

Daley-Morris, P. (2001). *Computers in the classroom: An introduction.* Kingston Jamaica, W.I.: The Chalkboard Press.

Dobbelstein, S., Levin, J. & Oosterbeck, H. (2002). The causal effect of class size on scholastic achievement: Distinguishing the pure class size effect from the changes in class composition. *Oxford bulletin of Economics and Statistics, 64*, 17-36.

Fraenkel, J. R., & Wallen, N. E. (2003). *How to design and evaluate research in education* (6th ed.). Boston: Mcgraw Hill.

Gall, M. D., Gall, J. P., & Borg, W. R. (2003). *Educational research: An introduction* (7th ed.). Boston: Allyn and Bacon.

Greene, J., & d'Oliviera, M. (2003). *Learning to use statistical testing in psychology* (2nd ed.). Buckingham, GB: Open University Press.

Hall, B. W., Ward, A. W., & Conner, C. B. (1988). Published educational research: An empirical study of its quality. *Journal of Educational Research*, 81, 182-198.

Harvey, G. (2000). *Excel for dummies* (2nd ed.). San Mateo, CA: IDG Books Worldwide Inc.

Hopkins, K. D., and Gullickson, A. R. (1992). *Response rates in survey research: A meta-analysis of the effects of monetary gratuities.* Paper presented at the annual meeting of the American Educational Research Association, New Orleans.

Kearl, M. (2004). *The research paper.* Retrieved Jan. 25, 2005 from http://www.trinity.edu/mkearl/research.html

Leedy, P. D., & Ormrod, J. E. (2001). *Practical research.* Upper Saddle River, NJ: Prentice-Hall.

Matalon, B. (1999). *Are culture tests really fair to Jamaican children?* Institute of Education Annual, 2, 3-20.

Matalon, B. (1990). *The influence of success or failure on learned helplessness behaviours in Jamaican children.* Unpublished doctoral dissertation, University of Miami, Florida.

Pagano, R. (2006). *Understanding statistics in the behavioural sciences.* NYC: Wadsworth.

Rosnow, R. L. & Rosnow, M. (2002). *Writing Papers in Psychology* (4th ed.). Pacific Grove, CA: Brooks/Cole

Sinione Dobbelsteen, S., Levin, J., & Oosterbeek, H. (2002). *The causal effect of class size on scholastic achievement: Distinguishing pure class size effect from the effect of changes in class composition.* Oxford Bulleting of Economics and Statistics, 64 (17), 305-349.

Stouffer, S. A. (1949). *An analysis of conflicting social norms.* American Social Psychology, 14, 707-717.

Tabachnik, B. G., & Fidell, L. S. (2000). *Using multivariate statistics* (4th ed.). Needham Heights, MA: Allyn and Bacon.

Wiersma, W. (2004). *Research methods in education: An introduction* (8th ed.). Upper Saddle River, NJ: Prentice-Hall.

Recommended Reading

For Style Guides

American Psychological Association. (2001). *Publication manual of the American Psychological Association* (5th ed.). Washington, DC: Author.

Chicago Press Staff. (2003). *Chicago manual of style* (16th ed.). Chicago: University of Chicago.

Gibaldi, J. (2003). *MLA handbook for writers of research* (5th ed.) NYC: Modern Language Association.

Gelford, H., & Walker, C. (Eds.). (2001). *Mastering APA style: Students' workbook and training guide.* Washington, DC: American Publication Association.

For Writing Guides

Lester, J. D., & Lester, D.L. Jr. (2004). *Writing research papers: A complete guide* (4th ed.). Glenview, IL: Scott, Foresman.

Strunk Jr,, W.& White, E. B. (2000). *The elements of style* (4th ed.). New York: Macmillan.

For Statistics

David, R. (2000). *Practical statistics for educators* (2nd ed.) NYS: University Press of America.

Jaisingh, L. R., & Rozakis, L. (2000). *Statistics for the utterly confused.* Boston: McGraw Hill.

Pallant, J. (2004). *SPSS survival manual.* Buckingham, GB: Open University Press.

Rowntree, D. (2000). *Statistics without tears: An introduction for non-mathematicians.* London, GB: Penguin Books.

Shannon, D. M., & Davenport, M. A. (2000). *Using SPSS to solve statistical problems: A self-instructional guide.* Upper Saddle River, NJ: Prentice-Hall.

Glossary

ABD: stands for All But Dissertation: This is what generally happens when students do not start to think about their research until after that have finished all their classes or have so much trouble trying to complete their research that they just do not complete it and fail to graduate.

Abscissa: the horizontal line or x axis of a graph.

A priori (planned) comparisons: determines what groups differ significantly from each other. To guard against Type 1 errors, use post hoc comparisons or the Bonferroni adjustment. Comparisons are planned in advance of the experiment and often arise from predictions based on theory and prior research.

A posteriori (post hoc) comparisons: explores differences between scores of each of groups or conditions. Comparisons are not planned prior to conducting the experiment and arise after the data has been analysed; use the Tukey's HSD (honestly significant difference) test or Scheffe's test.

Acquiescence bias: In responding to a questionnaire, a type of response set in which an individual agrees with items regardless of their content.

Alpha level: the threshold of possibility that is used as the critical region for rejecting or failing to reject the null hypothesis. The alpha level should be determined at the beginning of the research and is usually set at 0.05 or 0.01. The Greek letter "a" is the symbol used when writing the alpha level.

Alternate hypothesis: states that the difference in scores between conditions is due to the actions of the independent variables (written H_A or H_1).

Analysis of covariance (ANCOVA): used when you want to statistically control for the possible effects of a confounding variable (the covariate); useful when you suspect that your groups differ on some variable that may impact the effect that the independent variables have on the dependent variable. ANCOVA removes the effect of the covariate.

Analysis of variance (ANOVA): a statistical procedure used to determine whether the difference between the mean scores of two or more factors on a dependent variable is statistically significant; tells whether there is a significant difference between the means of the group; used in independent group designs and repeated measures designs and when one or more factors (groups that have been classified on several independent variables) are investigated in the same experiment; Also gives interaction effects. (See one-way ANOVA, two-way ANOVA, GLM).

Attribute variables: preexisting conditions or attributes of subjects or things; describes characteristics or attitudes of a variable, e.g., gender, religious preference, age, sex, grade level, life style, colour/size/weight of object, etc.

Bar graph: frequency distribution of nominal or ordinal data that are plotted using a bar for each category: numbers on the ordinal (the height of the bar) represents the frequency or number of that category; the types or groups can be arranged along the horizontal axis (abscissa) in any order.

Bivariate correlation coefficient: any type of statistic that describes the magnitude of the relationship between two variables.

Bimodal distribution: when a distribution has two modes instead of one mode as in the normal curve.

Bonferroni adjustment (to the alpha level): a method designed to protect against making Type 1 errors which involves setting the alpha level to a more stringent value for all the comparisons you plan to make. This usually involves dividing the alpha level by the number of comparisons. For example, if you set the alpha level at 0.05 and planned to make three comparisons, then the new alpha level would be $0.05 \div 3 = 0.016$.

C-alpha: see *Cronbach's alpha.*

Case study method: in depth study of one individual or one group of individuals.

Categorical variable: a characteristic that has been measured as a nominal scale; see nominal variable.

Causal-Comparative research: used to try to discover the possible causes and effects of a variable upon a second variable.

Central tendency: represents the most typical values: mean, median and mode.

Chi-square (χ^2): a non-parametric test most often used with nominal data; used for analysing frequencies; measures the discrepancy between the observed frequency and the expected frequency for each of the cells in a one-way or two-way table.

Coefficient of determination (R^2): the square of Pearson r; shows the proportion of the variability of one variable (Y) that is accounted for by the other variable (X) (see Pearson r).

Concurrent validity: the extent to which an individual's sores on one test correspond to scores on a similar test.

Confidence interval: a range of values that contains the population value.

Confidence limits: the upper and lower values that contain the boundaries of the confidence interval.

Confounding variables: effects of the independent variables are confused with one or more variables that should have been held in check making it impossible to tell whether results are valid or due to some other causes. (see also *contaminating variables*).

Construct: an abstract concept that is inferred from commonalities among observed phenomena and can serve as an explanatory term (as for example: government, affiliation-motivation); constructs that can not be directly observed but are defined based on observations.

Construct validity: the extent to which inferences from a test score accurately reflect the construct that the test is supposed to measure.

Contaminating variables: unwanted influences on the independent variables that should be controlled by the researcher (e.g., time of day...late in day subjects may be tired and perform poorly; level of hunger, etc.) (see also *confounding variables*).

Content validity: refers to how well the particular sampling of behaviours used to measure a characteristic reflects performance in an entire domain of behaviours that constitutes that characteristic.

Continuous variable: one that can have an infinite number of values between adjacent units on the scale (e.g., weight, height, time, etc.)

Control group: In quantitative research, a group of participants who receive no treatment or some form of alternative treatment so that the effect of extraneous variables can be determined; scores from the control group provide a basis for comparison with other groups of participants who received the treatment.

Correlation: the relationship between two variables with the major interest being the direction and degree of that relationship.

Correlation coefficient: a mathematical expression that expresses quantitatively the magnitude and direction of the relationship between two variables; can vary from +1 to -1 (e.g., Pearson r, Spearman rank order coefficient)

Criterion-related validity: type of validity, specifically predictive and concurrent validity, that involve an explicit standard against which claims for a test can be judged.

Correlation ratio: a mathematical expression that provides a more accurate index of the magnitude of the relationship between two measured variables than other correlational statistics through the use of correlational statistics.

Correlational research: an investigation to determine the degree and direction of relationship between two variables.

Cronbach alpha coefficient (C-alpha): a measure of the internal consistency of a test, based on the extent to which test-takers who answer a test item one way respond to other similar items the same way.

Cross-sectional research: research in which subjects are placed into groups according to age and are compared on a certain variable (e.g., looking at attitudes towards something using groups of teenage subjects, middle-aged subjects and older subjects).

Curvilinear relationship: a relationship between two variables in which the relationship (when graphed on a scatter plot) can be most accurately represented in a curved line.

Degrees of freedom (*df*): determined by the population and indicates the number of independent pieces of information (number of scores) a sample of observations can provide for the purpose of statistical inference. The df is one less than the total number of subjects (N-1); used in statistical analyses to compute variance and standard deviation. The SPSS programme automatically computes the *df* when it does statistical analyses.

Dependent variable: a measurement that changes in response to changes made to the independent variable. In a hypothesised cause and effect relationship, the dependent variable is the "presumed" effect.

Descriptive research: In quantitative research, a type of investigation that measures the characteristics of a sample or population on prespecified variables. In qualitative research, detailed depictions of what is happening now or what has happened in the environment being studied.

Descriptive statistics: techniques used to describe or characterise the obtained data; a summary of certain aspects of the results so they can be easily understood by the reader. (See *Central tendency, variability, dispersion, shape of distribution*).

Deviation score: tells how far away the raw score is from the mean of its distribution ($x - \bar{x}$).

Dichotomy: a categorical variable that only has two values (e.g., gender).

Discrete variable: one in which there are no possible values between adjacent units on the scale (e.g., number of pages in a book; number of children in a family).

Dispersion: indicates the variability or spread of the data for a set of results. Includes the range, mean deviation (rarely used) and variance.

Effect size: a measurement to indicate the magnitude of a treatment effect; not influenced by sample size.

Eta^2 (η^2): see *effect size.*

Excel: A statistical programme found in most computer programmes that is designed to create data bases from worksheets.

Experimental methods: manipulating one or more variables to determine the effect on some other variables.

Explained variance (R^2): In correlation, a statistic that specifies the percentage of the variance in variable X that can be predicted from the variance in variable Y. The greater the value of R^2, the greater the amount of explained variance.

External validity: the extent to which the results of a research study can be generalised to individuals and situations beyond those involved in the study.

Extraneous variable: In experiments, any aspect of the situation, other than the treatment variable, that can influence the dependent variable and that can, if not controlled, make it impossible to determine whether the treatment variable is responsible for any observed effect on the dependent variable. (See also, *confounding variables*).

Face validity: the extent to which a causal, subjective inspection of a test's items indicates they cover the content the test is claimed to measure.

Factor: in a factor analysis of a set of variables, a mathematical expression of a feature shared by a particular subset of the variable (e.g., grade levels)

Factorial analysis: a statistical procedure used to explain variability among observed variables in terms of factors for assessing the effects of two or more factors in one experiment; allows you to condense a large set of variables or scale items down to a smaller, more manageable number of dimensions or factors; used often when developing scales and measures to identify the underlying structure. In a factorial experiment, the treatments used are combinations of the levels of the factors. A two-way ANOVA allows the researcher, in one experiment, to evaluate the effect of two independent variables and the interaction between them. See *GLM.*

Frequency-count recording: measurement of the number of times that each observational variable occurs during an event.

Frequency distribution (*f*): presents the score values and their frequency of occurrence; makes it easier to understand and interpret scores.

Halo effect: the tendency for the observer's early impressions of an individual being observed to influence the observer's ratings of all variables involving that same individual.

Hawthorne effect: an observed change in research participants' behaviour based on their awareness of participating in an experiment, their knowledge of the researcher's hypothesis, or their response receiving special attention.

Hierarchal (sequential) multiple regression: all the independent or predictor variables are entered into the equation in the order specified by the researcher based on theoretical grounds. Variables or sets of variables are entered in steps or blocks and each independent variable is assessed in terms of what it adds to the predictor variable, after the previous variables are controlled for. The relative contribution of each block of variables is also assessed.

Histogram: represents frequency distributions using interval or ratio data; class intervals are plotted on the horizontal axis beginning and ending at the real limits of the interval with the point being plotted over the midpoint of each interval; the height of the bar represents the frequency of the data.

Homogeneity of Variance (HOV): the assumption that samples are obtained from populations that were normally distributed; that there are equal variances across samples. If one variance is very much larger than the other, it is possible that the assumption of HOV is violated. See also *Levene's test for equality of varian*ce.

Hypothesis: the researcher's prediction, derived from theory or speculation, about how two or more measured variables will be related to each other or about the outcome of an experimental manipulation or treatment.

Independent groups design: individuals randomly assigned to one of two (or more) groups; each subject is tested only once.

Independent variable: a variable that is manipulated or selected by a researcher to determine whether the dependent variable varies according to the different assigned values an influence on, another variable (called the dependent variable). In a hypothesised cause-and-effect relationship, the independent variable is the possible cause.

Inferential statistics: techniques that use obtained sample data to infer to the population; involves probability and inference tests, such as Student's *t*-test or ANOVA.

Informed consent: the ethical requirement that a researcher tells all potential participants about the study's procedures, the information they will be asked to disclose to the researcher and the intended uses of that information.

Intact group: a collection of persons who must be studied as members of a previously defined group (e.g., all the students in a classroom) rather than as individuals who have been randomly selected to participate in a study.

Interaction effect: in an ANOVA, when the value of dependent variables is not the same at each level of the grouping variables; when the effect of one variable is influenced by the level of another variable.

Internal consistency: an approach to estimating test reliability that examines the extent to which individuals who respond one way to a test item tend to respond the same way to other similar items on the test.

Internal validity: in experiments, the extent to which extraneous variables have been controlled by the researcher so that any observed effects can be attributed to the treatment variable.

Interval scale: the numeric value assigned indicates order of merit and meaningfully reflects relative distances between points along a given interval between measures; has the same meaning at any point along the scale. (John is twice as tall as Jane).

Item analysis: a set of procedures for determining the difficulty, the validity and the reliability of each item in the test.

Kurtosis: the degree of 'peakedness' to which observations cluster around a central point of a distribution of scores.

Kolmogorov-Smirnov Test: a non-parametric test used to test the hypothesis that the population distribution from which the data sample is drawn conforms to a hypothetical distribution.

Kruskal-Wallis Test: a non-parametric procedure used for determining whether the observed difference between the distribution of scores for more than two groups on a measured variable X is statistically significant; used as a substitute for a one-way parametric ANOVA.

Levene's test for equality of variance: used to test if K samples have equal variances – variances are equal across groups or samples.

Likert-type scale: a unidimensional rating scale used mainly for questionnaires in which people's responses indicate the degree of positive or negative attitudes, perceptions, feelings, etc.

Linear relationship: a relationship between two variables in which the relationship (when graphed on a scatter plot) can be most accurately represented in a straight line.

Line of best fit: in correlational studies, the line on a scattergram that represents and summarises the best prediction of each person's Y score from their X scores.

Longitudinal research: observations of the same subjects over a period of time that can last from about two weeks to many years.

LSD Option: post-hoc multiple comparisons that do not make any connections for Type 1 errors.

Main effect: in an ANOVA, the effect of an independent variable averaged over the levels of the other variables; the influence of a treatment variable by itself (one that is not in interaction with any other variable) on a dependent variable.

Mann-Whitney U Test: an inference test (a non-parametric test) for analysing the degree of separation between the groups in an independent groups design; uses ordinal data; compares scores of two groups to determine if chance alone is a reasonable explanation for the difference between the group scores or whether the difference is statistically significant. The lower the U_{obt} value, the greater the separation.

Matched-subject design: subjects are matched in pairs (according to some specific characteristic) and then randomly assigned to one or more groups. For example, in research looking at a reading programme, subjects could be matched according to intelligence, age, gender.

Mean (also called the average): the average of a set of scores represented by $\bar{X}$. It is the "balance point" of the distribution. It is also the measure that best reflects the total of the scores and is responsive to the exact position of score in the distribution. It is used in many statistical procedures.

$$\bar{X} = \frac{\text{sum of all scores}}{N}$$

Mean deviation: the difference between a score and the mean of a set of scores divided by the total number of scores (rarely used).

Measure of Central Tendency (Descriptive Statistics): a single number (e.g., the mean) that is representative of an entire set of numbers: numbers that tend to cluster around the "middle" of a set of values.

Measurement error: in Classical Test theory, the difference between an individual's true score on a test and the scores that the individual actually obtains on it when it is administered over a variety of conditions.

Median: the value chosen in a set of scores so that it has the same number of scores above it as below it; the scale value below which 50% of all scores fall. It is less affected by extreme scores than the mean.

Meta-analysis: the use of a particular statistical analysis to identify trends in the statistical results of a set of studies concerning similar research problems.

Mode: the most frequently occurring value in a set of scores. It of little use beyond the descriptive level because it is not stable from one distribution to the next.

Multiple correlation coefficient (R): a mathematical procedure fro determining the magnitude of the relationship between a criterion variable and some combination of two or more predictor variables in a multiple regression analysis; used to explore the predictive ability of a set of independent variables on one continuous dependent variable.

Multiple regression: a statistical procedure for determining the magnitude of the relationship between a criterion variable (one continuous variable) and some combination of two or more independent or predictor variables; used to provide information about how well a set of variables is able to predict a particular outcome; which variable in a set of variables is the best predictor of an outcome; whether a particular predictor variable is still able to predict an outcome when the effects of another variable are controlled for. (See *standard multiple regression; hierarchal or sequential multiple regression, stepwise multiple regression*)

Multivariate Analysis of Variance (MANCOVA): used to compare groups on a number of different but related dependent variables; can be used with one-way, two-way and higher factorial designs involving one, two, or more independent variables.

Multivariate correlation: any statistical analysis (e.g., multiple regression or factor analysis) that expresses the relationship among three or more variables.

n: the number of participants within a group.

N: the total number of participants taking part in the research.

Negative relationship: shows an inverse relationship between two variables (a high score has a corresponding low score or a low score has a corresponding high score)

Negatively skewed distribution: see skewed distribution

Newmann-Keuls Test: a post hoc test that allows us to make all possible pair-wise comparisons among the sample means.

Nominal scale: (think of "names") a measure in which numbers represent categories that have no order or quantitative value (e.g., coding gender: males = 1; females = 2); usually used with qualitative variables; observations are sorted into categories by the principle of equivalence (e.g., gender – males and females; types of cheese – Edam and Gouda; religious affiliation - protestant, Catholic, Muslim, and Hindu). This means that no one person or thing is better than the other but is just a way of sorting so we can tell the difference.

Non-parametric test of statistical significance: a type of test of significance that does not make assumptions about the distribution and form of scores on the measured sample.

Normal curve: a theoretical distribution of population scores; a distribution of scores that forms a bell-shaped curve when plotted on a graph.

Normal distribution: mean, median and mode are all clustered at the centre

Normed-referenced measurement: an approach to testing in which an individual's score on a test is interpreted by comparing it to the scores earned by the norming group.

Null hypothesis: a prediction stating that no differences will be found between two measured variables (written H_0).

Objectivity: in testing, the extent to which scores on a test are undistorted by biases of those who administer and score it.

Observational methods: collecting information about behaviour without trying to change anything (Can be non-participant observation such as watching children through a one-way mirror)

100mm line scale: a 100mm line anchored at each end by bipolar opposite adjectives used mainly in questionnaires.

One-tailed test of statistical significance: a mathematical procedure for determining whether a null hypothesis that specifies the direction of the difference between two groups (or other prediction involving only one tail of a probability distribution) can be rejected at a given alpha level.

One-way ANOVA: used when you are looking at the impact of only one independent variable on the dependent variable; informs if scores of groups differ but does not tell where significance difference is (use post hoc comparisons).

Operationally defined construct: a concept that is defined by specifying the activities used to measure or manipulate it.

Order effect: in experiments where each research participant receives more than one treatment; the influence of the order in which the treatments are administered on the dependent variable.

Ordinal scale: a measure in which observations are ranked in order of magnitude with numeric ranks expressing a "greater than" or "lesser than" relationship but with no implication about how much

greater or how much lesser. In other words, by using an ordinal scale, we can state that A>B, A=B or that A<B as, for example, John is taller than Jane. This statement does not state how much taller.

Ordinate: the vertical line or y-axis on a graph.

Outlier: a research participant or other unit of analysis whose score on a measure is markedly different from the other scores in the sample or population.

p: see *probability value.*

Parameter: any number that describes a characteristic of a population's score on a measure.

Parametric test of statistical significance: a type of test of statistical significance that makes certain assumptions about the distribution and form of scores on the measured variable; assumptions about underlying population distribution of data (i.e., normal distribution). Use randomization techniques so scores are considered as representative of some population. Can use continuous, discrete or categorical variables.

Partial correlation coefficient: a statistic that expresses the magnitude of the relationship between two measured variables (X and Y) after the influence of another measured variable on either X or Y (but not on both) has been removed; an extension of a Pearson correlation that allows you to control for the effects of a confounding variable.

Pearson r: a mathematical expression that shows the direction and magnitude to which paired scores occupy the same or opposite positions within their own distribution; developed to determine the relationship between two variables; to determine whether a correlation exists in the population; can also be interpreted in terms of the variability of one variable (Y) accounted for by another. variable (X). May be positive or negative and the *r* value can range from 0.0 to 1.0.

Phi coefficient: a measurement of the magnitude of the relationship between two dichotomous variables in a chi-square analysis.

Pilot study: a small-scale, preliminary investigation that is conducted to develop and test measures or procedures that will be used in a research study.

Plagiarism: the direct lifting of another's words for use in one's own report without giving any credit to the original writer.

Point biserial correlation: a measure of association between a continuous variable and a dichotomous variable.

Population: a complete set of observations or measurements about which we would like to be able to draw conclusions; total number of parts from which a sample is chosen.

Positive relationship: shows a direct relationship between two variables; a high score has a corresponding high score and a low score has a corresponding low score).

Positively skewed distribution: see s*kewed distribution.*

Post-test: a measure that is administered following an experimental or control treatment or other intervention in order to determine the effects of the intervention.

Power of an experiment: the probability that the result of an experiment will allow rejection of the null hypothesis if the independent variable has a real effect.

Prediction research: a type of investigation that seeks to predict future events, conditions, or accomplishments from variables measured at an earlier time.

Predictive validity: the extent to which scores on a test administered at one point in time accurately forecast the test-taker's scores on another measure administered at a later point in time.

Pretest: a measure that is administered prior to an experimental or treatment condition or other intervention.

Pretesting a questionnaire: Administering a questionnaire to a small group of people to determine whether items are unambiguous, etc.

Probability (p): a proportion; refers to the level of significance following statistical analyses (see alpha); the likelihood that a statistical result was not obtained by chance.

Q-Q plot: (quartile-quartile) a scatter plot of the quartiles of the first data on the horizontal axis paired with the quartiles of the second set of scores set on the longitudinal axis. Outliers will appear as dots that are far away from the overall pattern of points.

Quasi-experiment: a type of experiment in which research participants are not randomly assigned to the experimental, treatment and/or control groups.

Questionnaire: an instrument that presents a set of items to which all individuals in a sample are asked to respond.

Random assignment: the process of assigning individuals or groups (e.g., classrooms) to the experimental/treatment conditions such that each individual or group has an equal chance of being in any one condition.

Random sample: subjects drawn in an unbiased way as a sample from some defined population. This means that each member of the population has an equal chance of being included in the research (e.g., 50 students drawn at random from all first year college students). Using a random sample enables the researchers to generalise results and not have results only applicable to the subjects who have taken part in the research. This is central to much of statistical reasoning.

Random sampling: The selection of all members of a population for a research project so that each participant has an equal and independent chance of being selected.

Range: the difference between the highest and lowest scores. (Range = highest score - lowest score).

Ratings by observers: must be reliable (e.g., class room tests, measures of achievement, motivation, etc.) Can use correlation coefficients to show reliability of observer ratings, etc.

Ratio scale: this has all the properties of an interval scale as well as having a absolute zero. (With the ground level being zero, John is 6 feet tall and Jane is three feet tall; the Kelvin Scale which has an absolute zero so that the difference between 2° and 4° is the same as between 9° and 10°).

Raw score: an individual score on a measure as determined by the scoring key, without any further statistical manipulation.

Relevant (nuisance) variables: can influence the dependent variables in an experiment by not considering it to be important cause or effect (e.g., like not considering the effect of intelligence of students when looking at the effect of a reading programme). A good researcher tries to hold these nuisance variables in check. (see also: *confounding variables, contaminating variables*).

Reliability: refers to the consistency of the research; involves the extent to which measurements of some attribute or construct are collected in a systematic manner so that these measurements are consistent, stable and can be reproduced (e.g., other researchers would arrive at similar results if they studied the same concept).

Repeated-measures design: a single subject appears in each experimental condition. Note that problems can arise, however, in deciding the order in which each subject participates in the experimental condition. One solution could be counter-balancing the order of presentation of the conditions to the subjects.

Replication: the process of repeating a research study with a different group of participants using similar conditions with the purpose of increasing confidence in the original's study findings.

Response set: in testing, a predisposition to give the same type of answer to some or all of the items in a test rather than consider an answer to each item based on careful consideration of that item's content.

Results: need to be reliable so use good measuring instruments (like using steel or wooden measuring tape against an old cloth stretched one!)

Sample: individuals chosen from the population to participate in a study and who are believed to be representative of the general population; a small part of anything.

Sampling error: the deviation of a sample statistic from its population value.

Scales: see nominal, categorical and ratio scales, also Likert-type, 100mm line, and Semantic differences scales.

Scatter plot: a pictorial representation (a graph) of the correspondence between two pairs of values.

Scheffe test: a type of *t*-test for multiple comparisons.

SD: see *standard deviation*.

Semantic Differential (Charles Osgood) scale: a 7 point bipolar scale that is anchored at each end by pairs of opposite adjectives used mainly in questionnaires.

Shotgun research: a type of quantitative investigation that involves studying a large number of variables simply because they are there or easily measured rather than carefully considering how the variables relate to the hypothesis and research design.

Single-sample experimental designs: one or more of the null hypothesis population parameters (the mean and/or the standard deviation) must be specified; both the *z* and the *t*-tests are appropriate.

Skewed distribution: Positive skew means that more extreme scores are to the right and that the mean, median and mode are "bunched up" to the left of the graph. Negative skew means that more extreme scores are at the left and the mean, median and mode are "bunched up" to the right of the graph.

Spearman rank order coefficient: (rho) used for linear relationship when one or both variables are only of ordinal scaling.

Social desirability set: in testing, a type of response set in which individuals answer items in such a way as to cast themselves in a favourable light or as they think a "good" person would reply.

Solomon four-group design: a type of experiment involving two treatment groups and two control groups so that the researcher can determine the effect of both the treatment variable and the pretest on the dependent variable.

Split-half reliability correlation coefficient: the magnitude of relationship between individual's scores on two parts of a test which are usually formed by placing all the even numbered items in the first part and the odd numbered items in the second part.

SPSS: Statistical Package for the Social Sciences a comprehensive, integrated collection of computer programmes that is available for managing, analysing and displaying data.

Standard deviation: (SD) the squared root of variance; gives the average dispersion about the mean of the distribution; the most commonly used measures of variability. Defined in terms of deviation from the mean and responsive to the exact position of each score in the distribution

Standard error of measurement: a statistic that is used to estimate the probable range within which an individual's true score falls.

Standard multiple regression: all the independent (or predictor) variables are entered into the equation simultaneously and evaluated in terms of its predictive power over and above that offered by all the other independent variables; used when you need to know how much unique variance in the dependent variable that each of the independent variables explained.

Statistics: mathematical techniques for summarising or analysing numerical data.

Statistical inference: a set of procedures for determining whether the researcher's null hypothesis can be rejected at a given alpha level.

Statistical power: the probability that a particular test of statistical significance will lead to the rejection of a null hypothesis.

Step-down multiple regression: a type of multiple regression analysis in which, from among a set of measured predictor variables, the one that leads to the largest increase in R is next added to the prediction equation.

Step-wise multiple regression: the researcher provides a list of variables and allows the SPSS programme to select which variables it will enter, and the order in which they will be entered into the equation, based on a set of statistical criteria.

Student's *t*-test: (see *t-test*)

Subjects: (also called participants, population, respondents): people who take part in the research. Not used in today's reporting.

Survey methods: collecting information through questionnaires and/or surveys.

Synchronic research: investigates variables in a cross-sectional slice of time and refers to a particular variable only as it exists in the here and now but gives no information as to its development and growth patterns (see also cross-sectional research).

_t_-distribution: a probability distribution that is used to determine the level of significance of an obtained t value for the difference between two scores.

_t_-test: used to determine whether the means of two sets of measurements differ significantly from each other. Paired samples *t*-test (repeated measures) are used when two sets of scores are measured on the same subject (usually at different times). Independent-samples *t*-test are used when one set of measures are taken from two different sets of people or things.

Test of statistical significance: a mathematical procedure for determining whether a null hypothesis can be rejected at a given alpha level.

Test-retest reliability: the assessment of the degree to which test scores are similar or stable over time as opposed to the degree to which scores fluctuate upon repeated testings.

Theoretical construct: a concept, embedded within a theory, that is inferred from observed phenomena and related to other concepts in the theory.

Theory: an explanation of the commonalities and the relationships among observed phenomena in terms of causal structures and processes that are presumed to underlie them.

Three-Way ANOVA: used to test the impact of three independent grouping variables on one dependent variable and to test for interaction effects.

Treatment variable (independent or experiment variable): in experimental research, the variable manipulated in order to determine its effect on one or mode dependent variables.

True score: in classical test theory, the actual amount of the characteristic measured by the test (e.g., ability, attitude, personality trait) that the test taker possesses.

Two-way ANOVA: used to test the impact of two independent grouping variables on one dependent variable and to test for the interaction effect.

Tukey's HSD (honestly significant difference) test: allows us to compare all possible pairs of mean while maintaining the Type 1 error for making the complete set of comparisons at *a*.

Two-tailed test of statistical significance: a mathematical procedure for determining whether a null hypothesis that does not specify the direction of the difference between two groups (or other prediction involving both tails of a probability distribution) can be rejected at a given alpha level.

Type 1 error: a conclusion or decision to reject the null hypothesis when the null hypothesis is true.

Type 11 error: a conclusion or decision to retain the null hypothesis when the null hypothesis is false.

Validity: refers to how the test scores are used and interpreted and not the instrument itself. Determine the validity of a test through (1) content validity, (2) criterion-related validity, (3) construct-related validity and (4) predictive validity.

Variable: a quantitative expression of a construct that can vary in quantity or quality in an observed phenomena.

Variability: reveals the extent to which scores differ from one another (see *variance and standard deviation*)

Variance: a measure of the extent to which scores in a distribution deviate from the mean; calculated by squaring the standard deviation of the score distribution; the mean squared deviation of a set of scores; the square of the standard deviation. Not widely used in descriptive statistics but useful in inferential statistics.

Wilcoxon Matched Pairs Signed Ranks test: a non-parametric procedure used with a correlated groups design to determine whether the observed difference between the distribution of scores is statistically significant; serves as an alternative to the *t*-test when the assumptions of the *t*-test have not been met.

z scores: (also called standard scores) a transformation of the raw score that tells us how many standard deviation units the raw score is above or below the mean; can be used to compare scores that are not generally directly comparable (e.g., height and shoe size; examination results and IQ score) as long as the measuring scales allow computation of mean and standard deviation.

***z* test:** appropriate in situations in which both mean and standard deviations of the null hypothesis population are known.

Subject Index

ABD's 1
Abcsissa 36, 160, 320
Abstract of a thesis 269, 272-4
Alpha levels 162, 331
Alpha, as a measure of test reliability 33, 232
Alternate-form reliability 120
American Psychological Association Publication Manual
    134, 141, 315, 311
Analysis of covariance, *see ANCOVA*
Analysis of variance 218-42
    reading an ANOVA table 238-42
Analytical purpose of research 3
ANCOVA 29, 186, 219
Appendices 290
Argumentative/critical purpose of research 2
Arithmetic mean (average) 153

Bar chart, *see bar graph*
Bar graph 167, 170-2
    SPSS programme for 171-2
Bias, *see reliability*
Biserial correlation 183
    see point biserial correlation
Bivariate correlations 159-183
Bonferroni 222, 228, 231

C-alpha 192-8, 321
    acceptable level of 195
    SPSS programme for 193-5
Categorical variables 156, 168, 322
    see also nominal variables
Causal-comparative research 4, 72-3
Central tendency, measures of 152
Chicago 311
Chi-square design 38, 43, 46, 76-7, 255-9, 321
    frequency counts in cells 256
    interpretation of 258
    SPSS programme for 257
    test of goodness of fit 77
    2X2 research design 256-8
    2X3 research design 258-9
Children as research participants 124
Choosing a topic 6
Citations 12, 295-7
Classical Test Theory 119
Coding data 12, 21, 24, 138-9, 146-7
    coding variables in SPSS 146
    for missing variables 92, 140
Coefficient of correlation 68, 320
    for contrasts 223, 230
    of determination 184
    of equivalence 120
    of reliability (R^2) 184

of stability 119
Confidentiality 84, 90, 99, 104, 117, 123, 126-7, 321
Confounding variables 28-9, 48, 61, 67, 132, 184, 321
    controlling for 29
Consent form 127
Consistency questions 90-1, 93
Constructs 9, 29, 74, 112, 116, 122, 321
    theoretical 29-30
Construct-related validity 121, 330
Content-related validity 121
Contaminating variables, *see confounding variables*
Contingency table 256
Continuous measurements 24, 149, 154
Contrasts 220, 223-224, 231
    interpretation of 229-230
    SPSS statistical analysis of 221-224
    see also multiple comparisons
Control groups 52, 65, 217, 323
    in experimental designs 65
Copying files from SPSS to a word programme 156
Correlation coefficients 180, 183
    Pearson *r* 150-2, 180-2
        SPSS programme for 150-2, 180-1
    Spearman's rho 259
        SPSS Programme for 259
    See also multivariate statistics
Correlation matrix 210
Correlational research design 4-5, 26, 68-73, 74
    commonly made mistakes in 74
    planning for 69
Covariates, *see partial correlation*
Cover letter 98, 125-127, 132, 282, 290
Criterion-related validity 121-122, 321
Cronbach's alpha, *see C-alpha*
Cross-sectional research design 62, 234, 321
Cross tabs (SPSS programme)
    to determine frequencies 148-9, 150
    in chi-square 150

Data entry 138
    in Excel 139-43
    in SPSS 143-5
Data reduction 190-208
Debriefing 125
Deception 124-5
Decision chart 46
    explanation of 43-45
Degree of freedom 212, 322
Dehoaxing, *see debriefing*
Demographic variables 21
Dependent variables 25, 26, 47, 52, 218
Descriptive research, 3

Descriptives SPSS programme 154-6
    for ANOVA 222-4
    for continuous variables 154-5
    frequency counts 147-8
    for three-way ANOVA 236-7
Designs, basic 35
    independent subjects
    matched pairs 59-60, 78, 326
    repeated measures 61
    simple experimental 48-9
    simple factorial 54-5
Deviation 153
Dichotomous measurements 24, 150, 159, 173, 183, 255, 326
Directional hypothesis 17
    see also alternate hypothesis
Discrete variables 24
Dispersion, measures of 153
Distribution free research, *see non-parametric research*
Dissertation, *see thesis*
Do-able research 1, 8
Doc Centre 13

EBSCO 14
Effect size 214, 224, 226-7, 239
    in statistical power analysis 226
    interpretation of 227
EIA Factor model of Teacher Motivation 199-200
Eigenvalues 202, 203
End Notes 14
Environmental variables 28
ERIC 14
Error of measurement 119
Eta squared, *see effect size*
Ethical standards 122-125
Experimental research designs 5, 47-59
    checklist for 66
    factorial 52-57
    independent subjects 59
    matched pairs 59
    pretest/treatment/post-test 49
    quasi-experimental 61
    repeated measures 61
    tables for 57-8
Experimenter effects (bias) 119
Explanatory purpose research 3
Exploratory data analysis, *see data reduction*
Extraneous variables 317
Excel programme 138, 142

F-test (variance ratio), *see ANOVA*
Factorial analysis 52-57, 218-42
Factorial research designs, explanation of 52
Forced alternative, *see forced choice*
Forced choice questions 85-6

Formula wizard in Excel 141, 142
Frequency count 143, 148
    SPSS programme for 47
    SPSS programme explore option for 176
    SPSS programme graph option for 173
    piecharts 167-70
    SPSS programme for 168-9
Friedman test 43, 46, 78, 266-7
    SPSS programme for 266
    interpretation of 267

GAMTEAP Principles 96-101, 106-12, 125,192-208
Generalisability 36, 87
Goodness of Fit test 77, 256
GLM, *see two-way and three-way ANOVA* 233
Graphs 173-9
    SPSS programme for, *see histograms*

H_A, *see alternate hypothesis*
H_0, *see null hypothesis*
Harmonic means, *see Tukey's b*
High discriminatory response format 88
Histograms 155, 167, 168, 173-8, 319
    SPSS programme explore option for 176-9
    SPSS programme frequency option for 174-5
    SPSS programme graph option for 173
Homeogeneity of variance (HOV)
    tests for 205, 215, 221, 229, 230, 319
Human subject protection, *see ethics*
Hypothesis 16-20, 319
    alternative 19
    null 17, 18
    steps in formulating 17

Independent samples design 59, 78
Independent variables 25,26
Indicators 30
Inferential statistics 319
Informed consent 124
Intact groups 38, 61
Item analysis 183, 320
Item – open-ended 87
Item reliability coefficients 183
Interaction effects 52-4, 240-241, 248-64, 323
    explanation of 52-54
    interpretation of 248-264
    SPSS programme for, see Three-way ANOVA
Intercept 239
Internal consistency of test scores 120
Internal validity in a subtest 7
Inter-observer ratings 120
Interquartile range 153
Interval measurements 21, 22, 23, 320

Key words 274
Kolmogorov-Smirnov test 156-7, 320
    SPSS programme for 156
Kruskal-Wallis test 43, 46, 79, 265-6
    SPSS programme for 265
Kurder-Richardson formulas 127
Kurtosis 155, 176-7

Labels for variables in SPSS 142, 147
Level of significance 157-8
Levene's test 43, 215-16
    for equality of variance 222-3,
    for homogeneity of error variance 229, 236, 237-8
Lie scales 90, 91
Likert-type scales 92-94
Linear regression design 73
Line of best fit 320
Literature review 278, 291
    in thesis/project 278-9
    purpose of 278
    in research proposals 131-2
    steps in 11-5
Longitudinal research 63
Low discriminatory response formats 88-9

Main effects 53, 242-47
Mann-Whitney U test 43, 46, 78, 261-3
    SPSS programme for 261
    interpretation of 262-3
MANOVA 28, 29, 208, 219, 324
Matched pairs design 59
    see matched subjects
Mean, arithmetic 153
Measurement errors 119-21
    see also Classical Test Theory
Median 153
Methods section in thesis 280-2, 291
Missing data, coding for 140
Mode 153
Multiple comparisons 222, 231
    see also multiple contrasts
    interpretations of 227, 229-31
    SPSS statistical programme for 221-3

N (of total population) 52
n (of subsets of population) 52
Narrowing down the topic 7-10
Nominal measurements 22
Nondirectional hypothesis (See H_0)
Nonparametric research 40-41
    examples of 40-41
Normal curve 36
Normal distribution 36, 156-7
    shape of 36
Non-parametric research (NPAR) 46

Chi Square 46, 255-9
Mann-Whitney 46, 261-3
Wilcoxon 46, 263-4
Null hypothesis 17
Nuisance variables, *see confounding variables*

Organismic variables 28
One hundred millimeter scale 94-5
One-way ANOVA 43, 52, 218-27, 230, 326
    explanation of 219
    SPSS programme with contrasts for 221-4
    interpretation of 224
Open-ended question items 85
Operational definitions 29-31
Order effects 61
Ordered discrete variables 25
Ordinal measurements 22
Organismic variables 21
Osgood Semantic Differences scale 94-5
Outliers 179-80
    SPSS programme for 180

p, see probability values
Parameters 35, 41
Parametric research designs 35, 43, 47-67
    comparison with Npar tests 41
Partial correlations 183-91
    interpretation of 189-90
    SPSS programme for 187-8
Pearson *r* 43, 46,150-2
    SPSS programme for 150, 180-2
Perception variables 26-7
    in responses to questionnaires 86-7
Perfect linear relationship 69
Piecharts 167-70
    SPSS programme for 168-9
Pilot testing of a questionnaire 114-5
Phi coefficient 322
Plagiarism 12, 295, 296, 323
Point bi-serial correlation 188
Population 35, 36, 39
Positive correlation 160, 165, 166
Post hoc *t*-tests 222-3, 227, 231-2, 316
Post-test 40, 45, 50, 60
Prediction research, *see simple linear research designs*
Preliminaries (in thesis writing) 271-4
Pretest 40, 45, 50, 60
    of questionnaire items 114-5
Pretest/treatment/post-test research design 49
Prevalence variables 26-7
    in responses to questionnaire 86-7
Primary sources 2
Privacy, protection of 122-3
Probability values 157-8
Process trail 112

in questionnaire item writing 113-4
Product moment correlation, *see Pearson r*
Proposal writing 128-135
Protection of human subjects,
    see Human subjects protection
Pseudo-academic language 294
Psych Info, 14
Psychology of questionnaire responding, see GAMTEAP
Publication manuals
    APA 12, 13, 130, 134, 287, 298, 311
    MLA 12, 297, 311
    Chicago 311
Purpose of research 2

Q-Q plot 181
Qualrus 14
Qualitative research 5-6
    difference between qualitative and quantitative
Research 5
    evaluation of 6
Quantitative variables 15
Quasi-experimental research designs 61-62
    checklist for 66
Questionnaire design 82-4
    construction of items 85-9
    formatting items 98-111
    GAMTEAP Principles of 106-12
    increasing reliability of 192-7
    look of 101-11
    optimal return rate for 82
    pilot-testing of 114-5
    preplanning items for 112-3
    uses of 83-4

r, see Pearson
r², see reliability coefficient
Random assignment 38-9
Randomisation techniques 38
Random sampling 38
Range 153
Rank difference correlation, *see Spearman's rho*
Rating scales 92
Ratio 23
Raw data, entering into Excel 138-40
References 14, 134-5, 289
    organisation of 12-3
    conventional format for 297-8
Related or non-related 45
Related measures, *see paired samples*
Reliability 119-20
    analysis of questionnaire items 192-7
Reliability coefficient 183
Repeated measures research design 61
Replication of research 1, 282, 324
Representative sample 36

Reverse scoring questionnaire items 98-90
Response set 89, 90
Review of literature, *see Literature review*
Rho, *see Spearman's rho*
Rotated component matrix 204

Sample
    generalisability of 37
    representative 36
    size 37-38
    stratified 37
Scales 22-3, 92-4
    interval 22
    nominal 22
    ordinal 22
    ratio 23
    Likert-type 92-4
    One-hundred millimetre scale 94-5
    Osgood Semantic Differential 94-5
Scattergrams, *see Scatterplots*
Scatterplots 160-7
    estimating correlations from 164-6
    SPSS programme for 161-3
Scree plot 200-3
    SPSS programme for 200-2
Secondary sources 2
Self-administered questionnaire 82
Semantic differential scale 27
Signed ranks test 40
Significance level 157-8
Significance level 157
Skewness 152, 155, 177-8, 321
    SPSS programme for 155
Solomon four-group design 64-66
Space saving, in questionnaires 97
Spearman's rho 46, 75, 259
    SPSS programme for 260
Split-half reliability 120
SPSS 138-43
Standard deviation 153
Standards for Education and Psychological Testing 121
Statistical Package for the Social Sciences, *see SPSS*
Survey research 81

t-test 43, 46, 209-15
    for independent samples 43, 213-15
    interpreting results 216-17
    for paired samples 43, 213-15
    interpreting results 211-12
Tables for research designs 57-9
Tables for the thesis 284-5, 298-9
Task variables, 28
Tau, *see Kendall's tau*
Test-retest reliability 119

Tests of between-subjects effects,
    s*ee two- and three-way ANOVA*
Theoretical constructs, s*ee constructs*
Thesis statement 31
Thesis writing 275-289
Three-way ANOVA 233-40
    explanation of 218
    SPSS programme for 235-6
    interpretation of 238-242
    interaction effects 240
    main effects 239
Treatment variable 47
Tukey's b statistical test, 223, 228, 238, 231
Two-way ANOVA 43, 218, 233
    explanation of 218
Type 1 error, 37, 231-232
Type II error, 37, 231-232

Unidimensional scale 164
Unordered dichotomous variables 24
Unrelated samples *t*-test, *see Independent samples*

Validity 121-2
    content-related 121
    construct related 74, 121
    criterion related 122
Variability measures of 153
Variables 21-29
    coding for 21
Variance 153
Varimax factor analysis 199-108
    SPSS programme for 200-01
    interpretation of 206-8
Verb tense in
    in thesis writing 271, 275

White space in questionnaire 101-2
Wilcoxon signed ranks test 43, 46, 77-8, 263-4
    SPSS programme for 264
    interpretation of 264-5
Word maps 48

Z score, *see K-S tests*
Zero correlations 165, 166, 167

www.ingramcontent.com/pod-product-compliance
Lightning Source LLC
Chambersburg PA
CBHW080244030426
42334CB00023BA/2696